Graphics Programming
in Turbo C 2.0

Graphics Programming
in Turbo C 2.0

Ben Ezzell

Addison-Wesley Publishing Company, Inc.

Reading, Massachusetts   Menlo Park, California   New York

Don Mills, Ontario   Wokingham, England   Amsterdam   Bonn

Sydney   Singapore   Tokyo   Madrid   San Juan

Many of the designations used by manufacturers and sellers to distinguish their products are claimed as trademarks. Where those designations appear in this book, and Addison-Wesley was aware of a trademark claim, the designations have been printed in initial caps or all caps.

Library of Congress Cataloging-in-Publication Data

Ezzell, Ben.
    Graphics Programming in Turbo C 2.0 / [Ben Ezzell].
        p.   cm.
    Inludes index.
    ISBN 0-201-19443-0
    1. Computer graphics.   2. Turbo C (Computer program)   I. Title.
T385.E986   1989
006.6'869--dc 19   88-33685
                                                   CIP

Cover design by Doliber Skeffington

Text design by Bruce Jones Design

ABCDEFGHIJ-AL-89
First Printing, February, 1989

In Memorium

To Knud Gellert (1937-1988)
He would have appreciated the irony.

ACKNOWLEDGMENTS

For their assistance in preparing this book, I would like to thank Borland International; in part for supplying advance test versions of their latest releases, for providing the custom video driver and font editor programs that round out an already excellent product and, most importantly, for producing a fast, efficient and versatile Turbo C. It has been a real pleasure working with it.

I would also like to add a special thanks to Nan Borreson for her capable assistance in putting me in touch with the right people; to Paul Chui for his very capable comments, criticisms and suggestions and to Grant Larkin for his comments and criticisms as well. While I have not followed all of the suggestions and comments offered, they were — none the less — appreciated and considered.

And thanks also to the Hewlett-Packard Corporation for supplying a ColorPro plotter for testing and development; again with specific thank you's to James Gabrisch and to Peter Petrogeorge, each for their timely assistance.

A final thank you to Hewlett-Packard's Technical Assistance personnel who, on hearing the plotter was to be used to bit-map a color screen image to paper, protested, "Impossible! It wasn't designed that way!"

You were right ... almost ...

I thank you one and all.

Ben Ezzell — November 1988

CONTENTS

FOREWORD

Graphics and Turbo C are ideal partners.

Turbo C's fast, device-independent graphics routines allow programmers to create high-quality graphics with minimal fuss and a speed that is addictive. As a result, Turbo C is the environment of choice for graphics programmers.

Now Graphics Programming in Turbo C 2.0 gives readers the chance to explore the world of graphics programming as never before possible. Practical routines for animation, printer output, mouse control, turtle graphics and more are developed using Turbo C's built-in graphics. These functions enhance the existing library of graphics functions and are designed to be easily incorporated into any graphics program.

Ben Ezzell's Graphics Programming in Turbo C 2.0 is a welcome addition to the library of books supporting Turbo C and an indispensable reference for everyone interested in Turbo C graphics.

Paul Chui
Turbo C Technical Support Coordinator
Borland International

INTRODUCTION

INTRODUCTION TO GRAPHICS PROGRAMMING

A very brief decade ago, the term graphics meant something created by the art department — by hand — and photographed or engraved for reproduction on a printing press. Graphics — when the term was used relative to a computer at all — meant some elaborate arrangement of screen characters or, in some cases, a display using the alternate graphics character set.

True graphics, however, appeared quickly but in these early stages, were also an element that said ''this computer is designed for games'' and had the implication that any computer supporting a true graphic display was not capable of serious computing applications (an unstated implication that was also quite generally correct).

With the early microcomputers, graphics capabilities meant that much of the CPU's capability was being diverted to create or to maintain a graphics display. Also, that a great deal of memory (somewhere in the system) was being devoted to an elaborate display capability at a time when RAM memory was relatively expensive, memory addressing was limited (64K maximum) and low resolution TVs comprised virtually all of the ''color''-capable monitors.

Because the quality of the resulting ''graphics'' display was — at its very best — barely good enough for simple games, the term graphics — to serious programmers — might have been better spelled with four letters. Graphics, in these early days, was a cuss word — a toy to entertain obnoxious ten-year-olds and the company board-of-directors, but devoutly to be avoided by serious programmers and having no place what-so-ever in any real programming application (unless, you had the power of a Cray supercomputer and the video resolution of Disney Studios).

But times change. And, with computers, times change rapidly, dizzily, with generations passing almost in the blink of an eye and what was true yesterday, is old-hat today and history tomorrow.

And graphics have changed. CPUs are faster, more memory can be addressed, storage densities are higher, RAM is cheaper, video monitors are better and color — ah, color — has changed from four-color palettes to kilobyte palettes selected from a quarter-meg of hues with display capabilities running to kilo-pixel vertical and horizontal resolutions.

Suddenly graphics are not *just* a toy.

Now, don't get me wrong — graphics are still a wonderful toy: excellent for amusing even smart ten-year-olds and marvelous for impressing board members!

But graphics are much more than just a toy.

First, this book is being typeset using Ventura Publisher™ — a typesetting software system which allows both the author (myself) and his editor (Chris) and his production editor (Amy) to see exactly what the book will look like *before* it is printed!

But this is not a task that can be executed using the conventional ASCII alphanumeric display. Instead, each character is drawn on the screen, using detailed graphics images and a variety of typefaces and sizes, positioned proportionally as each will actually be printed — an electronic analog of a proposed paper image ... but also one which can be edited, adjusted, revised, amended, deleted, spaced, formatted and changed ... and with results that I can see instantly as I work — not later after sending the output to the printer.

Thus, I can see how various tables appear — are they correctly aligned? — does the material fit? — is the result clear and easy to read? — before it becomes a matter of explaining the problem to my production editor so that she can explain it to the typesetter ... etc ... etc. (Of course, in this case, there is no typesetter — in the human sense — involved because the same software that is used on Chris' and Amy's and my computers sends these same instructions directly to a 2000-line-resolution Linographic for the actual typesetting.)

And, if I want a box on the page, instead of specifying where the box is positioned and then entering the dimensions of the box and requesting shading or line width or all of those other details, I use a graphics mouse to point out the corner positions desired for a box (watching it appear as I do so) or, to reposition an existing image or adjust or duplicate ... etc. Not incidentally, many of the illustrations appearing in this book were created using the Ventura Publisher software and its interactive graphics ... and could not have been created as easily and conveniently in any other fashion.

And, in this case, graphics are anything but a toy ...

This is just one application out of many. In CAD (Computer Aided Design) applications, graphics capabilities are absolutely required. However, if you aren't an engineer, this may seem like a pretty remote application.

And games — no matter how well designed — may simply leave you cold.

So, what else is there?

Would you believe a whole world?

Human Information Inputs

Visual

Tactile

Audio

Olifactory

Humans are visually oriented. On the norm, we are far more capable of assimilating detailed visual information than any other kind and, depending on the type of information required, a graphic display may easily provide more information in a clearer manner.

For example, suppose I tell you that 75 percent of the information you receive from the outside world is visual, 15 percent is tactile, 8 percent audio and 2 percent olifactory. (Note: these percentages are arbitrary and for purposes of illustration only.)

You can read the preceding information but do the figures listed above tell you as much as quickly as a single glance at the bar graph above?

Granted, the hard figures, the percentages, convey more absolute information than the bar graph but the chart, the graphic information, provides a clearer intuitive recognition and will be remembered long after the figures quoted are forgotten, and this is one of the reasons for the popularity of business graph displays.

Add color and, unless you are among the rare individuals who are totally color blind, the information will be retained even longer and recalled more vividly.

Or suppose that you want to learn to play Blackjack — there are several interactive computer instruction games for this and other card games, but which do you think would be easier to pay attention to: a simple alphanumeric instruction set or a graphics display that showed the hand being dealt?

If gambling isn't your field of interest, consider other types of educational programming. Computers have a tremendous advantage in educational applications: they're infinitely patient, never get upset and are capable of providing individual attention in a manner that does not intimidate the student ... but, unless the program can also hold the student's attention, it is worthless.

Graphics are an excellent key to provide information that is clearer, more easily assimilated and longer remembered than simple text. Add colors, flashing patterns, sound effects (and headsets) and a simple remedial math drill can become a game.

On a more advanced level, physical principles can be graphically illustrated and at least one interactive program allows construction of simple machines and devices on screen, then shows the results in action. A juvenile CAD system that is instructive and the kids love it.

And there are serious business applications as well.

Several of the major airlines now use interactive graphics for their ticket agents. When the agent is booking a seat on a flight, an interactive graphics display shows a schematic of the seating arrangements, indicating which seats are already booked and which are available. The agent uses a mouse to select a seat for the customer without having to remember seat numbers, which are on the aisle and which are on the right and left sides. Because they can see all this information in an instant, error results decline dramatically.

Imagine the same type of graphics interactive display applied to the registration desk at a large hotel. The clerk, when registering a guest, could pick out a room on the display, showing the guest the room layout and where it is located in the hotel. A map could be quickly printed showing where the room was located relative to the elevators, staircases, etc. Another application could be customizing city maps to show points of special interest to the guest or where a particular resturant is located.

In the near future, I hope I may be able to have a graphic map display in my vehicle which will not only show me where I am (using satellite navigation aids), but will also be able to show where traffic is tied up in a strange city (since I travel a lot) and to suggest alternate routes to my destination. (Note: if you're working on this, please include the wilderness areas — I like quiet mountains.)

It would be presumptuous for me to attempt to define all of the possible applications for graphics programming (it would also be tedious and take entirely too much space). I'll finish this introduction; therefore, by briefly mentioning a few other possibilities, such as: interactive display of chemical reactions and bonds, anatomical displays, visual engine models, pinball construction sets, architectural design programs allowing prospective home owners to view house plans from inside, books on disk that could enlarge pages for those with poor eyesight ... for a start.

And don't forget the up-coming possibilities inherent in CD-ROMs. They're on the horizon and coming closer ... and graphics will combine with still and moving photography, massive text storage, freeze-frame and windows and ... well, use your own imagination — there's a lot of room and many possiblities.

I've mentioned a few possibilities out of thousands — but the possibilities are not the topic of this book: this book is about the tools with which to make possiblities become realities: graphics images, turtle graphics, BGI graphics drivers, graphics character fonts, mouse graphics interfacing, graphics screen output devices — and more — a full chest of tools with the applications left to your choice. So, good luck and have fun!

P.S. Oh yes, remember the bar graph presented earlier? Do you remember the percentages quoted two paragraphs above the bar graph? Are you sure of the amounts? Point taken?

CHAPTER 1

INTRODUCTION TO VIDEO GRAPHICS

In the Beginning

When the first microcomputers appeared, an 8-bit CPU and bus architecture with 16K of RAM were fairly standard, clock speeds of 2 Megahertz were considered fast, and video displays handling 80 characters and 25 lines were the absolute tops. If you wanted graphics displays, a ROM-based graphics character set was your only alternative to the familiar ASCII characters. Few, if any, provisions were offered for direct access to the video memory. CPU and system memory limitations made what access was available, difficult to use.

For the most part, this early world was divided into two parts: the serious computers that concentrated on efficient memory usage and fast processing speeds, and the game-oriented systems that sacrificed much of their potential capability in favor of elaborate monochrome or color graphics capabilities.

Later, with more powerful CPUs and operating systems and faster speeds, greater degrees of freedom became available. To use Heath/Zenith's Z-100 series (the original MS-DOS system) for an example, three banks of video memory were available, each providing 32K or 64K RAM to control the Red, Blue and Green color guns (total 192K). If your Z-100 had only one of the three banks of memory (by default the green bank), then you were limited to a monochrome display. If you had all three banks of video RAM, but only a monochrome monitor, then color was simulated by "shades of grey" and with a high-resolution color monitor, you had the breathtaking choice of eight colors (black, blue, violet, red, orange, green, yellow and white).

More important, however, was the fact that you had a pixel-addressable video memory with a display range of 640 pixels horizontal and 225 pixels vertical. For text, the display was 80 characters (columns) by 25 lines. There was, however, no distinction necessary between text and graphics modes: both were the same. Text characters were 8 pixels wide, 9 pixels high (including distenders — the portions of lower case characters that extend below the line, as with g, j, p, q and y) and were created by a ROM character set which was written directly to the video RAM.

You could also write (and read) individual pixels in video RAM, intermixing these with standard characters without changing modes or disabling one type of display in favor of another.

IBM's design approach, while essentially using the same CPU, 16-bit architecture and MS-DOS, used an initially minimalist hardware configuration. Thus, the first IBM PCs were provided with a rather scanty video RAM (about 4K) limited only to non-graphic displays. If you wanted graphics capabilities, the CGA (Color Graphics Adapter) was available as an add-on that provided either high-resolution graphics (640x200 pixels) with a 2-color display (monochrome), or a low-resolution (320x200), 4-color display using a choice of four, predefined palettes. This was a bit like Henry Ford's statement that you could have a Model-T in any color ... as long as it was black.

Changing the video adapter, however, was quite a bit easier than repainting a car. And so, a host of third-party developers looked at the price of RAM chips, warmed up their soldering irons and went into business creating more advanced video cards like the Hercules, AT&T and Telmar video adapters.

This proliferation of video hardware (which now includes at least 10 different standard video adapters) has presented problems for the programmer. Each different design of video hardware supports a different set of capabilities. It may use different memory addresses and may or may not support multiple graphics pages (and/or multiple text pages) and video modes ranging from 320x200 to 1024x768 pixel displays and from monochrome to 256 color displays.

Of course, the initial question facing every graphics programmer is identifying which video adapter is installed in a machine.

One option has always been to ask the user to select the video mode that will be used. This can be a poor choice because even professional programmers are not always certain with what hardware they are working. The average user may not even know if they have a graphics adapter at all, much less what type or capabilities might be present. The alternate choice is to have your software query the hardware to determine the present configuration.

If a standard for hardware identification existed, this would be a simple matter. Unfortunately for programmers, the rapid proliferation of video adapter hardware has occurred without any formalized provisions for identification. In a previous book, **Programming the User Interface**, I discussed several tests for the presence or absence of CGA/EGA video adapters and some of the problems inherent in correctly identifying hardware.

Happily, the release of Turbo C version 1.5 (and Turbo Pascal 4.0) has relieved much of the indecision in identifying, supporting and using the various video adapter cards currently in use. Also, judging by Borland's past performance, it seems fairly safe to assume that future video adapters will be similarly supported (see also Appendix D — **The BGI Driver Toolkit).**

Unhappily, this more than welcome support for diverse video capabilities has also resulted in creating confusion over how to use these new tools and what to do with a plethora of new capabilities.

This book has been written to untangle the confusion.

Video Adapter Types

Turbo C (version 1.5 and above) and Turbo Pascal (version 4.0 and above) each provide comprehensive support for all major video card types currently in use. In this book, I will be discussing and illustrating graphics in Turbo C only. If you are using Turbo Pascal, corresponding functions are provided, using essentially the same function and procedure names and operating in effectively the same manner.

Contemporary video cards range from the text-only original video systems to the ultra-high resolution IBM-8514 (popular with typesetting or CAD software applications) with a variety of resolutions lying between the two. Obviously, the higher resolution video cards must be matched with monitors that have corresponding pixel resolution. This is a hardware matter and, as a programmer, for all practical purposes, you may simply assume the hardware present corresponds to the identification returned by Turbo C's **detectgraph** function. Any discrepancies in matching between video cards and monitors, etc., are the user's responsibility and should not be the programmer's concern.

Video Modes

Every PC, XT or AT is equipped with some type of video adapter card. In the very basic video card, you may have the MDA (Monochrome Display Adapter) which supports text-only display. If this is the case, you will not be able to program or use graphics without upgrading your system.

The first step up is the popular CGA (Color Graphics Adapter) card, and then higher resolutions and wider options are provided by the Hercules Monochrome Graphics Adapters, MCGA (Multi Color Graphics Array) and EGA (Enhanced Graphics Adapter) video adapters. For more advanced graphics capabilities, such as for typesetting or CAD applications, the AT&T (400-line Graphic Adapter), VGA(Variable or Video Graphics Array), PC-3270 and IBM-8514 video adapters all offer even higher pixel resolutions.

In Turbo C, graphics support for all of these types is provided in the form of six graphics interface (.BGI) units (ATT, CGA, EGAVGA, HERC, IBM8514 and PC3270) and four graphics fonts (GOTH.CHR, LITT.CHR, SANS.CHR and TRIP.CHR). As new video graphics cards appear, new .BGI units may be included for support while new .CHR fonts may be user-created (see Chapter 17 — **The Turbo Font Editor**) or purchased from commercial sources.

The graphics support units, however, are not included in the standard memory models (as distributed) — an omission made for the express purpose of speeding compilation time when graphics are not needed.

To use the graphics modules, two options exist. First, Borland has provided TLIB, the Turbo Librarian distributed with Turbo C version 1.5. Using TLIB, the graphics library (GRAPHICS.LIB) can be incorporated in one or more of the memory model libraries. Using TLIB is explained in more detail in Chapter 9.

Second and more common, a project (.PRJ) file can be created for each program, making GRAPHICS.LIB available for linking and allowing your program to load the appropriate .BGI files from disk as needed.

Also, with the release of Turbo C version 2.0, a new option appears (see Options/Linker/Graphics Library) that tells the linker to automatically search the Graphics Library without requiring a Project file.

If you are using graphics programming extensively, including GRAPHICS.LIB in your standard library is recommended. As a further option, the BGIOBJ utility (distributed with Turbo C version 1.5) can be used to convert .BGI graphics drivers and .CHR font files to object files, allowing you to link them directly to your program (thus also including them directly in your .EXE program).

For testing and development, GRAPHICS.LIB is conveniently called as a secondary library and the .BGI and .CHR files are accessed externally.

Including The Graphics Library

If you are using the Turbo C command line compiler (TCC.EXE) to compile a source program titled YOURPROG.C, the TCC command would be:

```
tcc yourprog graphics.lib
```

This assumes that YOURPROG.C and GRAPHICS.LIB are in the same directory as TCC and; therefore, no path specifications are required.

When using the Turbo C integrated compiler (TC.EXE), you will need to create and select a project file that will instruct the linker to access the external (GRAPHICS.LIB) library in addition to the standard library. This project file is quite simple and, for this application, requires only a single line:

yourprog graphics.lib

Here, if GRAPHICS.LIB is located in a different subdirectory from the compiler, you may either specify the path in YOURPROG.PRJ or include the path in the compiler environment configuration (use Alt-O for options menu, then select **E**nvironment).

In either case, you will have to enter the project name YOURPROG.PRJ (the .PRJ extension is optional and will be assumed if not specified) before selecting the RUN option or compiling your program to disk.

Note that the absence of library functions will not create an error message during compiler execution — only during the second, linker pass. As long as the compiler finds the graphics functions correctly defined in the GRAPHICS.H header file (be sure to *#include graphics.h* in your source listing), no error messages will be generated until the linker finds itself unable to actually access the library *or* if a structure or constant from GRAPHICS.H is referenced.

To specify a .PRJ file, enter Alt-P to pop-up the Project Menu. Now, select the first menu item (**P**roject name:) and either type in the correct project name or hit ENTER to display and use the arrow keys to select the appropriate .PRJ file.

Remember, if you have TC configured for autosave, the selected project will still be in effect the next time you use C. The Clear project option is used to cancel this selection, allowing you to compile and run a different program.

Disadvantages

Once a program has been compiled (from a project file or using the command line specification), the .EXE program can be distributed together with external .BGI and .CHR files required for operation. Together, these files require approximately 60K of disk space — not an excessive requirement in terms of storage. Relying, however, on external files for execution can create some difficulties.

First, a call to **initgraph** must include the drive/path specification where the .BGI (and .CHR) modules are located. If no path is specified, then the current directory is assumed. This routing information is usually supplied by the programmer and, if the required files are not found — a problem that can occur for a variety of reasons — your program *will terminate!*

Second, if the default (current) path is assumed and all external files are present and the program is called from another directory or drive, there could also be a crash!

Third, never depend on the user to be aware of the importance of any external files. They may love your program and guard it jealously but, as soon as space becomes a problem, may ignorantly erase necessary external files. It happens: be prepared.

Alternatively, you can link the .BGI and .CHR files directly into the graphics library, increasing your .EXE program in size by about 30K (see Chapter 9), but making the drivers and fonts a part of your .EXE program rather than of the external files.

Knock, Knock! What's There?

The first step in your graphics program is to initialize the appropriate graphics driver. For a list of supported graphics video cards, drivers and graphics modes, see Table 1-1.

Table 1-1 : Video Modes Supported By Turbo C 2.0

GRAPHICS[1] DRIVER CONSTANT	NUMBER VALUE	GRAPHICS MODE(S)	KEY[2] VALUE	COLUMN X ROW	PALETTE[3] OR COLORS	VIDEO PAGES
DETECT	0	(requests **initgraph** to execute autodetection)				
CGA	1	CGAC0	0	320 x 200	C0	1
		CGAC1	1	320 x 200	C1	1
		CGAC2	2	320 x 200	C2	1
		CGAC3	3	320 x 200	C3	1
		CGAHI	4	640 x 200	2 colors	1
MCGA	2	MCGAC0	0	320 x 200	C0	1
		MCGAC1	1	320 x 200	C1	1
		MCGAC	2	320 x 200	C2	1
		MCGAC3	3	320 x 200	C3	1
		MCGAMED	4	640 x 200	2 colors	1
		MCGAH	5	640 x 480	2 colors	1
EGA	3	EGALO	0	640 x 200	16 colors	4
		EGAHI	1	640 x 350	16 colors	2
EGA64	4	EGA64LO	0	640 x 200	16 colors	1
		EGA64HI	1	640 x 350	4 colors	1
EGAMONO	5	EGAMONOHI	3	640 x 350	2 colors	1 - 2 [4]
IBM8514[5]	6	IBM8514LO	0	640 x 480	256 colors	1
		IBM8514HI	1	1024 x 768	256 colors	1
HERC	7	HERCMONOHI	0	720 x 348	2 colors	4
T400	8	ATT400C0	0	320 x 200	C0	1
		ATT400C1	1	320 x 200	C1	1
		ATT400C2	2	320 x 200	C2	1
		ATT400C3	3	320 x 200	C3	1
		ATT400MED	4	640 x 200	2 colors	1
		ATT400HI	5	640 x 400	2 colors	1
A	9	VGALO	0	640 x 200	16 colors	4
		VGAMED	1	640 x 350	16 colors	2
		VGAHI	2	640 x 480	16 colors	1
PC3270	10	PC3270HI	0	720 x 350	2 colors	1

1. The *graphic_drivers* and *graphic_modes* names are constants defined in GRAPHICS.H, as are the corresponding numerical values and mode values (see note 2).

2. Mode settings returned by **initgraph**, **detectgraph** or **getgraphmode**.

3. C0..C3 refer to the predefined 4-color palettes — see **setpalette**.

4. With 64K on an EGAMONO card, only one video page is supported; with 256K, two video pages are supported.

5. Autodetection will not correctly recognize the IBM-8514 graphics card. Instead, **initgraph** or **detectgraph** will identify the IBM-8514 card as a VGA graphics card which the IBM-8514 will emulate correctly (IBM8514LO is equivalent to VGAHI). To use the higher resolution mode (IBM8514HI — 1024x768 pixels), assign the value IBM8514 (numerical value 6 — defined in GRAPHICS.H) to the graphdriver variable before calling **initgraph**. Do not use **detectgraph** or DETECT with **initgraph**. See also text notes on IBM-8514 and **setrbgpalette**.

detectgraph

Normally, the **detectgraph** function is called by **initgraph**, but it can also be called independently.

```
#include <graphics.h>
int    graphdriver = DETECT, graphmode;
main
{
detectgraph( &graphdriver, &graphmode );
......
}
```

If a problem occurs, *graphdriver* returns an error code; otherwise, *graphdriver* identifies the appropriate driver type and *graphmode* returns the highest valid video mode for this driver.

Note: for **detectgraph**, no driver path is required (see **initgraph**).

The **detectgraph** function does *not* initialize any graphics settings. The principal reason for calling **detectgraph** directly would be to use **initgraph** to call a specific graphics driver or to select a graphics mode that **initgraph** would not call by default. Alternatively, a different mode can be called after initializing by using the **setgraphmode** function.

Value returned: *graphdriver* returns driver type or error code; *graphmode* returns highest valid video mode.

Portability: IBM PCs and compatibles only, corresponding functions exist in Turbo Pascal.

initgraph

Using Turbo C, the **initgraph** function is provided to set the initial graphics parameter values, load the proper graphics driver and set the system to the desired graphics mode.

```
#include <graphics.h>
int   graphdriver = DETECT, graphmode;
char *driverpath = "";
main
{
     initgraph( &graphdriver, &graphmode, driverpath );
     ......
}
```

Setting *graphdriver* as zero (see example) instructs **initgraph** to call *detectgraph(graphdriver,graphmode)* so it can determine the type (and settings) of the video graphics adapter installed. If an error occurs, **graphdriver* returns an error code indicating the type of error:

Table 1-2: Initialization Graphic Error Codes

CODES	INTERPRETATION
−2	Cannot detect graphics card
−3	Cannot locate graphics driver file(s)
−4	Invalid driver (or not recognized)
−5	Insufficient memory to load graphics driver

The **detectgraph** and **graphresult** functions return these same error codes.

If no error occurs, then the internal error code is set to zero and **initgraph** allocates memory for the appropriate graphics driver, loads the required .BGI file from disk and sets the default graphics parameter values. Also, *graphdriver* returns the driver type; *graphmode* returns the mode setting.

Alternatively, *graphdriver* and *graphmode* can be specified (either by using the appropriate numerical constants or by using the driver and mode names as defined in <GRAPHICS.H>).

In either case, *driverpath* shows the drive/path where the .BGI graphics drivers are located. If *driverpath* is null (as shown in the example), then these files must be located in the default directory. If they are located in a different directory, then the complete path specification should be shown as:

```
char *driverpath = "\\TURBOC\\DRIVERS";
```

Note the use of the double backslash (\\). Because the backslash character is used to set escape sequences (as in \n for carriage returns or \a for a bell), the \\ is required to include a backslash in a string.

The *driverpath* set by **initgraph** is also used by **settextstyle** to search for the character font (.CHR) files. Both .BGI and .CHR files must be located in the same directory.

Value returned: *graphdriver* returns driver type or error code; *graphmode* returns highest valid video mode.

Portability: IBM PCs and compatibles only, corresponding functions exist in Turbo Pascal.

Graphics Error Functions

As mentioned, if a graphics video card is not present, if the graphics drivers are not found or if some other error occurs during detection of initialization, an error code is returned by **detectgraph** or **initgraph**. There are, however, other conditions where a graphics error can occur and the functions **graphresult** and **grapherrormsg** are provided to test and to display appropriate error results and messages.

graphresult

The function **graphresult** returns a numerical error code set by the last graphics operation that has reported an error. This will be an integer value in the range −15..0 . Since, when **graphresult** is called, the error condition is reset to zero, the value returned should be stored in a local variable, then tested for further action.

```
#include <graphics.h>
int   errornumber;
errornumber = graphresult();
```

Value returned: error code (−15..0), see Table 1-3 for interpretation.

Portability: IBM PCs and compatibles only, corresponding functions exist in Turbo Pascal.

Table 1-3: Graphics Error Messages

ERROR CODE	GRAPHICS_ERROR CONSTANT [1]	CORRESPONDING ERROR MESSAGE STRING
0	grOk	No error
−1	grNoInitGraph	(BGI) graphics not installed (use **initgraph**)
−2	grNotDetected	Graphics hardware not detected
−3	grFileNotFound	Device driver file not found (.BGI file)
−4	grInvalidDriver	Invalid device driver file
−5	grNoLoadMem	Not enough memory to load driver
−6	grNoScanMem	Out of memory in scan fill
−7	grNoFloodMem	Out of memory in flood fill
−8	grFontNotFound	Font file not found (.CHR file)
−9	grNoFontMem	Not enough memory to load font
−10	grInvalidMode	Invalid graphics mode for selected driver
−11	grError	Graphics error (*generic error*)
−12	grIOerror	Graphics I/O error
−13	grInvalidFont	Invalid font file
−14	grInvalidFontNum	Invalid font number
−15	grInvalidDeviceNum	Invalid device number

1. The *graphics_errors* constants and error messages are defined in GRAPHICS.H.

grapherrormsg

The **grapherrormsg** function returns a pointer to the appropriate error message string. These strings are defined in the graphics library (**GRAPHICS.LIB**), however, a separate error message routine can be created to display a more complete or more informative error message if desired.

```
#include <graphics.h>
int   errornumber;
errornumber = graphresult();
printf(" %s ",grapherrormsg(errornumber));
```

Value returned: none.
Portability: IBM PCs and compatibles only, corresponding functions exist in Turbo Pascal.

installuserdriver

The **installuserdriver** (version 2.0 or later, only) allows installation of a custom or vendor-added device driver to the BGI internal table. See Appendix D for information on creating custom BGI drivers.

```
#include <graphics.h>
char *driver_name;
int  driver, mode;
int huge detect_driver()
{
    int  found, defaultmode;
    found = ...                    /* detect hardware tests as required */
    if( !found ) return( grError );         /* not found, return error */
    defaultmode = ...              /* determine default graphics mode */
    return( defaultmode );
}
main()
{
    driver = installuserdriver( "DRIVER", detect_driver() );
```

```
if( grOk != graphresult() )
{
    /* error message -- driver table is full */
    exit( 1 );
}
initgraph( &driver, &mode );
....
```

Value returned: Driver number parameter for use by **initgraph**.

Portability: Turbo C version 2.0 or later, IBM PCs and compatibles only, corresponding functions exist in Turbo Pascal version 5.0 or later.

Other Graphics Mode Functions

With the exceptions of the HERCMONO and PC3270 video drivers, each video driver supports two or more video modes that offer varying pixel resolutions or different color palettes. To handle mode inquiries and change operating modes, Turbo C provides several functions:

getdrivername

The **getdrivername** function (version 2.0 or later) returns a pointer to a string identifying the current graphics driver.

```
#include <graphics.h>
char *driver_name;
driver_name = getdrivername();
```

getmodename

The **getmodename** function (version 2.0 or later) returns a pointer to a string identifying the current graphics mode.

```
#include <graphics.h>
char *mode_name;
mode_name = getmodename();
```

Value returned: pointer to string.

Portability: Turbo C version 2.0 or later, IBM PCs and compatibles only, corresponding functions exist in Turbo Pascal version 5.0 or later.

getgraphmode

The **getgraphmode** function returns an integer value showing the current (operational) graphics mode that was set by **initgraph** or **setgraphmode**.

```
#include <graphics.h>
int   currentmode;
currentmode = getgraphmode();
```

Value returned: current graphics mode.

Portability: IBM PCs and compatibles only, corresponding functions exist in Turbo Pascal.

getmoderange

The **getmoderange** function is called with an integer value specifying the graphics driver (may be an integer variable or one of the constants defined in GRAPHICS.H) and returns two values defining the minimum and maximum valid modes supported by the indicated driver.

```
#include <graphics.h>
int   graphdriver, lomode, himode;
getmoderange( graphdriver, &lomode, &himode );
```

If the value passed as *graphdriver* is invalid, then both *lomode* and *himode* return −1.

Value returned: maximum and minimum valid modes or −1 error code.

Portability: IBM PCs and compatibles only, corresponding functions exist in Turbo Pascal.

graphdefaults

The **graphdefaults** function resets all graphic settings to their default values (the values originally set by **initgraph** and defined in GRAPHICS.H). This includes: resetting the viewport (graphics window) to the entire screen;

moving the current position to 0,0; resetting default palette colors, background color and drawing color; resetting the default file and pattern styles and resetting the default text font and justification modes.

```
#include <graphics.h>
graphdefaults();
```

Value returned: none.

Portability: IBM PCs and compatibles only, corresponding functions exist in Turbo Pascal.

setgraphmode

Graphics mode must have been previously initialized by **initgraph**. The **setgraphmode** function must be called with a graphics mode that is valid for the current device driver (use **getgraphmode** to find current mode value or **getmoderange** to check permissible values). When called, **setgraphmode** selects a new graphics mode, clearing the screen and resetting all graphics variables to their default values (see **graphdefaults**).

```
#include <graphics.h>
int   modenumber;
setgraphmode(modenumber);
```

The **setgraphmode** function can also be used with the **restorecrt** function to switch back and forth between text and graphics displays. Note: **initgraph** must be called before either of these functions can be used.

```
#include <graphics.h>
int   currentmode;
currentmode = getgraphmode();
restorecrtmode();                          /* text mode           */
setgraphmode(currentmode);                 /* graphics mode */
```

If **setgraphmode** is called with a value that is invalid for the current device driver, **graphresult** will return a value of −10 (grInvalidMode).

Value returned: none, see **graphresult** for error codes.

Portability: IBM PCs and compatibles only, corresponding functions exist in Turbo Pascal.

restorecrtmode

The **restorecrtmode** function resets the system video to the original text mode detected by the call to **initgraph**. This can be used with **setgraphmode** to alternate between text and graphics displays.

```
#include <graphics.h>
restorecrtmode();
```

Value returned: none, see **graphresult** for error codes.

Portability: IBM PCs and compatibles only, corresponding functions exist in Turbo Pascal.

closegraph

The **closegraph** function restores the system to normal text mode originally detected by **initgraph**. This also calls **_graphfreemem** to deallocate the memory that was used by the graphics system for drivers, fonts and the internal buffer.

```
#include <graphics.h>
closegraph();
```

If you wish to switch back and forth between text and graphics, use the **restorecrtmode** and **setgraphmode** functions. Alternatively, graphics memory allocation can be changed using the **_graphfreemem** and **_graphgetmem** functions.

Value returned: none, see **graphresult** for error codes.

Portability: IBM PCs and compatibles only, corresponding functions exist in Turbo Pascal.

```
                    /*              FIRSTGRP.C                    */
             /* demo for initializing graphics mode in Turbo C version 1.5 */
#ifdef __TINY__
#error Graphics demos will not run in the tiny model.
#endif
#include    <conio.h>
#include    <stdio.h>
#include    <stdarg.h>
#include    <graphics.h>
char *DriverNames[]= { "Detect", "CGA", "MCGA", "EGA",
                        "EGA64", "EGAMono", "IBM8514",
                        "HercMono", "ATT400", "VGA", "PC3270" };
char *Fonts[]       = { "Default", "Triplex", "Small", "SansSerif", "Gothic" };
char *LineStyles[]  = { "Solid", "Dotted", "Center", "Dashed", "User-Defined" };
char *FillStyles[]  = { "Empty", "Solid", "Line Fill", "Light Slash",
                        "Slash", "Back Slash", "Light Back Slash",
                        "Hatch", "XHatch", "Interleave", "Wide Dot",
                        "Close Dot" };
char *TextDirect[]  = { "Horizontal", "Vertical" };
char *HorizJust[]   = { "Flush Left", "Centered", "Flush Right" };
char *VertJust[]    = { "Bottom", "Centered", "Top" };
int   GraphDriver, GraphMode;           /* graphics driver and mode value  */
double  AspectRatio;                    /* pixel aspect ratio on screen    */
int     xasp, yasp;                     /* factors for aspect ratio        */
int     MaxX, MaxY;                     /* maximum screen resolution       */
int     MaxColors;                      /* maximum colors available        */
int     ErrorCode = 0;                  /* variable for graphics errors    */
struct  palettetype palette;            /* used for palette info           */

void TestGraphicError()
{
    ErrorCode = graphresult();          /* check the result                */
    if( ErrorCode != grOk )             /* if an error occurs then         */
    {
        closegraph();                   /* report error                    */
```

```
        printf(" Graphics System Error: %s\n",        /* using text mode       */
                grapherrormsg( ErrorCode ) );
        exit( 1 );                                     /* and exit to DOS       */
    }
}

void ChangeTextStyle(int font, int direction, int charsize)
{
    graphresult();                                     /* clear error code */
    settextstyle(font, direction, charsize);
    TestGraphicError();                                /* check for errors */
}

void StatusLine( char *msg )                           /* display status line at bottom */
{
    int Height;
    setviewport( 0, 0, MaxX, MaxY, 1 );                /* open display viewport */
    setcolor( MaxColors - 1 );                         /* start with max color  */
    ChangeTextStyle( DEFAULT_FONT, HORIZ_DIR, 1 );
    settextjustify( CENTER_TEXT, TOP_TEXT );
    setlinestyle( SOLID_LINE, 0, NORM_WIDTH );
    setfillstyle( EMPTY_FILL, 0 );
    Height = textheight( msg );                         /* get char height */
    bar( 0, MaxY-(Height+4), MaxX, MaxY );
    rectangle( 0, MaxY-(Height+4), MaxX, MaxY );
    outtextxy( MaxX/2, MaxY-(Height+2), msg );
    setviewport( 1, Height+5, MaxX-1, MaxY-(Height+5), 1 );
}

void DrawBorder()                    /* draw solid line around current viewport (window) */
{
    struct viewporttype vp;
    setcolor( MaxColors - 1 );                          /* set draw color as white */
    setlinestyle( SOLID_LINE, 0, NORM_WIDTH );
    getviewsettings( &vp );
    rectangle( 0, 0, vp.right-vp.left, vp.bottom-vp.top );
}
```

19

```
void ReportWindow( char *header )                    /* setup window for graphics report */
{
    int Height;
    cleardevice();                                   /* clear graphics screen */
    setcolor( MaxColors - 1 );
    setviewport( 0, 0, MaxX, MaxY, 1 );              /* setup viewport */
    Height = textheight( header );                   /* get character height */
    ChangeTextStyle( DEFAULT_FONT, HORIZ_DIR, 1 );
    settextjustify( CENTER_TEXT, TOP_TEXT );
    outtextxy( MaxX/2, 2, header );
    setviewport( 0, Height+4, MaxX, MaxY-(Height+4), 1 );
    DrawBorder();
    setviewport( 1, Height+5, MaxX-1, MaxY-(Height+5), 1 );
}

char *GetMode()                                      /* return mode as string for display */
{
    static char Buffer[40];
    switch( GraphDriver )
    {
        case CGA:  if( GraphMode == CGAHI ) return( "CGAHI" );
                       else    {
                                   sprintf( Buffer, "CGAC%d", GraphMode );
                                   return( Buffer );
                               }

        case MCGA : switch( GraphMode )
        {
            case MCGAMED    : return( "MCGAMed" );
            case MCGAHI     : return( "MCGAHi"  );
            default         : sprintf( Buffer, "MCGAC%d", GraphMode );
                               return( Buffer );
        }

        case EGA            : switch( GraphMode )
        {
```

```
        case EGALO          : return( "EGALo" );
        case EGAHI          : return( "EGAHi" );
} break;

case EGA64              : switch( GraphMode )
                          {
        case EGA64LO : return( "EGA64Lo" );
        case EGA64HI : return( "EGA64Hi" );
} break;

case EGAMONO            : return( "EGAMonoHi" );

case IBM8514            : switch( GraphMode )
{
    case IBM8514LO     : return( "IBM8514Lo" );
    case IBM8514HI     : return( "IBM8514Hi" );
} break;

case HERCMONO          : return( "HercMonoHi" );

case ATT400            : switch( GraphMode )
{
case ATT400MED         : return( "ATT400Med" );
case ATT400HI          : return( "ATT400Hi" );
        default        : sprintf( Buffer, "ATT400C%d", GraphMode );
                         return( Buffer );

}

case VGA               : switch( GraphMode )
{
    case VGALO         : return( "VGALo"  );
    case VGAMED        : return( "VGAMed" );
    case VGAHI         : return( "VGAHi"  );
} break;

case PC3270            : return( "PC3270HI" );
}
```

```
        return( "Device unknown" );
}

void Pause()                                        /* wait for a key entry */
{
        static char msg[] = "Press any key...";
        StatusLine( msg );                          /* put msg on screen      */
        if ( kbhit() != 0 ) getch();
        getch();
        cleardevice();                              /* clear the screen       */
}

/*              gprintf is used like printf except the output is sent to       */
/*              the screen in graphics mode at the specified co-ordinate,       */
/*              then current position is moved for next line output            */
void gprintf( int *xloc, int *yloc, char *fmt, ... )
/*              note ellipsis indicating variable ^ argument list */
{
        va_list  Argptr;                                    /* argument list    */
        char Workstr[140];                                  /* string for output */
        struct textsettingstype textinfo;

        va_start( Argptr, format );                         /* set up argument list */
        vsprintf( Workstr, fmt, Argptr );                   /* create output string */
        outtextxy( *xloc, *yloc, Workstr );                 /* print the output  */

        gettextsettings( &textinfo );                       /* get output orientation */
        if ( textinfo.direction )
                *xloc += textheight(Workstr) + 2;           /* move CP horiz */
        else *yloc += textheight(Workstr) + 2;              /* move CP vert   */

        va_end( Argptr );                                   /* close argument list */
}

void StepColor()                /* steps display colors through valid range */
{
        int Color;
```

```
    Color = getcolor() - 1;
    if ( !Color ) Color = getmaxcolor();
    setcolor( Color );
}

void ReportStatus()                                    /* report the current system configuration */
{
    struct viewporttype   viewinfo;                               /* parameters for inquiry */
    struct linesettingstype  lineinfo;
    struct fillsettingstype  fillinfo;
    struct textsettingstype  textinfo;
    struct palettetype     palette;
    char *driver, *mode;                                        /* mode and driver strings */
    int x, y;
    x = 10;
    y = 4;
    ReportWindow( "Graphic Status Report" );
    getviewsettings( &viewinfo );                               /* read parameter values */
    getlinesettings( &lineinfo );
    getfillsettings( &fillinfo );
    gettextsettings( &textinfo );
    getpalette( &palette );
    settextjustify( LEFT_TEXT, TOP_TEXT );
    Driver = DriverNames[ GraphDriver ];
    Mode = GetMode();                                          /* get current video mode */
    StepColor();
    gprintf( &x, &y, "Graphics device     : ( %d ) %-10s",GraphDriver, Driver );
    StepColor();
    gprintf( &x, &y, "Graphics mode       : ( %d ) %-10s", GraphMode, Mode );
    StepColor();
    gprintf( &x, &y, "Screen resolution   : (  0,  0, %2d, %2d )",getmaxx(), getmaxy() );
    StepColor();
    gprintf( &x, &y, "Current view port   : ( %2d, %2d, %2d, %2d )",
                          viewinfo.left, viewinfo.top,
                          viewinfo.right, viewinfo.bottom );

    StepColor();
```

```
    gprintf( &x, &y, "Clipping              : %s",viewinfo.clip ? "ON" : "OFF" );
    StepColor();
    gprintf( &x, &y, "Current position (CP)  : ( %2d, %2d )",getx(), gety() );
    StepColor();
    gprintf( &x, &y, "Max color / This color : %2d / %2d",MaxColors, getcolor() );
    StepColor();
    gprintf( &x, &y, "Line thick / style     : %2d / %s",
            lineinfo.thickness,
            LineStyles[ lineinfo.linestyle ] );
    StepColor();
    gprintf( &x, &y, "Fill color / style     : %2d / %s",
            fillinfo.color, FillStyles[ fillinfo.pattern ] );
    StepColor();
    gprintf( &x, &y, "Character size / font   : %2d / %s",
            textinfo.charsize, Fonts[ textinfo.font ] );
    StepColor();
    gprintf( &x, &y, "Text direction         :    %s",TextDirect[ textinfo.direction ] );
    StepColor();
    gprintf( &x, &y, "Horizontal justify     :    %s", HorizJust[ textinfo.horiz ] );
    StepColor();
    gprintf( &x, &y, "Vertical justify       :    %s", VertJust[ textinfo.vert ] );
    StepColor();
    gprintf( &x, &y, "Aspect Ratio  ( x/y )   : %d / %d = %5.3f",
            xasp, yasp, AspectRatio );
    Pause();
}

void Initialize()                       /* initialize graphics system and report errors */
{
    GraphDriver = DETECT;                           /* Request auto-detection   */
    initgraph( &GraphDriver, &GraphMode, "" );
    TestGraphicError();                             /* check graphics errors    */
    getpalette( &palette );                         /* read palette parameters */
    MaxColors = getmaxcolor() + 1;                  /* read maximum color range*/
    MaxX = 380;                                     /* set viewport (window) size  */
    MaxY = 174;
```

```
    getaspectratio( &xasp, &yasp );                    /* read the hardware aspect    */
    AspectRatio = (double)xasp / (double)yasp;
}                                                      /* calculate aspect ratio      */

main()
{
    Initialize();                                      /* set graphics mode           */
    ReportStatus();                                    /* show graphics settings      */
    closegraph();                                      /* set text mode               */
}
```

CHAPTER 2

VIEWPORT, SCREEN AND PAGE FUNCTIONS

Setting Up the Graphics Viewport

Just as windowing and screen management routines are provided for text display modes, similar control features are provided for graphics display modes. These include the **cleardevice** and **clearviewport** functions (graphics equivalents of **clrscr**), **setviewport** (equivalent to **window**), **getviewsettings** and the **setactivepage** and **setvisualpage** functions.

Not all of these graphics functions have text mode equivalents. There are several text mode functions that are not provided with graphics mode equivalents. Even when a graphics function appears similar to the text mode equivalent, it may or may not (most often not) operate identically to the text function.

The first of these screen management functions is:

cleardevice

```
#include <graphics.h>
cleardevice();
```

The **cleardevice** function erases the entire graphics screen — regardless of viewport settings — and moves the current position (CP) to the screen home (0,0) position. This does not affect the active viewport (if any is in use). The viewport settings remain unchanged, however, the screen clearing has not been limited to just the viewport. No values are returned and no error condition should be generated.

While **cleardevice** is similar to the text command **clrscr**, because the text function is window sensitive (can be used to clear only the currently active window), the **cleardevice** command resets the entire *active* graphics screen, but does not affect alternate graphics screens (if any are supported by the present graphics hardware).

Remember: text functions such as **clrscr** do not work in graphics modes and vice versa.

See also **clearviewport**, **setactivepage** and **setvisualpage**.

clearviewport

```
#include <graphics.h>
clearviewport();
```

The **clearviewport** function erases the current viewport (graphics window), moving current position (CP) to home position (0,0) within the viewport setting. Unlike the **cleardevice** function, **clearviewport** is limited to a specific area of the screen and operates like the text **clrscr** command with an active window setting.

See also **getviewsettings** and **setviewport**.

setviewport

```
#include <graphics.h>
int  xleft, ytop, xright, ybottom, clipflag;
setviewport( xleft, ytop, xright, ybottom, clipflag );
```

The **setviewport** function is roughly equivalent to the text **window** function and is used to set an active viewport. The coordinates (*xleft, ytop, xright, ybottom*) are absolute screen coordinates and affect only the active graphics page (see **setactivepage**).

The last argument passed to **setviewport** is the *clipflag*. If *clipflag* is non-zero, clipping will be in effect and all drawings will be restricted to the current viewport. If *clipflag* is zero, drawings may extend, without limitation, beyond the viewport perimeters.

Please note: the viewport limits do not affect the **getimage** or **putimage** commands and a pixel image being written to the screen will not be truncated at the viewport perimeter, regardless of the *clipflag* setting.

If invalid coordinates are passed to **setviewport**, then **graphresult** will return a value of −11 (graphics error or generic error) and the previous viewport settings (if any) will remain in effect. Both the **initgraph** and **setgraphmode** functions initialize the current viewport to the entire graphics screen as defined by the current mode setting.

See also **clearviewport** and **getviewsettings**.

getviewsettings

```
#include <graphics.h>
struct viewporttype viewport;
getviewsettings( &viewport );
```

The **getviewsettings** uses a record structure *viewporttype*, which is defined in GRAPHICS.H as:

```
struct viewporttype
{
    int left, top, right, bottom;
    int clipflag;
};
```

The structured variable *viewport* returns the current graphics window coordinates and the *clipflag* setting. The coordinates returned are absolute screen coordinates.

Where *clipflag* is non-zero, drawings are truncated at the current viewport margins. See **setviewport** for further details.

See also **clearviewport**, **initgraph**, **setgraphmode** and **setviewport**.

Multiple Graphics Pages

Several graphics video cards offer support for two to four pages of graphics display (most without restricting color or resolution). To allow use of these capabilities, Turbo C provides two functions: **setactivepage** which selects the active graphics output page and **setvisualpage** which selects the graphics page actually appearing on the screen. These are most often used for graphics animation.

These commands are valid only with the following drivers and modes:

Table 2-1: Graphics Modes Supporting Multiple Pages

GRAPHICS DRIVER	DRIVER VALUE	GRAPHICS MODE	MODE VALUE	RESOLUTION XAXIS x YAXIS	COLORS AVAILABLE	GRAPHICS PAGES
EGA	3	EGALO	0	640 x 200	16	4
		EGAHI	1	640 x 350	16	2
EGAMONO	5	EGAMONOHI	3	640 x 350	2	4[1]
HERCMONO	7	HERCMONOHI	0	720 x 348	2	2
VGA	9	VGALO	0	640 x 200	16	4
		VGAMED	1	640 x 350	16	2[2]

1. The EGAMono card must have 256K RAM to support multiple video pages, some EGAMono cards have only 64K RAM

2. The VGAHI mode (640 x 480) supports only *one* graphics page.

Remember: where multiple graphics pages are supported, the graphics pages are numbered from zero and page zero is active by default. Where multiple graphics pages are not supported, the **setactivepage** and **setvisualpage** commands will simply not operate. By default, page zero will remain as the active output page and the active visual page.

Relying on this default behavior is not necessarily the best approach to handling multiple video pages. In many cases, it might be better to know how many — if any — video pages are available and have your program respond accordingly. The procedure, **VideoPages**, returns zero if no alternate video pages are available, and an integer value if more than one video page is supported.

```
#include <graphics.h>

int GraphDriver, GraphMode;                          /* graphics driver and mode value */


int VideoPages(void)
{
    switch( GraphDriver )
    {
        case EGA                :switch ( getgraphmode() )
        {
            case EGALO          :return( 4 );
            case EGAHI          :return( 2 );
        } break;
        case EGAMONO            :return( 0 );         /* see note 1 */
        case HERCMONO           :return( 2 );
        case VGA                :switch ( getgraphmode() )
        {
            case VGALO          :return( 4 );
            case VGAMED         :return( 2 );
            case VGAHI          :return( 0 );
        } break;
    }
    return( 0 );                                     /* see note 2 */
}
```

1. Some EGAMono cards support four video pages, but mode and driver settings do not identify which cards have 256K RAM and which have only 64K RAM. Thus, the best default value returned is 0. This can be changed if your application requires a different response.

2. All remaining drivers and modes identify themselves as supporting single video pages. Newer video cards may require modification of this selection table.

setactivepage

```
#include <graphics.h>
int pagenum;
setactivepage( pagenum );
```

The **setactivepage** function selects which graphics page (*pagenum*) will be used for output by all graphics functions. This does not affect which graphics page is currently being displayed (see **setvisualpage**), but does allow graphics operations to be directed to an "invisible" page. They can then be displayed either by using the **getimage** and **putimage** functions (use the latter after changing the active page to match the visual page) or by changing the displayed page.

setvisualpage

```
#include <graphics.h>
int pagenum;
setvisualpage( pagenum );
```

The **setvisualpage** function selects the specified graphics page (*pagenum*) for active display. This is not necessarily the same as the active output graphics page (see **setactivepage**), but is useful for switching the display between different graphics pages. The change is immediate and requires only one screen refresh cycle for a complete display change.

The **setactivepage** and **setvisualpage** functions are demonstrated in ANIMATON.C in Chapter 10.

CHAPTER 3

COLOR/PALETTE FUNCTIONS

Graphics Color Selection

In addition to knowing which graphics card and which graphics driver to use, you also need to know what palettes or colors are supported.

With the CGA, MCGA and ATT400 drivers in 320x200 pixel modes, color selections are limited to the four-color, predefined color palettes (C0, C1, C2 and C3). With higher resolutions, some graphics cards offer 16 colors, while others offer either two or four colors, however, the color selection is independent of the predefined palettes.

Finally, with the IBM-8514, a palette of 256 colors becomes possible, with tint selection from a total of 262,144 shades. The color and palettes functions following are not compatible with the IBM8514 driver — see the **IBM-8514 Video Graphics Card.**

getmaxcolor

```
#include <graphics.h>
int MaxColors;
MaxColors = getmaxcolor() + 1;
```

The **getmaxcolor** function returns the maximum valid color number (or palette size −1) for the current graphics mode. This is valid in both high and low resolution modes. Thus, in a low resolution (320x200) mode, **getmaxcolor** will return a value of 3 — one less than the number of colors in the predefined palettes. In high resolution modes such as EGAHI, the value returned will be 15 and, in monochrome modes such as ATT400HI, a value of 1 will be returned.

Please note: normally the value indicates only the number of separate palette colors that can be used and not the maximum color values. This function is not valid in the IBM8514 mode.

See also **setcolor**.

setcolor

```
example:   #include <graphics.h>
           int forecolor;
           forecolor = getmaxcolors();
           setcolor( forecolor );
```

The **setcolor** function selects the current drawing color or foreground color.

In low resolution CGA modes (320x200 pixel), the color selected is the palette color number and not the actual color value. Thus in CGAC2 mode, **setcolor(0)** selects the background color (see **setpalette**), **setcolor(1)** selects GREEN (color value 2), **setcolor(2)** selects RED (color value 4) and **setcolor(3)** selects BROWN (color value 6).

In high resolution modes, the color values can be either the symbolic names (which are defined in GRAPHICS.H) or the numerical values. If the **setpalette** or **setallpalette** functions have been used to change the palette color values, the symbolic color names may not produce the expected results.

The current color selected is used for drawing and for graphics text output. The current fillcolor, however, may be different from the current drawing color (see Chapter 5 and Chapter 6).

The colors selected are retrieved from a record of structure *palettetype* as *palette.color[colornumber]*. The structure *palettetype* is defined in GRAPHICS.H as:

```
struct palettetype
{
        unsigned    char size;
        signed   char colors[ MAXCOLORS + 1 ];
};
```

The constant MAXCOLORS is defined as 15.

See **setpalette** for predefined color palettes. See also **getcolor** and **setbkcolor**.

getcolor

```
#include <graphics.h>
int forecolor;
forecolor = getcolor();
```

The **getcolor** function returns the current drawing (foreground) color. In low resolution modes using color palettes, the value returned will be the palette number, not the actual color value.

In high resolution (16 color) modes, the value returned will correspond to the color values unless the **setpalette** or **setallpalette** functions have been used to change the palette values.

See **setcolor** for color values; see **setpalette** for palette colors. See also **getbkcolor**.

setbkcolor

```
#include <graphics.h>
int backcolor;
backcolor = 0;
setbkcolor( backcolor );
```

The function **setbkcolor** selects the background color values by changing the first entry in the active color palette (*palette.color[0] = backcolor*) to the specified color value — see also **setpalette**.

When **setbkcolor** is called with a new value, the background color on the entire screen is changed. Note: if this new background color corresponds to the color of an image already on the screen, the image will be effectively invisible, but the image information is *not* lost. When the background color is changed to a contrasting color, the invisible image will again become clear.

The argument *backcolor* can be either the symbolic color name or the color value. The following color names are enumerated in GRAPHICS.H as:

Table 3-1: Background Color Values

NAME	VALUE	NAME	VALUE
BLACK	0	DARKGREY	8
BLUE	1	LIGHTBLUE	9
GREEN	2	LIGHTGREEN	10
CYAN	3	LIGHTCYAN	11
RED	4	LIGHTRED	12
MAGENTA	5	LIGHTMAGENTA	13
BROWN	6	YELLOW	14
LIGHTGREY	7	WHITE	15

In low resolution (320x200) color palette modes, only the first entry in the palette (*palette.color[0]*) can be changed — see **setpalette**.

In high resolution 16-color modes (EGA/VGA), any or all palette colors can be changed using the **setpalette** and **setallpalette** functions. If this is done, the symbolic color names sometimes provide the expected results.

getbkcolor

```
#include <graphics.h>
int backcolor;
backcolor = getbkcolor();
```

Because the background color is always *palette.color[0]*, the **getbkcolor** function returns the current background color *value*, not the palette entry number.

See also **getcolor** and **setbkcolor**.

getpalette

```
#include <graphics.h>
struct palettetype palette;
getpalette( &palette );
```

The **getpalette** function fills the *palette* structure with current palette information (settings). The structure *palettetype* is defined in GRAPHICS.H as:

```
struct palettetype
{
    unsigned char size;
    signed   char colors[ MAXCOLORS + 1 ];
};
```

Palette.size gives the number of colors valid for the current graphics driver and mode, while *palette.color* is an array of *size* of bytes containing the color values for each entry in the palette.

Table 3-2: Color Values

(CGA) NAME	VALUE	(EGA/VGA) NAME	VALUE
BLACK	0	EGA_BLACK	0
BLUE	1	EGA_BLUE	1
GREEN	2	EGA_GREEN	2
CYAN	3	EGA_CYAN	3
RED	4	EGA_RED	4
MAGENTA	5	EGA_MAGENTA	5
BROWN	6	EGA_BROWN	20
LIGHTGREY	7	EGA_LIGHTGREY	7
DARKGREY	8	EGA_DARKGREY	56
LIGHTBLUE	9	EGA_LIGHTBLUE	57
LIGHTGREEN	10	EGA_LIGHTGREEN	58
LIGHTCYAN	11	EGA_LIGHTCYAN	59
LIGHTRED	12	EGA_LIGHTRED	60
LIGHTMAGENTA	13	EGA_LIGHTMAGENTA	61
YELLOW	14	EGA_YELLOW	62
WHITE	15	EGA_WHITE	63

Note: most, if not all, EGA/VGA graphics cards will accept either the CGA or the EGA/VGA symbolic color names and color values that appear in the preceding list. CGA graphics cards, however, may respond unexpectedly to the EGA/VGA color values.

See **setallpalette** and **setpalette**. See also Appendix E — **A 256-Color .BGI Driver**.

setpalette

```
#include <graphics.h>
int palette_index, color;
setpalette( palette_index, color );
```

With any of the 320x200 pixel video graphics modes (CGA, MCGA or AT&T), color selections are limited to predefined 4-color palettes: C0, C1, C2 and C3. In each palette, the background color (*palette.color[0]*) can be user-defined, but colors 1..3 cannot be changed. In every other graphics mode, all colors can be redefined.

Table 3-3: Predefined Palettes and Colors

PALETTE	COLOR0	COLOR1	COLOR2	COLOR3
C0	black	lightgreen	lightred	yellow
C1	black	lightcyan	lightmagenta	white
C2	black	green	red	brown
C3	black	cyan	magenta	lightgrey

The IBM-8514 graphics card and IBM8514 driver support a color palette of 256 colors chosen from a total of 262,144 (256K) color values. No symbolic constants are defined for this driver, but the IBM-8514 card can also emulate VGA modes. See the **IBM-8514 Video Graphics Card** for further details.

setallpalette

```
#include <graphics.h>
struct palettetype newpalette;
setallpalette( &newpalette );
```

The **setallpalette** function assigns *newpalette* as the current palette with all new color assignments effected immediately. The colors for *newpalette* must be assigned using **setpalette**.

In low resolution (320x200) graphics modes using the predefined color palettes, the **setallpalette** command is not valid since only the background palette color is assignable. Note: changing graphics modes — as from CGAC0 to CGAC2 — to change color palettes erases (resets) the graphics screen.

See also **getpalette**.

IBM-8514 Video Graphics Card

setrbgpalette

```
#include <graphics.h>
int  colornum, redval, blueval, greenval;
setrbgpalette( colornum, redval, blueval, greenval );
```

The **setrbgpalette** routine is provided for use with the IBM-8514 graphics card and IBM8514 driver, supporting a color palette of 256 colors chosen from a total of 262,144 (256K) color values.

The **detectgraph** function will not identify the IBM-8514 card correctly but will instead identify this hardware configuration as VGA compatible. The VGA driver is recommended for maximum compatibility (see **initgraph**) when the extended resolution of the IBM8514HI mode is not required.

No symbolic constants are defined for this driver. Instead, each color is defined by three, six-bit values for the red, green and blue components.

The *colornum* argument sets the palette color (0..255) to be defined by the *redval*, *blueval* and *greenval* arguments. Only the six most significant bits from the low byte of each color argument are used (values from 0 to 252 in steps of four). For example, arguments of 252, 253, 254 and 255 are treated identically since the six most significant bits are the same.

The other palette manipulation routines in the graphics library are invalid with the IBM8514 driver in the IBM8514HI (1023x768 pixel) mode. This includes **setallpalette**, **setpalette** and **getpalette**. Also, the **floodfill** routine is not valid with this driver and mode.

CHAPTER 4

SCREEN POSITION FUNCTIONS

Graphics Screen Positions

In graphics modes, the familiar 80 by 25 screen coordinates are replaced by pixel coordinates and may vary — depending on hardware — from 320 horizontal by 200 vertical, to as high as 1024 horizontal by 768 vertical (with newer and higher resolutions appearing almost daily).

Because of this variety of screen resolutions, most graphics programs begin by checking the hardware for the appropriate drivers (see FIRSTGRP.C — Chapter 1). They then use functions such as **getmaxx** and **getmaxy** to determine the screen size, adjusting subsequent operations to fit within these screen limits.

getmaxx/getmaxy

```
#include <graphics.h>
int MaxX, MaxY;
MaxX = getmaxx();
MaxY = getmaxy();
```

The **getmaxx** and **getmaxy** functions return the maximum x-axis and y-axis screen coordinate (maximum CP) for the current graphics driver and mode. For example, in EGAHI mode (640x350), **getmaxx** returns 639 (0..639) and **getmaxy** returns 349 (0..349). Both are independent of viewport settings.

See also **getviewsettings**, **getx** and **gety**. Similar information is available in text modes using the **gettextinfo** function.

getx/gety

```
#include <graphics.h>
int xpos, ypos;
xpos = getx();
ypos = gety();
```

The **getx** and **gety** functions return the current position (CP) horizontal and vertical pixel coordinates. These coordinates are the position relative to the current viewport. If no viewport has been set, the default viewport includes the entire screen.

See also **getviewsettings**, **moverel** and **moveto**. Similar information is available in text modes using **wherex** and **wherey**.

moveto

```
#include <graphics.h>
int x, y;
moveto( x, y );
```

The **moveto** function moves the current position (CP) to the absolute screen pixel coordinates specified by (*x,y*) and relative to the current viewport settings where (0,0) is the upper left corner. Note: the resulting CP is *not* limited by the current viewport settings or by the maximum and minimum screen coordinates.

If no viewport settings have been made, the default settings include the entire screen. See also **moverel**.

In text modes, **gotoxy** provides the equivalent function.

moverel

```
#include <graphics.h>
int xdev, ydev;
moverel( xdev, ydev );
```

For graphics application, a relative move is often handier than an absolute move. For this, the **moverel** function shifts the new current position (CP) a relative distance from the old current position using the offset specified by (*xdev,ydev*). Note: the resulting CP is *not* limited by the current viewport settings or by the maximum and minimum screen coordinates.

See also **moveto**.

CHAPTER 5

PIXEL, DRAWING AND IMAGE FUNCTIONS

While lines and curves are useful for many drawing applications, some images can only be created by manipulating individual pixels and, of course, the line and curve functions could hardly operate without pixel write procedures. Using pixel functions on a macro scale, entire images can be saved, rewritten, erased or combined with existing screen images.

Pixel Functions

putpixel

```
#include <graphics.h>
int xpos, ypos, color;
putpixel( xpos, ypos, color );
```

The **putpixel** function sets the pixel specified by (*xpos,ypos*) to the color indicated. In graphics modes using predefined palettes, *color* must be in the range 0..3 where 0 provides the background color value. In full palette color modes, either color names (defined in GRAPHICS.H) or color values may be used.

See also **getpixel**.

getpixel

```
#include <graphics.h>
int x, y;
color = getpixel( x, y );
```

The **getpixel** function returns the color palette index of the indicated pixel at (*x,y*). Note: this may or may not correspond to the actual color value.

See also **getimage** and **putpixel**.

Line Drawing Functions

Turbo-C provides three drawing functions — **line**, **lineto** and **linerel** — for straight lines. The coordinate points used for these lines are integer coordinates (positive or negative) that are plotted relative to the current viewport coordinates, but need not be restricted to the viewport limits. If the viewport clipflag is non-zero, the lines drawn will be truncated at the viewport borders.

If clipflag is zero, lines are truncated only at the limits of the screen though the endpoint coordinates and the resulting current position (CP) may still lie outside the viewport and/or the screen limits.

line

```
#include <graphics.h>
int xstart, ystart, xend, yend;
line( xstart, ystart, xend, yend );
```

The **line** function draws a line beginning at the first coordinate pair (*xstart,ystart*) and ending at the second coordinate pair (*xend,yend*). It uses the current drawing color, line style and thickness. The current position (CP) is not changed.

See also **linerel** and **lineto**.

lineto

```
#include <graphics.h>
int xpos, ypos;
lineto(xpos,ypos);
```

The **lineto** function draws a line beginning at current position (CP) and ending at the coordinates specified (*xpos,ypos*). The current drawing color, line style and thickness are used and CP is reset to (*xpos,ypos*).

See also **line** and **linerel**.

linerel

```
#include <graphics.h>
int xdev, ydev;
linerel( xdev, ydev );
```

The **linerel** function draws a line from CP to a point offset from CP by the horizontal and vertical distances specified by (*xdev,ydev*). The line is drawn using the current color, line style and thickness. CP is updated to (*CPX + xdev* , *CPY + ydev*).

See also **line** and **lineto**.

Line Styles

For graphics drawing, two line thicknesses and several line styles are provided. You can also define a custom line style using a 16-pixel pattern. The line thickness and pattern settings are used by **arc**, **bar**, **bar3d**, **circle**, **drawpoly**, **ellipse**, **line**, **linerel**, **lineto**, **pieslice** and **rectangle**.

Turbo C version 2.0 (and Turbo Pascal version 5.0) also provide a new function, **setwritemode**.

setlinestyle

```
#include <graphics.h>
unsigned linepattern;
int  style, width;
setlinestyle( style, linepattern, width );
```

The **setlinestyle** function sets the current line width and style. The style and width operators (*line_styles* and *thickness*) are enumerated in GRAPHICS.H (see Table 5-1).

Table 5-1: Line Styles

NAME	VALUE	DESCRIPTION
SOLID_LINE	0	solid line (default)
DOTTED_LINE	1	dotted line
CENTER_LINE	2	centered dash line
DASHED_LINE	3	ashed line
USERBIT_LINE	4	user-defined style

Table 5-2: Line Widths

NAME	VALUE	DESCRIPTION
NORM_WIDTH	1	1 pixel width (default)
THICK_WIDTH	3	3 pixels width

Note: a line width of 2 can also be assigned, but any value greater than 3 results in a graphics error and causes the line style and width to be set to the default settings.

The remaining argument, *linepattern*, is a 16-bit pattern defining a custom bit pattern to be used for drawing the line. The *linepattern* argument is applicable only if *style = USERBIT_LINE* (numerical value 4). If *style !=* *USERBIT_LINE*, then *linepattern* must still be supplied, but is not used.

When a user-defined pattern is used, each pixel corresponding to a one-bit in the pattern is turned on, while pixels corresponding to a zero-bit are left off. Thus, if *linepattern = 0xFFFF*, a solid line is drawn and, if *linepattern = 0x9999*, a dashed line alternating two pixels on, two pixels off will result. For a long-dashed line, *linepattern = 0xFF00* or *0xF00F* might be used.

If invalid parameters are passed to **setlinestyle**, **graphresult** will return a value of −11 (*graphics error* or *generic error*) and the current line style will remain in effect.

See also **getlinesettings.**

setwritemode

```
#include <graphics.h>
int  writemode;
setwritemode( writemode );
```

The **setwritemode** function sets the screen writing mode for line drawing in graphic modes. Two constants are defined: COPY_PUT and XOR_PUT.

The COPY_PUT setting uses the assembly language MOV instruction, overwriting existing screen pixels. The XOR_PUT setting uses the XOR command to combine new lines with existing screen images. If a line is drawn twice using the XOR_PUT setting, the line is erased, and the screen's original appearance is restored.

Note: **setwritemode** currently works only with **line, linerel, lineto, rectangle** and **drawpoly**.

getlinesettings

```
#include <graphics.h>
struct linesettingstype lineinfo;
getlinesettings( &lineinfo );
```

The **getlinesettings** function returns *lineinfo* with the current line style, pattern (*upattern*) and thickness. The structure *linesettingstype* is defined in GRAPHICS.H as:

```
struct linesettingstype
{
        int linestyle;
        unsigned upattern;
        int thickness;
};
```

See **setlinestyle** for styles and thickness.

Rectangles, Bar Graphs and Polygons

While any of the following geometric forms can be created using the line drawing function, it is more convenient to have functions providing faster handling for common shapes.

rectangle

```
#include <graphics.h>
int xleft, ytop, xright, ybottom;
rectangle( xleft, ytop, xright, ybottom );
```

The **rectangle** function draws a square or rectangle as defined by the corner coordinates passed as arguments. The figure is drawn using the current line style, thickness and color. If one or more corners do not fall within the current viewport limits and the clipflag is set, then only the portion of the figure that fits within the viewport will be created.

See also **bar**.

bar

```
#include <graphics.h>
int  left, top, right, bottom;
bar( left, top, right, bottom );
```

The **bar** function draws a square or rectangle as defined by the corner coordinates passed as arguments. Unlike the figure created by the **rectangle** function, the **bar** figure is not outlined, but uses the current fill pattern and fill color (not the drawing color). For an outlined bar, use **bar3d** with a depth setting of zero.

See also **getcolor**, **getfillsettings**, **getlinestyle**, **rectangle** and **setfillpattern**.

bar3d

```
#include <graphics.h>
int  left, top, right, bottom, depth, topflag;
bar3d( left, top, right, bottom, depth, topflag );
```

The **bar3d** function outlines a three-dimensional rectangular bar using the current line style and drawing color, and then fills in the faces of the figure using the current fill pattern and fill color.

The bar's depth is given in pixels (normally about 25 percent of the width) and is set back at an x/y ratio of 1:1 (approximately 45 degrees adjusted by the screen aspect ratio).

If the topflag parameter is passed as zero, no top is added to the bar. This allows for bars to be stacked.

If desired, a more elaborate figure can be created. Each face of the figure can be filled with a different color and/or pattern using the **floodfill** function. If this is desired, use the **setfillpattern** function to select EMPTY_FILL before calling **bar3d**.

See also **bar**, **getcolor**, **getfillsettings**, **getlinestyle** and **rectangle**.

drawpoly

```
#include <graphics.h>
int points;
int figure1[] = { 100,100, 110,120, 100,130, 120,125,
                  140,140, 130,120, 140,110, 120,115, 100,100 };
int figure2[] = { 180,100, 210,120, 200,130, 220,125,
                  240,140, 230,120, 240,110, 220,115, 220,100 };
points = sizeof ( figure1 ) / ( 2 * sizeof ( int ) );
drawpoly( points, figure1 );
drawpoly( sizeof( figure2 ) / ( 2 * sizeof( int ) ), figure2 );
```

The **drawpoly** function draws the outline of a polygon using current color settings and line style.

The *points* argument gives the number of vertices for the polygon and *poly* points to a sequence of integer pairs, each pair defining the x/y coordinates for a vertex of the polygon.

In order to draw a closed figure with *n* vertices, *points* = *n+1* and the *nth* (final) coordinate pair is equal to the *0th* (first) coordinate pair.

In the example, *figure1* defines a four-pointed star. Instead of assigning a constant to *points*, the number of points in the figure is calculated from *sizeof(figure)* divided by two times *sizeof(int)* (because each point requires two integer coordinates).

The second figure, *figure2*, changes the four-pointed star into an open line figure, but is still created in the same manner.

See also **getlinesettings**, **getcolor**, **fillpoly** and **setgraphbufsize**.

fillpoly

```
#include <graphics.h>
int figure1[] = { 75, 0, 100, 50, 150, 75, 100,100,
                  75,150, 50,100, 0, 75, 50, 50, 75, 0 };
int figure2[] = { 75, 50, 100, 75, 75,100, 50, 75 };
fillpoly( sizeof ( figure1 ) / ( 2 * sizeof ( int ) ), figure1 );
fillpoly( sizeof ( figure2 ) / ( 2 * sizeof ( int ) ), figure2 );
```

The **fillpoly** function draws the outline of a polygon using current color settings and line style and then fills the polygon using the current fill pattern and fill color.

The *points* argument gives the number of vertices for the polygon and *poly* points to a sequence of integer pairs, each pair defining the x/y coordinates for a vertex of the polygon.

In order to draw a closed figure with *n* vertices, *points* = *n+1* and the *nth* (final) coordinate pair is equal to the *0th* (first) coordinate pair.

In the example, *figure1* defines a four-pointed star. Instead of assigning a constant to *points*, the number of points in the figure is calculated from *sizeof(figure1)* divided by two times *sizeof(int)* (because each point requires two integer coordinates).

The second figure, *figure2*, creates an open square. Note, however, that **fillpoly** will close the figure by connecting the start and end points, then fill the enclosed region.

Unlike **floodfill**, the fill algorithm used by **fillpoly** does not depend on a continuous outline to define the area; therefore, broken line styles are acceptable and will simply fill the area defined by the polygon — which includes overwriting any other figure lying within the new boundary.

If an error occurs, **graphresult** returns –6 (*out of memory in scan fill*).

See also **drawpoly**, **getfillsettings**, **setfillpattern**, **getcolor** and **setgraphbufsize**.

Video Aspect Ratio

Each graphics driver and graphics mode has an associated *aspect ratio* — the ratio between vertical and horizontal pixel sizes and spacing. A figure which appears round on one screen (and graphics card/mode) may appear crushed or elongated when using different graphics hardware.

In order to insure that geometric figures appear on the screen, more or less as intended, the screen *aspect ratio* should be used to calculate and to correct the distortions created by differences in hardware/graphics cards.

getaspectratio

```
#include <graphics.h>
int xasp, yasp;
double AspectRatio;
getaspectratio( &xasp, &yasp );
AspectRatio = (double) xasp / (double) yasp;
```

Each graphics driver and graphics mode has an associated aspect ratio determined by the relative height and width of the pixels. For example, using an EGA graphics card (*EGAHI*), an aspect ratio of 0.775 is found (*xasp = 7750, yasp = 10000*) since the EGA pixels are roughly 1/3 taller than they are wide. On the other hand, using a VGA graphics card, the aspect ratio is found to be 1.000 (*xasp = 10000, yasp = 10000*), with the pixels appearing to be square. As you can see, there's a considerable difference between the two screen presentations.

The **getaspectratio** returns integer values for the x- and y-axis aspects. The aspect ratio is calculated as *xasp/yasp* and is used automatically as a scaling factor with the **arc**, **circle** and **pieslice** routines in order to normalize the appearance of circles and circular arcs on the screen.

With the **ellipse** routine, the aspect scaling ratio must be included, otherwise, no adjustment is applied. The aspect ratio can also be used with other geometric figures to correct scaling and appearance.

Note: The y-axis aspect factor is normalized to 10,000 and, in general, *xasp <= 10,000* (most screens' pixels are taller than they are wide).

setaspectratio

```
#include <graphics.h>
int xasp, yasp;
setaspectratio( xasp, yasp );
```

Each graphics driver and graphics mode has an associated aspect ratio determined by the relative height and width of the pixels, used to insure that circles appear round, etc. If circles appear elliptical, however, the monitor may be out of alignment and require mechanical (electronic) adjustment. Adjustment can be accomplished by using the **setaspectratio** function (Turbo C version 2.0 or later) to change the aspect ratio.

Circles, Curves and Arcs

Curves are the hardest figures to create, requiring relatively complex calculations to determine the points composing them. Thus, the functions **circle**, **ellipse** and **arc** offer no small convenience in creating curved figures.

The **circle** function creates a complete circle, while **arc** and **ellipse** are called with start and end angles and may produce complete (closed) curves or only partial arcs.

The **getarccoords** function returns the start, end and center coordinates of the last call to **arc** or **ellipse**, allowing lines to be drawn to the ends of arcs. The **pieslice** function uses a combination of these capabilities to create an arc with lines drawn from the end points to the center.

The start and end angles for **arc**, **ellipse** and **pieslice** are given in degrees, with 0° and 360° at the right, 90° at the top, 180° at the right and 270° at the bottom.

Figure 5-1: Drawing Arc Angles

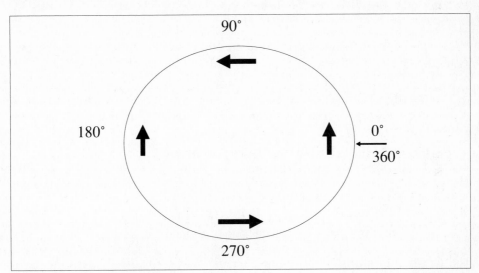

The angles for arc, ellipse and pieslice run counterclockwise (widershins) beginning with 0°/360° at the right, 90° at the top, 180° at the left and 270° at the bottom.

To draw a closed arc or ellipse, simply specify a start angle of 0° and an end angle of 360°. Angles greater than 360° can be used as arguments, but will be reduced to 0°..360°. For example, a starting angle of 300° and an end angle of 450° will draw an arc from the 300° point to the 90° point.

Of course, the same arc can be drawn by simply specifying 300° and 90° as the start and end points. There is no inherent requirement for the end angle to be greater than the start angle, although allowing angles greater than 360 degrees can simplify many programming procedures.

Note: the **arc**, **circle**, **ellipse** and **pieslice** functions do not use the current line style. All curves are drawn as solid lines using the current drawing color.

circle

```
#include <graphics.h>
int xcenter, ycenter, radius;
circle( xcenter, ycenter, radius );
```

The **circle** function draws a complete arc from 0° to 360°. The circle is drawn using the current drawing color and radius specified (in pixels) and is centered at the given screen coordinates.

Unlike **ellipse**, **circle** is called with a single radius argument and; therefore, the screen aspect ratio is automatically applied to adjust the results for producing a correct (circular) appearance.

See also **arc**, **ellipse**, **getaspectratio** and **pieslice**.

arc

```
#include <graphics.h>
int  xcenter, ycenter, startangle, endangle, radius;
arc( xcenter, ycenter, startangle, endangle, radius );
```

The **arc** function draws a circular curve with the specified radius between the angles specified and centered at the given x and y coordinates. The start and end angles are in degrees (0..360). The center coordinates and the radius are both in pixels. The current drawing color and line style are used. Correction for the screen aspect ratio is handled automatically.

See also **circle**, **ellipse**, **getaspectratio** and **pieslice**.

ellipse

```
#include <graphics.h>
int xcenter, ycenter, startangle, endangle, xradius, yradius;
ellipse( xcenter, ycenter, startangle, endangle, xradius, yradius );
```

or:

```
ellipse( xcenter, ycenter, startangle, endangle,
xradius, yradius * AspectRatio );
```

The **ellipse** function is similar to **arc** except in that separate radii are specified for the x- and y-axes. The elliptic arc is centered at the given x and y coordinates, beginning and terminating at the specified start and end angles and using the current drawing color. For a complete (closed) ellipse, use a start angle of 0° and an end angle of 360°.

Unlike **arc** and **circle**, correction for the screen aspect ratio is not applied automatically. If proportional radii, rather than specific pixel distances are required, the y-axis distance should be adjusted as *yradius * AspectRatio*.

See also **arc**, **circle**, **fillellipse**, **pieslice** and **sector**.

getarccoords

```
#include <graphics.h>
struct arccoordstype  arcinfo;
getarccoords( &arcinfo );
```

The **getarccoords** function returns the end point and center coordinates of the last call to **arc** or **ellipse**. The structure *arccoordstype* is defined in GRAPHICS.H as:

```
struct arccoordstype
{
    int x, y;
    int xstart, ystart, xend, yend;
};
```

The info structure defines the center point (*x,y*) coordinates of the arc, the starting point coordinates (*xstart,ystart* — these are pixel coordinates, not the angle) and the end point (*xend,yend*) of the arc. These values are used by the **pieslice** function, and can be used to draw chords, radii or other lines meeting the ends of the arc.

If the **circle** function was the last curve function called, then **getarccoords** will return the center coordinates of the circle and the (*xstart,ystart*) and (*xend,yend*) coordinates will be the 0° position on the circle.

fillellipse

```
#include <graphics.h>
int xcenter, ycenter, xradius, yradius;
fillellipse( xcenter, ycenter, xradius, yradius );
```

The **fillellipse** function(Turbo C version 2.0 or later) draws an ellipse using xcenter, ycenter as the center point and xradius and yradius as the horizontal and vertical axes, filling the ellipse with the current fill color and fill pattern. Unlike the **ellipse** function, start and end angle arguments are not supported and an elliptical arc cannot be drawn — see **sector**.

See also **arc**, **circle**, **ellipse** and **pieslice**.

pieslice

```
#include <graphics.h>
int xcenter, ycenter, startangle, endangle, radius;
pieslice( xcenter, ycenter, startangle, endangle, radius );
```

The **pieslice** function creates an arc, draws lines from the end points to the center point and then fills in the completed pieslice. The figure outline is drawn using the current drawing color and current line style for the radius lines. It is then filled using the current fill pattern and fill color (see **floodfill**). Screen aspect ratio adjustment is automatic.

See also **arc**, **circle**, **ellipse**, **getaspectratio** and **sector**.

sector

```
#include <graphics.h>
int xcenter, ycenter, startangle, endangle, xradius, yradius;
sector( xcenter, ycenter, startangle, endangle, xradius, yradius );
```

The **sector** function creates an elliptical arc, draws lines from the end points to the center point and then fills in the completed figure. The sector outline is drawn using the current drawing color and current line style for the radius lines, then filled using the current fill pattern and fill color (see **floodfill**). Screen aspect ratio adjustment is automatic.

See also **arc**, **circle**, **ellipse**, **fillellipse**, **getaspectratio** and **pieslice**.

Fill Patterns and Fill Colors

Several functions are provided to handle fill patterns, to fill enclosed areas and to create custom fill patterns; including **floodfill**, **getfillpattern**, **getfillsettings**, **setfillpattern** and **setfillstyle**.

floodfill

```
#include <graphics.h>
int xpoint, ypoint, bordercolor;
floodfill( xpoint, ypoint, bordercolor );
```

The **floodfill** function fills a bounded (enclosed) region defined by the specified *bordercolor* (normally this will be the current drawing color). The (*xpoint,ypoint*) coordinates specify some point to be filled within the area, using the current fill pattern and fill color.

If the start point is outside a bounded region, the exterior region (limited by the borders set by viewport) will be filled. If any break occurs in the line defining the region, then the fill will leak. Only a very small break is required.

For future compatibility, **fillpoly**, instead of **floodfill**, is recommended where possible.

If an error occurs, **graphresult** will return a value of –7 (*out of memory in flood fill*).

See also **fillpoly**, **getfillsettings**, **getlinesettings** and **setgraphbufsize**.

setfillpattern

```
#include <graphics.h>
int color;
char diamond[8] = { 0x10, 0x38, 0x7C, 0xFE,
                    0x7C, 0x38, 0x10, 0x00 };
setfillpattern( diamond, color );
```

The **setfillpattern** selects an 8x8, user-defined fill pattern in the specified color. In the example, *diamond* is a sequence of eight bytes, each byte corresponding to eight pixels in the pattern. One bits turn on pixels, zero bits turn off pixels. The example pattern *diamond* creates a small, 7x7 diamond pattern with a one pixel border at right and bottom.

After **setfillpattern** is called to establish the user-defined pattern, **setfillstyle** must be called to make USER_FILL (12) the current pattern.

A few other possible patterns are:

```
char checker[8] = { 0xAA, 0x55, 0xAA, 0x55,
                    0xAA, 0x55, 0xAA, 0x55 };
char chains1[8] = { 0x6F, 0x40, 0xA0, 0xA0,
                    0xA0, 0x40, 0x6F, 0x00 };
char chains2[8] = { 0x3C, 0xC3, 0xA0, 0x90,
                    0x90, 0xA0, 0x3C, 0xC3 };
```

See also **getfillpattern**, **getfillstyle** and **setfillstyle**.

setfillstyle

```
#include <graphics.h>
setfillstyle( SOLID_FILL, GREEN );
```

The **setfillstyle** function sets the current fill pattern and fill color. Note: *fill* color and *drawing* color are separate and may have different values. Fill patterns are defined in GRAPHICS.H as:

Table 5-3: Fill Patterns

PATTERN NAME	VALUE	DESCRIPTION
EMPTY_FILL	0	background color
SOLID_FILL	1	solid fill
LINE_FILL	2	fill with ————
LTSLASH_FILL	3	fill with ////
SLASH_FILL	4	fill with ////, thick
BKSLASH_FILL	5	fill with \\\\ , thick
LTBKSLASH_FILL	6	fill with \\\\
HATCH_FILL	7	light crosshatch
XHATCH_FILL	8	heavy crosshatch
INTERLEAVE_FILL	9	interleaving lines
WIDE_DOT_FILL	10	wide-spaced dots[1]
CLOSE_DOT_FILL	11	close-spaced dot[1]
USER_FILL	12	user-defined pattern

1. May appear incorrectly in some references as WIDEDOT_FILL and CLOSEDOT_FILL. Labels given here correspond to definitions in GRAPHICS.H.

All patterns except EMPTY_FILL use the current fill color. Note: pattern 12 (USER_FILL) can only be called *after* **setfillpattern** has established a user-defined fill pattern.

See also **fillpoly**, **floodfill**, **getfillpattern** and **getfillstyle**.

getfillpattern

```
#include <graphics.h>
char fillpatterninfo[8];
getfillpattern( &fillpatterninfo );
```

The **getfillpattern** function copies a user-defined fill pattern, set by **setfillpattern**, to the memory space occupied by *fillpatterninfo*.

See **setfillpattern**.

getfillsettings

```
#include <graphics.h>
struct fillsettingtype fillinfo;
getfillsettings( &fillinfo );
```

The **getfillsettings** function returns information in *fillinfo* about the current fillpattern settings. The structure *fillsettingtype* is defined in GRAPHICS.H as:

```
struct fillsettingtype
{
    int pattern;                    /* predefined pattern numbers only */
    int color;
};
```

See also **getfillpattern**, **setfillpattern** and **setfillstyle**.

The Internal Graphics Buffer

As noted previously, several of the graphics functions can return error messages indicating insufficient buffer memory to accomplish their tasks. When this happens, the **setgraphbufsize** function can be used to allocate additional buffer memory.

setgraphbufsize

```
#include <graphics.h>
unsigned bufsize, oldbufsize;
oldbufsize = setgraphbufsize( bufsize );
```

Several of graphics routines use a memory buffer created by **initgraph** via **_graphgetmem**. The default buffer size is 4K (4096 bytes), but this can be decreased to save space or increased if more buffer memory is required.

The **setgraphbufsize** function must be called *before* calling **initgraph**. Also, **setbufgraphsize** returns the original buffer size.

Image Manipulation

In addition to drawing functions, procedures are supplied for copying, erasing, duplicating and manipulating screen images. For any type of animation, these are essential. For less elaborate applications, they are useful in image replication.

imagesize

```
#include <graphics.h>
unsigned size;
size = imagesize(ulx, uly, lrx, lry);
```

The **imagesize** function returns the size in bytes required to store the bit image specified by the screen coordinates. If the size required for the image is greater than 64K, a value of 0xFFFF (unsigned 65535 or signed −1) is returned.

See also **getimage** and **putimage**.

getimage

```
#include <graphics.h>
void far *bitimage;
int xleft, ytop, xright, ybottom;
unsigned  size;
size = imagesize( xleft, ytop, xright, ybottom );
bitimage = far malloc( size );
getimage( xleft, ytop, xright, ybottom, bitimage);
```

The **getimage** function saves the pixel image from the screen area that is specified by the four parameters. The **initsize** function is used to calculate the memory required and the **malloc** function allocates memory for image storage (memory allocation must be less than 64K).

See also **imagesize** and **putimage**.

putimage

```
#include <graphics.h>
void far *bitimage;
int xleft, ytop, ops;
putimage( xleft, ytop, bitimage, ops );
```

The **putimage** function writes a previously saved bit image to the screen, with the upper-left corner of the image appearing at (*xleft,ytop*). The *ops* parameter controls how each image pixel (color) is combined with the existing screen pixels. The *ops* options are enumerated in GRAPHICS.H in *putimage_ops* as:

Table 5-4: Image Put Options

NAME	VALUE	DESCRIPTION
COPY_PUT	0	image is copied to screen, replacing existing pixels
XOR_PUT	1	image is eXclusive-**OR**'d with existing pixels
OR_PUT	2	image is inclusive-**OR**'d with existing pixels
AND_PUT	3	image is **AND**ed with existing pixels
NOT_PUT	4	copies the inverse bit-image to the screen.

The program PUT-DEMO.C will demonstrate how the various **putimage** options operate. PUT-DEMO is written for color monitors (EGA or VGA preferred), but can be adapted to run on monochrome systems, though the color overlay effects will not be as visible or may be markedly different.

I suggest running the program as it stands, then experimenting with different color values and fill patterns.

COPY_PUT: Each pixel in the image is mapped directly to the screen, thereby replacing any existing image pixels. Note: this includes image pixels that are blank (background). An entirely blank image can be used to erase other images or portions of the screen. More often, however, the **XOR_PUT** option is used to ''unmap'' an existing image.

XOR_PUT: Each existing screen pixel's value is e**X**clusively **OR**'d with the corresponding image byte and then the result is written back to the screen. When an image is XOR'd with a existing screen image, the result is a composite of the two.

In PUT-DEMO.C, notice that the LIGHTCYAN pixels (1011) XOR'd with the BLUE (0001) background become LIGHTGREEN (1010), while LIGHTRED **XOR**'d with BLUE (0001) becomes LIGHTCYAN (1011) and the results appear cleanly against the background image.

If the same image is then XOR'd a second time, it cancels itself bit by bit, and the original screen is restored. This option is particularly useful for animation where an image needs to be over an existing screen, then erased again to leave the original screen in place. This put-option will be used heavily in the ANIMATON.C demo (see Chapter 10).

OR_PUT: This might also be called EITHER/OR since each image byte is **OR**'d with corresponding screen pixel and the result is written back to the screen. Remember, each bit in each pixel is **OR**'d with the bits in the image, so the result is a color composite of the background and the image.

In the example program, PUT-DEMO.C, notice how LIGHTCYAN pixels (1011) **OR**'d with BLUE (0001) remain LIGHTCYAN (1011), while LIGHTRED (1100) OR'd with the BLUE (0001) background becomes LIGHTMAGENTA (1101).

AND_PUT: Here only the bits which are 'on' in *both* the screen pixel and the image byte are on in the result. Notice how the blank background in the Star image wipes out both the Box outline and the fill color — except where the Star image actually overlies the Box. Also, the LIGHTRED (1100) **AND**'d with LIGHTBLUE (1001) becomes DARKGREY (1000).

NOT_PUT: This is essentially the same as **COPY_PUT** except that the image is bit inverted — all BLACK (0000) pixels in the image become WHITE (1111), etc. The background image is simply overwritten and lost.

See also **imagesize** and **getimage**.

```
        /*          PUT-DEMO.C — Demonstration of putimage options          */
#ifdef __TINY__
#error Graphics demos will not run in the tiny model.
#endif

#include <conio.h>
#include <stdio.h>
#include <stdlib.h>
#include <alloc.h>
#include <graphics.h>

int     GraphDriver,                        /* graphics device driver      */
        GraphMode,                          /* graphics mode value         */
        MaxColors,                          /* maximum colors available    */
        ErrorCode = 0;                      /* reports any graphics errors */
void    *Star, *Box;                    /* image pointers                  */

void *SaveImage( int left, int top, int right, int bottom )
{
    void    far *image;                     /* local image pointer         */

    image = far malloc( imagesize( left, top, right, bottom ) );
    getimage( left, top, right, bottom, image );        /* save the image  */
    putimage( left, top, image, XOR_PUT );              /* erase the image */
    return( image );                                    /* return image ptr */
}

void CreateImages()
{
    int  pstar[] = { 100,100, 110,120, 100,130, 120,125, 140,140,
                130,120, 140,110, 120,115, 100,100 };
    int  pbox[] = { 100,100, 100,140, 140,140, 140,100, 100,100 };

    setcolor( LIGHTRED );
    setfillstyle( LINE_FILL, LIGHTCYAN );
    fillpoly( sizeof( pstar ) / ( 2 * sizeof( int ) ), pstar );
    Star = SaveImage( 100, 100, 140, 140 );
```

```
setcolor( LIGHTGREEN );
setfillstyle( SOLID_FILL, LIGHTBLUE );
fillpoly( sizeof( pbox ) / ( 2 * sizeof( int ) ), pbox );
Box  = SaveImage( 100, 100, 140, 140 );

setcolor( WHITE );

putimage(  10,    10,    Star,       COPY_PUT    );
outtextxy(  60,    25,    "+" );
putimage(  80,    10,    Box,        COPY_PUT    );
putimage( 200,    10,    Box,        COPY_PUT    );
putimage( 200,    10,    Star,       COPY_PUT    );
outtextxy( 130,    25,                "COPY_PUT"  );

putimage(  10,    60,    Star,       COPY_PUT    );
outtextxy(  60,    75,    "+"                     );
putimage(  80,    60,    Box,        COPY_PUT    );
putimage( 200,    60,    Box,        COPY_PUT    );
putimage( 200,    60,    Star,       AND_PUT     );
outtextxy( 130,    75,                " AND_PUT"  );

putimage(  10,   110,    Star,       COPY_PUT    );
outtextxy(  60,   125,    "+"                     );
putimage(  80,   110,    Box,        COPY_PUT    );
putimage( 200,   110,    Box,        COPY_PUT    );
putimage( 200,   110,    Star,       NOT_PUT     );
outtextxy( 130,   125,                " NOT_PUT"  );

putimage( 310,    10,    Star,       COPY_PUT    );
outtextxy( 360,    25,    "+"                     );
putimage( 380,    10,    Box,        COPY_PUT    );
putimage( 500,    10,    Box,        COPY_PUT    );
putimage( 500,    10,    Star,       OR_PUT      );
putimage( 500,    10,    Star,       XOR_PUT     );
outtextxy( 430,    15,                "  OR_PUT"  );
outtextxy( 430,    25,                "     and  " );
```

```
    outtextxy(   430,   35,                    " XOR_PUT"   );

    putimage(    310,   60,    Star,    COPY_PUT    );
    outtextxy(   360,   75,    "+"                  );
    putimage(    380,   60,    Box,     COPY_PUT    );
    putimage(    500,   60,    Box,     COPY_PUT    );
    putimage(    500,   60,    Star,    OR_PUT      );
    outtextxy(   430,   75,             "   OR_PUT" );

    putimage(    310,   110,   Star,    COPY_PUT    );
    outtextxy(   360,   125,   "+"                  );
    putimage(    380,   110,   Box,     COPY_PUT    );
    putimage(    500,   110,   Box,     COPY_PUT    );
    putimage(    500,   110,   Star,    XOR_PUT     );
    outtextxy(   430,   125,            " XOR_PUT"  );
}

void Initialize()                            /* initialize graphics system and report errors */
{
    GraphDriver = DETECT;                             /* request auto-detection       */
    initgraph( &GraphDriver, &GraphMode, "" );
    ErrorCode = graphresult();                        /* test initialization results  */
    if ( ErrorCode != grOk )                  /* if error occurred during init  */
    {
        printf(" Graphics System Error: %s\n",
                grapherrormsg( ErrorCode ) );
        exit( 1 );
    }
    MaxColors = getmaxcolor() + 1;                    /* read maximum color range */
}

void Pause()                                          /* wait for key to be pressed */
{
    if( kbhit ) getch();
    getch();
}
```

```
main()
{
    Initialize();                    /* set graphics mode      */
    CreateImages();                  /* create and save images */
    Pause();
    closegraph();                    /* restore text mode      */
}
```

CHAPTER 6

GRAPHICS TEXT FUNCTIONS

Once a graphics mode has been set, the conventional text displays are no longer available; and labels and text information can only be displayed using graphics text displays.

In graphics modes, however, graphics text display operates quite differently from conventional text display. For example, in graphics modes, the conventional character screen positions (column and row coordinates) no longer apply and an individual character can appear almost anywhere on the screen. Special provisions are therefore required for tracking the screen display position, deciding where the next display line should appear and writing graphics text to the screen. These include the functions **outtext** and **outtextxy**.

Because character sizes can be varied and different vertical and horizontal justifications are offered and, because text can be displayed in both vertical and horizontal orientations, the line offset and display positions become more than a little confusing. These variable settings are controlled by **settextstyle**, **settextjustify** and **setusercharsize**.

With these variables and complications in mind, several functions have been provided to make it easier to keep track of display positions, font sizes and string widths. These include **gettextsettings**, **textheight** and **textwidth**.

Because I want to be able to display program variables and other changing data, as well as string constants, I need graphics equivalents for the conventional text functions. These capabilities will be discussed in Chapter 8, with the functions **erasestr, printf** and **gprintc** offering examples of advanced graphics text handling functions.

Also, with Turbo C version 2.0 (and Turbo Pascal version 5.0), the **installuserfont** function allows new graphics fonts and user-created fonts to be incorporated in your programs. See also Chapter 17 — **The Turbo Font Editor**.

The first task is simply to be able to write to the screen while in graphics mode:

Text Functions

outtext

```
#include <graphics.h>
outtext( "Display string for viewport" );
```

The **outtext** function displays a string in the viewport (graphics window), beginning at CP. The current font selection, drawing color, character size, text orientation (direction) and justification are used.

If horizontal justification is LEFT_TEXT and direction is HORIZ_DIR (default settings for graphics text display), then CP's x-axis coordinate is advanced by *textwidth(textstring)* — otherwise the CP is not altered.

See also **gettextsettings**, **gprintf**, **gprintc**, **outtextxy**, **setcolor**, **settextsettings**, **textheight** and **textwidth**.

outtextxy

```
#include <graphics.h>
int x, y;
outtextxy( x, y, "Display string for viewport" );
```

The **outtextxy** function displays a string in the viewport (graphics window), beginning at the coordinates specified by (*x,y*) relative to the viewport settings. The current font selection, drawing color, character size, text orientation (direction) and justification are used.

The current position's (CP) coordinates are not affected.

See also **gettextsettings**, **gprintf**, **gprintc**, **outtext**, **setcolor**, **settextsettings**, **textheight** and **textwidth**.

The **outtext** and **outtextxy** functions provide the basic text I/O handling in graphics modes. More advanced graphics text I/O and text formatting capabilities will be demonstrated shortly using the **gprintf** and **gprintc** functions.

Graphics Text Styles/Justification/Sizing

Where conventional text modes offer the display equivalent of a typewritten page, graphics text modes come closer to providing a typeset display. This enhancement is capable of changing fonts, selecting different horizontal and vertical justifications, changing character sizes and even running text displays vertically instead of horizontally.

settextstyle

```
#include <graphics.h>
int font, direction, charsize;
settextstyle( font, direction, charsize );
```

The function **settextstyle** sets the current graphics text *font*, the *direction* for the text display (horizontal or vertical) and the *charsize*.

The standard *font_names* are defined in GRAPHICS.H as:

Table 6-1: Graphics Text Fonts

NAME[1]	VALUE	DESCRIPTION
DEFAULT_FONT	0	bit-mapped 8x8 font
TRIPLEX_FONT	1	stroked triplex font
SMALL_FONT	2	stroked small font
SANS_SERIF_FONT	3	stroked sans-serif font
GOTHIC_FONT	4	stroked gothic font

1. For additional fonts, see also Chapter 17 — **The Turbo Font Editor.**

The DEFAULT_FONT is built into the graphics system. Of the other fonts, only one is kept in memory at any time and the .CHR files for the selected font must be located in the directory or subdirectory indicated by **initgraph** as *driverpath* before it can be loaded.

Multiple fonts, however, can be linked to your program using the BGIOBJ utility (see **Linking Graphics Drivers/Fonts** — Chapter 7). In this case, the **registerbgifont** function is used to select the font required.

By default, graphics text direction is horizontal, but can be set to vertical (rotated 90° counterclockwise). The two graphics text directions are defined in GRAPHICS.H as:

Table 6-2: Graphics Text Directions

NAME	VALUE	DESCRIPTION
HORIZ_DIR	0	left to right (*default*)
VERT_DIR	1	bottom to top

In vertical orientation, the text string begins at the bottom and runs up. No provisions currently exist for a string display running down the page or for an inverted string (upside down, running right to left), but these could be created using the image rotation techniques demonstrated in Chapter 12.

For bit-mapped font(s): *charsize* may be 0..10. Values zero and one display 8x8 pixel rectangles, value two displays a 16x16 pixel rectangle, etc., up to 10 times normal size.

For stroked fonts: *charsize = 0* magnifies the stroked font by the default factor of 4 or by the user-defined size factors set by **setusercharsize**. The maximum valid *charsize* is 10.

If invalid values are passed to **settextjustify**, **graphresult** will return −11 (*general error*) and the current text settings will remain unchanged.

See also **settextjustify**, **textheight** and **textwidth**.

installuserfont

```
#include <graphics.h>
int  USER_FONT = 0;
USER_FONT = installuserfont( "\FontPath\FontName.CHR" );
```

The **installuserfont** (Turbo C version 2.0) function loads a .CHR (stroked) font that is not built into the BGI system, and returns a font ID number which can be passed to **settextstyle** to select the font.

Up to 20 external fonts can be installed at any time. If the internal font table is full, a value of -11 (*grError*) is returned.

See also Chapter 17 — **The Turbo Font Editor**.

settextjustify

```
#include <graphics.h>
int  hjustify, vjustify;
settextjustify( hjustify, vjustify );
```

The **settextjustify** function selects horizontal and vertical text justification. The default values are LEFT_TEXT, TOP_TEXT (0,2) and the justification terms *text_just* are defined in GRAPHICS.H as:

Table 6-3: Text Justification Terms

(HORIZONTAL JUSTIFY)		(VERTICAL JUSTIFY)	
NAME	VALUE	NAME	VALUE
LEFT_TEXT	0	BOTTOM_TEXT	0
CENTER_TEXT	1	CENTER_TEXT	1
RIGHT_TEXT	2	TOP_TEXT	2

For horizontal justification, LEFT_TEXT displays the text string to the right starting at CP, CENTER_TEXT displays the text string centered right/left at CP, and RIGHT_TEXT displays the text string to the left, ending at CP.

For vertical justification, BOTTOM_TEXT aligns the bottom of the character string with CP, CENTER_TEXT aligns the center of the display string at CP and TOP_TEXT aligns the top of the string with CP.

When justification is set as LEFT_TEXT and *direction* = HORIZ_DIR, the current position's *x* setting is advanced after a call to **outtext** or **gprintf** by **textwidth(string)**.

See also **settextstyle**.

Figure 6-1: Text Justification

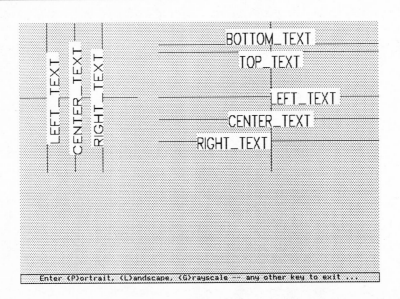

Several options for text alignment are supported as shown above. Notice that the CENTER_TEXT line (vertical orientation at left) is centered according to the total font height. This includes blank header space above the characters. All alignments include this header space, as well as a brief margin following the end of a string (or a single character).

setusercharsize

```
#include <graphics.h>
int xmult, xdiv, ymult, ydiv;
setusercharsize( xmult, xdiv, ymult, ydiv );
```

The **setusercharsize** function provides user-defined character magnification for stroked fonts only! This does not function with the DEFAULT_FONT characters and the font adjustment parameters are active only if **settextstyle** has been called to set *charsize = 0*.

When **setusercharsize** is called to select custom character scaling, the resulting width is defined as *xmult/xdiv*, the resulting height as *ymult/ydiv*.

For example, to create a display with characters scaled to a height of three (24 pixels) and twice as wide as they are tall (48 pixels), **setusercharsize** would be called with:

```
xmult = 6;   xdiv = 1;
ymult = 3;   ydiv = 1;
setusercharsize( xmult, xdiv, ymult, ydiv );
```

Alternatively, for tall and narrow characters —

```
xmult = 3;   xdiv = 2;
ymult = 6;   ydiv = 1;
setusercharsize( xmult, xdiv, ymult, ydiv );
```

— would produce characters 12 pixels wide and 48 pixels tall.
See also **gettextsettings**.

Text Settings Information

With the variety of choices in fonts, text direction, and vertical and horizontal justification, it is helpful to be able to find out what the current settings are and also to determine how wide and how tall a text string is using the current settings. For these applications, three functions are provided: **gettextsettings**, **textheight** and **textwidth**.

gettextsettings

```
#include <graphics.h>
struct textsettingstype textinfo;
gettextsettings( &textinfo );
```

The **gettextsettings** function fills *textinfo* with the current text font, direction, size, and horizontal and vertical justification. The structure *textsettingstype* is defined in GRAPHICS.H as:

```
struct textsettingstype
{
      int font;        int direction;
      int charsize;
      int horiz;       int vert;
};
```

See also **outtext**, **textheight**, **textwidth** and **settextstyle**.

textheight/textwidth

```
#include <graphics.h>
int charheight, charwidth;
charheight = textheight( "Text String" );
charwidth = textwidth( "Text String" );
```

The **textheight** function returns the height of a string in pixels, using the current font size, scaling factors and text direction. This may be the height of a single character or the height of an entire string. When a single character is used, an uppercase character is customary — even though the information returned is based on calculated size, rather than actual display size (i.e. − a ''u'' will return the same size as ''U'').

The **textwidth** function returns the width of a string in pixels, using the current font size, scaling factors and text direction. This may be the width of a single character or, more often, the width of an entire string.

CHAPTER 7

ADVANCED C GRAPHICS

The Graphics Library

With the release of version 1.5 of Turbo C, a graphics function library has been supplied (GRAPHICS.H) as a supplement to the standard memory model libraries. Turbo C provides several standard libraries that are memory model specific and, when using Turbo C's Integrated Development Environment (TC.EXE), the appropriate memory model is loaded automatically, corresponding to the memory model selected (see menu under **O**ptions/Compiler/Model).

The graphics library, however, is separate and is not automatically included at compile time. For this reason, there are two options when using graphics functions with Turbo C: using .PRJ files or incorporating GRAPHICS.LIB in one or more of the standard libraries.

Before proceeding, remember that the graphics header file must be called in each module of your source code before any graphics functions can be used. Thus, the source line *#include <graphics.h>*, should appear in all code modules.

Also, the graphics functions will not work using the TINY memory model because of limited memory. Larger memory models make more memory available for your program.

Graphics Using .PRJ (project) Files

The simplest method of including the graphics library (using TC.EXE, the Integrated Development Environment) at compile time is to use a .PRJ file.

For example, in a program named PROGNAME.C, you would create a project file, PROGNAME.PRJ, which includes the line:

progname graphics.lib

It's all quite simple. To compile, you simply select the pull-down **Project** menu and enter the project name *PROGNAME* (the extension *.PRJ* is optional and will be assumed by default). Now select **Compile** (Alt-C) and proceed.

With the release of Turbo C version 2.0, a new option (Option/Linker/Graphics Library) instructs the linker to automatically search the Graphics Library without requiring a project file.

Or, using the command line version of Turbo C (TCC.EXE), you would simply include the graphics library in your command:

tcc progname graphics.lib

Again, quite simple.

Remember though, you must specify that the graphics library is to be included or you will find an astonishing number of errors reported by the linker.

Adding GRAPHICS.LIB to the Standard Libraries

As an alternative to using .PRJ files or to calling GRAPHICS.LIB from the command line, Turbo C version 2.0 provides an option that instructs the linker to automatically search for the Graphics Library without requiring a project file. Use the **O**ptions/**L**inker/**G**raphics library menu settings.

In version 1.5, the graphics library can be incorporated into one or more of the standard libraries using the TLIB.EXE, the Turbo object code librarian (distributed with Turbo C version 1.5 — see Appendix B in **Turbo C Additions and Enhancements**).

To add the graphics library to a specific memory model, the **Cx.LIB** file and **GRAPHICS.LIB** file should be in the same directory/subdirectory before entering the command: *tlib cx +graphics.lib<CR>*, where *c*x identifies the specific memory model to use.

If you prefer to add the graphics library to all of the memory model libraries, you might create a .BAT file reading:

```
tlib cs  +graphics.lib
tlib cc  +graphics.lib
tlib cm +graphics.lib
tlib cl   +graphics.lib
tlib ch  +graphics.lib
```

The disadvantage of incorporating the graphics library is getting a slightly longer compile time on non-graphic programs ... but this is a minor matter and hardly rates as an inconvenience.

Note: you might like to link the graphics drivers and graphics fonts *before* incorporating the graphics library.

Linking Graphics Drivers/Fonts

By default, Turbo C (and Turbo Pascal) use dynamically linked graphics drivers (*.BGI files) and graphics fonts (*.CHR files). While the use of external drivers and fonts offers advantages in limiting compiled program size and flexibility for adding new drivers and fonts at later dates, there are two decided disadvantages to depending on external files for operation.

First, when using external drivers and fonts, the drive and directory path where the external utilities are located must be specified by the programmer at compile time (see **initgraph** — Chapter 1). If the specified path or drive is changed at a later time, then the program must be recompiled with the new information.

Second, while the .BGI and .CHR files can be distributed with your compiled program, these extra files are subject to accidental erasure and to other hazards ... any of which can result in a dissatisfied user.

There is an alternative — linking the drivers and fonts directly as a part of the graphics library so that no external files are required. After this is done, the drivers and fonts will be a part of the .EXE code produced by the C compiler. At this point, the graphics library can be added to the standard libraries, included using a .PRJ file, or linked by a command line specification as detailed previously.

However, in order to link the driver and font files, the BGIOBJ utility must first be called to convert the .BGI and .CHR files to .OBJ files (see Appendix D in **Turbo C Additions and Enhancements**).

The BGIOBJ utility is invoked as:

```
bgiobj <source>
```

It produces an object file with the same name as *source* but the extension .OBJ. Thus, CGA.BGI produces CGA.OBJ and TRIP.CHR produces TRIP.OBJ.

Once the .OBJ file(s) are created, TLIB is invoked:

```
tlib graphics +cga +trip
```

It adds the CGA driver and TRIP font to GRAPHICS.LIB. Note: the extensions .LIB and .OBJ are understood and do not need to be specified.

You can also use the following two .BAT files:

ADD-DRVR.BAT file for adding graphics drivers to GRAPHICS.LIB

```
bgiobj cga
bgiobj egavga
bgiobj herc
bgiobj att
bgiobj pc3270
bgiobj ibm8514
tlib graphics +cga +egavga +herc +att +pc3270 +ibm8514
```

ADD-FONT.BAT file for adding graphics fonts to GRAPHICS.LIB

```
bgiobj trip
bgiobj litt
bgiobj sans
bgiobj goth
tlib graphics +trip +litt +sans +goth
```

Using the Linked Drivers/Fonts

To use graphics drivers and fonts after linking with the graphics library, there is one other requirement that does not appear when using external drivers and fonts: the driver(s) and/or font(s) must be registered *before* calling **initgraph**.

Several of these functions appear in both near and far versions (as **register...** and **registerfar...**). The **registerfar...** functions and the /F option (see **The /F Option** in Appendix D of the **Turbo C version 2.0 Reference Guide**) provide more memory for your programs by registering drivers and fonts at *far* segment address.

registerbgidriver/registerfarbgidriver

```
#include <graphics.h>
if ( registerbgidriver( <DRIVER_name> ) < 0 ) exit(1);
```

The **registerbgidriver** function is used to register a linked-in graphics driver. If the specified graphics driver is not found, a negative error code is returned; otherwise, the internal driver number is returned.

Table 7-1: Graphics Drivers

DRIVER FILE	NORMAL SYMBOLIC NAME	FAR[1] SYMBOLIC NAME
CGA.BGI	CGA_driver	CGA_driver_far
EGAVGA.BGI	EGAVGA_driver	EGAVGA_driver_far
HERC.BGI	Herc_driver	Herc_driver_far
ATT.BGI	ATT_driver	ATT_driver_far
PC3270.BGI	PC3270_driver	PC3270_driver_far
IBM8514.BGI	IBM8514_driver	IBM8514_driver_far

1. See the next section, **Linker Error With Drivers and Fonts** for explanation on **registerfarbgidriver** and *far* driver symbolic names.

/* DRIVER.I — call RegisterDrivers() */

```
#include <graphics.h>
void RegisterDrivers()
{
    if( registerbgidriver( CGA_driver     ) < 0 )    exit(1);
    if( registerbgidriver( EGAVGA_driver) < 0 )    exit(1);
    if( registerbgidriver( Herc_driver    ) < 0 )    exit(1);
    if( registerbgidriver( ATT_driver     ) < 0 )    exit(1);
    if( registerbgidriver( PC3270_driver  ) < 0 )    exit(1);
    if( registerbgidriver( IBM8514_driver ) < 0 )    exit(1);
}

main()
{
    RegisterDrivers();
    Initialize();
    ....
    closegraph();
}
```

Portability: IBM PCs and compatibles only, corresponding functions exist in Turbo Pascal.

See preceding for information on creating linked-in graphics drivers.

registerbgifont/registerfarbgifont

```
#include <graphics.h>
if ( registerbgifont( name_font ) < 0 ) exit(1);
```

The **registerbgifont** function is used to register a linked stroked font character set. If the specified font is not found, a negative error code is returned; otherwise, the registered font number is returned.

Table 7-2: Graphics Fonts

FONT FILE	NORMAL SYMBOLIC NAME	FAR SYMBOLIC NAME
TRIP.CHR	triplex_font	triplex_font_far
LITT.CHR	small_font	small_font_far
SANS.CHR	sanserif_font	sanserif_font_far
GOTH.CHR	gothic_font	gothic_font_far

1. See next section, **Linker Error With Drivers and Fonts** for explanation on **registerfarbgifont** and _far_ font symbolic names.

/* FONTS.I — call RegisterFonts() */

```
#include <graphics.h>
void RegisterFonts()
{
        if( registerbgifont( triplex_font  ) < 0 )    exit(1);
        if( registerbgifont( small_font        ) < 0 )    exit(1);
        if( registerbgifont( sanserif_font   ) < 0 )    exit(1);
        if( registerbgifont( gothic_font  ) < 0 )    exit(1);
}

main()
{
        RegisterDrivers();
        RegisterFonts();
        Initialize();
        ....
        closegraph();
}
```

Portability: IBM PCs and compatibles only, corresponding functions exist in Turbo Pascal.

See preceding for information on creating linked-in graphics fonts.

Linker Errors With Drivers and Fonts

It is possible for a linker error to occur when using linked graphics drivers and fonts. The error message, *Segment exceeds 64K*, or similar will appear; a problem which is most likely to occur with **tiny**, **small** or **compact** memory models.

When BGIOBJ creates .OBJ files, they all use the same memory segment, **_TEXT**. If too many files are linked and the segment exceeds the 64 size limit, then an error will occur.

If this happens, the /**F** option should be used with BGIOBJ to create new memory segments of the form **FILENAME_TEXT**, leaving the default segment free for other applications. Doing so will have two immediate effects.

First, an **F** will be appended to the .OBJ file names. Thus CGA.BGI would produce CGAF.OBJ instead of CGA.OBJ and the TLIB commands would need to be altered accordingly. Note: the source file names must also be seven characters or less in length to allow for this addition.

Second, the public names have **_far** appended and the *register-farbgidriver* and *registerfarbgifont* functions will be needed in the **RegisterDrivers** and **RegisterFonts** routines.

```
if( registerfarbgidriver( Herc_driver_far   ) < 0 )   exit(1);
if( registerfarbgifont( triplex_font_far    ) < 0 )   exit(1);
```

See Appendix D in either the **Turbo C 1.5 Additions and Enhancements** or **Turbo C 2.0 Reference Guide** for further details.

Custom Graphics Memory Management

Provision does exist for customizing the graphics memory management procedures. This should not, however, be attempted lightly. The following two functions are included here solely for completeness.

_graphfreemem

```
#include <graphics.h>
unsigned size;
int *memptr;
_graphfreemem( &memptr, size );
```

Normally, **_graphfreemem** is called by **closegraph** to deallocate the memory reserved for drivers, fonts and internal buffers. By default, **_graphfreemem** calls the **free** function, however, custom memory management can be created by defining a new **_graphfreemem**. The new **_graphfreemem** function must be declared matching the standard function (see Chapter 4, **Turbo C 1.5 Additions and Enhancements**).

See also **_graphgetmem**.

_graphgetmem

```
#include <graphics.h>
unsigned size;
_graphgetmem( size );
```

Normally, **_graphgetmem** is called by **initgraph** to allocate memory space for graphic drivers, graphic character fonts and internal buffers. By default, **_graphgetmem** uses the **malloc** function to set memory allocation but custom memory management can be created by defining a new **_graphgetmem** function. The new **_graphgetmem** function must be declared matching the standard function — see Chapter 4, **Turbo C 1.5 Additions and Enhancements.**

See also **_graphfreemem**.

PART TWO

USING TURBO C GRAPHICS

In the first section of this book, I discussed the various Turbo C graphics commands and briefly illustrated some of them. In the next section, these commands will be used to create graphics and utilities and to demonstrate how various procedures and applications can be created.

The demonstrations will include combining text and graphics, creating two- and three-dimensional graph displays for business applications, simple animation techniques, turtle graphics, image manipulation with rotations in two and three dimensions, image file storage, using a mouse with graphics displays and creating custom graphics fonts. Also, because programs must operate on a variety of hardware with varying resolutions and color capabilities, some techniques for adapting to various hardware will also be shown.

Caveat

Most of these demonstrations have been created specifically for use with EGA or higher resolution graphics hardware using a color monitor. When practical, additional code has been included for adaptation to CGA or monographic equipment, however, some modification of the source codes may be necessary for lower resolution modes.

While lower resolution and monochrome equipment is graphics capable, 640x350 color provides a good minimum standard for demonstrating graphics applications.

If these applications and demonstrations were written to operate only under the limitations of the lowest common resolutions and color capabilities, a great deal of real capability would necessarily be ignored.

The EGA vertical resolution of 350 pixels provides space to show far more detail than is possible with 200 pixels (though the 1024 vertical resolution of the IBM-8514 would be nice). A palette of 16 colors certainly shows more visual information than monochrome. The utilities demonstrated here will make use of these capabilities whenever possible, even though they are not universally available.

CHAPTER 8

COMBINING TEXT WITH GRAPHICS

While some earlier computer designs did not differentiate between text and graphics, contemporary MS-DOS systems do not permit mapping the ROM-based character set(s) directly into a graphics display. To overcome this limitation, both Turbo C and Turbo Pascal provide a default bit-mapped graphics character set which is effectively a replacement for the ROM character set. The set includes the extended ASCII characters (ASCII 0x80..0xFF) which provide foreign characters such as the English pound sign, the Japanese yen sign, the accented vowels, and the graphics and math characters.

Note: these extended ASCII characters are not included in the current stroked fonts and; therefore, attempts to print extended character codes using stroked fonts are simply ignored. The graphics fonts distributed with the Turbo Font Editor, however, (see Chapter 17 for details) do include — for the most part — extended ASCII character set equivalents.

These graphics character fonts are not merely replacements for the ROM based characters. In graphics modes, text displays can be much more elaborate than possible under text modes.

Four, fancy stroked typefaces — Gothic, Sans Serif, Triplex (Roman) and Small — are supplied. String character positions can be adjusted by pixel instead of character positions; both the default and the stroked typefaces can be enlarged up to 10 times normal; the stroked typefaces can be proportioned to be taller or wider; and strings may be set flush left, centered, or flush right and displayed vertically as well as horizontally.

Further, while the default font is a fixed width font (all characters are the same basic width), the stroked fonts are proportional (i.e.– a capital 'W' is proportionally wider than a lowercase 'i') and character placement and string spacing reflect these, providing a better appearance than typewriter style text.

But there are also a few limitations: the two principal output functions **outtext** and **outtextxy**, discussed in Chapter 6, each write a string to screen — **outtext** using the default CP and **outtextxy** accepting a screen position for the text output. Both of these functions accept only a string for output; there is no direct provision for printing variables or building strings for output as supported in text modes by the **printf** and **cprintf** functions, however, it is possible to create analogous functions to serve these same purposes.

The gprintf function

The **gprintf** function has been used in most, if not all, of the previous demo programs and a slightly different version of **gprintf** appears in the BGIDEMO program distributed with Turbo C version 1.5. In neither case, however, has the operation of the **gprintf** function been explained in any detail.

In brief, **gprintf** is used like **printf** to accept a variable number of arguments and to combine these together in creating a string which is output to the screen. Unlike **printf**, **gprintf** is called with output coordinates, is usable only in the graphics mode and does not function in the text mode. Depending on the text direction (horizontal or vertical) either the xloc or yloc coordinate is returned with the appropriate offset so that the next string printed will be correctly aligned.

The first trick is to accept a variable argument list and to then use it to create the appropriate output string. This is provided in the declaration of **gprintf** and in the local variables:

```
void gprintf( int *xloc, int *yloc, char *fmt, ... )
{
        va_list  argptr;
```

The first two arguments passed to **gprintf** are the output coordinates: the x- and y-axis location (CP). The third argument, *char *fmt,* is a pointer to a string which may be simply an alphanumeric set of characters or may be a format string; that is, a string which includes format specifications for subsequent arguments.

The ellipsis (...), which ends the argument list, indicates that an undetermined number of arguments may, or may not, be included. The actual number of arguments passed in each call to **gprintf** is determined by the number of format specifications included in *fmt*.

Note: if your actual argument list is longer than the number of arguments required by the format specifications, no error message will appear and the excess arguments will be ignored. On the other hand, if there is a shortage of arguments, the compiler will issue an error message accordingly.

The *va_list* data type is shown in **stdarg.h** and declares an array containing information which will be needed to access the argument list.

The remaining local variables are *str[140]*, a buffer string of 140 characters to hold the eventual output string; *textinfo* which will be used to check the text direction and *pos_adj* which is initially set equal to *xloc*.

```
char        str[140];
struct      textsettingstype textinfo;
int         pos_adj = *xloc;
```

The **va_start** function initializes the argument pointer array (*argptr*) to point to *fmt*, the format string, which is the last *fixed* parameter passed to **gprintf**. The **va_start** function must be called before any call to **va_arg** or **va_end**.

```
va_start( argptr, fmt );
vsprintf( str, fmt, argptr );
```

The **vsprintf** function behaves very much like the familiar **printf** except that output goes to a null-terminated (ASCIIZ) string buffer (*str*) which uses the **va_arg** array and the argument format instructions in *fmt*. It is the programmer's responsibility to insure that the *str* buffer is large enough to hold the created string.

If no optional arguments (except the string *fmt* itself) are passed to **gprintf**, then *str* equals *fmt*.

Once the output string is created in the *str* buffer, **gettextsettings** gets the current text justification and direction instructions.

```
gettextsettings( &textinfo );
```

Version 1.5 Position Correction

The text justification information is used for several purposes. Originally, in Turbo C version 1.5, there was no thought of using the text justification settings with the vertical text direction (an oversight which has been corrected with the release of version 2.0).

In vertical orientation, however, the text justification settings do affect the display position of the output string ... but with the string displaced left by the height of the text string.

For example, with a string height of 20 pixels, in RIGHT_TEXT justification, the base of the character string appears 20 pixels to the left of the x-axis position. In CENTER_TEXT justification, the base of the string appears 10 pixels left of the x-axis position and, in LEFT_TEXT, the base of the string appears at the x-axis position (the string should appear left-flush to the right of the x-axis position — not right-flush at the left).

Thus, for all stroked fonts (but not for the bit-mapped font), a horizontal adjustment to the right — equal to textheight — is required to correctly position the output string. In CENTER_TEXT, the positioning can be improved by reducing the adjustment by $1/8$ of the textheight.

```
#if(_TURBOC_ == 0x150)
{
    if( textinfo.direction && textinfo.font )
    {
        pos_adj += textheight( str );
        if( textinfo.horiz == CENTER_TEXT )pos_adj -= textheight( str ) / 8;
```

```
                }
        }
        #endif
```

Next, **outtextxy** writes *str* to the screen in graphics mode, using *pos_adj* and **yloc* to determine the string output position. The graphics string is written using the current text style, font, drawing color and text justification settings.

```
outtextxy( pos_adj, *yloc, str );
switch ( textinfo.direction )
{
        case    HORIZ_DIR : *yloc += textheight( str ) + 2; break;
        case    VERT_DIR  : *xloc += textheight( str ) +  2; break;
};
```

With the screen output finished, *textinfo.direction* is tested again to decide whether to update the x-axis or y-axis coordinate in order to be ready for the next screen output. In graphics text output, including a \n in the format string to end the output string with a carriage_return/line_feed combination would be essentially ineffective. Instead, **gprintf** automatically provides the graphics analog of a line feed by updating the appropriate x-axis or y-axis position coordinate.

```
                va_end( argptr );
        }
```

Lastly, **va_end** is called to close the pointer to the argument list. This is basic housekeeping that follows any call to **va_start**. Failure to close with this function might cause unexpected behavior in subsequent operations.

The gprintc function

The **gprintc** function operates almost the same as **gprintf**, but with one important difference. In text modes, when a string is written to the screen, any existing text at the output position is simply overwritten. In graphics modes, this is not the case and, when **gprintf** is used, the output text is written over the existing screen image. Only the pixels which actually comprise the string characters are written and the background pixels remain unchanged. Thus, depending on the existing screen image, the resulting output may, or may not, be legible.

This can be true when a new graphics string is written over an existing graphics string.

To correct this problem without the difficulty of erasing and recreating the entire screen, the function **gprintc** is provided and it includes a call to the **erasestr** function.

```
void gprintc( int *xloc, int *yloc, char *fmt, ... )
{
        .....
        gettextsettings( &textinfo );
        erasestr( *xloc, *yloc, str );
        .....
        outtextxy( pos_adj, *yloc, str );
        .....
}
```

Other than calling **erasestr** with the position information and a copy of the formatted output string, **gprintc** functions precisely the same as **gprintf**.

The gprintxy function

Both the **gprintf** and **gprintc** functions require the x- and y-axis coordinates to be passed, as pointers, to variables so that the changed coordinates can be returned for the next string output. This is not, however, always convenient and; therefore, the **gprintxy** function is also included in GPRINT.I.

The **gprintxy** function differs in accepting screen coordinates that are passed as values — no deposit, no return — but, otherwise acts exactly the same as **gprintc**. Thus, **gprintxy** can be called as:

```
gprintxy( 10, 10, "Something to print with a number %d ", number );
```

While the same call to **gprintc** would require:

```
int  x = 10, y = 10;
gprintc( &x, &y, "Something to print with a number %d ", number );
```

In many applications, this difference will matter little but, at other times, such as in a quick graphics line display for debugging, the **gprintxy** function can provide a tremendous convenience.

The erasestr function

The **erasestr** function is provided to erase the appropriate area of the screen before writing a string to the screen. This is principally intended to remove a block of graphics background which would interfere with the string image, however, this function can also be used to erase a string or portion of a string if necessary.

From **gprintc**, **erasestr** is called with the x-axis and y-axis coordinates that will be used to position the output string.

```
void erasestr( int xloc, int yloc, char *str )
{
```

While the *textinfo* structure has already been accessed from **gprintc**, this information is not directly available to **erasestr** and, instead of passing the data in the call to **erasestr**, a local information structure is loaded with the justification settings and text output direction.

```
struct    textsettingstype textinfo;
int       xdim, ydim;
void      *textimage;
gettextsettings( &textinfo );
```

According to the text output direction, the x and y dimensions of the output string are assigned to the appropriate variables. Also, for horizontal output, the *xloc* variable is decreased to provide a one-pixel offset for the erase area. For vertical output, the *yloc* variable is increased for the same reason.

```
            switch ( textinfo.direction )
      {
            case HORIZ_DIR :  xdim = textwidth( str );
                              ydim = textheight( str );
                              xloc− −;                    break;
            case  VERT_DIR :  ydim = textwidth( str );
                              xdim = textheight( str );
                              yloc++;                     break;
      }
```

In the next steps, the *xloc* variable is adjusted according to the horizontal justification setting.

```
switch ( textinfo.horiz )
{
      case    LEFT_TEXT :                    break;
      case CENTER_TEXT : xloc −= xdim / 2;  break;
      case   RIGHT_TEXT : xloc −= xdim;      break;
}
```

The *yloc* variable is adjusted using the vertical justification setting.

```
switch ( textinfo.vert )
{
      case BOTTOM_TEXT : yloc −= ydim;        break;
      case CENTER_TEXT : yloc −= ydim / 2;     break;
      case TOP_TEXT :                          break;
}
```

Before any attempt is made to erase a screen area, two tests are done to insure that the *xloc* and *yloc* coordinates fall within the valid screen area. If the *xloc* or *yloc* coordinates fall outside the screen area, then nothing would be erased from the screen because the subsequent calls to the **getimage** and **putimage** functions would be attempting to use coordinates that did not exist in video memory.

If necessary, *xloc* and *yloc* are adjusted to insure they lie within the screen limits and, at the same time, the *xdim* and *ydim* offsets are changed to compensate appropriately.

```
while( xloc < 0 ) { xloc++; xdim− −; }
while( yloc < 0 ) { yloc++; ydim− −; }
```

Now it's time to actually erase a block of screen. The first step is to allocate memory for *textimage* according to the screen area which will be cleared. The function **imagesize** uses the *xloc*, *yloc*, *xdim* and *ydim* variables to return an unsigned integer that indicates the number of bytes required for the selected image.

```
textimage = far malloc( imagesize( xloc, yloc, xdim, ydim ) );
```

Next, **getimage** is called to store the screen area image in *textimage*, then **putimage** returns the image using the *XOR_PUT* option to clear it. This leaves a blank screen in the desired area.

```
getimage( xloc, yloc, xloc + xdim, yloc + ydim, textimage );
putimage( xloc, yloc, textimage, XOR_PUT );
```

Lastly, the **free** function is used to release the memory allocated for *textimage*. The *textimage* pointer variable can not be referenced outside of the **erasestr** function. Memory which has been allocated locally, however, does remain allocated until it is specifically released — and it must be released while the *textimage* pointer is still available — before exiting **erasestr**.

```
        free( textimage );
}
```

When **erasestr** is called again, a new block of memory will be allocated and a new *textimage* pointer assigned. If memory was repeatedly allocated without being released, the system memory would be quickly exhausted and subsequent calls to this or other functions would produce error results.

The erase_block function

The necessary screen area could have been erased by rewriting the individual pixels using the background color as an alternative to using the image functions.

```
void erase_block( int left, int top, int right, int bottom )
{
        int        i, j, k = getbkcolor();
        for ( i=left; i<=right; i++ )
            for ( j=top; j<=bottom; j++ )
                putpixel( i, j, k );
}
```

This second option does save the small amount of memory which is allocated in the preceding **erasestr** function. The trade-off, however, is that this function is slower in execution than using the **getimage** and **putimage** functions.

Alternative applications

It was mentioned earlier that the **erasestr** function could also be used to erase a string or portion of a string if desired. This statement was only half true: it can certainly be used to erase an existing string. The second application, erasing a portion of a string, is slightly less practical since **erasestr** has not been specifically designed for it.

Both of these functions can be accomplished, but there are a couple of prerequisites that must be recognized. First, the text style, fonts and justification must be the same as when the string was originally written. Second, the original drawing color must be in effect. Third, the screen coordinates where the original string was written must be known. And fourth, the string itself must be known.

If any of these first three items have changed, an attempt to erase an existing string or a portion of an existing string will have unexpected results.

In graphics modes, there is no convenient method of ''reading'' a text string back from the screen, as can be done in text modes.

Now, assuming that the text settings and color are correct and that the original screen coordinates are known, the first operation is to erase an existing string. It is a simple operation — just call **erasestr** directly, using the x and y screen coordinates, and the string; the appropriate area of the screen will be XOR'd with itself, leaving the screen blank and ready for a rewrite or whatever is desired.

In the second application — erasing a portion of a string — the easiest method is to begin by erasing the entire string and then to rewrite the portion of the string which is desired. While several elaborate schemes could be constructed for erasing specific graphics characters or substrings, all of these would require far more processing and time.

Word processing, per se, is not the topic of the book and using graphics fonts and text display is hardly the simplest method of programming a word processor or similar application. However, you may find it necessary to employ text-editing procedures along with a graphics application. If so, here are a few hints:

The best approach would be to treat the screen image as a mapped copy of the actual text array in memory, using some indexing scheme to identify a correspondence between a ''line'' of text in memory and its graphics position on the screen.

If the bitmapped DEFAULT_FONT is being used, the screen position for any character is relatively easy to calculate because all characters are fixed width. If the stroked fonts are being used, then the **textwidth** function would be the optimum method of deciding where a particular string should end.

Also, the screen can not be scrolled up or down in the usual manner. While it would be possible to use the **getimage** and **putimage** to move a major portion of the screen image, you might find the memory requirements are excessive. If so, a simpler method would be to move some smaller portion of the screen, using multiple moves to shift as much of the screen as necessary. A similar technique can be used for left and right scrolling.

Listings for GPRINT.I

```
/*          ERASESTR: Used to erase a portion of the screen before a new string          */
/*                 is written to the screen or simply to remove a string from the screen          */
void erasestr( int xloc, int yloc, char *str )
{
    struct textsettingstype  textinfo;                              /* text settings information */
    int   xdim, ydim;
    void      *textimage;                                           /* image pointer   */
    gettextsettings( &textinfo );                          /* check graphic text settings */
    switch ( textinfo.direction )                          /* get dimensions of area   */
    {
        case HORIZ_DIR :  xdim = textwidth( str );
                          ydim = textheight( str );
                          xloc– –; break;
        case VERT_DIR :   ydim = textwidth( str );
                          xdim = textheight( str );
                          yloc++;  break;
    }
    switch ( textinfo.horiz )                       /* adjust horizontal position          */
    {
        case   LEFT_TEXT :                              break;
        case   CENTER_TEXT :   xloc –= xdim / 2;        break;
        case   RIGHT_TEXT :    xloc –= xdim;            break;
    }
    switch ( textinfo.vert )                             /* adjust vertical position   */
    {
        case   BOTTOM_TEXT :   yloc –= ydim;        break;
        case   CENTER_TEXT :   yloc –= ydim / 2;    break;
        case   TOP_TEXT :                           break;
    }
    while( xloc < 0 ) { xloc++; xdim– –; }               /* if position is offscreen    */
    while( yloc < 0 ) { yloc++; ydim– –; }               /* move back to valid area */
    textimage = malloc( imagesize( xloc, yloc, xdim, ydim ) );
    getimage( xloc, yloc, xloc+xdim, yloc+ydim, textimage );
```

102

```
        putimage( xloc, yloc, textimage, XOR_PUT );
        free( textimage );                               /* release the memory allocated */
}                                                        /* end ERASESTR            */


/*              GPRINTF: Used like PRINTF except the output is sent to the screen        */
/*                  in graphics mode at the specified co-ordinate. Depending on text     */
/*              direction, the xloc or yloc coordinate is returned offset according      */
/*                              to the string (font) height.                             */


void gprintf( int *xloc, int *yloc, char *fmt, ... )
{
    va_list argptr;                                      /* argument list pointer    */
    char    str[140];                                    /* buffer to build string into */
    struct textsettingstype  textinfo;                   /* text settings information */
    int  pos_adj = *xloc;                                /* default position for adjust */
    va_start( argptr, format );                          /* initialize va_functions  */
    vsprintf( str, fmt, argptr );                        /* add elements to str buffer */
    gettextsettings( &textinfo );                        /* check graphic text settings */
    #if (_TURBOC_ == 0x150 )          /*      correction for Turbo C version 1.5 only */
    {
        if( textinfo.direction && textinfo.font )        /* adjust position for */
        {                                                /* vertical text with  */
            xloc += textheight( str );                   /* stroked fonts       */
            if( textinfo.horiz == CENTER_TEXT )
                xloc − = textheight( str ) / 8;          /* offset for better center */
        }
    }
    #endif
    outtextxy( pos_adj, *yloc, str );                    /* write string in graphics mode */
    switch ( textinfo.direction )                        /* adjust offset for next string */
    {
        case HORIZ_DIR : *yloc += textheight( str ) + 2;   break;
        case  VERT_DIR : *xloc += textheight( str ) + 2;   break;
    };
    va_end( argptr );                                    /* close va_functions    */
```

```
}                                                      /* end GPRINTF */

/*          GPRINTC: Used like GPRINTF except the area where the text will be          */
/*                  written to the screen is first reset to the background color.       */
void gprintc( int *xloc, int *yloc, char *fmt, ... )
{
    va_list  argptr;                                   /* argument list pointer    */
    char     str[140];                                 /* buffer to build string into  */
    struct   textsettingstype  textinfo;               /* text settings information*/
    int      pos_adj = *xloc;                          /* default position for adjust  */

    va_start( argptr, format );                        /* initialize va_functions */
    vsprintf( str, fmt, argptr );                      /* add elements to str buffer  */
    gettextsettings( &textinfo );                      /* check graphic text settings */
    #if (_TURBOC_ == 0x150 )        /*       correction for Turbo C version 1.5 only   */
    {
        if( textinfo.direction && textinfo.font )           /* adjust position for */
        {                                                   /* vertical text with  */
            xloc += textheight( str );                      /* stroked fonts       */
            if( textinfo.horiz == CENTER_TEXT )
                xloc - = textheight( str ) / 8;             /* offset for better center */
        }
    }
    #endif
    erasestr( *xloc, *yloc, str );                     /* erase the area first     */
    outtextxy( pos_adj, *yloc, str );                  /* write string in graphics mode */
    switch ( textinfo.direction )                      /* adjust offset for next string */
    {
        case HORIZ_DIR : *yloc += textheight( str ) + 2;  break;
        case  VERT_DIR : *xloc += textheight( str ) + 2;  break;
    };
    va_end( argptr );                                  /* close va_functions      */
}                                                      /* end GPRINTC */
```

```
/*GPRINTXY: Used like GPRINTC except the area where screen coordinates*/
/*   are passed by value rather than passed by address pointer.        */
void gprintxy( int xloc, int yloc, char *fmt, ... )
{
    va_list argptr;                             /* argument list pointer      */
    char   str[140];                            /* buffer to build string into */
    struct  textsettingstype textinfo;          /* text settings information  */
    va_start( argptr, format );                 /* initialize va_functions    */
    vsprintf( str, fmt, argptr );               /* add elements to str buffer */
    gettextsettings( &textinfo );               /* check graphic text settings */
    #if (_TURBOC_ == 0x150 )        /*       correction for Turbo C version 1.5 only  */
    {
        if( textinfo.direction && textinfo.font )            /* adjust position for */
        {                                                    /* vertical text with  */
            xloc += textheight( str );                       /* stroked fonts       */
            if( textinfo.horiz == CENTER_TEXT )
                xloc -= textheight( str ) / 8;               /* offset for better center */
        }
    }
    #endif
    erasestr( xloc, yloc, str );                /* erase the area first       */
    outtextxy( xloc, yloc, str );               /* write string in graphics mode */
    va_end( argptr );                           /* close va_functions         */
}                                               /* end GPRINTXY               */


    /* end GPRINT.I */
```

Listing for PRN_DEMO.C

```
/* PRN_DEMO.C — show horizontal and vertical text justification        */

#ifdef __TINY__
#error GRAPHICS will not run in the tiny model.
#endif

#include <dos.h>
#include <math.h>
#include <conio.h>
#include <stdio.h>
#include <stdlib.h>
#include <stdarg.h>
#include <graphics.h>
#include "gprint.i"                        /* provides additional graphics print functions */


int     GraphDriver;                       /* The Graphics device driver     */
int     GraphMode;                         /* The Graphics mode value        */
int     MaxX, MaxY;                        /* The maximum resolution of the screen */
int     MaxColors;                         /* The maximum # of colors available    */
int     ErrorCode = 0;                     /* Reports any graphics errors    */
struct  palettetype palette;               /* Used to read palette info      */


void Initialize()
{
    GraphDriver = DETECT;                              /* Request auto-detection  */
    initgraph( &GraphDriver, &GraphMode, "" );
    ErrorCode = graphresult();                         /* Read result of initialization */
    if ( ErrorCode != grOk )                   /* Error occurred during init      */
    {
        printf(" Graphics System Error: %s\n",
                    grapherrormsg( ErrorCode ) );
        exit( 1 );
    }
```

```
    getpalette( &palette );                      /* Read the palette from board    */
    MaxColors = getmaxcolor() + 1;                        /* Read maximum colors */
    MaxX = getmaxx();                            /* set viewport (window) size     */
    MaxY = getmaxy();
}

void StatusLine( char *msg )
{
    int height;
    setcolor( MaxColors – 1 );                   /* Set current color to white     */
    settextstyle( DEFAULT_FONT, HORIZ_DIR, 1 );
    settextjustify( CENTER_TEXT, TOP_TEXT );
    height = textheight( "H" );                  /* Determine current height       */
    rectangle( 0, MaxY–(height+4), MaxX, MaxY );
    outtextxy( MaxX/2, MaxY–(height+2), msg );
}

void Pause()
{
    static char msg[] = "Press any key ...";
    StatusLine( msg );                           /* Put msg at bottom of screen    */
    while( kbhit() ) getch();
    getch();
}

main()
{
    int i, xax = 50, yax = 100;

    Initialize();
    setfillstyle( CLOSE_DOT_FILL, BLUE );
    bar( 0, 0, MaxX, MaxY );
    if( MaxColors > 4 ) setcolor(RED);
    line( 0, yax, getmaxx()/3, yax );
    settextstyle( 3, VERT_DIR, 3 );
    if( MaxColors > 4 ) setcolor(GREEN);
    line( xax, yax–100, xax, yax+100 );
```

```
if( MaxColors > 4 ) setcolor(WHITE);
settextjustify( LEFT_TEXT, CENTER_TEXT );
gprintc( &xax, &yax, "LEFT_TEXT" );

xax = 100;
if( MaxColors > 4 ) setcolor(GREEN);
line( xax, yax–100, xax, yax+100 );
if( MaxColors > 4 ) setcolor(WHITE);
settextjustify( CENTER_TEXT, CENTER_TEXT );
gprintc( &xax, &yax, "CENTER_TEXT" );

xax = 150;
if( MaxColors > 4 ) setcolor(GREEN);
line( xax, yax–100, xax, yax+100 );
if( MaxColors > 4 ) setcolor(WHITE);
settextjustify( RIGHT_TEXT, CENTER_TEXT );
gprintc( &xax, &yax, "RIGHT_TEXT" );
if( MaxColors > 4 ) setcolor(GREEN);

xax = 450;
line( xax, yax–100, xax, yax+100 );
settextstyle( 3, HORIZ_DIR, 3 );

yax = 30;
if( MaxColors > 4 ) setcolor(RED);
line( xax–200, yax, xax+200, yax );
if( MaxColors > 4 ) setcolor(WHITE);
settextjustify( CENTER_TEXT, BOTTOM_TEXT );
gprintc( &xax, &yax, "BOTTOM_TEXT" );

yax = 40;
if( MaxColors > 4 ) setcolor(RED);
line( xax–200, yax, xax+200, yax );
if( MaxColors > 4 ) setcolor(WHITE);
settextjustify( CENTER_TEXT, TOP_TEXT );
gprintc( &xax, &yax, "TOP_TEXT" );
```

```
    yax = 100;
    if( MaxColors > 4 ) setcolor(RED);
    line( xax–200, yax, xax+200, yax );
    if( MaxColors > 4 ) setcolor(WHITE);
    settextjustify( LEFT_TEXT, CENTER_TEXT );
    gprintc( &xax, &yax, "LEFT_TEXT" );

    yax = 130;
    if( MaxColors > 4 ) setcolor(RED);
    line( xax–200, yax, xax+200, yax );
    if( MaxColors > 4 ) setcolor(WHITE);
    settextjustify( CENTER_TEXT, CENTER_TEXT );
    gprintc( &xax, &yax, "CENTER_TEXT" );

    yax = 160;
    if( MaxColors > 4 ) setcolor(RED);
    line( xax–200, yax, xax+200, yax );
    if( MaxColors > 4 ) setcolor(WHITE);
    settextjustify( RIGHT_TEXT, CENTER_TEXT );
    gprintc( &xax, &yax, "RIGHT_TEXT" );

    Pause();
    closegraph();                              /* Return the system to text mode    */
}
```

CHAPTER 9

BUSINESS GRAPH DISPLAYS

Business applications often require graphic displays to show sales figures, financial information, stock price fluctuations and almost any other type of numerical data. The reasons for this demand for graphic displays are simple: a graph display makes information easier to understand than a column of figures and a graph offers convenient visual comparisons making trends, irregularities and shifts much more obvious than the numbers themselves. Also, graph displays are simply far more impressive than mere alphanumerical displays.

Given the vagaries of human nature, this last consideration — a visually impressive display — usually far outweighs the first two.

Thus, the business graphs demonstrated here have been created with visual appeal in mind, using colors and fill patterns where possible and, in some cases, have been designed to be more visually impressive than visually informative. Granted, this is a purely subjective distinction, but it is also one that you will need to be aware of when creating graphs and selecting the styles of display, patterns and colors to be used.

A Cautionary Note

So geographers, in Afric-maps,
With savage pictures fill their gaps;
And o'er unhabitable downs
Place elephants for want of towns.
— J. Swift

When creating any graph display, restraint is the best virtue. It is not only possible to include too much information in a graph, but it is frequently common for the resulting graphic display to be rendered unintelligible because of an excess of artistic style, information, attempted cross-correlation or a combination of all.

Remember, the first purpose of a graph is to present information in a manner and style that shows convenient correlations between different figures. This primary function, information, should not be overshadowed and defeated by colors, patterns, labels, logos or other elements intended to make the information eye-catching.

Concentrate on the information first, the entertainment second.

The Business Graph Demos

While there are at least several hundred types and styles of business graphs possible, five basic graph displays will be illustrated in this chapter: pie graphs, bar graphs, multiple bar graphs, 3-D bar graphs and line graphs. (To print graph displays, see Chapter 15.)

The first four graph types — pie, bar, multiple bar and 3-D bar graphs — have been combined in a single demo program, while the line graph demo is created separately for reasons that will be discussed later. Each of the first four graph styles will present the same data but in a different format. The demo program will pause after each graph, waiting for a key stroke. The last graph demo (3-D graphs) will show several displays with different depths, pausing after each display.

The data used for the demo has been written as two arrays; one of *integer* and one of *char*. In actual practice, this information would be read from external sources such as spreadsheet data, database files, internally created data arrays or from data files specifically created by your own program(s).

```
int      Accounts[4][9] = { 1985, 133, 35, 33, 17, 29, 15, 17, 32,
                            1986, 122, 41, 30, 25, 18, 24, 43, 21,
                            1987, 111, 65, 57, 14, 17, 39, 32, 17,
                            1988, 100, 60, 70, 12, 16, 13, 17, 12 };
```

```
char        *AccTypes[9]   = { "      ", "Motor", "Acsry", "Reprs", "Govmt",
                              "Lease", "Tires", "Paint", "Misc"   };
```

The dummy data sets shown are an anonymous corporation's figures for four years' income, broken down by eight categories. This data was selected simply for simulation and you may experiment with the graph displays by changing the figures in any fashion.

The Pie Graph Displays

Four separate pie graphs (see Figure 9-1), one for each year's data, are created using the function **Draw_Pie_Graphs** to position the four displays. Three parameters are used, the first specifying the array index for the year, the second and third specifying the x and y screen positions where the pie graph will be centered.

```
void Draw_Pie_Graphs()
{
        cleardevice();
        graphdefaults();
        rectangle( 0, 0, MaxX, MaxY );
        if( GraphDriver == CGA )
{
            Pie_Graph( 0, 150,  55);
            Pie_Graph( 1, 450,  55);
            Pie_Graph( 2, 150, 140);
            Pie_Graph( 3, 450, 140);
}
        else
        {
            Pie_Graph( 0, 150,  80);
            Pie_Graph( 1, 450,  80);
            Pie_Graph( 2, 150, 250);
            Pie_Graph( 3, 450, 250);
        }
}
```

For CGA systems, a separate set of screen coordinates has been provided, however, EGA or higher resolution with color is recommended.

When the **Pie_Graph** function is called, several local variables are established: total is initialized as zero and will be used to determine the total value of all of the data elements so that the slices can be apportioned correctly; m is initialized as 135 and will be used to position the year label; s and t are initialized as zero and will be used for start and terminate angles for each slice.

```
void Pie_Graph( int dataset, int x, int y )
{
        int i, m = 135, r, s = 0, t = 0, HJust, VJust;
        int total = 0;
        int Blank_Line = 0x0000;
        int CapColor;
        struct arccoordstype arcrec;
```

The variable *Blank_Line* is also initialized as zero and will be used to draw an invisible line for positioning labels around the pie graph. The elaboration of 0x0000 is not actually necessary — a simple 0 would suffice — but, to define a less empty line style, a four digit hexadecimal specification is usually necessary and this form has been followed here.

In the first step, all of the items for the current year (dataset) are totalled and the radius, r, is set to $1/4$ of total.

```
        for (i=1; i<=8; i++)
        total += Accounts[dataset][i];
        r = total / 4;
```

Because there are only eight items for each year, the actual integer can be used in the loop. In other circumstances, the number of elements might vary from application to application, a different method of controlling the loop might be preferred. This could be using an index element, *Elements*:

```
        for (i=1; i<=Elements; i++)
```

Or by calculating the number of elements:

```
for (i=1; i<=(sizeof(Accounts)/years*sizeof(integer)); i++)
```

Now that there is a radius, you can put a label for the year on the screen (before drawing the pie graph). Instead of arbitrarily positioning the label — and having to create a new label position for each data set — it is preferable to be able to calculate the proper position.

Because you know the radius (r), you could calculate a position from this bit of data, but there is a more elegant method that will be used repeatedly as the pie graph is drawn. When **Pie_Graph** was called, the variable m was initialized at 135, an angle which will be toward the top left of the eventual pie graph.

The line style is set to *Blank_Line*, which was previously defined as 0x0000, and the fill style is set to 0 (EMPTY_FILL) and fill color to 0 (BLACK).

```
setlinestyle( USERBIT_LINE, Blank_Line, NORM_WIDTH );
setfillstyle( 0, 0 );
```

Next, the pieslice function is called with the x and y center coordinates to draw a pie slice beginning at the angle m and ending at the angle $m+1$ with a radius of $r+10$. A minimum angle width of one degree is required or pieslice will simply do nothing. Also, using a radius 10 pixels greater than the one which will be used for the pie graph, yields a position outside the eventual graph image.

```
pieslice(x,y,m,m+1,r+10);          /* must have a minimum width of one degree*/
getarccoords( &arcrec );
```

The pie slice drawn in this case will be invisible, but it does yield a screen position that can be retrieved by calling **getarccoords**. Before doing anything with this information, however, the current color, text style, direction and justification need to be set.

```
if( MaxColors > 4 ) setcolor( WHITE );
settextstyle( SANS_SERIF_FONT, HORIZ_DIR, 2 );
```

```
settextjustify( RIGHT_TEXT, BOTTOM_TEXT );
```

Now, the **gprintf** function can be called with the *xend* and *yend* coordinates in *arcrec* and the year data, which is the 0th element in each *Accounts[dataset]*, is written to the screen.

```
gprintf( &arcrec.xend, &arcrec.yend, "%d", Accounts[dataset][0] );
```

Remember, **getarccoords** returns a data record that contains the start and end x and y screen coordinates for the last call to any of the **arc**, **circle**, **ellipse** or **pieslice** functions.

This particular method of calculation to determine an appropriate screen position for a label, will be used several times while the pie graph is being drawn in order to position a label correctly for each pie slice.

Before proceeding, the default text style is selected and, if practical, the drawing color is reset.

```
settextstyle( DEFAULT_FONT, HORIZ_DIR, 1 );
if( MaxColors > 4 ) setcolor( EGA_YELLOW );
```

At this point, the actual pie slices are drawn, again using a loop for a known number of data elements:

```
for (i=1; i<=8; i++)
{
```

The fill style and color are arbitrarily changed for each slice. In this application, on a monochrome system, the fill color setting can be ignored, though the drawing color is not so cavalierly inconsequential. Also, the line settings are reset to a solid line before a new pie slice is created.

```
setfillstyle( i, i );
if( MaxColors > 4 ) setcolor( WHITE );
setlinestyle( SOLID_LINE, 0, NORM_WIDTH );
```

The end angle for the pie slice is calculated as the proportional angle. As you will notice, all of the calculations are being carried out as double values for accuracy, with the final result being returned to an integer value since the pieslice function does not accept float or double. Also, the calculated value has been incremented by 0.5, before truncation, to round the results to the nearest integer instead of the next lower integer.

```
t += (int) ( 360 * (double) Accounts[dataset][i]
                / (double) total + 0.5 );
```

If any angle is returned greater than 360 degrees — an error that is unlikely except on the final slice — then the value is arbitrarily fixed at 360 to prevent a confusing display. Likewise, if the last pie slice does not complete the circle, if *t* is less than 360, then a correction is made to keep the pie graph neatly finished. This type of error is not unlikely when a number of angles are calculated, each being rounded to the nearest integer value, however, the cumulative error should not exceed one degree per slice. In this example, a maximum error of eight degrees would be possible.

```
if ( t > 360 ) t = 360;
if ( i == 8 ) if ( t < 360 ) t = 360;
```

Depending on your application, you may wish to arrange matters so that the correction is added to the largest individual slice or so that the error is apportioned among the various slices.

Next, the actual pie slice is created using the x and y center coordinates, the start angle *s*, the end angle *t* and the radius *r*.

```
pieslice( x, y, s, t, r );
```

Now it is time to reset the line style to *Blank_Line* and to reset the fill style and fill color to EMPTY_FILL and BLACK. Also, the working *CapColor* is set to the bright equivalent of the fill color used for the last pie slice (*i+8*) and, if practical, the drawing color is set to *CapColor*.

```
setlinestyle( USERBIT_LINE, Blank_Line, NORM_WIDTH );
setfillstyle( 0, 0 );
CapColor = i+8;
if ( CapColor > WHITE ) CapColor = DARKGREY;
if( MaxColors > 4 ) setcolor( CapColor );
```

At this point, the program is repeating the same operation that was used to position the year number before this pie graph was started, but with a slight difference. The angle *m* becomes the mid-angle between the start and end angles (*s* and *t*) of the current pie slice and, again, an invisible pie slice is drawn and **getarccoords** returns the screen coordinates for the endpoints of this invisible slice.

```
m = ( t – s ) / 2 + s;
pieslice( x, y, m, m+1, r+5 );
getarccoords( &arcrec );
```

The next step arranges the vertical and horizontal text justification settings so that the label for the current pie slice will be positioned appropriately outside the pie graph. Also, **outtextxy** is called to write the label *AccTypes[i]* to the screen.

```
if ( arcrec.xend > x ) HJust = LEFT_TEXT;
            else HJust = RIGHT_TEXT;
if ( arcrec.yend > y ) VJust = TOP_TEXT;
            else VJust = BOTTOM_TEXT;
settextjustify( HJust, VJust );
outtextxy( arcrec.xend, arcrec.yend, AccTypes[i] );
```

Finally, the current end angle becomes the start angle for the next pie slice and the loop continues.

```
    s = t;
    }
}
```

Exploded Pie Graphs

The technique that was used to position the labels for the pie graph can also be used to produce an Exploded Pie Graph — a pie graph in which one or more segments are offset from the center to emphasize a specific segment.

Figure 9-1: Pie Graph

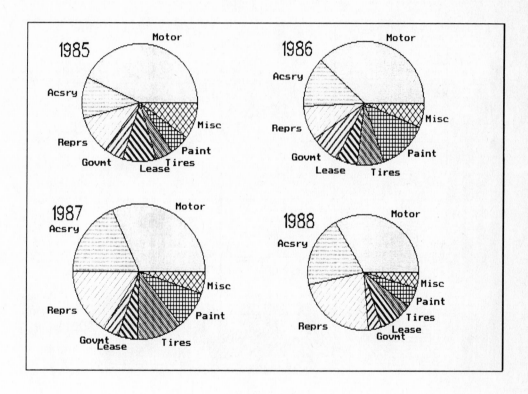

Line Graph showing a four-year financial breakdown for a fictional company. The graph was created by GRAPHALL.C in color on an EGA screen, then downloaded to a laserjet printer in GREYSCALE mode using the LJ-GRAPH utility demonstrated in Chapter 14.

Figure 9-2: Bar Graph

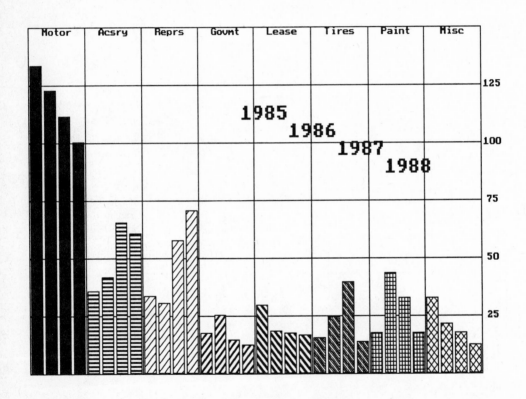

Bar Graph showing a four-year financial breakdown for a fictional company. The graph was created by GRAPHALL.C in color on an EGA screen, then downloaded to a laserjet printer in LANDSCAPE mode using the LJ-GRAPH utility demonstrated in Chapter 14.

In order to keep the symmetry of the overall pie graph, the offset must be at the correct angle, the mid-angle of the slice.

The following example code will provide a five pixel radius offset by first creating an invisible pie slice.

```
setlinestyle( USERBIT_LINE, Blank_Line, NORM_WIDTH );
setfillstyle( 0, 0 );
m = ( t – s ) / 2 + s;
pieslice( x, y, m, m+1, 5 );
getarccoords( &arcrec );
```

Then the fill style and drawing colors are reset.

```
setfillstyle( i, i );
if( MaxColors > 4 ) setcolor( WHITE );
setlinestyle( SOLID_LINE, 0, NORM_WIDTH );
```

And the offset pie slice is created, centered on the *arcrec* coordinates of the invisible slice.

```
pieslice( arcrec.xend, arcrec.yend, s, t, r );
```

The label for this slice will also require its position to be calculated with the additional five units radius, in order to be proportionally located.

Bar Graph

While pie graphs are visually more impressive, bar graphs offer a clearer visual comparison of magnitude. Most often, bar graphs are drawn vertically — as in the demonstration program — but may also be presented horizontally.

While the **Pie_Graph** function does not compensate for horizontal resolutions less than 640 pixels, the function **Bar_Graph** (see Figure 9-2)adjusts the graphic presentation to fit both the vertical and horizontal resolutions of the screen and graphics mode in use. It begins by setting width to *MaxX* and height to *MaxY*.

```
void Bar_Graph( )
{
int width = MaxX, height = MaxY, left = 0, top = 0;
int i, j, hstep, vstep, bottom, x, y, barhigh;
```

Now a viewport (window) is created, leaving a margin at the top which is necessary for the labels that will later be written along the side. Then *width* is decremented by 30 to leave space for amount labels. The horizontal graph step (*hstep*) is calculated from the width variable to provide for 32 columns and the vertical step (*vstep*) is calculated from the height variable. Finally, *bottom* variable is set to six times the vertical step (*vstep*).

```
setviewport( left, top+5, left+width, top+height+5, 0 );
width −= 30;
hstep = width/32;
vstep = height/6;
bottom = vstep*6;
```

In this particular instance, the graph is being divided vertically into six increments, each increment to be 25 units (which might be dollars, pounds, yen in hundreds, thousands or similar units). In an application where the range of values is not known in advance, you might prefer your program to test for the highest value that would be displayed and then create graph increments accordingly, numbering the vertical scale marks as appropriate. (See The **Line_Graph** Function for an example.)

Horizontally, the bars will be grouped in units of four, placing each type of entry, from each of the four year's data, together. Vertical markers are drawn every fourth *hstep*:

```
if( MaxColors > 4 ) setcolor( GREEN );
for ( i=0; i<=hstep*32; i+=hstep*4 ) line( i, 0, i, vstep*6 );
```

Horizontal scale lines are drawn for each *vstep*:

```
if( MaxColors > 4 ) setcolor( CYAN );
for ( i=0; i<=bottom; i+=vstep )  line( 0, i, hstep*32, i );
```

And, with the scaling grid completed, the *bottom* variable is moved up one pixel so that the bars will not overwrite the base of the grid:

```
bottom– –;
```

Now the drawing color, text style and fonts are set and the unit increments (the horizontal lines) are labeled beginning with 150 at the top, decreasing in steps of 25 until 0 is reached at the bottom.

```
if( MaxColors > 4 ) setcolor( WHITE );
settextstyle( DEFAULT_FONT, HORIZ_DIR, 1 );
settextjustify( CENTER_TEXT, CENTER_TEXT );
for ( i=0; i; i++ )
{
        x = hstep*32 + 15;
        y = i*vstep;
        gprintf( &x, &y, "%d", 150–i*25 );
}
```

Now, with the background grid complete, it's time to create the bars themselves. The height of the bar will be calculated as a vertical offset from *bottom*, scaled as 25 units per vertical step.

```
for ( i=1; i<=8; i++ )
{
        for ( j=0; j; j++ )
        {
                barhigh = bottom – Accounts[j][i]
                          * (double) vstep / (double) 25;
```

If the current video system is color capable in high resolution, then a new outline color (drawing color) and fill color are used for each year's bar. Otherwise, only the fill style is changed and the draw and fill colors are kept as WHITE (*MaxColors–1*).

```
                if( MaxColors > 4 ) setcolor( j+1 );
                if( MaxColors > 4 ) setfillstyle( i, j+1 );
                        else setfillstyle( i, MaxColors–1 );
```

Even though a two-dimensional graph is being created, the **bar3d** function is used, but with a depth of 0 specified. The **bar** function does not draw an outline, but only creates a bar using the fill style and color. The **bar3d** function provides an outline in the current drawing color and creates a better appearance. Alternatively, the **rectangle** function could have been called to draw an outline and then **bar** called to fill in the area, however, the effects would have been almost identical, but slower.

```
        bar3d( (i–1)*hstep*4 + j*hstep + 2,        barhigh,
               (i–1)*hstep*4 + j*hstep + hstep–2, bottom, 0, 0 );
    }                                              /* end of loop for j */
```

As the last step within this loop, after each set of four bars for the four years' data have been drawn, the drawing color is reset to WHITE and a label is written at the top of the bar graph column.

```
        if( MaxColors > 4 ) setcolor( WHITE );
        outtextxy( i*hstep*4–hstep*2, 5, AccTypes[i] );
    }                                              /* end of loop for i */
```

Finally, if high resolution and color are supported, then the four years (year numbers) are added to the screen, the colors corresponding to the drawing color and fill color used for each year's bars. If the system is monochrome, then there is little purpose in this unless you simply want to show the years. You might, however, modify the code to draw a small block by each year number, using the corresponding year's fill style.

```
    if( MaxColors > 4 )
    {
        x = MaxX/2;
        y = MaxY/4;
        settextstyle( DEFAULT_FONT, HORIZ_DIR, 2 );
        for (i=0; i; i++)
        {
            setcolor(i+1);
            gprintf( &x, &y, "%d", Accounts[i][0] );
```

```
        x+=textwidth (" ");
        }
    }
}
```

Multiple Bar Graphs

While combining several years' data in a single bar graph allows for convenient comparison between different years, it also makes the comparison between the different categories within each year, difficult. It also complicates viewing each year as a whole. There are times when separate graphs for each year are more useful (and sometimes more impressive) than a single, combined graph. The function **Draw_Multi_Graphs** creates four graphs on a single screen, one for each year's data.

```
void Draw_Multi_Graphs()
{
        Multi_Bar_Graph( 0, 0, 0);
        Multi_Bar_Graph( 1, MaxX/2, 0);
        Multi_Bar_Graph( 2, 0, MaxY/2 );
        Multi_Bar_Graph( 3, MaxX/2, MaxY/2 );
}
```

Like **Bar_Graph**, the function **Multi_Bar_Graph** adjusts the graphic presentation to fit both the vertical and horizontal resolutions of the screen and graphics mode in use, beginning by setting width to *MaxX/2* and height to *MaxY/2–13*. The height setting includes a 13 pixel margin and the width setting includes a 30 pixel margin so that the graphs do not butt against each other, allowing for better visual appearance.

```
void Multi_Bar_Graph( int dataset, int left, int top )
{
        int    width  = MaxX/2–30;
        int    height = MaxY/2–13;
        int    i, hstep, vstep, bottom, x, y;
double  scale;
```

The viewport (window) and scaling factors are set up essentially the same as in the **Bar_Graph** function, except that only eight bars will be arranged horizontally and a vertical scaling factor is calculated as the variable scale, instead of executing a separate scaling calculation each time.

```
setviewport( left, top+5, left+width, top+height+5, 0 );
hstep = width/8;
vstep = height/6;
tom = vstep*6;
scale = (double) vstep / 25;
```

A background grid is then written with scale factors along the right margin.

```
if( MaxColors > 4 ) setcolor( GREEN );
for ( i=0; i<=hstep*8; i+=hstep ) line( i, 0, i, vstep*6 );
if( MaxColors > 4 ) setcolor( CYAN );
for ( i=0; i<=bottom; i+=vstep )  line( 0, i, hstep*8, i );
if( MaxColors > 4 ) setcolor( WHITE );
settextstyle( DEFAULT_FONT, HORIZ_DIR, 1 );
settextjustify( CENTER_TEXT, CENTER_TEXT );
for ( i=0; i; i++ )
{
        x = hstep*8 + 15;
        y = i*vstep;
        gprintf( &x, &y, "%d", 150–i*25 );
}
```

The graph is created for the selected year's data, similar to **Bar_Graph,** but with one principal difference. Because single bars will need to be labeled and these will not be wide enough for horizontal text labels, the vertical text direction is selected and the labels will be written centered horizontally over each bar and flush against a point that is five pixels below the top of the viewport.

If you are using an EGA or higher resolution system, you should notice that the labels appear clearly in white even though some partially overlie a colored bar. This is also the reason why the **bar** function, instead of the **bar3d** function, was used: because an outline might have made the overlying captions more difficult to read. In monochrome modes, however, this becomes a major problem and an alternative will be shown momentarily.

```
settextstyle( DEFAULT_FONT, VERT_DIR, 1 );
settextjustify( CENTER_TEXT, TOP_TEXT );
for ( i=0; i<=7; i++ )
{
    if( MaxColors > 4 ) setfillstyle( i+1, i+1 );
    else setfillstyle( i+1, MaxColors-1 );
    bar( i*hstep+2,  bottom-scale*Accounts[dataset][i+1]-1,
        (i+1)*hstep-2, bottom-1 );
    outtextxy( i*hstep+hstep/2, 5, AccTypes[i+1] );
}
```

As a last step, the year data is written to each graph:

```
settextstyle( SANS_SERIF_FONT, HORIZ_DIR, 2 );
settextjustify( CENTER_TEXT, BOTTOM_TEXT );
x = width/2;
y = height/2-4;
gprintf( &x, &y, "%d", Accounts[dataset][0] );
}
```

Improving The Monochrome Display

Now, there is a problem, as mentioned, with monochrome display modes where a label overwrites a bar, resulting in the label not being legible. There is, however, a simple method you can use with a monochrome display that cures this problem. First, in the function **Multi_Bar_Graph**, add a variable declaration for a pointer to caption.

```
void        *caption;
```

The viewport, text and color settings are made as before and the background grid lines are drawn. Then, in the loop before drawing the bar, the **erasestr** function (defined in Chapter 8 and included in **gprint.i**) is called to erase the area where the label will be written and the label is sent to the screen.

```
for ( i=0; i<=7; i++ )
{
        x = i*hstep+hstep/2;
        y = 5;
        erasestr( x, y, AccTypes[i+1] );
        outtextxy( x, y, AccTypes[i+1] );
```

Next, memory space is allocated for caption:

```
caption = malloc( imagesize( x, y, textheight(AccTypes[i+1]),
                    textwidth(AccTypes[i+1]) ) );
```

And, because horizontal justification was set to CENTER_TEXT, x is offset by half the string height of *AccTypes[i+1]* to insure that the correct image area is read.

```
x -= textheight(AccTypes[i+1])/2;
```

Now the **getimage** function reads the label image from the screen as caption, then **putimage** uses the XOR_PUT option to erase the label, momentarily.

```
getimage( x, y, x+textheight(AccTypes[i+1]),
            y+textwidth(AccTypes[i+1]), caption );
putimage( x, y, caption, XOR_PUT );
```

The bar is drawn as before:

```
if( MaxColors > 4 ) setfillstyle( i+1, i+1 );
else                setfillstyle( i+1, MaxColors-1 );
bar( i*hstep+2,  bottom-scale*Accounts[dataset][i+1]-1,
    (i+1)*hstep-2, bottom-1 );
```

And then **putimage** is called again with the XOR_PUT option to eXclusively-**OR** the *caption* image with the screen image. The result is that the portion of the label which overlies a bar is now a visible black on white instead of an invisible white on white.

```
putimage( x, y, caption, XOR_PUT );
```

Finally, the memory allocated to caption is released.

```
free( caption );
}
```

This same modification can be used with color displays but — warning — the effects may not be precisely what you expect. Remember, eXclusively-**OR**ing WHITE with WHITE produces BLACK, but eXclusively-**OR**ing WHITE with BLUE produces YELLOW, etc.

Incidentally, if you are using an EGA/VGA system, delete the line in the **Initialize** function in the **GRAPHALL.C** demo that reads:

```
GraphDriver = DETECT;
```

Add the instructions:

```
GraphDriver = CGA;
GraphMode = CGAHI;
```

This will force your system to emulate a CGA system and to demonstrate the difficulties in a monochrome display. This is also a good way to test your programs to see how they will execute on a CGA system, without having to move your program to another computer.

Three-Dimensional Graphs

While Turbo C provides the **bar3d** function for a three-dimensional bar graph (see Figure 9-3), actually creating a 3-D graph display can be slightly more complicated.

Figure 9-3: Three-dimensional Bar Graph

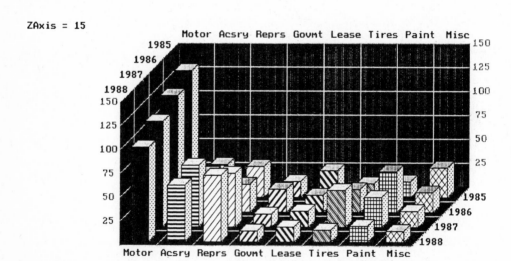

Three-dimensional bar graph showing a four-year financial breakdown for a fictional company. The graphics image was created by GRAPHALL.C in color on an EGA screen, then downloaded to a laserjet printer in GREYSCALE mode using the LJ-GRAPH utility demonstrated in Chapter 14.

Figure 9-4: Line Graph

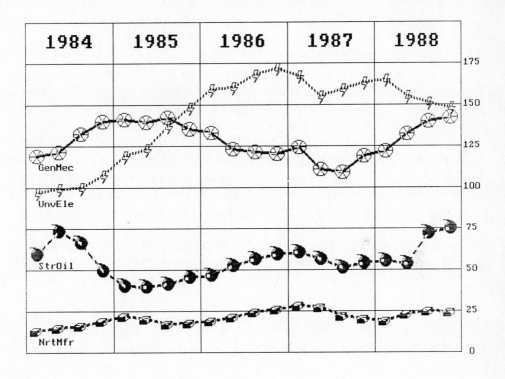

Line graph showing four stocks with bit-images added to deliniate points on graph. The graphics image was created by LINEGRAF.C in color on an EGA screen, then downloaded to a laserjet printer in PORTRAIT mode using the LJ-GRAPH utility demonstrated in Chapter 14.

In its simplest form, a 3-D bar graph would simply be a flat bar graph with the bars drawn using **bard3d** to provide an illusion of depth, but with only a single horizontal row of bars.

If you are going to use the three-dimensional effect, at some point you're probably going to want to display several rows of bars with the illusion of depth in the arrangement of the rows, as well as in the bars themselves. This creates further complexity.

First, the 3-D bars created by **bar3d** can be generated with different depths. Second, for best appearance, a three-dimensional graph requires a three-dimensional setting, with scaling lines and an overall appearance of depth corresponding to the depth aspect of the individual bars. Third, everything must be tied together in an consistent whole, rather than appearing to be merely an assemblage of scattered parts.

In a purely rational sense, a 3-D bar graph is not as informative as a series of flat bar graphs. Visually, it is difficult to discern clearly the relative heights of the various bars and how a specific bar aligns with the background scale lines. The more important consideration here is that the three-dimensional graph is visually very impressive.

The same data that has been presented in the form of pie and bar graphs, will now be displayed in the form of four rows and eight ranks of three-dimensional columns against a scaled three-dimensional field. Also, for purposes of demonstration, **Graphs_3D** will show the same graph data using a series of *ZAxis* depths in steps of five — from 15 to 40 pixels.

The variables *XAxis* and *YAxis* , which will be the horizontal and vertical scale increments, are assigned values scaled to fit within the current screen size limits, while *XOrg* and *YOrd* provide the screen origin point for all three axis. The graph width (*XWidth*) and height (*YHeight*) are now set to multiples of *XAxis* and *YAxis* which will remain constant. *ZDepth* will be recalculated for each graph display as the *ZAxis* increment size is changed.

```
void Graphs_3D()
{
        XAxis = MaxX/13;
```

```
YAxis = MaxY/14;
XOrg = MaxX/3;
YOrg = MaxY/2;
XWidth = 8 * XAxis;
YHeight = 6 * YAxis;
scale = (double) YAxis / 25;
```

Then **Graphs_3D** loops as long as the display produced by the *ZAxis* value does not exceed the screen limits.

```
for( ZAxis=15; (YOrg+4*ZAxis)axY; ZAxis+=5 )
    Three_D_Graph();
}
```

The function **Three_D_Graph** creates each graph display, first clearing the screen and setting the z-axis depth (*ZDepth*) for the current *ZAxis*.

```
void Three_D_Graph()
{
    int x, y;
    cleardevice();
    ZDepth  = 4 * ZAxis;
```

A caption is displayed in the upper left corner of screen, showing the current *ZAxis* size; the display background is created by **Graph_Field** and the scale lines for each axis are labeled by **Show_Labels**. The bar graph elements are drawn by the **Show_Accounts** function and the program pauses for a keystroke before creating the next graph display.

```
settextjustify( LEFT_TEXT, TOP_TEXT );
setcolor( MaxColors − 1 );
x = 10; y = 10;
gprintf( &x, &y, "ZAxis = %d", ZAxis );
Graph_Field();
Show_Labels();
Show_Accounts();
Pause();
}
```

The elements of the overall graph display have been broken down into separate tasks in order to reduce a complex program to manageable proportions.

The Graph_Field Function

The first of these tasks is the **Graph_Field** function, which creates a three-dimensional backdrop for the graph, complete with grid lines for all three axes. If color is supported, then the **Fill_Plane** function is used to create three solid planes, rather like three sides of a box, in blue, red and yellow. These planes will form the background for the display. **Fill_Plane** is simply a convenient enhancement of the **fillpoly** function and will be explained in a moment.

```
void Graph_Field()
{
        int i;
        if ( MaxColors > 4 )
        {
            Fill_Plane(  XOrg, YOrg, XOrg+XWidth, YOrg,
                         XOrg+XWidth, YOrg–YHeight, XOrg,
                         YOrg–YHeight, SOLID_FILL, LIGHTBLUE );
            Fill_Plane(  XOrg, YOrg, XOrg–(ZDepth/AspR), YOrg+ZDepth,
                         XOrg–(ZDepth/AspR), YOrg+ZDepth–YHeight,
                         XOrg, YOrg–YHeight,
                         SOLID_FILL, LIGHTRED );
            Fill_Plane(  XOrg, YOrg, XOrg+XWidth, YOrg,
                         XOrg+XWidth–(ZDepth/AspR), YOrg+ZDepth,
                         XOrg–(ZDepth/AspR), YOrg+ZDepth,
                         SOLID_FILL, YELLOW );
        }
```

Next, three lines are drawn from the screen origin point at *XOrg/YOrg*. If the background planes were created, these lines simply delineate the planes.

If the system is using monochrome display, then these axis lines and the grid lines following will serve to create the backdrop.

```
line( XOrg, YOrg, XOrg+XWidth, YOrg );               /* X-axis */
line( XOrg, YOrg, XOrg,  YOrg–YHeight );              /* Y-axis */
line( XOrg, YOrg, XOrg–ZDepth/AspR, YOrg+ZDepth );
                                                     /* Z-axis */
```

If you will notice, the z-axis line (above) is adjusted for the screen aspect ratio, *AspR*. This same adjustment will appear in all positioning calculations involving the z-axis to keep the z-axis angle constant (approximately 45°) for all screen resolutions.

```
                                      /*      X-axis grid lines */
if ( MaxColors > 4 ) setcolor(GREEN);
for ( i = XOrg + XAxis; i <= XOrg + XWidth; i += XAxis )
{
line( i, YOrg, i, YOrg–YHeight );
line( i, YOrg, i–ZDepth/AspR, YOrg+ZDepth  );
}
                                      /*      Y-axis grid lines */
if ( MaxColors > 4 ) setcolor(CYAN);
for ( i = YOrg – YAxis; i >= YOrg – YHeight; i –= YAxis )
{
line( XOrg, i, XOrg+XWidth, i );
line( XOrg, i, XOrg–ZDepth/AspR, i+ZDepth );
}
                                      /*      Z-axis grid lines */
if ( MaxColors > 4 ) setcolor(RED);
for (i = ZAxis; i <= ZDepth; i += ZAxis)
{
    line( XOrg–i/AspR, YOrg+i, XOrg–i/AspR+XWidth,  YOrg+i );
    line( XOrg–i/AspR, YOrg+i, XOrg–i/AspR, YOrg–YHeight+i );
}
}
```

The Fill_Plane Function

The **Fill_Plane** function is simply a convenient method of passing a set of calculated points to be assigned to an integer array (*polygon*), before calling the **fillpoly** function. This is faster than using the **floodfill** function and will be used several times in this demonstration program to fill large or small areas with either solid colors or patterns. The color value passed (*FColor*) is tested for validity and defaults to WHITE if monochrome graphics are being used.

```
void Fill_Plane( int X1, int Y1, int X2, int Y2,
                 int X3, int Y3, int X4, int Y4,
                 int FStyle, int FColor )
{
        int polygon[10];

        polygon[0] = polygon[8] = X1;
        polygon[1] = polygon[9] = Y1;
        polygon[2] = X2;                        polygon[3] = Y2;
        polygon[4] = X3;                        polygon[5] = Y3;
        polygon[6] = X4;                        polygon[7] = Y4;
        if ( MaxColors  4 ) FColor = MaxColors − 1;
        setfillstyle(FStyle,FColor);
        fillpoly(5,polygon);
}
```

The Show_Labels Function

The **Show_Labels** function displays labels for all three axes of the display, beginning with the vertical (y-axis) magnitude scales along both the right and left sides of the display. The right side positions are relatively easy to calculate since they are simply stepped from the *YOrg* position with an x-axis offset equal to *XOrg + XWidth + 15*.

The left side, however, requires both a y-axis offset which is easily calculated as *ZDepth − i * YAxis*, and an x-axis offset (left from *XOrg*), which is slightly more complicated, but is calculated as $XOrg - ZDepth / AspR - 15$. Remember, the $ZDepth$ variable is plotted at an angle so the actual screen offset must be calculated using the screen aspect ratio $AspR$ to maintain the 45° screen angle for the z-axis.

```
void Show_Labels()
{
        int i, j, k, l, m;
        settextjustify(CENTER_TEXT,CENTER_TEXT);


        j = XOrg + XWidth + 15;
        l = XOrg - ZDepth / AspR - 15;
        for ( i=1; i; i++ )
        {
                k = YOrg - i * YAxis;
                gprintf( &j, &k, "%d", i*25 );
                m = YOrg + ZDepth - i * YAxis;
                gprintf( &l, &m, "%d", i*25 );
        }
```

The *AccTypes* labels are written horizontally across the top and bottom of the graph:

```
        if ( MaxColors > 4 ) setcolor(LIGHTBLUE);
        j = XOrg + 25;
        l = j - ( ZDepth / AspR );
        m = YOrg + ZDepth + 8;
        k = YOrg - YHeight - 8;
        for ( i=1; i<=8; i++ )
        {
                outtextxy( j, k, AccTypes[i] );
                outtextxy( l, m, AccTypes[i] );
                j += 50;
                l += 50;
        }
```

The year dates are written at an angle along the z-axis:

```
if ( MaxColors > 4 ) setcolor(LIGHTGREEN);
for ( i=0; i<=3; i++ )
{
        j = XOrg – ( i * ZAxis + ZAxis / 2 ) / AspR + 2;
        m = YOrg + i * ZAxis + ZAxis / 2;
        k = m – YHeight;
        l = j + XWidth;
        settextjustify( LEFT_TEXT, TOP_TEXT );
        gprintf( &l, &m, "%4d", Accounts[i][0] );
        settextjustify( RIGHT_TEXT, BOTTOM_TEXT );
        gprintf( &j, &k, "%4d", Accounts[i][0] );
}
}
```

The Show_Accounts Function

The bars for each year could have been drawn using a double loop and incrementing the colors for each year. Instead, four separate loops are used here, permitting the assignment of specific colors for each year's bars.

```
void Show_Accounts()
{
        int i;
        if ( MaxColors > 4 ) setcolor( EGA_YELLOW );
        for (i=1; i<=8; i++)
            Add_Bar( i–1, 0, Accounts[0][i] * scale, LIGHTCYAN, CYAN );
        for (i=1; i<=8; i++)
            Add_Bar( i–1, 1, Accounts[1][i] * scale, LIGHTRED, RED );
        for (i=1; i<=8; i++)
            Add_Bar( i–1, 2, Accounts[2][i] * scale, LIGHTBLUE, BLUE );
        for (i=1; i<=8; i++)
            Add_Bar( i–1, 3, Accounts[3][i] * scale, LIGHTGREEN, GREEN );
}
```

The Add_Bar Function

The **Add_Bar** function is used to create and to position the three-dimensional graph bars. The *BarWidth* and *BarDepth* variables that set the size of the bar, are initialized as half the x-axis and z-axis step sizes. Making each bar smaller than the spacing between the bars, offers a better visual effect and also permits seeing between bars so that taller bars do not completely hide smaller bars that lie behind them.

```
void Add_Bar( int left, int bottom, int height, int Color1, int Color2 )
{
        int top, right;
        int BarWidth = XAxis / 2;
        int BarDepth = ZAxis / 2;
        if ( MaxColors  4 )
        {
              Color1 = MaxColors – 1;
              Color2 = MaxColors – 1;
        }
```

The fill style for each bar is incremented from left to right. If the display is in monochrome, this helps to make the bars easier to distinguish.

```
        setfillstyle( left+1, Color1 );
```

The left and bottom variables began as integers in the 1..8 and 1..4 ranges describing step positions, but are now converted to the actual screen offset positions while *right* and *top* provide the remaining corner parameters.

```
        left   = XOrg + ( left * XAxis )
                   – ( ( ( bottom + 0.75 * ZAxis / XAxis ) * ZAxis ) / AspR );
        bottom = YOrg + ( ( bottom + 0.75 ) * ZAxis );
        right = left + BarWidth;
        top = bottom – height;
```

At this point, the **bar3d** function could, very conveniently, be used to create the display bars for this graph. There is, however, one flaw in this: the z-axis angle produced by **bar3d** does not always match the z-axis angle produced by the screen aspect. For this reason, **bar3d** is called with a 0 depth and the **Fill_Plane** function is called to create each bar's side and top.

```
bar3d( left, top, right, bottom, 0, 0 );
Fill_Plane(  right, top,
             right+BarDepth/AspR, top–BarDepth,
             right+BarDepth/AspR, bottom–BarDepth,
             right, bottom,
             CLOSE_DOT_FILL, Color1 );
Fill_Plane(  left, top,
             right, top,
             right+BarDepth/AspR, top–BarDepth,
             left+BarDepth/AspR, top–BarDepth,
             SOLID_FILL, Color2 );
}
```

If you would like to experiment, simply comment out the two **Fill_Plane** calls, set **bar3d**'s depth as *BarDepth/AspR* and change the final parameter from 0 to 1, in order to put a top on the bar.

The Line Graph Display

The previous demos used the same data set for each graph form. Line graphs, however, are normally used to show a half-dozen or fewer data sets, with each containing a large number of sequential data points. For demonstration, four data sets will be used, each containing 20 sequential data points. As with the previous demo, for convenience, the data points are contained in a 4 by 20 matrix though, in actual practice, the graph data would probably be read from some external source or generated within the program.

```
int     Accounts[4][20] =
                { 119, 121, 132, 140, 141, 139, 142, 135, 133, 123,
                  121, 120, 124, 111, 109, 119, 122, 132, 140, 142,
                  97,  99,  100, 107, 119, 123, 137, 148, 159, 160,
                  168, 172, 167, 155, 159, 163, 165, 155, 151, 148,
```

```
                  59,  73,  66,  49,  40,  39,  41,  45,  46,  52,
                  56,  59,  60,  56,  51,  54,  55,  53,  72,  75,
                  13,  15,  16,  19,  22,  20,  17,  18,  19,  21,
                  24,  26,  28,  27,  22,  20,  19,  23,  25,  24 };
int       Years[5]     = { 1984, 1985, 1984, 1987, 1988 };
char      *AccTypes[4] = { "GenMec", "UnvEle", "StrOil", "NrtMfr" };
```

Again, to make the graph visually impressive, a set of four graphic images (see Figure 9-4) will be used in the plot and the procedure **Create_Images** is used to construct them. In other circumstances, you might prefer to create a series of images separately and to store these as disk files, calling the various images as required.

```
void      *grimage[3];
main()
{
          Initialize();                          /* set graphics mode*/
          Create_Images();
          Line_Graph();
          Pause();
          closegraph();                          /* restore text mode*/
}
```

The Create_Images Function

This function is used to generate and to save a series of graphic images that will be used to emphasize points on the line graph. The array *figure* is a set of points describing a small stylized lightning bolt.

```
void Create_Images()
{
          int i;
          int figure[] = {   10, 5, 15, 5, 12, 10, 17, 10,
                             10, 18, 12, 13, 8, 13, 10, 5 };
```

The wheel or gear image is created from a series of small pie segments. Please realize that any small arc figure will be grainy. If you need a more detailed figure, it would be best to create an integer bit image after designing your figure on graph paper.

```
if ( MaxColors > 4 ) setcolor(2);
for( i=0; i<=5; i++ )
        pieslice( 10,10, i*60, (i*60)+60, 10 );
grimage[0] = malloc( imagesize( 0, 0, 20, 20 ) );
getimage( 0, 0, 20, 20, grimage[0] );
putimage( 0, 0, grimage[0], XOR_PUT );
```

The lightning bolt image uses the data points in figure and the **fillpoly** function with the fill style set to EMPTY_FILL.

```
setfillstyle( EMPTY_FILL, 0 );
if ( MaxColors > 4 ) setcolor(3);
fillpoly( sizeof(figure) / ( 2 * sizeof(int) ), figure );
grimage[1] = malloc( imagesize( 0, 0, 20, 20 ) );
getimage( 0, 0, 20, 20, grimage[1] );
putimage( 0, 0, grimage[1], XOR_PUT );
```

The oil drop image is created in outline by the **arc** and **ellipse** functions. Then **floodfill** is called, using SOLID_FILL and the current (drawing) color, to complete the image.

```
if ( MaxColors > 4 ) setcolor(4);
setfillstyle( SOLID_FILL, getcolor() );
arc( 10,  10, 105, 360, 8 );
ellipse( 0,  5, 300, 90, 8, 3 );
ellipse( 3, 10,  0, 90, 16, 8 );
floodfill( 10, 10, getcolor());
grimage[2] = malloc( imagesize( 0, 0, 20, 20 ) );
getimage( 0, 0, 20, 20, grimage[2] );
putimage( 0, 0, grimage[2], XOR_PUT );
```

The box image is the simplest of the four, and uses the **bar3d** function to create a small cube.

```
        if ( Max Colors > $ ) setcolor (5);
        bar3d( 0, 10, 10, 15, 5, 1);
        grimage[3] = malloc( imagesize( 0, 0, 20, 20));
        getimage( 0, 0, 20, 20, grimage[3]);
        putimage( 0, 0, grimage[3], XOR_PUT0;
}
```

In each case, memory is allocated for the image using **malloc** and **imagesize**, the getimage stores the screen image and **putimage** uses the XOR_PUT option to erase the screen for the next drawing. (See Chapter 10 for further details on image manipulation.)

The **Line_Graph** function begins by testing the data to find the highest value that requires plotting (*MaxVal*) and the viewport (window) is set to provide a top margin so there is space for labels.

```
void Line_Graph()
{
        int       width = getmaxx(), height = getmaxy(),
                  left = 0, top = 0, i, j, hstep, vstep, vsteps,
                  bottom, x, y, MaxVal = 0;
        double    scale;

        for( i=0; i; i++ )
                for( j=0; j ; j++ )
                if ( Accounts[i][j] > MaxVal ) MaxVal = Accounts[i][j];
        setviewport( left, top+5, left+width, top+height+5, 0 );
```

Next, vertical and horizontal steps are set to fit with the current screen resolution and with *MaxVal*.

```
        width −= 30;
        hstep  = width / 20;
        vsteps = ( MaxVal / 25 ) + 2;
```

```
vstep  = height / vsteps;
bottom = vstep * vsteps;
scale  = (double) vstep / (double) 25;
```

A series of vertical bars are drawn to mark off the years and each year is labeled.

```
if ( MaxColors > 4 ) setcolor( GREEN );
for ( i=0; i<=hstep*32; i+=hstep*4 ) line( i, 0, i, vstep*vsteps );
if ( MaxColors > 4 ) setcolor( WHITE );
settextjustify( CENTER_TEXT, CENTER_TEXT );
settextstyle( DEFAULT_FONT, HORIZ_DIR, 2 );
for( i=0; i; i++ )
{
        x = i * hstep * 4 + 2 * hstep;
        y = vstep / 2;
        gprintf( &x, &y, "%d", Years[i] );
}
```

Then a set of horizontal bars are drawn and labeled with amounts in steps of 25 to complete the graph background grid.

```
settextjustify( CENTER_TEXT, CENTER_TEXT );
for ( i=0; i<=bottom; i+=vstep )
{
        if ( MaxColors > 4 ) setcolor( BLUE );
        line( 0, i, hstep*20, i );
        if ( MaxColors > 4 ) setcolor( WHITE );
        x = hstep*20 + 15;
        y = i;
        gprintf( &x, &y, "%d", ((bottom−i)/vstep)*25 );
}
```

Each set of data is plotted separately, using a different color and line style. This plot begins by setting the current position (CP) relative to the first horizontal graph position (*hstep/2+3*) and the adjusted vertical position

(*bottom – scale*Accounts[i][0]+8*) and calling **outtext** to put a label on the
screen. Then the CP is set to the actual first plot position.

```
settextjustify( LEFT_TEXT, TOP_TEXT );
for ( i=0; i; i++ )
    {
    setlinestyle( i, 0, 3 );
    if ( MaxColors > 4 ) setcolor(i+2);
    moveto( hstep/2+3, bottom – scale*Accounts[i][0]+8 );
    outtext( AccTypes[i] );
    moveto( hstep/2,bottom – scale*Accounts[i][0] );
```

The data plot begins with the appropriate image (symbol) centered on the
plot position, then a line is drawn to the next graph position. When the loop
is finished, a final symbol is added at the end plot position.

```
for ( j=1; j ; j++ )
    {
    putimage( getx()–10, gety()–10, grimage[i], XOR_PUT );
    lineto( hstep/2+j*hstep, bottom–scale*Accounts[i][j] );
    }
    putimage( getx()–10, gety()–10, grimage[i], XOR_PUT );
    }
}
```

If you would prefer a simpler display, instead of the **putimage** functions,
a three by three "dot" could also be used to show the plot position:

```
for( x = –1; x <= 1; x++ )
            for( y = –1; y <= 1; y++ )
                putpixel( getx(), gety(), getcolor() );
```

```
/*          GRAPHALL.C — multiple graph demos          */


#ifdef __TINY__
#error Graphics demos will not run in the tiny model.
#endif

#include <conio.h>
#include <stdio.h>
#include <stdlib.h>
#include <stdarg.h>
#include <graphics.h>
#include "gprint.i"

int       GraphDriver;                              /* graphics device driver  */
int       GraphMode;                                /* graphics mode value     */
int       MaxColors;                        /* maximum colors available        */
int       ErrorCode = 0;                    /* reports any graphics errors     */
double AspR;                                        /* screen aspect ratio     */
int       XWidth, YHeight, ZDepth;
int       XAxis, YAxis, ZAxis;
int       XOrg, YOrg, MaxX, MaxY;
double  scale;
int    Accounts[4][9] = { 1985, 133, 35, 33, 17, 29, 15, 17, 32,
                          1986, 122, 41, 30, 25, 18, 24, 43, 21,
                          1987, 111, 65, 57, 14, 17, 39, 32, 17,
                          1988, 100, 60, 70, 12, 16, 13, 17, 12  };
char *AccTypes[9] = { "   ", "Motor", "Acsry", "Reprs", "Govmt",
                   "Lease", "Tires", "Paint", "Misc"        };

void Initialize()                       /* initialize graphics system and report errors */
{
  int xasp, yasp;
  GraphDriver = DETECT;                                 /* request auto-detection   */
  initgraph( &GraphDriver, &GraphMode, "" );
  ErrorCode = graphresult();                            /* test initialization results */
  if ( ErrorCode != grOk )                        /* if error ocurred during init        */
```

```
    {
        printf(" Graphics System Error: %s\n",
                    grapherrormsg( ErrorCode ) );
        exit( 1 );
    }
    MaxColors = getmaxcolor() + 1;                    /* read maximum color range        */
    getaspectratio(&xasp,&yasp);
    AspR = (double) xasp / (double) yasp;
    MaxX = getmaxx();
    MaxY = getmaxy();
}

void Pause()
{
    if( kbhit() ) getch();
    getch();
}

void Pie_Graph( int dataset, int x, int y )
{
    int i, m = 135, r, s = 0, t = 0, HJust, VJust;
    int total = 0;
    int Blank_Line = 0x0000;
    int CapColor;
    struct arccoordstype arcrec;
    for (i=1; i<=8; i++)
        total += Accounts[dataset][i];
    r = total / 4;
    setlinestyle( USERBIT_LINE, Blank_Line, NORM_WIDTH );
    setfillstyle( 0, 0 );
    pieslice(x,y,m,m+1,r+10);
                                        /* must have a minimum width of one degree */
    getarccoords( &arcrec );
    if( MaxColors > 4 ) setcolor( WHITE );
    settextstyle( SANS_SERIF_FONT, HORIZ_DIR, 2 );
    settextjustify( RIGHT_TEXT, BOTTOM_TEXT );
```

147

```
    gprintf( &arcrec.xend, &arcrec.yend, "%d", Accounts[dataset][0] );
    settextstyle( DEFAULT_FONT, HORIZ_DIR, 1 );
    if( MaxColors > 4 ) setcolor( EGA_YELLOW );
    for (i=1; i<=8; i++)
    {
        setfillstyle( i, i );
        if( MaxColors > 4 ) setcolor( WHITE );
        setlinestyle( SOLID_LINE, 0, NORM_WIDTH );
        t += (int) ( 360 * (double) Accounts[dataset][i]
                        / (double) total + 0.5 );
        if ( t > 360 ) t = 360;
        if ( i == 8 ) if ( t <360 ) t = 360;
        pieslice(x,y,s,t,r);
        setlinestyle( USERBIT_LINE, Blank_Line, NORM_WIDTH );
        setfillstyle( 0, 0 );
        CapColor = i+8;
        if ( CapColor > 15 ) CapColor = 7;
        if( MaxColors > 4 ) setcolor( CapColor );
        m = ( t − s ) / 2 + s;
        pieslice(x,y,m,m+1,r+5);                    /* minimum width one degree */
        getarccoords( &arcrec );
        if ( arcrec.xend > x) HJust = LEFT_TEXT;
                    else HJust = RIGHT_TEXT;
        if ( arcrec.yend > y) VJust = TOP_TEXT;
                    else VJust = BOTTOM_TEXT;
        settextjustify( HJust, VJust );
        outtextxy( arcrec.xend, arcrec.yend, AccTypes[i] );
        s = t;
    }
}
void Draw_Pie_Graphs()
{
    cleardevice();
    graphdefaults();
    rectangle( 0, 0, MaxX, MaxY );
    if( GraphDriver == CGA )
```

```
    {
        Pie_Graph( 0, 150,  55);
        Pie_Graph( 1, 450,  55);
        Pie_Graph( 2, 150, 140);
        Pie_Graph( 3, 450, 140);
    }
    else
    {
        Pie_Graph( 0, 150,  80);
        Pie_Graph( 1, 450,  80);
        Pie_Graph( 2, 150, 250);
        Pie_Graph( 3, 450, 250);
    }
}

void Bar_Graph( )
{
    int width = MaxX, height = MaxY, left = 0, top = 0;
    int i, j, hstep, vstep, bottom, x, y, barhigh;

    cleardevice();
    graphdefaults();
    setviewport( left, top+5, left+width, top+height+5, 0 );
    width −= 30;
    hstep = width/32;
    vstep = height/6;
    bottom = vstep*6;
    if( MaxColors > 4 ) setcolor( GREEN );
    for ( i=0; i<=hstep*32; i+=hstep*4 ) line( i, 0, i, vstep*6 );
    if( MaxColors > 4 ) setcolor( CYAN );
    for ( i=0; i<=bottom; i+=vstep )  line( 0, i, hstep*32, i );
    bottom− −;
    if( MaxColors > 4 ) setcolor( WHITE );
    settextstyle( DEFAULT_FONT, HORIZ_DIR, 1 );
    settextjustify( CENTER_TEXT, CENTER_TEXT );
    for ( i=0; i; i++ )
```

```
    {
        x = hstep*32 + 15;
        y = i*vstep;
        gprintf( &x, &y, "%d", 150–i*25 );
    }
    for ( i=1; i<=8; i++ )
    {
        for ( j=0; j; j++ )
        {
            barhigh = bottom – Accounts[j][i] * (double) vstep / (double) 25;
            if( MaxColors > 4 ) setcolor( j+1 );
            if( MaxColors > 4 ) setfillstyle( i, j+1 );
                        else setfillstyle( i, MaxColors–1 );
            bar3d( (i–1)*hstep*4 + (j*hstep) + 2, barhigh,
                    (i–1)*hstep*4 + (j*hstep) + hstep–2, bottom, 0, 0 );
            if( MaxColors > 4 ) setcolor( WHITE );
            outtextxy( i*hstep*4–hstep*2, 5, AccTypes[i] );
        }
    }
    if( MaxColors > 4 )
    {
        x = MaxX/2;
        y = MaxY/4;
        settextstyle( DEFAULT_FONT, HORIZ_DIR, 2 );
        for (i=0; i; i++)
        {
            setcolor(i+1);
            gprintf( &x, &y, "%d", Accounts[i][0] );
            x += textwidth(" ");
        }
    }
}

void Multi_Bar_Graph( int dataset, int left, int top )
{
    int  width  = MaxX/2–30;
```

```
int   height = MaxY/2–13;
int   i, hstep, vstep, bottom, x, y;
double  scale;

setviewport( left, top+5, left+width, top+height+5, 0 );
hstep = width/8;
vstep = height/6;
bottom = vstep*6;
scale = (double) vstep / 25;
if( MaxColors > 4 ) setcolor( GREEN );
for ( i=0; i<=hstep*8; i+=hstep ) line( i, 0, i, vstep*6 );
if( MaxColors > 4 ) setcolor( CYAN );
for ( i=0; i<=bottom; i+=vstep )  line( 0, i, hstep*8, i );
if( MaxColors > 4 ) setcolor( WHITE );
settextstyle( DEFAULT_FONT, HORIZ_DIR, 1 );
settextjustify( CENTER_TEXT, CENTER_TEXT );
for ( i=0; i; i++ )
{
    x = hstep*8 + 15;
    y = i*vstep;
    gprintf( &x, &y, "%d", 150–i*25 );
}
settextstyle( DEFAULT_FONT, VERT_DIR, 1 );
settextjustify( CENTER_TEXT, TOP_TEXT );
for ( i=0; i<=7; i++ )
{
    if( MaxColors > 4 ) setfillstyle( i+1, i+1 );
                  else setfillstyle( i+1, MaxColors–1 );
    bar( i*hstep+2,   bottom–scale*Accounts[dataset][i+1]–1,
        (i+1)*hstep–2, bottom–1 );
    outtextxy( i*hstep+hstep/2, 5, AccTypes[i+1] );
}
settextstyle( SANS_SERIF_FONT, HORIZ_DIR, 2 );
settextjustify( CENTER_TEXT, BOTTOM_TEXT );
x = width/2;
y = height/2–4;
```

```
            gprintf( &x, &y, "%d", Accounts[dataset][0] );
    }

    void Draw_Multi_Graphs()
    {
        cleardevice();
        graphdefaults();
        Multi_Bar_Graph( 0, 0, 0);
        Multi_Bar_Graph( 1, MaxX/2, 0);
        Multi_Bar_Graph( 2, 0,      MaxY/2);
        Multi_Bar_Graph( 3, MaxX/2, MaxY/2);
    }

    void Fill_Plane(   int X1, int Y1, int X2, int Y2,
                       int X3, int Y3, int X4, int Y4,
                       int FStyle, int FColor        )
    {
        int polygon[10];

        polygon[0] = polygon[8] = X1;
        polygon[1] = polygon[9] = Y1;
        polygon[2] = X2;                      polygon[3] = Y2;
        polygon[4] = X3;                      polygon[5] = Y3;
        polygon[6] = X4;                      polygon[7] = Y4;
        if ( MaxColors  4 ) FColor = MaxColors − 1;
        setfillstyle(FStyle,FColor);
        fillpoly(5,polygon);
    }

    void Graph_Field()
    {
        int i;

        if ( MaxColors > 4 )
        {
        Fill_Plane(  XOrg, YOrg, XOrg+XWidth, YOrg,
                     XOrg+XWidth, YOrg−YHeight, XOrg, YOrg−YHeight,
```

```
                    SOLID_FILL, LIGHTBLUE );
        Fill_Plane(  XOrg, YOrg, XOrg-(ZDepth/AspR), YOrg+ZDepth,
                    XOrg-(ZDepth/AspR), YOrg+ZDepth-YHeight,
                    XOrg, YOrg-YHeight, SOLID_FILL, LIGHTRED );
        Fill_Plane(  XOrg, YOrg, XOrg+XWidth, YOrg,
                    XOrg+XWidth-(ZDepth/AspR), YOrg+ZDepth,
                    XOrg-(ZDepth/AspR), YOrg+ZDepth,
                    SOLID_FILL, YELLOW );
    }
    line(XOrg,YOrg,XOrg+XWidth,YOrg);                      /* X-axis */
    line(XOrg,YOrg,XOrg,YOrg-YHeight);                     /* Y-axis */
    line(XOrg,YOrg,XOrg-ZDepth/AspR,YOrg+ZDepth);          /* Z-axis */
    if ( MaxColors > 4 ) setcolor(GREEN);        /* X-axis position lines */
    for ( i=XOrg+XAxis; i<=XOrg+XWidth; i+=XAxis )
    {
        line( i, YOrg, i, YOrg-YHeight );
        line( i, YOrg, i-ZDepth/AspR, YOrg+ZDepth );
    }
    if ( MaxColors > 4 ) setcolor(CYAN);         /* Y-axis position lines */
    for ( i=YOrg-YAxis; i>=YOrg-YHeight; i-=YAxis )
    {
        line( XOrg, i, XOrg+XWidth, i );
        line( XOrg, i, XOrg-ZDepth/AspR, i+ZDepth );
    }
    if ( MaxColors > 4 ) setcolor(RED);          /* Z-axis position lines */
    for (i=ZAxis; i<=ZDepth; i+=ZAxis)
    {
        line(XOrg-i/AspR,YOrg+i,XOrg-i/AspR+XWidth,YOrg+i);
        line(XOrg-i/AspR,YOrg+i,XOrg-i/AspR,YOrg-YHeight+i);
    }
}
void Show_Labels()
{
    int i, j, k, l, m;
    settextjustify(CENTER_TEXT,CENTER_TEXT);
    j = XOrg + XWidth + 15;
```

```
        l = XOrg - ZDepth / AspR - 15;
        for ( i=1; i<>; i++ )
        {
            k = YOrg - i * YAxis;
            gprintf( &j, &k, "%d", i*25 );
            m = YOrg + ZDepth - i * YAxis;
            gprintf( &l, &m, "%d", i*25 );
        }
        if ( MaxColors > 4 ) setcolor(LIGHTBLUE);
        j = XOrg + 25;
        l = j - ( ZDepth / AspR );
        m = YOrg + ZDepth + 8;
        k = YOrg - YHeight - 8;
        for ( i=1; i<=8; i++ )
        {
            outtextxy( j, k, AccTypes[i] );
            outtextxy( l, m, AccTypes[i] );
            j += 50;
            l += 50;
        }
        if ( MaxColors > 4 ) setcolor(LIGHTGREEN);
        for ( i=0; i<=3; i++ )
        {
            j = XOrg - ( i * ZAxis + ZAxis / 2 ) / AspR + 2;
            m = YOrg + i * ZAxis + ZAxis / 2;
            k = m - YHeight;
            l = j + XWidth;
            settextjustify( LEFT_TEXT, TOP_TEXT );
            gprintf( &l, &m, "%4d", Accounts[i][0] );
            settextjustify( RIGHT_TEXT, BOTTOM_TEXT );
            gprintf( &j, &k, "%4d", Accounts[i][0] );
        }
    }

    void Add_Bar( int left, int bottom, int height, int Color1, int Color2 )
    {
```

```
    int top, right;
    int BarWidth = XAxis / 2;
    int BarDepth = ZAxis / 2;
    if ( MaxColors  4 )
    {
        Color1 = MaxColors – 1;
        Color2 = MaxColors – 1;
    }
    setfillstyle( left+1, Color1 );
    left  = XOrg + ( left * XAxis )
                – ( ( ( bottom + 0.75 * ZAxis / XAxis ) * ZAxis ) / AspR );
    bottom = YOrg + ( ( bottom + 0.75 ) * ZAxis );
    right  = left + BarWidth;
    top  = bottom – height;
    bar3d( left, top, right, bottom, 0, 0 );
    Fill_Plane( right, top,
                right+BarDepth/AspR, top–BarDepth,
                right+BarDepth/AspR, bottom–BarDepth,
                right, bottom,
                CLOSE_DOT_FILL, Color1 );
    Fill_Plane( left, top,
                right, top,
                right+BarDepth/AspR, top–BarDepth,
                left+BarDepth/AspR, top–BarDepth,
                SOLID_FILL, Color2 );
}

void Show_Accounts()
{
    int i;
    if ( MaxColors > 4 ) setcolor( EGA_YELLOW );
    for (i=1; i<=8; i++)
        Add_Bar( i–1, 0, Accounts[0][i] * scale, LIGHTCYAN, CYAN );
    for (i=1; i<=8; i++)
        Add_Bar( i–1, 1, Accounts[1][i] * scale, LIGHTRED, RED );
    for (i=1; i<=8; i++)
```

```
                Add_Bar( i–1, 2, Accounts[2][i] * scale, LIGHTBLUE, BLUE );
        for (i=1; i<=8; i++)
                Add_Bar( i–1, 3, Accounts[3][i] * scale, LIGHTGREEN, GREEN );
}

void Three_D_Graph()
{
        int x, y;
        cleardevice();
        ZDepth  = 4 * ZAxis;
        settextjustify( LEFT_TEXT, TOP_TEXT );
        setcolor( getmaxcolor() );
        x = 10; y = 10;
        gprintf( &x, &y, "ZAxis = %d", ZAxis );
        Graph_Field();
        Show_Labels();
        Show_Accounts();
        Pause();
}

void Graphs_3D()
{
        cleardevice();
        graphdefaults();
        XAxis = MaxX/13;
        YAxis = MaxY/14;
        ZAxis = 10;
        XOrg  = MaxX/3;
        YOrg  = MaxY/2;
        XWidth  = 8 * XAxis;
        YHeight = 6 * YAxis;
        scale = (double) YAxis / 25;
        for( ZAxis=15; (YOrg+4*ZAxis)axY; ZAxis+=5 )
            Three_D_Graph();
}
```

```
/*********************** MAIN GRAPH************************/
main()
{
    Initialize();                                /*  set graphics mode      */
    Draw_Pie_Graphs();
    Pause();
    Bar_Graph();
    Pause();
    Draw_Multi_Graphs();
    Pause();
    Graphs_3D();
    closegraph();                                /*  restore text mode      */
}
```

```
            /* LINEGRAF.C — Sample LINE-GRAPH using Turbo-C Graphics */
#ifdef __TINY__
#error Graphics demos will not run in the tiny model.
#endif
#include <conio.h>
#include <stdio.h>
#include <stdlib.h>
#include <stdarg.h>
#include <graphics.h>
#include <gprint.i>
int  GraphDriver;                               /* graphics device driver  */
int  GraphMode;                                 /* graphics mode value      */
int  MaxColors;                                 /* maximum colors available */
int  ErrorCode = 0;                             /* reports any graphics errors */
void    *grimage[3];
int  Accounts[4][20] = { 119, 121, 132, 140, 141, 139, 142, 135, 133, 123,
                         121, 120, 124, 111, 109, 119, 122, 132, 140, 142,
                         97, 99, 100, 107, 119, 123, 137, 148, 159, 160,
                         168, 172, 167, 155, 159, 163, 165, 155, 151, 148,
```

```
                         59, 73, 66, 49, 40, 39, 41, 45, 46, 52,
                         56, 59, 60, 56, 51, 54, 55, 53, 72, 75,
                         13, 15, 16, 19, 22, 20, 17, 18, 19, 21,
                         24, 26, 28, 27, 22, 20, 19, 23, 25, 24 };
int    Years[5]      = { 1984, 1985, 1984, 1987, 1988 };
char *AccTypes[4]    = { "GenMec", "UnvEle", "StrOil", "NrtMfr" };

void Initialize()                        /* initialize graphics system and report errors */
{
     GraphDriver = DETECT;                        /* request auto-detection   */
     initgraph( &GraphDriver, &GraphMode, "" );
     ErrorCode = graphresult();                   /* test initialization results */
     if ( ErrorCode != grOk )             /* if error occurred during init    */
     {
         printf(" Graphics System Error: %s\n", grapherrormsg( ErrorCode ) );
         exit( 1 );
     }
     MaxColors = getmaxcolor() + 1;       /* read maximum color range      */
}

void Pause()
{
     if( kbhit() ) getch();
     getch();
}

void Line_Graph()
{
     int  width = getmaxx(), height = getmaxy(), left = 0, top = 0;
     int  i, j, hstep, vstep, vsteps, bottom, x, y, MaxVal = 0;
     double  scale;
     for( i=0; i; i++ )
         for( j=0; j ; j++ )
             if ( Accounts[i][j] > MaxVal ) MaxVal = Accounts[i][j];
     setviewport( left, top+5, left+width, top+height+5, 0 );
     width -= 30;
     hstep  = width / 20;
```

```
vsteps = ( MaxVal / 25 ) + 2;
vstep  = height / vsteps;
bottom = vstep * vsteps;
scale  = (double) vstep / (double) 25;
if ( MaxColors > 4 ) setcolor( GREEN );
for ( i=0; i<=hstep*32; i+=hstep*4 ) line( i, 0, i, vstep*vsteps );
if ( MaxColors > 4 ) setcolor( WHITE );
settextjustify( CENTER_TEXT, CENTER_TEXT );
settextstyle( DEFAULT_FONT, HORIZ_DIR, 2 );
for( i=0; i; i++ )
{
    x = i * hstep * 4 + 2 * hstep;
    y = vstep / 2;
    gprintf( &x, &y, "%d", Years[i] );
}
settextjustify( CENTER_TEXT, CENTER_TEXT );
for ( i=0; i<=bottom; i+=vstep )
{
    if ( MaxColors > 4 ) setcolor( BLUE );
    line( 0, i, hstep*20, i );
    if ( MaxColors > 4 ) setcolor( WHITE );
    x = hstep*20 + 15;
    y = i;
    gprintf( &x, &y, "%d", ((bottom−i)/vstep)*25 );
}
settextjustify( LEFT_TEXT, TOP_TEXT );
for ( i=0; i; i++ )
{
    setlinestyle(i,0,3);
    if ( MaxColors > 4 ) setcolor(i+2);
    moveto( hstep/2+3, bottom − scale*Accounts[i][0]+8 );
    outtext( AccTypes[i] );
    moveto( hstep/2,bottom − scale*Accounts[i][ 0] )
                    /*instead of putimage, create a 'dot' around the plot position */
                        /* for ( x + −1; x <<= 1; x++ 0*/
                        /*for ( y + −1; y<<=1; y++ ) */
```

159

```
                                        /* put pixel ( getx(), gety (), getcolor () ); */
            putimage( getx()–10, gety()–10, grimage[i], XOR_PUT );
            lineto( hstep/2+j*hstep, bottom – scale*Accounts[i][j] );
        }
        putimage( getx()–10, gety()–10, grimage[i], XOR_PUT );
    }
}

void Create_Images()
{
    int i;
    int figure[] = { 10, 5, 15, 5, 12,10, 17,10,
                     10,18, 12,13,  8,13, 10, 5 };
    setfillstyle(EMPTY_FILL,0);                           /*wheel/gear*/
    if ( MaxColors > 4 ) setcolor(2);
    for( i=0; i<=5; i++ )
        pieslice( 10,10, i*60, (i*60)+60, 10 );
    grimage[0] = malloc( imagesize( 0, 0, 20, 20 ) );
    getimage( 0, 0, 20, 20, grimage[0] );
    putimage( 0, 0, grimage[0], XOR_PUT );
    if ( MaxColors > 4 ) setcolor(3);                     /*lightning bolt*/
    fillpoly( sizeof(figure) / ( 2 * sizeof(int) ), figure );
    grimage[1] = malloc( imagesize( 0, 0, 20, 20 ) );
    getimage( 0, 0, 20, 20, grimage[1] );
    putimage( 0, 0, grimage[1], XOR_PUT );
    if ( MaxColors > 4 ) setcolor(4);                     /*oil drop*/
    setfillstyle(SOLID_FILL,getcolor());
    arc( 10,  10, 105, 360, 8 );
    ellipse( 0,  5, 300, 90, 8, 3 );
    ellipse( 3, 10,   0, 90, 16, 8 );
    floodfill(10,10,getcolor());
    grimage[2] = malloc( imagesize( 0, 0, 20, 20 ) );
    getimage( 0, 0, 20, 20, grimage[2] );
    putimage( 0, 0, grimage[2], XOR_PUT );
    if ( MaxColors > 4 ) setcolor(5);                     /*box*/
    bar3d( 0,10,10,15,5,1);
```

```
    grimage[3] = malloc( imagesize( 0, 0, 20, 20 ) );
    getimage( 0, 0, 20, 20, grimage[3] );
    putimage( 0, 0, grimage[3], XOR_PUT );
}
main()
{
    Initialize();                                          /* set graphics mode   */
    Create_Images();
    Line_Graph();
    Pause();
    closegraph();                                          /* restore text mode   */
}
```

CHAPTER 10

SIMPLE ANIMATION TECHNIQUES

The word "animation" — moving graphic images — might first bring to mind cartoon images from the Saturday TV channels. Or you might settle on advertising animation where a computer is able to eat a stick of gum or to drink a soda by plugging into the bottle. Or you may be an aficionado of the arcade graphic animations where, for the mere fourth part of a dollar, swarms of saucers, ninjas and fantasy monsters present themselves for electronic combat.

These are all animations and are computer generated in whole or in part. Graphic animation, however, is not a product of the computer age. Over a century ago, the zeoscope combined a series of pictures to create a moving animation. Graphic images appeared in the margins of books where the pages could be riffled to create a moving picture. Decades of cartoons have been created by combining carefully hand-drawn images to create masterpieces ranging from Wylie Coyote and Roadrunner to Fantasia.

Today, much of the drudgery of cartoon animation is handled by computer graphics programs, but the animation processes used may still be categorized as two types: combined images and morphological images.

Combined images are images built up from a stockpile or library of image parts as used in the demo program ANIMATE1.C. In this very simple demo, "George" is created first as a head and torso image. This initial image is saved, then additions are made to create a second image with one arm swinging forward and the other back. By combining these simple images, George is able to saunter through the maze, swinging his arms as he walks in a moderately convincing graphic animation.

More complex actions — such as picking up an object or doing a broadjump — would require a different set of images and the program that allows George to walk has only a very simple set of rules and responses.

The second type of animation is the morphological image: the image that is created in response to a set of programming rules instead of being selected from a series of stored images. In the second animation demo ANIMATE2.C, a simple stick figure (in this case limited to a head and two legs) will walk along a cluttered plane. However, instead of a series of images, each figure is created from a simple set of links describing a basic skeleton with hinge points and each follows a limited set of response rules.

In a sense, this figure is a robot who can walk without falling over and — as Samuel Johnson once said of dancing dogs — the fascination lies not in it being done well, but merely that it can be done at all. Essentially the same is true of the robot — it walks, if not well.

Unlike the series of prewritten images, however, the robot image can be programmed to respond to a variety of situations and to create images to adapt to different circumstances. There are, however, drawbacks. The programmer must create decision trees and loops to adapt to the varying circumstances and the calculations required for each image are more extensive than those required to simply place the appropriate image in the correct screen position.

Image Animation

Depending on your hardware graphics card, your system may support two or more pages of graphics video memory with the zero page being the default both for visual display and for graphics mode operations. In Turbo C, the **setvisualpage** and **setactivepage** provide access to the alternate video pages, if supported by the hardware. The **setactivepage** function selects which video graphics page will be written to by all graphics operations. The **setvisualpage** function selects which graphics video page is actually displayed.

Remember: the active page and the visual page are not necessarily the same page. Graphics operations can be carried out on any supported page whether it is visible or not and any supported page can be switched to active, visible, display instantly. The actual time required to ''switch'' visual pages is less than 1/50 of a second (varying according to hardware capabilities).

The demo program ANIMATE1.C will begin by switching the active graphics page (assuming your graphics card supports alternate video pages) to go ''backstage'', and create a series of images out of sight. Once this is finished and our actor is ready, the active graphics page will be reset to match the active visual page and a maze will be drawn on screen with George appearing at the upper left of the maze. At this point, the cursor controls (or a mouse) can be used to walk George through the maze.

Note: this is not a case of ''dragging'' an image across the screen. As George moves in different directions, the image is animated using a series of three poses to create the appearance of a man walking as seen from above. Since these operations can be carried out very quickly, the screen action is slowed, using the **delay** function, to approximate a realistic walking pace.

Before anything else, the program begins with definitions that will control the movement directions:

```
#define  RIGHT  0
#define  LEFT    1
#define  UP      2
#define  DOWN  3
```

And a second set which control George's poses as he moves:

```
#define  NSTEP  0
#define  LSTEP  1
#define  RSTEP  2
```

And two arrays of pointers for the graphics images that will be used:

```
void    *Flash[3];
void    *Man[4][3];
```

The first array (Flash) will be used to provide a visual response whenever George runs into something, while the second array (Man) provides three different poses of George facing in four directions.

The program begins by using the **Initialize** function to set up the graphics screen mode; then, because creating the images will require a few seconds, it writes a message to the active screen display before calling **setactivepage** to switch to an alternate video page as the active graphics page.

```
main()
{
        Initialize();                           /*        set graphics mode        */
        outtextxy(10,10," One Moment Please ");
        setactivepage( 1 );
```

If your hardware does not support alternate video pages, this selection command will simply be ignored and the graphics images will be visible during their construction. The time required is the same in either case, but it is a bit more elegant to keep the nuts and bolts assembly work out of sight. If you are curious, this selection can be commented out to allow the image creation process to proceed in plain view.

The **CreateImages** function constructs the graphics images that will be used, then the active video graphics page is reset to the default page and the screen is cleared. Alternatively, the **setvisualpage** function could have been used to change the visual (displayed) graphics video page to match the active video page. The results would be the same.

```
        CreateImages();
        setactivepage( 0 );
        clearviewport();
```

Now the maze for the game is created on screen and the game proceeds.

```
        CreateMaze();
        StartGame();
```

The **ClearImages** function is used before exiting to release the memory allocated to store the several graphics images. In this particular application, memory release is not absolutely necessary since exiting the program will take care of this, but it is still good practice to provide for proper memory management.

```
ClearImages();
closegraph();
}
```

CreateImages

The **CreateImages** function creates and saves a series of graphic images, beginning with a series of integer arrays (pflash# and ##arm_#) that describe elements used in the images.

```
void CreateImages()
{
        int  i, j, MaxColor = getmaxcolor();
        int pflash1[] = { 100, 40, 110, 60, 100, 70, 120, 65,
                        140, 80, 130, 60, 140, 50, 120, 65, 100, 40 };
        int pflash2[] = { 120, 40, 110, 55,  90, 60, 110, 65,
                        120, 80, 130, 65, 150, 60, 130, 65, 120, 40 };
        int pflash3[] = { 140, 40, 130, 60, 140, 70, 120, 65,
                        100, 80, 110, 60, 100, 50, 120, 55, 140, 40 };
        int bkarm_u[] = { 100, 62, 102, 68, 105, 70, 108, 69, 109, 65 };
        int ftarm_u[] = { 140, 62, 143, 52, 130, 47, 125, 52 };
        int bkarm_r[] = { 121,145, 128,147, 130,150, 129,153, 125,154 };
        int ftarm_r[] = { 117,176, 106,176, 100,165, 107,160 };
```

The **randomize** function is used to seed the random number generator. Then the drawing color, fill style and fill color are selected randomly for each of the *pflash#* images.

```
randomize();
setcolor( random( MaxColor ) + 1 );
setfillstyle( random(11) + 1, random ( MaxColor ) + 1 );
```

Figure 10-1: Basic Figure Animation — Initial Image

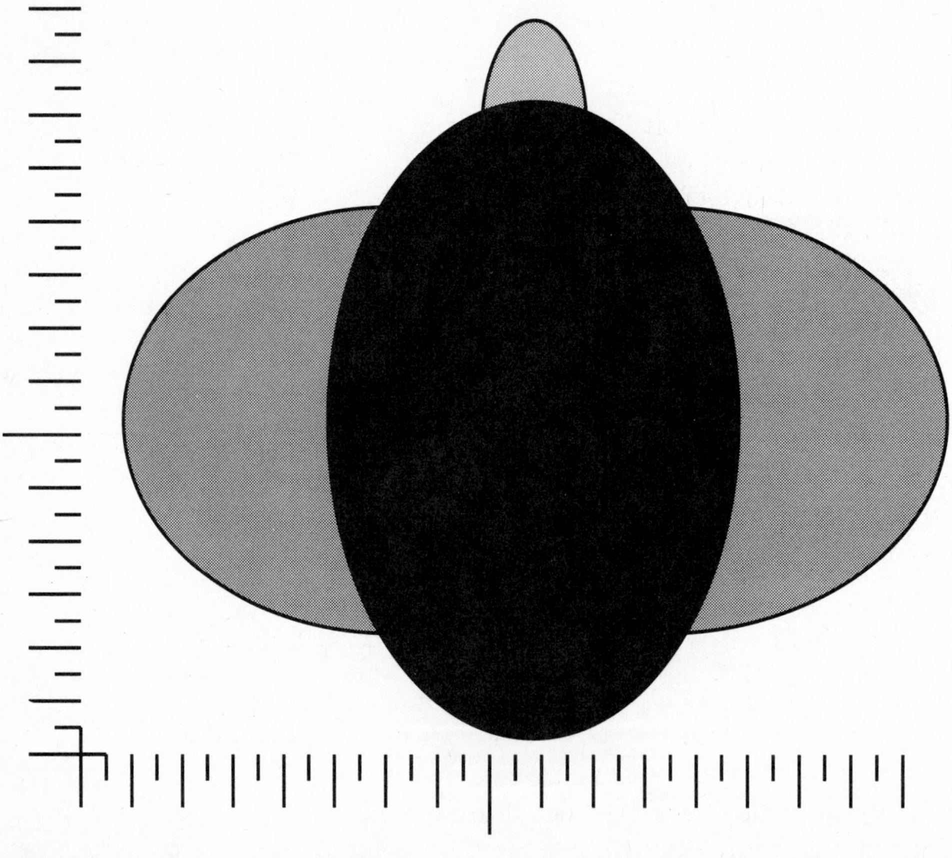

This initial image (see Figure 10-1) consists of four ellipses. The head is an ellipse with a vertical radius of 12 and a horizontal radius of eight. Each shoulder is an ellipse with a vertical radius of eight and a horizontal radius of 12 with centers offset four pixels right and left. Last, the nose is a smaller ellipse with a vertical radius of four and a horizontal radius of two.

This image will be inverted (top to bottom) to create the downfacing image but, instead of rotating for right and left facing images, these will be created by transposing the axis coordinates and radii and using AspR (aspect resolution) to adjust the X/Y resolution.

When calling the **fillpoly** function, instead of having to know the size of the integer array for each polygon, the size passed to **fillpoly** is calculated as *sizeof(pflash#)* divided by two times *sizeof(int)*, because two integer values are required for each polygon point.

```
fillpoly( sizeof( pflash1 )/( 2 * sizeof( int ) ), pflash1 );
```

The **SaveImage** function will be described further in a moment but, in brief, it returns a pointer to a memory image. The four parameters describe the screen coordinates for the image to be saved.

```
Flash[0] = SaveImage( 100, 40, 140, 80 );
```

Essentially, the same sequence of operations is repeated for the *pflash2* and *pflash3* arrays.

George's images begin with a series of ellipses to create two heads with noses and shoulders; one head with the long axis horizontal, the other vertical. The **floodfill** function fills in the images using SOLID_FILL for the heads and HATCH_FILL for the shoulders.

```
setcolor( MaxColor );
setfillstyle( SOLID_FILL, MaxColor );
ellipse(  120,  60,  0, 360, 10, 10 );
floodfill( 120,  60, MaxColor );
ellipse(  220, 160,  0, 360, 13,  7 );
floodfill( 220, 160, MaxColor );
ellipse(  120,  51,  0, 180,  3,  3 );
ellipse(  207, 160, 90, 270,  3,  2 );
setfillstyle( HATCH_FILL, MaxColor );
ellipse(  128,  60, 270, 90, 12,  6 );
```

```
ellipse(  112,  60,  90, 270, 12,  6 );
floodfill( 105,  60, MaxColor );
ellipse(  220, 154,   0, 180,  8,  9 );
floodfill( 220, 150, MaxColor );
ellipse(  220, 166, 180, 360,  8,  9 );
floodfill( 220, 170, MaxColor );
```

Figure 10-2: Basic Figure Animation — Secondary Image

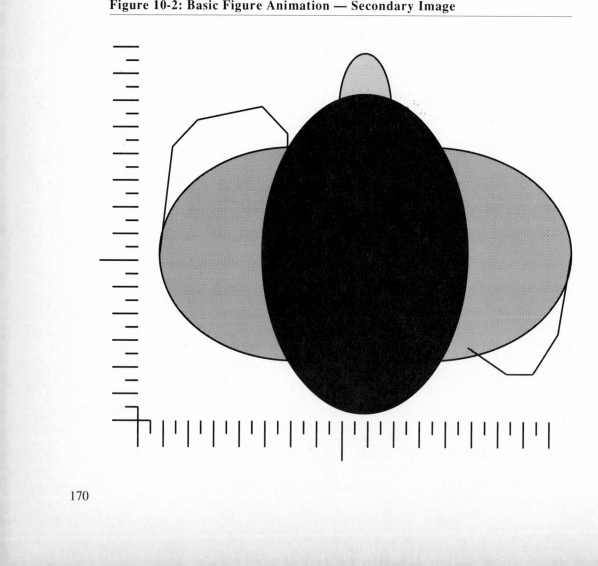

In lieu of duplicating efforts to draw separate heads facing left and right and up and down, two of the existing images are mapped, pixel by pixel, to create matching reversed images.

```
for ( i=100; i<=145; i++)
for ( j= 45; j<= 70; j++)
putpixel( 345–i, 120–j, getpixel( i, j ) );
for ( i=204; i<=235; i++)
for ( j=145; j<=175; j++)
putpixel( 345–i, j, getpixel( i, j ) );
```

And the four end products are saved as individual images.

```
Man[ UP ][ NSTEP ]    = SaveImage( 100,  45, 140,  70 );
Man[ DOWN ][ NSTEP ] = SaveImage( 205,  50, 245,  75 );
Man[ LEFT ][ NSTEP ]  = SaveImage( 203, 140, 234, 180 );
Man[ RIGHT ][ NSTEP ] = SaveImage( 111, 140, 142, 180 );
```

So far, four stationary images have been created. Now two of these will be used as the basis for further images by adding arms to the bodies (see Figure 10-2).

In Figure 10-2 arms are added to the initial image, then the image will be rotated up/down and right/left to create two pairs of movement images. The right/left facing image will have arms added, then run through the same pixel transformation.

The end results will be a set of 12 images in sets of three (stationary, right arm forward, left arm forward) facing four directions (up, right, left and down) for movement through the maze.

While this is an extremely simple animation, the basic principles required for greater elaborations are amply demonstrated. The fillstyle is set to CLOSE_DOT_FILL and **fillpoly** is called to add the two arms to the image.

```
setfillstyle( CLOSE_DOT_FILL, MaxColor );
putimage( 100, 45, Man[ UP ][ NSTEP ], COPY_PUT );
fillpoly( sizeof( bkarm_u )/( 2 * sizeof(int) ), bkarm_u );
fillpoly( sizeof( ftarm_u )/( 2 * sizeof(int) ), ftarm_u );
putimage( 100, 45, Man[ UP ][ NSTEP ], OR_PUT );
```

Note that **putimage** has been called twice; first with the COPY_PUT option and the second time with the OR_PUT option. With the first call, using COPY_PUT, the image is written to the screen, replacing any existing pixels at the image location. Next, the **fillpoly** function is used to add arms as new elements to this screen image.

There is, however, a minor problem with **fillpoly** (see Figure 10-3).

The problem is that **fillpoly** does not follow the existing outlines when adding the fill pattern. Instead, **fillpoly** calculates the area to fill by assuming a line between the first point plotted and the last and fills everything within the polygon area. This is also a portion of the original image — which is not what is desired. The line shading on the arms of George in Figure 10-3 shows the area of the original image that will be overwritten by the **fillpoly** function.

Instead of trying to close the polygon in such a manner as to avoid this overwrite, the **putimage** function is called a second time, using OR_PUT, to restore the overwritten pixels, leaving the final image as desired.

The first call to **putimage** could be omitted since it has no effect on the operations carried out by **fillpoly** and the final call to **putimage** will insert the head and body image. The first call, however, was used as a convenience to line up the arms correctly and was left in the code to allow you to examine the results produced by the interaction with **fillpoly**.

At this point, the image has one arm in front of the body and the other swung back. Now, it will be transposed to create three other images; one also facing up but with the arms reversed; the other two facing down with the left and right arms alternately in front and in back.

```
for ( i=100; i<=145; i++)
for ( j= 45; j<= 70; j++)
{ putpixel( 345–i,    j, getpixel( i, j ) );
        putpixel( 345–i, 220–j, getpixel( i, j ) );
        putpixel(    i, 220–j, getpixel( i, j ) ); }
```

And the final four images are saved individually:

```
Man[ UP ][ LSTEP ]  = SaveImage( 100, 45, 145, 70 );
Man[ UP ][ RSTEP ]  = SaveImage( 200, 45, 245, 70 );
```

```
Man[ DOWN ][ LSTEP ] = SaveImage( 100, 150, 145, 175 );
Man[ DOWN ][ RSTEP ] = SaveImage( 200, 150, 245, 175 );
```

Figure 10-3: The fillpoly Problem

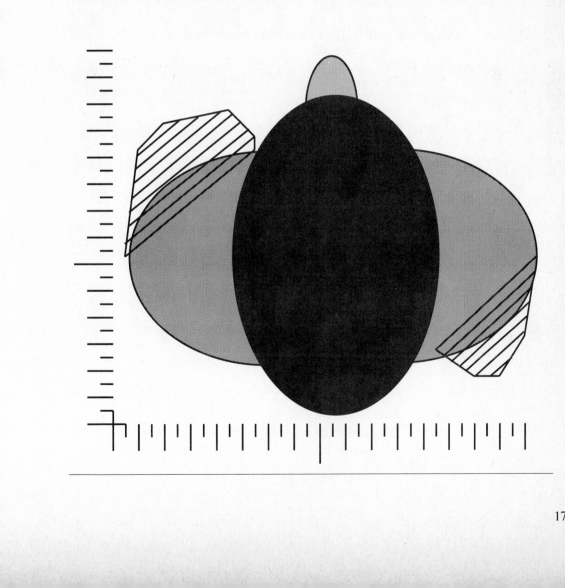

Next, using the original left-facing image, the same process is repeated, arms are added and the result is transposed three ways, to create the final set of four images.

```
putimage( 100, 140, Man[ LEFT ][ NSTEP ], COPY_PUT );
fillpoly( sizeof( bkarm_r )/( 2 * sizeof(int) ), bkarm_r );
fillpoly( sizeof( ftarm_r )/( 2 * sizeof(int) ), ftarm_r );
putimage( 100, 140, Man[ LEFT ][ NSTEP ], OR_PUT );
for ( i=100; i<=132; i++)
for ( j=144; j<=177; j++)
{ putpixel( 345–i, j, getpixel( i, j ) );
   putpixel( 345–i, 220–j, getpixel( i, j ) );
   putpixel( i, 220–j, getpixel( i, j ) ); }
Man[ LEFT ][ RSTEP ] = SaveImage( 100, 144, 132, 177 );
Man[ LEFT ][ LSTEP ]  = SaveImage( 100,  43, 132,  76 );
Man[ RIGHT ][ LSTEP ] = SaveImage( 213,  43, 245,  76 );
Man[ RIGHT ][ RSTEP ]= SaveImage( 213, 144, 245, 177 );
}
```

SaveImage

The **SaveImage** function is called with four parameters specifying the corners of a rectangle on the screen. **SaveImage** uses the **imagesize** function to calculate the memory necessary and uses the function **malloc** to allocate memory for the image area specified, also assigning a local pointer **image** to the memory location.

```
void *SaveImage( int left, int top, int right, int bottom )
{
        void *image;
        image = malloc( imagesize( left, top, right, bottom ) );
```

The **getimage** function transfers the screen image to the memory area pointed at by *image*, then **putimage** uses the XOR_PUT option to erase the screen image and then the image pointer is returned to the calling function.

```
getimage( left, top, right, bottom, image );
```

```
        putimage( left, top, image, XOR_PUT );
        return( image );
}
```

At this point, memory has been allocated for the graphic image, the screen image information has been written to this memory location and the pointer to the location has been returned in order to be assigned to the appropriate pointer variable (so the local pointer *image* can be forgotten).

CreateMaze

The **CreateMaze** function writes a maze to the screen. The maze elements are described as a series arrays of integers specifying pairs of points.

```
void CreateMaze()
{
        int    i, j;
        int    maze1[]  = { 200, 40,  50, 40,  50,160, 100,160 };
        int    maze2[]  = { 100, 80, 100,120, 200,120, 200,240 };
        .
        .
        .
        int    maze16[] = { 550,120, 550,200, 450,200, 450,280, 550,280 };
        int    maze17[] = { 500,240, 600,240 };
        struct viewporttype vp;
```

This maze data could be retrieved from an external file or even generated by an appropriate algorithm. For purposes of demonstration, it is easiest to provide the data as shown.

The viewport (window) is set to the entire screen — in this case, EGA or higher resolution is assumed — and a brief instruction is written at the bottom.

```
        setcolor( MaxColors – 1 );
        setviewport(0,0,639,349,1);                    /*Set draw color to white*/
        settextstyle( DEFAULT_FONT, HORIZ_DIR, 1 );
        outtextxy(  20, 330, "Use Arrow Keys to move 'George' or"
```

" <Q>uit to exit program");

Now the viewport is reduced in size and a border is drawn around the area.

```
setviewport(0,0,600,320,1);
setlinestyle( SOLID_LINE, 0, NORM_WIDTH );
getviewsettings( &vp );
rectangle( 0, 0, vp.right – vp.left, vp.bottom – vp.top );
```

The final step is to draw the walls of the maze and to add labels for the start and finish points.

```
outtextxy( 10, 20, "START" );
drawpoly( sizeof( maze1  )/( 2 * sizeof(int) ), maze1  );
drawpoly( sizeof( maze2  )/( 2 * sizeof(int) ), maze2  );
   .
   .
   .
drawpoly( sizeof( maze16 )/( 2 * sizeof(int) ), maze16 );
drawpoly( sizeof( maze17 )/( 2 * sizeof(int) ), maze17 );
outtextxy( 550, 300, "FINISH" );
}
```

In this case, the **drawpoly** function is used instead of **fillpoly** because you only want lines drawn without fill to be added. The operation is otherwise the same as described in the **Create_Images** function.

Note: no record of the maze construction nor of the position of the walls is necessary — the program will not depend on any such record for operation. Instead, the screen image itself will be tested to decided if movements are valid or not.

StartGame

Now, it is time for the actual game control, which begins with the **StartGame** function. Initially, **StartGame** calls the **Put_Image** function to put George on the screen at the start coordinates, then reads the keyboard (or a mouse) to direct George's movements on the screen. Only four keys will be accepted as input: the UP, DOWN, RIGHT and LEFT arrow keys and 'Q' for quit.

```
void StartGame()
{
        har ch;
        int  Quit = 0;
        Move = LastMove = RIGHT;
        Put_Image( NSTEP );
```

The variable *Quit* was initialized as zero (a Boolean false). Until *Quit* is true, the *while* loop will continue.

```
        while ( !Quit )
        {
                ch = getch();
                if ( ch == 0x00 )
            {
```

If the first key read is a NULL, then, presumably, one of the function keys was pressed and a second character code is read to decide which key. The four arrow keys (cursor keys) control George's movements, each calling the **Move_Image** function with the appropriate direction as a parameter.

```
                ch = getch();
                switch (ch)
                {
                    case 'M' : Move_Image( RIGHT );  break;
                    case 'K' : Move_Image( LEFT );  break;
                    case 'H' : Move_Image( UP );    break;
                    case 'P' : Move_Image( DOWN );  break;
                }
            }
```

Note that both **Q** and **q** are accepted as valid inputs. If *Quit* increments, then *Quit* becomes a Boolean true and the *while* loop exits.

```
                else if (ch == 'Q' || ch == 'q') Quit++;
        }
}
```

Move_Image

The **Move_Image** function is called with an argument *NextStep*, which specifies the direction for George to move. First, **Put_Image** is called to erase the current screen image. The *Move* variable, which controls direction and selects the set of images used, takes the value *NextStep* and **Put_Image** is called again to put George back on the screen, but facing in the correct direction.

```
void Move_Image( int NextStep )
{
        int i, XFake, YFake, XStep, YStep, XFlash, YFlash;
        Put_Image( NSTEP );
        Move = NextStep;
        Put_Image( NSTEP );
```

Before the two calls to **Put_Image**, George may have been facing the same direction as he will be after the calls but, rather than writing a test for direction, it is simple enough to erase the existing image and restore the desired image.

Depending on the direction of movement, several variables: *XFake*, *YFake*, *XStep*, *YStep*, *XFlash* and *YFlash* are assigned values that might be needed subsequently. It's easiest, however, to use one *switch* statement to set all six variables for the proper directions and then you don't have to worry about them anymore.

```
switch( Move )
{
    case RIGHT:    XFake  = 5;      YFake  = 0;
                   XStep  = 5;      YStep  = 0;
                   XFlash = 5;      YFlash = 0;    break;
    case LEFT:     XFake  = -5;     YFake  = 0;
                   XStep  = -5;     YStep  = 0;
                   XFlash = 2;      YFlash = 0;    break;
    case  UP:      XFake  = 0;      YFake  = -5;
                   XStep  = 0;      YStep  = -4;
```

```
                    XFlash = 0;     YFlash = 2;    break;
    case DOWN:      XFake = 0;      YFake = 5;
                    XStep = 0;      YStep = 4;
                    XFlash = 0;     YFlash = 0;    break;
}
```

The call to the **Test_Move** function decides if George can move in the direction requested.

```
    if ( !Test_Move() )
    {
```

If **Test_Move** returns a Boolean false, then **Put_Image** erases the stationary image, increments the position by *XFake* or *YFake* (one of these is always zero), places the stepping image (LSTEP) on the screen, and calls **FlashImage**.

```
    Put_Image( NSTEP );
    XPos += XFake;
    YPos += YFake;
    Put_Image( LSTEP );
    FlashImage( XPos+XFlash, YPos+YFlash );
```

Now, the LSTEP image is erased, the position coordinates are returned to their previous values and the NSTEP image is restored.

```
    Put_Image( LSTEP );
    XPos -= XFake;
    Pos -= YFake;
    Put_Image( NSTEP );
    }
```

In this manner, George takes a half step forward, bumps into the wall of the maze, flashing stars are superimposed cartoon-style (with sound effects) and, finally, George steps back and waits for the next instruction.

If **Test_Move** returns true, then George is free to move forward. This begins by erasing the stationary image (NSTEP) and incrementing the position coordinates.

```
else
{
        Put_Image( NSTEP );
        XPos += XStep;
        YPos += YStep;
```

In order to make the illusion of movement as smooth as possible, George's *LastMove* is tested to decide on which foot he should now be leading. Actually, George's feet are never seen — only the illusion of his arms swinging as he walks. If the sequence of his movements were not coordinated, the results would look very awkward indeed. Since *LastMove* will be either 1 or 2 (LSTEP or RSTEP), only a simple Boolean test is required.

```
        if( LastMove != LSTEP )
        {
```

Each time an arrow key is pressed (or a mouse sends the equivalent signal), George is going to take several steps on the screen. Instead of writing all the individual instructions necessary for each step and each position adjustment, a loop will run calls through to the **Take_Step** function to make George walk forward, with his last step the same as his first in this sequence and ending in the NSTEP (stationary) position.

```
        for ( i=1; i<=2; i++ )
        {
            Take_Step( XStep, YStep, LSTEP );
            Take_Step( XStep, YStep, NSTEP );
            Take_Step( XStep, YStep, RSTEP );
            Take_Step( XStep, YStep, NSTEP );
        }
        Take_Step( XStep, YStep, LSTEP );
        Put_Image( NSTEP );
```

```
            delay( TimeOut );
        }
```

The *XStep* and *YStep* variables have already been assigned the appropriate offsets for the movement direction (*Move*) and each call to **Take_Step** places the appropriate image on the screen, waits momentarily, erases the image and then increments the position coordinates.

If *LastMove* was LSTEP, then George starts off with RSTEP, running though the same sequences.

```
        else
        {
            for ( i=1; i<=2; i++ )
            {
                Take_Step( XStep, YStep, RSTEP );
                Take_Step( XStep, YStep, NSTEP );
                Take_Step( XStep, YStep, LSTEP );
                Take_Step( XStep, YStep, NSTEP );
            }
            Take_Step( XStep, YStep, RSTEP );
            Put_Image( NSTEP );
            delay( TimeOut );
        }
    }
}
```

The **Test_Move** function is the key decision mechanism for this game. It reads the screen pixels in the direction requested to decide if George is free to move. The *switch(Move)* directive decides which test is appropriate for the selected direction.

```
int Test_Move()
{
        int i;
```

Since the *XPos/YPos* coordinates are at the upper left corner of the image, different offsets and ranges need to be tested for each direction. The test itself is very simple: if any pixel tested is not zero (BLACK), then a zero value (FALSE) is immediately returned — end of test and the function exits, immediately returning a false result.

```
switch( Move )
{
case RIGHT: for ( i = XPos+47; i <= XPos+96; i++ )
                   if ( getpixel( i, YPos+5 ) ) return( 0 );   break;
case LEFT  : for ( i = XPos; i >= XPos–50; i– – )
                   if ( getpixel( i, YPos+5 ) ) return( 0 );   break;
case UP     : for ( i = YPos; i >= YPos–40; i– – )
                   if ( getpixel( XPos+5, i ) ) return( 0 );   break;
case DOWN: for ( i = YPos+37; i <= YPos+76; i++ )
                   if ( getpixel( XPos+5, i ) ) return( 0 );   break;
}
```

If no non-BLACK pixels were encountered by the selected test, then a one (TRUE) is returned and George is free to move forward.

```
        return( 1 );

}
```

In other applications, different test types may be required. This test is merely the most practical and serves nicely in the application. In other situations, however, you might find that you need to test for a specific color value, test several pixels for a condition or test against a separate ''map'' for responses based on information that is not visible on the screen. You might even use a combination of all of these.

The Take_Step Function

The **Take_Step** function is the principal movement function in this demo program and is called with three parameters. The *x* and *y* arguments are the horizontal and vertical movement increments that will determine the next screen image position. The *Step* argument is passed to **Put_Image** in order to control which image (NSTEP, LSTEP or RSTEP) will be used and to set the value for *LastMove*.

```
void Take_Step( int x, int y, int Step )
{
        Put_Image( Step );
        elay( TimeOut );
        Put_Image( Step );
        XPos += x;
        YPos += y;
        if( Step ) LastMove = Step;
}
```

The first call to **Put_Image** places the appropriate image on the screen and, after a time delay, the second call erases the image. Note also that the position is incremented only after the image is erased.

Put_Image

The **Put_Image** function places the desired image on the screen using the XOR_PUT option. If the image indicated by *Move* and *Step* is already on the screen, then XOR_PUT erases the image. If there is another image already on the screen, then the new image overlies the existing image without erasing it. If the current image is being XOR'ed with itself, then the original image is restored.

```
void Put_Image( int Step )
{
        int   x = XPos, y = YPos;
        switch( Move )
        {
            case RIGHT :
            case LEFT   : x+=8;  break;
            case UP     :
            case DOWN : y+=5;  break;
        }
```

```
            putimage( x, y, Man[ Move ][ Step ], XOR_PUT );
    }
```

For left and right facing images, the x-axis position is offset by eight pixels, for up and down, the y-axis is offset by five pixels. This does not affect the *XPos* and *YPos* screen coordinates, but simply improves positioning of the images within the maze walls.

FlashImage

The **FlashImage** function is called — following the finest cartoon traditions — when George runs into a wall. This function overwrites George's image with a series of irregular colored stars and adds random sound effects. Each flash is popped onto the screen, the sound effect is activated and the flash is XOR'd with itself and a new sound effect is generated.

The three flash images are cycled three times, but no time delay is used; therefore, the resulting screen image is a very brief multicolored star or series of stars that vanish before they are completely seen.

```
    void FlashImage( int x, int y )
    {
            int i, j, k;
            for( i=1; i<=3; i++ )
                for( j=0; j<3; j++ )
                    for( k=0; k<2; k++ )
                    {
                        putimage( x, y, Flash[j], XOR_PUT );
                        sound( random(100) + 100 );
                    }
            nosound();
    }
```

Before the function exits, the **nosound** function is called to cancel the last generated sound. Remember: each generated sound continues until a new **sound** command is called or until the **nosound** function is called to explicitly terminate the sound effects.

ClearImages

The final function used in this demonstration is the **ClearImages** function, which uses the **free** function to release the memory allocated for the various images.

```
void ClearImages()
{
        int i, j;
        for( i=0; i<=2; i++ )
            free( Flash[i] );
        for( i=0; i<=3; i++ )
            for( j=0; j<=2; j++ )
                free( Man[i][j] );
}
```

Once your program exits, these memory allocations should be released by a call to **closegraph**. It is good practice to explicitly release the memory allocated to the images. Also, in other applications, it may be advantageous to use the **free** function to release memory that was used for one application and make it available for another.

Morphological Animation

While the conventional animation technique's use of precreated images is fine for arcade games and simpler applications, the programmer is required to provide in advance for all contingencies and to individually create each of the required images. The alternative is, instead of creating individual images, to create rules for the construction of an image and then have the computer draw each image as needed, altering and rearranging them according to the situation's requirements.

In the second animation demo, ANIMATE2.C, Elmer is a stylized stick figure consisting of a triangular body and two legs. This is not a precreated image, however, but is drawn and erased according to a moderately simple series of program rules. The legs are links with defined limits of freedom and fixed lengths — literally, a skeleton much like your own.

In the demo, Elmer will stand up, then walk across the screen from left to right. To accomplish this, a total of more than 5,000 images will be written or erased. Standing up requires some 242 images and each step requires a series of 243 images.

The disadvantage to this approach is: first, that Elmer requires a great deal of calculation; second, the rules for Elmer's motion and position are complex; and third, the more complex the image, the greater the required processing time.

These disadvantages can be overcome by various methods. Movement rules can be simplified to minimize calculation and math co-processors will cut the time required for the calculations. The calculated image can be combined in part with stored images to reduce the complexity of calculations.

The big advantage is that the programmer can create rules and decision trees to govern the images and positions and can design these in a manner to provide flexibility that fixed images cannot emulate. The present demo does not have a complex set of responses, but the basic requirements are here. You are invited to try your hand at expanding this program and creating a more complex set of adaptations.

Warning: If you don't enjoy math, you are going to hate morphological animation! There are no easy solutions and you have to look at rules that require serious number crunching and a bit of skull work.

Thus warned, it's time to take a look at how image morphology is handled.

ANIMATE2.C begins with two constants: PI which will be used to convert angles from degrees to radians, and BRIEF which will provide a time delay constant. BRIEF can be increased or decreased according to the speed of your system.

```
const  double  PI = 3.1415;
const  int     BRIEF = 5;
```

A series of global variables will be used for the action points and to define the relations between the several portions of Elmer's anatomy.

```
int      rcolor, lcolor,                       /*right and left leg colors  */
         urangle, ulangle,                     /*upper right & left leg angles  */
         lxknee, lyknee, rxknee, ryknee,       /*coordinates for knees  */
         lrangle, llangle,                     /*lower right & left leg angles  */
         lxfoot, lyfoot, rxfoot, ryfoot,       /*coordinates for feet  */
         ujoint, ljoint,                       /*length of upper and lower legs  */
         xpos,  ypos;                          /*body coordinates (center)  */
```

Before getting into these special functions, a brief digression. In C, the conventional trigonometry functions accept angle arguments in radians, while Turbo C's graphics functions are configured to use arguments in degrees. For this application, it is more convenient to use angles in degrees even though the conventional trigometric functions will be used. For this reason, the function **rad** is created to convert an angle expressed in degrees to an angle expressed in radians.

```
double rad( int degrees )
{
        return( PI * degrees / 180 );
}
```

Simply for convenience, the functions **rsin** and **rcos** are provided to calculate the sin and cos values for angles in degrees. Note also that an integer argument (degrees) returns a double (decimal fraction) result.

```
double rsin( int degrees )
{
        return sin( rad( degrees ) );
}

double rcos( int degrees )
{
        return cos( rad( degrees ) );
}
```

The main program begins by using the same **Initialize** function as previous programs, then it sets initial values for the variables that describe Elmer's structure and beginning position.

```
main()
{
        int i;
        Initialize();
        urangle = 30;   ulangle = 30;
        lrangle = 0;    llangle = 0;
        ujoint = 30;    ljoint = 30;
        lxfoot = 30;    lyfoot = ryfoot = 150;
        rcolor = BLUE; lcolor = RED;
```

The **Create_Field** function draws a plane for Elmer to walk on and provides a few background structures for demonstration. **Start_Walker** puts Elmer on the screen in his beginning configuration (a folded squat), **Raise_Walker** allows Elmer to stand up and then **Walk_Right** is looped for the 20 steps necessary for Elmer to cross the screen.

```
        Create_Field();
        Start_Walker();
        Raise_Walker();
        for( i=1; i<=20; i++ ) Walk_Right();
        Pause();
        closegraph();                           /*      restore text mode */
}
```

In **main**, initial values were set for several of Elmer's definitions, but these may not be correct. Some of the values are better established by calculation than by a programmer's entry. This is another way of saying that it's easier to let the computer figure out how Elmer fits together, than to run out the angles and formulas on your pocket calculator and type them in. After all, why do it the hard way?

To begin, the position of the left foot is predefined and the left knee is considered to be directly above the foot (as per the defined length of the lower leg).

```
void Start_Walker()
{
        lxknee = lxfoot;
        lyknee = lyfoot–ljoint;
```

With the lower left leg and knee in position, the body coordinates are calculated according to the angle from vertical (*ulangle*) and the length of the upper joint (*ujoint*).

```
        xpos = lxfoot + rsin( ulangle ) * ujoint;
        ypos = lyfoot + rcos( ulangle ) * ujoint – ljoint;
```

The calculations continue down the right leg until the right knee and right foot are positioned.

```
        rxfoot = xpos + rsin( urangle ) * ujoint;
        rxknee = rxfoot;
        ryknee = ryfoot–ljoint;
        Body_Image( MaxColors-1 );
}
```

The last step is to put Elmer on the screen by calling **Body_Image**. The **Body_Image** function is called both to draw Elmer on the screen and, with a color value of 0, to erase Elmer again.

```
void Body_Image( int color )
{
        int i, j, left, right, top, bottom;
        setcolor( color );
        if( color ) setcolor(lcolor);
```

Beginning with the left leg, CP is set to the proper coordinates and a knot is drawn for Elmer's foot. A line is then drawn up to the knee and another knot is added for the knee.

```
moveto( lxfoot, lyfoot );
Plot_Knot();
lineto( lxknee, lyknee );
Plot_Knot();
```

The line continues up to the hip, changes color for the right leg and works back down to the right foot.

```
lineto( xpos, ypos );
if( color ) setcolor(rcolor);
lineto( rxknee, ryknee );
Plot_Knot();
lineto( rxfoot, ryfoot );
Plot_Knot();
```

The last task is drawing the body. Because Elmer's body does not bend or shift orientation, a simple set of **line** commands are sufficient for this portion of his anatomy.

```
if( color ) setcolor(MaxColors–1);
bottom = ypos+10;
top   = ypos–5;
left  = xpos–11;
right = xpos+11;
line( xpos, ypos, left,  top   );
line( xpos, ypos, right, top   );
line( xpos, ypos, xpos,  bottom );
line( left, top,  right, top   );
line( left, top,  xpos,  bottom );
line( right, top, xpos,  bottom );
}
```

The **Body_Image** function will be called more than 5,000 times to draw Elmer in different configurations as he moves on the screen. One alternative, to help speed operations, might be to draw this portion of the body once, save the screen image, then use the **put_image** function with the XOR_PUT option.

The **Plot_Knot** function draws a 3x3 pixel knot to define Elmer's feet and knees.

```
void Plot_Knot()
{
        int i, j, k = getcolor();
        for( i=-1; i<=1; i++ )
            for( j=-1; j<=1; j++ )
                putpixel( getx()+i, gety()+j, k );
}
```

The function **Raise_Walker** takes Elmer from his initial squatting position to an erect posture. When Elmer was first set up, his upper leg angle (*ulangle*) was initialized at 30 degrees. Now, he'll straighten up in one degree steps, with new knee and hip positions calculated for each one degree change, until he is fully erect with an upper leg angle of 150 degrees. Because both legs are assumed to be moving in the same way and at the same time, calculations are greatly simplified.

```
void Raise_Walker()
{
        while( ulangle<=150 )
        {
            ulangle++;
            Body_Image( 0 );
            lxknee = xpos - rsin( ulangle ) * ujoint;
            lyknee = ypos - rcos( ulangle ) * ujoint;
            lrangle=llangle=180*atan2((lxfoot-lxknee),(lyfoot-lyknee))/PI;
            lxknee = lxfoot - rsin( llangle ) * ljoint;
            rxknee = rxfoot + rsin( lrangle ) * ljoint;
            ryknee = lyknee = lyfoot - rcos( llangle ) * ljoint;
            ypos = lyknee + rcos( ulangle ) * ujoint;
            Body_Image( 15 );
            delay( BRIEF * 10 );
        }
```

The right and left angles are then equalized and, just in case of any remaining error, the lower angles (*lrangle* and *llangle*) are set to zero.

```
urangle = ulangle;
lrangle = llangle = 0;
}
```

Now that Elmer is standing, the **Walk_Right** function will be used to move him across the screen. When you try complicating Elmer's responses, you may wish to break this function down to a series of functions for calculating each movement element independently.

```
void Walk_Right()
{
        int    i;
```

The first element here involves swinging the right foot (the lower right leg) up 30 degrees:

```
for( i=1; i<=30; i++ )
{
    Body_Image( 0 );
    lrangle++;
    rxfoot = rxknee + rsin( lrangle ) * ljoint;
    ryfoot = ryknee + rcos( lrangle ) * ljoint;
    Body_Image( MaxColors–1 );
    delay(BRIEF);
}
```

Now that Elmer has his foot up, the left leg is ready to bend down until the right foot is back on the ground (or approximately so). Note: since Elmer weighs nothing, he doesn't have to worry about falling over and can balance without any adjustments. In other applications, it might be advisable to provide for a counter movement to better simulate natural motion. To keep this demo program simple, however, gravity is replaced by levity.

Again, the calculations begin with one foot (the left), go up to the hip and then down to the right foot.

```
for( i=1; i<=30; i++ )
{
        ody_Image( 0 );
        llangle++;
        lxknee = lxfoot + rsin( llangle ) * ljoint;
        lyknee = lyfoot – rcos( llangle ) * ljoint;
        xpos = lxknee + rsin( ulangle ) * ujoint;
        ypos = lyknee + rcos( ulangle ) * ujoint;
        rxknee = xpos + rsin( urangle ) * ujoint;
        ryknee = ypos – rcos( urangle ) * ujoint;
        rxfoot = rxknee + rsin( lrangle ) * ljoint;
        ryfoot = ryknee + rcos( lrangle ) * ljoint;
        Body_Image( MaxColors–1 );
        delay(BRIEF);
}
```

And now it's time to straighten up the right leg — with the left leg moving to compensate:

```
for( i=1; i<=30; i++ )                          /*bring right leg back to standing*/
{
        Body_Image( 0 );
        lrangle– –;
        rxknee = rxfoot – rsin( lrangle ) * ljoint;
        ryknee = ryfoot – rcos( lrangle ) * ljoint;
        xpos = rxknee – rsin( urangle ) * ujoint;
        ypos = ryknee + rcos( urangle ) * ujoint;
        lxknee = xpos – rsin( ulangle ) * ujoint;
        lyknee = ypos – rcos( ulangle ) * ujoint;
        lxfoot = lxknee – rsin( llangle ) * ljoint;
        lyfoot = lyknee + rcos( llangle ) * ljoint;
        Body_Image( MaxColors–1 );
        delay(BRIEF);
}
```

Finally, the left leg swings back to the standing position to complete Elmer's step:

193

```
for( i=1; i<=30; i++ )                /*        bring left leg back to standing        */
{
        Body_Image( 0 );
        llangle– –;
        lxfoot = lxknee – rsin( llangle ) * ljoint;
        lyfoot = lyknee + rcos( llangle ) * ljoint;
        Body_Image( MaxColors–1 );
        delay(BRIEF);
}
```

At this point, the coordinates and angles of each foot have been recalculated about 120 times and, inevitably, a certain amount of error has accumulated in the process. If you observe the resulting figure carefully, you may note that Elmer's right foot is slightly above the ground plane where he started and the left leg is approximately one pixel further off the ground than the right.

As he continues across the screen, if no correction is made, he will slowly walk up the screen as well as right.

If these positions were critical, the optimum choice would be to redesign the calculation path — specifically, redesign the loop conditions. For this application, however, a simple corrective **Ground_Image** function is quite sufficient to keep Elmer's feet firmly on the ground.

```
        Ground_Image();
}
```

The **Ground_Image** function simply allows gravity to take charge for a moment and pull Elmer back down to the ground by adjusting the five critical vertical coordinates.

```
void Ground_Image()
{
        while( !getpixel( lxfoot, lyfoot+3 ) )
        {
            Body_Image( 0 );
            lyknee++;   ryknee++;
```

```
            lyfoot++;    ryfoot++;
            ypos++;
            Body_Image( MaxColors-1 );
        }
    }
```

And this completes the initial task of taking Elmer for a walk.

Retaining A Background Image

When you run this demo, you will notice that Elmer walks across a plane that is cluttered by a set of boxes. Given the simplicity of the program, Elmer is quite oblivious to this clutter and, as Elmer's image is successively redrawn, the boxes are erased by the image of his leg.

Without going into the question of having Elmer see these obstacles and climb over them (though this is a good place for you to experiment with decision and response rules), there are two ways to avoid having the background image be erased.

One approach is to save an image of the background and, instead of using the **Body_Image** function with a BLACK color value to erase Elmer, simply use the **putimage** function with the COPY_PUT option to restore the background and erase Elmer at the same time. Then you can draw Elmer's new image for the next step.

To do this, you will need three new global variables:

```
nt   PositionTop, PositionLeft;
void  *Background;
```

The **Walk_Right** function would be changed to:

```
void Walk_Right()
{
        int   i;
        for( i=1; i<=30; i++ )
        {
                Erase_Image();                    /*replaces Body_Image( 0 );*/
```

195

```
            lrangle++;
            rxfoot = rxknee + rsin( lrangle ) * ljoint;
            ryfoot = ryknee + rcos( lrangle ) * ljoint;
            Get_Background();                    /*         add to restore background */
            Body_Image( MaxColors–1 );
            delay(BRIEF);
        }
        .
        .
        .

    }
```

The key to the operation is the **Get_Background** function, which would be written like this:

```
void Get_Background()
{
        int left, top, right, bottom = 150;
        if( lxfoot < lxknee )  left = lxfoot–5;
        else                   left = lxknee–5;
        if( rxfoot > rxknee ) right = rxfoot+5;
        else                   right = rxknee+5;
        if( lyknee < ypos )   top = ypos–7;
        else                   top = lyknee–5;
        PositionTop = top;
        PositionLeft = left;
        Background = malloc( imagesize( left, top, right, bottom ) );
        getimage( left, top, right, bottom, Background );
}
```

The *left* and *right* variables are tested for the maximum extent of Elmer's image and *top* for the height. Of course, a slight margin has been added on all sides and, for simplicity, *bottom* is fixed. *PositionTop* and *PositionLeft* are global variables for saving the corner coordinates.

The **Erase_Image** function uses **putimage** to restore the background using COPY_PUT, then releases the memory allocated to *Background*.

Remember, if memory is allocated repeatedly without being released, you will quickly run out of it!

```
void Erase_Image()
{
    putimage( PositionLeft, PositionTop, Background, COPY_PUT );
    free( Background );
}
```

Also remember, the **Get_Background** function must be called for the first time before Elmer is initially placed on the screen, but after Elmer's feet and knees have been calculated (see the **Start_Walker** function).

XOR_Line

A second option is to create an **XOR_Line** function. This is the equivalent of the **line** function in Turbo C but, instead of writing the pixel values directly to the screen, each calculated line pixel is XOR'd with the existing screen pixel. To do this, the first step is to calculate the line and **XOR_Line** is called exactly the same as the **line** function.

```
void XOR_Line( int x1, int y1, int x2, int y2 )
{
    int    i, j, k = getcolor();
    int    x = 10, y = 10;
    double slope;
```

The line calculation begins by testing the endpoints to find if the greater distance is on the x-axis or the y-axis.

```
    if( abs(x1–x2) > abs(y1–y2) )
    {
```

Then the endpoints are tested for order and, if the first point is greater than the second, both the x- and y-axis coordinates are swapped. This is done for simplicity of calculation, the final loop always proceeding from the lesser to greater value. Both coordinate pairs are exchanged so the line will retain the correct result.

```
if( x1 > x2 )
  {
        i = x1;  x1 = x2;  x2 = i;
        i = y1;  y1 = y2;  y2 = i;
  }
```

The variable *j* takes the x-axis difference and *slope* is calculated for the line.

```
        j = x2–x1;
        slope = (double) (y2–y1)/j;
```

Last, a loop proceeds through the x-axis range of the line and a y-axis point corresponding to each x-axis point is calculated from the slope value. The results are passed to the **XOR_Plot** function.

```
        for( i=1; i<=j; i++ )
            XOR_Plot( x1+i, y1+(int)(i*slope), k );
  }
  else
  {
```

The second case, where the y-axis distance is greater than the x-axis distance, proceeds in exactly the same way, but with an x-axis point calculated for each y-axis point.

```
        if( y1 > y2 )
        {
            i = y1;  y1 = y2;  y2 = i;
            i = x1;  x1 = x2;  x2 = i;
        }
        j = y2–y1;
        slope = (double) (x2–x1)/j;
        for( i=1; i<=j; i++ )
            XOR_Plot( x1+(int)(i*slope), y1+i, k );
```

```
        }
}
```

The **XOR_Plot** function uses the **putpixel** function to rewrite the screen but XOR's the specified color value with the pixel's present value.

```
void XOR_Plot( int x, int y, int color )
{
        putpixel( x, y, color ^ getpixel( x, y ) );
}
```

XOR equivalents for the **lineto** and **linerel** functions are also easily created and, if the same line is drawn a second time using an XOR function, then the first line is erased. The original background is left intact.

To use these in the ANIMATE2.C demo program, change all occurrences of **Body_Image(0)** to **Body_Image(MaxColors −1)** or simply change the **Body_Image** function to ignore or to remove the color argument.

Of course, there is one minor drawback to this approach: the **XOR_Line** function shown is considerably slower than Turbo C's **line** function. If you intend to use this extensively and speed is a consideration, you should write your XOR line equivalents in assembly language and optimize speed of operation.

If, however, you have Turbo C version 2.0, the **setwritemode** function can be used for this same purpose and executes with no particular loss of speed.

```
/*********************************************************/
/*ANIMATE1.C — Simple Animation using Turbo-C Graphics */
/*    — images and maze image are created for EGA or higher   */
/*    resolutions — CGA requires image and maze adjustments   */
/*     though the present demo will run as is on CGA systems.   */
/*    *********************************************   */

#ifdef __TINY__
#error Graphics demos will not run in the tiny model.
#endif

#include <conio.h>
#include <stdio.h>
#include <stdlib.h>
#include <stdarg.h>
#include <graphics.h>

#define RIGHT  0
#define LEFT   1
#define UP  2
#define DOWN  3

#define NSTEP  0
#define LSTEP  1
#define RSTEP  2

int    GraphDriver;                      /*      graphics device driver      */
int    GraphMode;                        /*      graphics mode value         */
int    MaxColors;                        /*      maximum colors available */
int    ErrorCode = 0;            /*    reports any graphics errors      */
int    XPos = 3, YPos = 3;               /*      initial position for maze    */
int    Move, LastMove;                   /*      movement directions        */
void   *Flash[3];                        /*      flash when hitting walls   */
void   *Man[4][3];               /*    images to run through maze       */
unsigned  TimeOut = 100;
```

```
void Initialize()
/*                      initialize graphics system and report errors                      */
{
    GraphDriver = DETECT;                   /*      request auto-detection         */
    initgraph( &GraphDriver, &GraphMode, "" );
    ErrorCode = graphresult();              /*      test initialization results    */
    if ( ErrorCode != grOk )                /*      if error occurred during init  */
    {
        printf(" Graphics System Error: %s\n",
            grapherrormsg( ErrorCode ) );
        exit( 1 );
    }
    MaxColors = getmaxcolor() + 1;          /*      read maximum color range       */
}

void *SaveImage( int left, int top, int right, int bottom )
{
    void  *image;

    image = malloc( imagesize( left, top, right, bottom ) );
    getimage( left, top, right, bottom, image);                 /* save the image */
    putimage( left, top, image, XOR_PUT )           /* erase the image        */
    return( image );                                /* return image ptr       */
}

void CreateImages()
{
    int  i, j, MaxColor = getmaxcolor();
    int  pflash1[] = { 100, 40, 110, 60, 100, 70, 120, 65,
                   140, 80, 130, 60, 140, 50, 120, 65, 100, 40 };
    int  pflash2[] = { 120, 40, 110, 55,  90, 60, 110, 65,
                   120, 80, 130, 65, 150, 60, 130, 65, 120, 40 };
    int  pflash3[] = { 140, 40, 130, 60, 140, 70, 120, 65,
                   100, 80, 110, 60, 100, 50, 120, 55, 140, 40 };
    int  bkarm_u[] = { 100, 62, 102, 68, 105, 70, 108, 69, 109, 65 };
    int  ftarm_u[] = { 140, 62, 143, 52, 130, 47, 125, 52 };
```

201

```
int  bkarm_r[] = { 121,145, 128,147, 130,150, 129,153, 125,154 };
int  ftarm_r[] = { 117,176, 106,176, 100,165, 107,160 };

randomize();
setcolor( random( MaxColor ) + 1 );
setfillstyle( random(11) + 1, random ( MaxColor ) + 1 );
fillpoly( sizeof( pflash1 )/( 2 * sizeof( int ) ), pflash1 );
Flash[0] = SaveImage( 100, 40, 140, 80 );

setcolor( random( MaxColor ) + 1 );
setfillstyle( random(11) + 1, random ( MaxColor ) + 1 );
fillpoly( sizeof( pflash2 )/( 2 * sizeof( int ) ), pflash2 );
Flash[1] = SaveImage(  90, 40, 150, 80 );

setcolor( random( MaxColor ) + 1 );
setfillstyle( random(11) + 1, random( MaxColor ) + 1 );
fillpoly( sizeof( pflash3 )/( 2 * sizeof( int ) ), pflash3 );
Flash[2] = SaveImage( 100, 40, 140, 80 );

setcolor( MaxColor );
setfillstyle( SOLID_FILL, MaxColor );
ellipse(  120,  60,  0, 360, 10, 10 );        /*      draw and fill heads     */
floodfill( 120,  60, MaxColor );
ellipse(  220, 160,  0, 360, 13,  7 );
floodfill( 220, 160, MaxColor );
ellipse(  120,  51,  0, 180,  3,  3 );        /*      now tack on noses       */
ellipse(  207, 160, 90, 270,  3,  2 );

setfillstyle( HATCH_FILL, MaxColor );         /*      change fill style */
ellipse(  128,  60, 270,  90, 12,  6 );       /*      add shoulders     */
floodfill( 135,  60, MaxColor );
ellipse(  112,  60,  90, 270, 12,  6 );
floodfill( 105,  60, MaxColor );
ellipse(  220, 154,  0, 180,  8,  9 );
floodfill( 220, 150, MaxColor );
ellipse(  220, 166, 180, 360,  8,  9 );
floodfill( 220, 170, MaxColor );
```

```
for ( i=100; i<=145; i++)
    for ( j= 45; j<= 70; j++)
        putpixel( 345–i, 120–j, getpixel( i, j ) );

for ( i=204; i<=235; i++)
    for ( j=145; j<=175; j++)
        putpixel( 345–i, j, getpixel( i, j ) );

Man[UP][NSTEP]    = SaveImage( 100,  45, 140, 70 );
Man[DOWN][NSTEP]  = SaveImage( 205,   50, 245,  75 );
Man[LEFT][NSTEP]  = SaveImage( 203, 140, 234, 180 );
Man[RIGHT][NSTEP] = SaveImage( 111, 140, 142, 180 );

setfillstyle( CLOSE_DOT_FILL, MaxColor );

putimage( 100, 45, Man[UP][NSTEP], COPY_PUT );
                                                      /*      add arms      */
fillpoly( sizeof( bkarm_u )/( 2 * sizeof(int) ), bkarm_u );
fillpoly( sizeof( ftarm_u )/( 2 * sizeof(int) ), ftarm_u );
```
/*   *fillpoly fills calculated outline between end points — may overwrite*   */
/*   *part of original image and boundary — restore original using* OR_PUT   */
```
putimage( 100, 45, Man[UP][NSTEP], OR_PUT );

for ( i=100; i<=145; i++)
    for ( j= 45; j<= 70; j++)
    {
        putpixel( 345–i,      j, getpixel( i, j ) );       /*      rotate left/right  */
        putpixel( 345–i, 220–j, getpixel( i, j ) );        /*      and invert to      */
        putpixel(    i, 220–j, getpixel( i, j ) );     }   /*      face down ...       */
                                                           /*      save all images    */
Man[UP][LSTEP]   = SaveImage( 100,  45, 145,  70 );
Man[UP][RSTEP]   = SaveImage( 200,  45, 245,  70 );
Man[DOWN][LSTEP] = SaveImage( 100, 150, 145, 175 );
Man[DOWN][RSTEP] = SaveImage( 200, 150, 245, 175 );
```

```
        putimage( 100, 140, Man[LEFT][NSTEP], COPY_PUT );
        fillpoly( sizeof( bkarm_r )/( 2 * sizeof(int) ), bkarm_r );  /*     add arms      */
        fillpoly( sizeof( ftarm_r )/( 2 * sizeof(int) ), ftarm_r );
        putimage( 100, 140, Man[LEFT][NSTEP], OR_PUT );

        for ( i=100; i<=132; i++)
            for ( j=144; j<=177; j++)
            {
                putpixel( 345–i, j, getpixel( i, j ) );          /*      rotate up/down  */
                putpixel( 345–i, 220–j, getpixel( i, j ) );      /*      and invert to   */
                putpixel( i, 220–j, getpixel( i, j ) ); }        /*      face right ...  */

        Man[LEFT][RSTEP]  = SaveImage( 100, 144, 132, 177 );
        Man[LEFT][LSTEP]  = SaveImage( 100,  43, 132,  76 );
        Man[RIGHT][LSTEP] = SaveImage( 213,  43, 245,  76 );
        Man[RIGHT][RSTEP] = SaveImage( 213, 144, 245, 177 );
}

void CreateMaze()
{
    int i, j;
    int maze1[]    = { 200, 40,  50, 40,  50,160, 100,160 };
    int maze2[]    = { 100, 80, 100,120, 200,120, 200,240 };
    int maze3[]    = { 0,200, 100,200 };
    int maze4[]    = { 150,160, 150,240, 50,240, 50,280 };
    int maze5[]    = { 150, 80, 300, 80 };
    int maze6[]    = { 250, 80, 250,160 };
    int maze7[]    = { 100,280, 100,320 };
    int maze8[]    = { 150,280, 250,280, 250,240, 300,240 };
    int maze9[]    = { 250, 40, 350, 40, 350, 80 };
    int maze10[]   = { 200,200, 300,200, 300,120, 400,120, 400, 80, 400,160 };
    int maze11[]   = { 300,280, 350,280, 350,160 };
    int maze12[]   = { 400,  0, 400, 40 };
    int maze13[]   = { 450,120, 450, 40, 550, 40, 550, 80 };
    int maze14[]   = { 500, 80, 500,160, 400,160, 400,240 };
    int maze15[]   = { 400,280, 400,320 };
    int maze16[]   = { 550,120, 550,200, 450,200, 450,280, 550,280 };
```

```c
int  maze17[]   = { 500,240, 600,240 };
struct viewporttype vp;

setcolor( MaxColors – 1 );                              /*       Set draw color to white     */
setviewport(0,0,639,349,1);
settextstyle( DEFAULT_FONT, HORIZ_DIR, 1 );
outtextxy(  20, 330, "Use Arrow Keys to move 'George' or"
                     " <Q>uit to exit program");

setviewport(0,0,600,320,1);
setlinestyle( SOLID_LINE, 0, NORM_WIDTH );
getviewsettings( &vp );
rectangle( 0, 0, vp.right – vp.left, vp.bottom – vp.top );

outtextxy( 10, 20, "START" );
drawpoly( sizeof( maze1  )/( 2 * sizeof(int) ), maze1  );
drawpoly( sizeof( maze2  )/( 2 * sizeof(int) ), maze2  );
drawpoly( sizeof( maze3  )/( 2 * sizeof(int) ), maze3  );
drawpoly( sizeof( maze4  )/( 2 * sizeof(int) ), maze4  );
drawpoly( sizeof( maze5  )/( 2 * sizeof(int) ), maze5  );
drawpoly( sizeof( maze6  )/( 2 * sizeof(int) ), maze6  );
drawpoly( sizeof( maze7  )/( 2 * sizeof(int) ), maze7  );
drawpoly( sizeof( maze8  )/( 2 * sizeof(int) ), maze8  );
drawpoly( sizeof( maze9  )/( 2 * sizeof(int) ), maze9  );
drawpoly( sizeof( maze10 )/( 2 * sizeof(int) ), maze10 );
drawpoly( sizeof( maze11 )/( 2 * sizeof(int) ), maze11 );
drawpoly( sizeof( maze12 )/( 2 * sizeof(int) ), maze12 );
drawpoly( sizeof( maze13 )/( 2 * sizeof(int) ), maze13 );
drawpoly( sizeof( maze14 )/( 2 * sizeof(int) ), maze14 );
drawpoly( sizeof( maze15 )/( 2 * sizeof(int) ), maze15 );
drawpoly( sizeof( maze16 )/( 2 * sizeof(int) ), maze16 );
drawpoly( sizeof( maze17 )/( 2 * sizeof(int) ), maze17 );
outtextxy( 550, 300, "FINISH" );
}

void FlashImage( int x, int y )
{
```

```
        int i, j, k;

        for( i=1; i<=3; i++ )
            for( j=0; j<3; j++ )
        for( k=0; k<2; k++ )
        {
            putimage( x, y, Flash[j], XOR_PUT );
            sound( random(100) + 100 );
        }
        nosound();
    }

    void Put_Image( int Step )
    {
        int  x = XPos, y = YPos;

        switch( Move )
        {
            case RIGHT  :
            case LEFT   :  x+=8;  break;
            case UP     :
            case DOWN :  y+=5;  break;
        }
        putimage( x, y, Man[ Move ][ Step ], XOR_PUT );
    }

    int Test_Move()
    {
        int i;

        switch( Move )
        {
            case RIGHT: for ( i = XPos+47; i <= XPos+96; i++ )
                        if ( getpixel( i, YPos+5 ) ) return( 0 );  break;
            case  LEFT: for ( i = XPos; i >= XPos–50; i– – )
                        if ( getpixel( i, YPos+5 ) ) return( 0 );  break;
            case    UP: for ( i = YPos; i >= YPos–40; i– – )
```

```
                        if ( getpixel( XPos+5, i ) ) return( 0 );   break;
            case  DOWN: for ( i = YPos+37; i <= YPos+76; i++ )
                        if ( getpixel( XPos+5, i ) ) return( 0 );   break;
    }
    return( 1 );
}

void Take_Step( int x, int y, int Step )
{
    Put_Image( Step );
    delay( TimeOut );
    Put_Image( Step );
    XPos += x;
    YPos += y;
    if( Step != NSTEP) LastMove = Step;
}

void Move_Image( int NextStep )
{
    int i, XFake, YFake, XStep, YStep, XFlash, YFlash;

    Put_Image( NSTEP );
    Move = NextStep;
    Put_Image( NSTEP );
    switch( Move )
    {
        case RIGHT:    XFake  = 5;  YFake  = 0;
                       XStep  = 5;  YStep  = 0;
                       XFlash = 5;  YFlash = 0;  break;
        case  LEFT:    XFake  = -5; YFake  = 0;
                       XStep  = -5; YStep  = 0;
                       XFlash = 2;  YFlash = 0;  break;
        case   UP:     XFake  = 0;  YFake  = -5;
                       XStep  = 0;  YStep  = -4;
                       XFlash = 0;  YFlash = 2;  break;
        case  DOWN:    XFake  = 0;  YFake  = 5;
                       XStep  = 0;  YStep  = 4;
```

```
                        XFlash = 0;   YFlash = 0;   break;
    }
    if ( !Test_Move() )
    {
        Put_Image( NSTEP );
        XPos += XFake;
        YPos += YFake;
        Put_Image( LSTEP );
        FlashImage( XPos+XFlash, YPos+YFlash );
        Put_Image( LSTEP );
        XPos -= XFake;
        YPos -= YFake;
        Put_Image( NSTEP );
    }
    else
    {
        Put_Image( NSTEP );
        XPos += XStep;
        YPos += YStep;
        if( LastMove != LSTEP )
        {
            for ( i=1; i<=2; i++ )
            {
                Take_Step( XStep, YStep, LSTEP );
                Take_Step( XStep, YStep, NSTEP );
                Take_Step( XStep, YStep, RSTEP );
                Take_Step( XStep, YStep, NSTEP );
            }
            Take_Step( XStep, YStep, LSTEP );
            Put_Image( NSTEP );
            delay( TimeOut );
        }
        else
        {
            for ( i=1; i<=2; i++ )
            {
```

```
                Take_Step( XStep, YStep, RSTEP );
                Take_Step( XStep, YStep, NSTEP );
                Take_Step( XStep, YStep, LSTEP );
                Take_Step( XStep, YStep, NSTEP );
            }
            Take_Step( XStep, YStep, RSTEP );
            Put_Image( NSTEP );
            delay( TimeOut );
        }
    }
}

void StartGame()
{
    char ch;
    int  Quit = 0;
    Move = LastMove = RIGHT;
    Put_Image( NSTEP );
    while ( !Quit )
    {
        ch = getch();
        if ( ch == 0x00 )
        {
            ch = getch();
            switch (ch)
            {
                case 'M' : Move_Image( RIGHT );  break;
                case 'K' : Move_Image( LEFT );  break;
                case 'H' : Move_Image( UP );    break;
                case 'P' : Move_Image( DOWN );  break;
            }
        }
        else if (ch == 'Q' || ch == 'q') Quit++;              /*      exit!    */
    }
}
```

```
void ClearImages()
{
      int i, j;

      for( i=0; i<=2; i++ )
          free( Flash[i] );
      for( i=0; i<=3; i++ )
          for( j=0; j<=2; j++ )
          free( Man[i][j] );
}

main()
{
      Initialize();                              /*      set graphics mode        */
      outtextxy(10,10," One Moment Please ");
      setactivepage( 1 );
      CreateImages();                            /*      create and save images   */
      setactivepage( 0 );
      clearviewport();
      CreateMaze();                              /*      build the maze           */
      StartGame();                               /*      now run the demo         */
      ClearImages();                             /*      free memory used         */
      closegraph();                              /*      restore text mode        */
}
```

```
/*          **************************************************  */
/*             ANIMATE2.C — Simple Animation using Turbo-C Graphics     */
/*                      and formula-generated images                    */
/*          **************************************************  */

#ifdef __TINY__
#error Graphics demos will not run in the tiny model.
#endif

#include <conio.h>
#include <stdio.h>
#include <stdlib.h>
#include <stdarg.h>
#include <math.h>
#include <graphics.h>

int    GraphDriver;                           /*      graphics device driver        */
int    GraphMode;                  /*      graphics mode value             */
int    MaxColors;                             /*      maximum colors available */
int    ErrorCode = 0;              /*      reports any graphics errors      */

const  double PI = 3.1415;
const  int       BRIEF = 5;                   /*      change value to slow images      */
int  rcolor, lcolor,                          /*        right and left leg colors      */
     urangle, ulangle,            /*      upper right & left leg angles    */
     lxknee, lyknee, rxknee, ryknee,          /*        coordinates for knees          */
     lrangle, llangle,            /*      lower right & left leg angles    */
     lxfoot, lyfoot, rxfoot, ryfoot,          /*        coordinates for feet           */
     ujoint, ljoint,              /*        length of leg joints           */
     xpos,  ypos;                 /*        body coordinates (center)      */

void Initialize()                  /*      initialize graphics system and report errors   */
{
     GraphDriver = DETECT;                    /*        request auto-detection       */
     initgraph( &GraphDriver, &GraphMode, "" );
     ErrorCode = graphresult();               /*        test initialization results  */
     if ( ErrorCode != grOk )      /*      if error occurred during init     */
```

211

```
        {
            printf(" Graphics System Error: %s\n",
                        grapherrormsg( ErrorCode ) );
            exit( 1 );
        }
        MaxColors = getmaxcolor() + 1;          /*        read max color range        */
    }

double rad( int degrees )
{
    return( PI * degrees / 180 );
}

double rsin( int degrees )
{
    return sin( rad( degrees ) );
}

double rcos( int degrees )
{
    return cos( rad( degrees ) );
}

void Pause()
{
    while( kbhit() ) getch();
    getch();
}

void Create_Field()
{
    int  base = 152;

    line( 0, base, 639, base );
    rectangle( 100, base−10, 120, base );
    rectangle( 150, base−15, 175, base );
    rectangle( 255, base−20, 300, base );
```

```
        rectangle( 375, base−10, 420, base );
}

void Plot_Knot()
{
    int i, j, k = getcolor();

    for( i=−1; i<=1; i++ )
        for( j=−1; j<=1; j++ )
            putpixel( getx()+i, gety()+j, k );
}

void Body_Image( int color )
{
    int i, j, left, right, top, bottom;

    setcolor( color );

    if( color ) setcolor(lcolor);
    moveto( lxfoot, lyfoot );
    Plot_Knot();
    lineto( lxknee, lyknee );
    Plot_Knot();
    lineto( xpos, ypos );
    Plot_Knot();
    if( color ) setcolor(rcolor);
    lineto( rxknee, ryknee );
    Plot_Knot();
    lineto( rxfoot, ryfoot );
    Plot_Knot();
    if( color ) setcolor(MaxColors−1);

    bottom = ypos+10;
    top    = ypos−5;
    left   = xpos−11;
    right  = xpos+11;
    line( xpos, ypos, left, top   );
```

```
        line( xpos, ypos, right, top   );
        line( xpos, ypos, xpos, bottom );
        line( left,  top,  right, top   );
        line( left,  top,  xpos, bottom );
        line( right, top,  xpos, bottom );
    }

    void Start_Walker()
    {
        lxknee = lxfoot;
        lyknee = lyfoot–ljoint;
        xpos = lxfoot + rsin( ulangle ) * ujoint;
        ypos = lyfoot + rcos( ulangle ) * ujoint – ljoint;
        rxfoot = xpos + rsin( urangle ) * ujoint;
        rxknee = rxfoot;
        ryknee = ryfoot–ljoint;
        Body_Image( MaxColors–1 );
    }

    void Raise_Walker()
    {
        while( ulangle<=150 )
        {
            ulangle++;
            Body_Image( 0 );
            lxknee = xpos – rsin( ulangle ) * ujoint;
            lyknee = ypos – rcos( ulangle ) * ujoint;
            lrangle = llangle = 180 * atan2( (lxfoot–lxknee),(lyfoot–lyknee) ) / PI;
            lxknee = lxfoot – rsin( llangle ) * ljoint;
            rxknee = rxfoot + rsin( lrangle ) * ljoint;
            ryknee = lyknee = lyfoot – rcos( llangle ) * ljoint;
            ypos = lyknee + rcos( ulangle ) * ujoint;
            Body_Image( 15 );
            delay(BRIEF*10);
        }
        urangle = ulangle;
```

```
    lrangle = llangle = 0;
}

void Ground_Image()
{
    while( !getpixel( lxfoot, lyfoot+3 ) )
    {
        Body_Image( 0 );
        lyknee++;   ryknee++;
        lyfoot++;   ryfoot++;
        ypos++;
        Body_Image( MaxColors–1 );
    }
}

void Walk_Right()
{
    int    i;

    for( i=1; i<=30; i++ )                  /*      swing right foot up 30 degrees      */
    {
        Body_Image( 0 );
        lrangle++;
        rxfoot = rxknee + rsin( lrangle ) * ljoint;
        ryfoot = ryknee + rcos( lrangle ) * ljoint;
        Body_Image( MaxColors–1 );
        delay(BRIEF);
    }

    for( i=1; i<=30; i++ )                  /*      adjust left leg to advance foot      */
    {
        Body_Image( 0 );
        llangle++;
        lxknee = lxfoot + rsin( llangle ) * ljoint;
        lyknee = lyfoot – rcos( llangle ) * ljoint;
        xpos = lxknee + rsin( ulangle ) * ujoint;
        ypos = lyknee + rcos( ulangle ) * ujoint;
```

215

```
        rxknee = xpos + rsin( urangle ) * ujoint;
        ryknee = ypos – rcos( urangle ) * ujoint;
        rxfoot = rxknee + rsin( lrangle ) * ljoint;
        ryfoot = ryknee + rcos( lrangle ) * ljoint;
        Body_Image( MaxColors–1 );
        delay(BRIEF);
    }

    for( i=1; i<=30; i++ )              /*       bring right leg back to standing     */
    {
        Body_Image( 0 );
        lrangle– –;
        rxknee = rxfoot – rsin( lrangle ) * ljoint;
        ryknee = ryfoot – rcos( lrangle ) * ljoint;
        xpos = rxknee – rsin( urangle ) * ujoint;
        ypos = ryknee + rcos( urangle ) * ujoint;
        lxknee = xpos – rsin( ulangle ) * ujoint;
        lyknee = ypos – rcos( ulangle ) * ujoint;
        lxfoot = lxknee – rsin( llangle ) * ljoint;
        lyfoot = lyknee + rcos( llangle ) * ljoint;
        Body_Image( MaxColors–1 );
        delay(BRIEF);
    }

    for( i=1; i<=30; i++ )              /*       bring left leg back to standing      */
    {
        Body_Image( 0 );
        llangle– –;
        lxfoot = lxknee – rsin( llangle ) * ljoint;
        lyfoot = lyknee + rcos( llangle ) * ljoint;
        Body_Image( MaxColors–1 );
        delay(BRIEF);
    }
    Ground_Image();
}

main()
```

```
{
    int i;

    Initialize();                                /*      set graphics mode      */

    urangle = 30;  ulangle = 30;                 /*      initial values for  */
    lrangle = 0;    llangle = 0;                 /*      charlie (walker)  */
    ujoint = 30;    ljoint = 30;
    lxfoot = 30;    lyfoot = ryfoot = 150;
    rcolor = BLUE;lcolor = RED;

    Create_Field();
    Start_Walker();
    Raise_Walker();
    for( i=1; i<=20; i++ ) Walk_Right();
    Pause();
    closegraph();                                /*      restore text mode */
}


/*      **************************************************      */
/*                  The XOR_Line And XOR_Plot Functions         */
/*      **************************************************      */
void XOR_Plot( int x, int y, int color )
{
    putpixel( x, y, color ^ getpixel( x, y ) );
}

void XOR_Line( int x1, int y1, int x2, int y2 )
{
    int   i, j, k = getcolor();
    int   x = 10, y = 10;
    double slope;

    if( abs(x1–x2) > abs(y1–y2) )
    {
        if( x1 > x2 )
```

```
                {
                    i = x1;   x1 = x2;   x2 = i;
                    i = y1;   y1 = y2;   y2 = i;
                }
                j = x2-x1;
                slope = (double) (y2-y1)/j;
                for( i=1; i<=j; i++ )
                    XOR_Plot( x1+i, y1+(int)(i*slope), k );
        }
        else
        {
            if( y1 > y2 )
            {
                    i = y1;   y1 = y2;   y2 = i;
                i = x1;   x1 = x2;   x2 = i;
            }
            j = y2-y1;
            slope = (double) (x2-x1)/j;
            for( i=1; i<=j; i++ )
                XOR_Plot( x1+(int)(i*slope), y1+i, k );
        }
    }
```

CHAPTER 11

TURTLE GRAPHICS

The original concept of Turtle Graphics was proposed by Seymour Papert and co-workers at MIT as a convenient method of creating graphics without requiring an understanding of Cartesian coordinates. This basic vision was a turtle capable of walking along a straight line for a specified distance at a specific angle and drawing a line in its track; rather like the line left by a turtle's tail after coming ashore on a sandy beach.

The basic concept proved very popular. On the one hand, even relatively young children could use the 'turtle' to program images and, on the other, experienced programmers found turtle graphics an excellent tool capable of creating interesting images using simple algorithms. These algorithms were much simpler than those required for similar results using Cartesian coordinate systems.

The turtle implemented here is designed to adapt to various screen and video capabilities; handling colors where hardware supported and adjusting movement to match video screen aspect ratios.

The TURTLE.I utility provides 29 functions for complete turtle capabilities. Not all of these are intended for direct use, some are written only to be called by other functions, but the complete source code for all of the functions is included. And, of course, you are invited to modify or revise these functions for your own mutant turtle applications.

Just as the other graphics functions, the turtle graphics operate within a window, but the turtle window is independent of your graphics viewport (window). Separate turtle windows and graphics viewports can be in use at the same time.

The turtle routines operate on *turtle coordinates*. The home position (at turtle coordinates 0,0), is in the center of the active turtle window — with positive turtle coordinates to the right (x-axis) and upwards (y-axis) and, with negative coordinates to the left (x-axis) and down (y-axis). The *turtle angles* follow mapping conventions and begin with 0° as up or NORTH, 90° to the right or EAST, 180° as down or SOUTH and 270° as left or WEST.

Both 0° and 360° are valid angles but all angles or rotations greater than 360° or less than 0° are translated into the range 0..360°. The four ordinal directions; NORTH, EAST, SOUTH and WEST, are constants defined in Turtle.I.

As you have probably noticed, the turtle coordinates and angles do not correspond with the angles and coordinates used in the Turbo C graphics system or the familiar screen coordinate system. By normal computer conventions (as dictated by the screen address requirements), y-axis values increase from top to bottom while the turtle y-axis values decrease over the same range. At the same time, the Turbo C graphics system considers the zero angle to lie horizontally to the right (EAST) with angles increasing counterclockwise, while the turtle angles place zero at the top (NORTH) with the angles increasing in a clockwise direction.

These rotations and directions are not completely arbitrary. The turtle angles and directions follow cultural conventions long established and, in part, almost instinctive: that the compass (or clock) rotates clockwise, that graphs increase going up, that the king is at the top of the mountain. Alternatively, the rotations and directions that have become familiar to the programmer were forged under different constraints.

Since the basic concept behind the turtle graphics was to design them to be accessible and acceptable to individuals who weren't "computer sophisticated", the turtle angles and directions/values were written to follow the common and familiar conventions. For the same reasons, this set of turtle commands continues to follow the earlier standards, the possible dangers of confusing an occasional programmer notwithstanding.

The Turtle Graphic Commands

The turtle graphics utility does presume that Turbo C has initialized the graphics system and selected a graphics driver and mode. This done, turtle graphics are initialized by their own function: **init_turtle**.

init_turtle

Syntax: init_turtle();

While turtle graphics do not require any special device drivers or modes aside from those provided by the normal graphics initialization, the **init_turtle** function does take care of several important tasks, beginning by calling the **create_turtle** function to draw a turtle cursor and to save an image of the cursor. The **init_turtle** function also calculates the current screen aspect ratio (*TAsp*), sets up an initial turtle window and sets several default conditions. These conditions include: pen color is the maximum valid color, the turtle cursor is set to visible, screen wrap is off, the turtle pen is down in drawing position and the initial heading is NORTH (0).

Correction for screen aspect ratio is automatically applied to the y-axis.

turtle_window

Syntax: turtle_window(x_center, y_center, width, height);

The **turtle_window** function defines an area of the screen as the active turtle graphics window. Unlike the graphics window function (**setviewport**), **turtle_window**'s first two arguments are the x and y *center* coordinates while the last two arguments provide the width and height for the window.

The window is always centered on the home coordinates (position 0,0 in turtle coordinates, but x_center, y_center in absolute screen coordinates) and is initially established to include the entire screen, less three pixels margin. This default margin is provided to insure that the **putimage** function which handles the turtle cursor, is not called with coordinates that fall outside the valid full screen limits — an error that would prevent the cursor from appearing correctly.

The **clear_turtle_screen** erases the turtle window; the **hide_turtle**, **show_turtle**, **no_wrap**, **wrap** and **turtle_delay** functions control the turtle display parameters.

clear_turtle_screen

Syntax: clear_turtle_screen();

The **clear_turtle_screen** function borrows the Turbo C graphics viewport functions to erase the turtle screen, restoring the original graphics viewport settings afterwards.

hide_turtle/show_turtle

Syntax: hide_turtle();
Syntax: show_turtle();

The **hide_turtle** and **show_turtle** functions disable and enable the turtle cursor display by setting the *visible* flag. In this program, initially, the turtle is visible — other turtle graphics programs prefer to start the turtle as hidden.

wrap/no_wrap

Syntax: no_wrap();
Syntax: wrap();

The **wrap** and **no_wrap** functions control the turtle response when the turtle window limits are reached. If **wrap** is in effect, the turtle reaches the window limits and it will reenter the window at the opposite border.

If **no_wrap** is in effect, the turtle is allowed to move beyond the turtle window limits (or even outside the screen limits entirely), but the turtle drawing will not extend beyond the window borders.

turtle_delay

Syntax: turtle_delay(milliseconds);

By default, the turtle moves as fast as possible, but speed is not always desired. The **turtle_delay** function allows you to specify a delay in milliseconds between turtle steps (between pixel movements).

Also, if the turtle is offscreen, outside of the turtle window, the time delay has been disabled. This can prevent long waits for elaborate 'nothings' that are taking place outside the active turtle window, but it does not otherwise affect the display or the offscreen reference points used for lines.

Turtle Movements

The turtle movements are controlled by three factors: position, distance and direction. The position functions provide for absolute moves, the distance functions provide for movements a specified distance along the current heading and the direction functions set the movement headings.

home

Syntax: home();

The **home** function moves the turtle cursor to the home coordinates (0,0) at the center of the turtle window without drawing a line in the process. If a **turtle_delay** time is in effect, the cursor will be moved immediately, but no further movements will occur until the delay time has elapsed.

set_position

Syntax: set_position(xaxis, yaxis);

The **set_position** function immediately moves the turtle cursor to the turtle coordinates specified. No line is drawn by this move. If a **turtle_delay** time is in effect, the cursor will be moved immediately, but no further movements will occur until the delay time has elapsed.

forward

Syntax: forward(distance);

The **forward** function is the heart of the turtle graphics. The turtle cursor is moved the distance specified from the current position along the current heading. Movement is in one pixel steps and, if the turtle pen is down (*draw* = TRUE), a line is drawn using the current *pencolor*. If the turtle pen is up, the turtle cursor is moved (if *visible* = TRUE) without drawing a line. If *visible* is FALSE, the turtle cursor is moved invisibly.

If *distance* is negative, then movement is executed in the direction opposite the current heading.

If a **turtle_delay** time is in effect, movement will halt after each step until the set delay time has elapsed. This movement delay is used regardless of the *draw* or *visible* flag settings.

The **forward** function uses the **rcos** and **rsin** functions to calculate the appropriate x-axis and y-axis distances and the **step_turtle** function to accomplish the actual movement.

```
void forward( int distance )
{
        int   i, xdistance, ydistance,
            xorg = xpos, yorg = ypos;
        double slope;
        xdistance = rsin( direction ) * distance;
        ydistance = rcos( direction ) * distance * TAsp;
```

Some turtle drivers do not adjust for screen aspect. In this application, the *TAsp* (aspect ratio) variable is used to adjust vertical and horizontal movements in order to maintain equal line lengths on the screen in each direction. A movement of 50 units on the x-axis causes the turtle to move 50 pixels. The same distance on the y-axis is adjusted by the aspect ratio for the current graphics driver and mode. See also the **drawstr** function.

The next step, after calculating the x and y offsets resulting from the *direction* and *distance*, is a series of decisions beginning by deciding which is greater, the *xdistance* or *ydistance*.

```
if( abs( xdistance ) > abs( ydistance ) )
{
```

When plotting a line, always begin with the axis with greater change, then for each point along this axis, calculate the minor axis position — and begin by calculating the *slope* of the line.

```
slope = (double) ydistance / xdistance;
```

If the *xdistance* is positive, an increasing loop is used and a y-axis position is calculated and plotted for each x-axis position.

```
if( xdistance > 0 )
      for( i=1; i<=xdistance; i++ )
            step_turtle( xorg + i, yorg + (int) ( i * slope ) );
```

Otherwise, a decreasing loop is used, but the calculations are the same.

```
else
      for( i=-1; i>=xdistance; i-- )
            step_turtle( xorg + i, yorg + (int) ( i * slope ) );
}
```

Alternatively, the x-axis positions are calculated along the y-axis.

```
else
{
        slope = (double) xdistance / ydistance;
        if( ydistance > 0 )
            for( i=1; i<=ydistance; i++ )
                step_turtle( xorg + (int) ( i * slope ), yorg + i );
        else
            for( i=-1; i>=ydistance; i-- )
            step_turtle( xorg + (int) ( i * slope ), yorg + i );
```

```
        }
    }
```

back

   Syntax: back(distance);

The **back** function moves the turtle according to the same rules as the **forward** function, except that movement is in the direction opposite the current heading. If *distance* is negative, then movement is forward.

drawstr

   Syntax: drawstr(int scale, char charstr[150])

The **drawstr** function differs from the **forward** and **back** functions in two important respects: first, no correction is applied for the screen aspect ratio and; second, all movements are executed in absolute pixel steps. The reason for this is that attempting to draw small, closed figures using the slope calculations tends to produce a cumulative error when decimal fractions are rounded to integers. The resulting endpoints; therefore, do not always match the start points, leaving somewhat jagged or open corners on the resulting figures. By using absolute pixel movements for small closed figures, these errors are eliminated and a smooth, finished appearance is created.

   The **drawstr** function accepts two parameters, a scale multiplier and an array of characters describing the turtle movements that create a figure, turtle character, logo or other drawing. For this type of drawing, turtle movement is restricted to eight directions, the four cardinal directions and the four diagonals lying between these (see the **turtle_write** function for details).

```
    void drawstr( int scale,  char charstr[150] )
    {
          int  distance, j, k, x, y;
```

   A loop steps through the *charstr* array, acting in response to each element in the instruction string:

```
for( j=0; j<=strlen(charstr); j++ )
{
        distance = scale;
        switch( charstr[j] )
        {
```

Figure 11-1: Plot Compass for Turtle Fonts

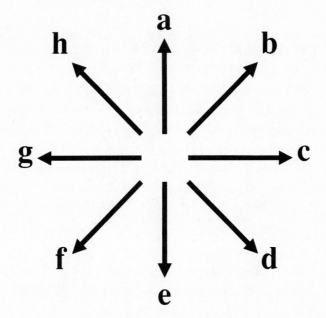

The instruction characters *a..h* set the step direction (see Figure 11-1). As long as either *x* or *y* is not zero, turtle movement will be executed after the switch/case selector is finished. Selecting a direction also causes the turtle to take one step in this direction.

```
case 'a':   x = 0;      y = -1;   break;
case 'b':   x = 1;      y = -1;   break;
case 'c':   x = 1;      y = 0;    break;
case 'd':   x = 1;      y = 1;    break;
case 'e':   x = 0;      y = 1;    break;
case 'f' :  x = -1;     y = 1;    break;
case 'g':   x = -1;     y = 0;    break;
case 'h':   x = -1;     y = -1;   break;
```

The instruction characters *m* and *p* call the **pen_up** and **pen_down** functions after setting both the *x* and *y* step increments to zero so that no turtle movement is executed in response.

```
case 'm':   x = 0;      y = 0;   pen_down();   break;
case 'p' :  x = 0;      y = 0;   pen_up();     break;
```

And the instruction characters *2..0* continue movement in the active direction, setting the *distance* according to the scale and the multiplier.Because the instruction which set the direction also resulted in one turtle step (with *distance* equal to *scale*), a movement instruction of *1* is ignored entirely, an instruction of *2* is accepted, but no action is taken, leaving the value for *distance* = (2 – 1) * *scale* (which is already the value of *distance)* so only a break statement is needed. Instructions *3* through *9* multiply distance by one less than the instruction integer and an instruction of *0* is taken as the equivalent of 10, making *distance* equal *scale* times 9 (10–1).

```
case '2':                             break;
case '3':    distance = scale * 2;    break;
case '4':    distance = scale * 3;    break;
case '5':    distance = scale * 4;    break;
case '6':    distance = scale * 5;    break;
case '7':    distance = scale * 6;    break;
case '8':    distance = scale * 7;    break;
case '9':    distance = scale * 8;    break;
case '0':    distance = scale * 9;    break;
```

```
      default :     x = 0;  y = 0;
   }
```

The default case in the switch statement sets null values for the *x* and *y* step values in any case where the instruction character is not recognized; therefore, preventing error movements. This might be applicable if you wanted to delimit your instruction strings using spaces, commas, dashes or even several characters, simply to make the instructions easier to read.

Finally, the turtle is stepped along the appropriate heading for the distance set.

```
            for( k=1; k<=distance; k++ ) step_turtle( xpos + x, ypos + y );
      }
   }
```

set_heading

Syntax: set_heading(degrees);

The **set_heading** function sets the current heading to an absolute value. The argument *degrees* can be any integer value, or the four cardinal directions (NORTH, EAST, SOUTH and WEST) defined in TURTLE.I can be used.

If a negative value is passed to **set_headings** or if the variable *degrees* is greater than 360°, then the **correct_direction** function corrects the heading value to the range 0..360°.

turn_left/turn_right

Syntax: turn_left(angle);
Syntax: turn_right(angle);

The **turn_left** function (counterclockwise) decreases the current heading by *angle* degrees. The **turn_right** function (clockwise) increases the current heading by *angle* degrees. In either function, a negative argument reverses the direction, the current angle is changed and both **turn_left** and **turn_right** use the **correct_direction** function to insure that the resulting turtle heading remains within the 0..360° range.

Turtle Drawing

The turtle graphics utility provides three functions to control the drawing: **set_pen_color** to select the turtle drawing color and, **pen_down** and **pen_up** to lower and raise the 'pen' during movements.

set_pen_color

Syntax: set_pen_color(color);

The **set_pen_color** function selects the turtle drawing color and accepts the color names defined in graphics.h. In monochrome modes (CGAHI for example), the drawing color is limited to BLACK or WHITE. In palette selection modes (CGAC0 for example), the drawing colors are limited to the predefined palette selections. Otherwise, the drawing color may be any valid, supported color.

pen_up/pen_down

Syntax: pen_down();
Syntax: pen_up();

The **pen_up** and **pen_down** functions operate exactly as the function names imply, setting the *draw* flag to FALSE or TRUE respectively. If *draw* is FALSE (set by **pen_up**), turtle movements do not draw a line. If *draw* is TRUE (set by **pen_down**), turtle movements draw a line in the current *pencolor*.

Turtle Information

Functions are also provided to return information about the turtle settings and coordinates.

heading

> Syntax: angle = heading();

The **heading** function returns an integer value reporting the current turtle heading.

turtle_where

> Syntax: if(turtle_where()) ... ;

The **turtle_where** function returns a Boolean value: TRUE if the current turtle position is within the turtle window limits, FALSE if the turtle is outside the window limits.

xcor/ycor

> Syntax: xaxis = xcor();
> Syntax: yaxis = ycor();

The **xcor** and **ycor** functions return the x-axis and y-axis turtle cursor coordinates.

Turtle Graphics Demo (TURTLE.C)

Turtle Graphics are excellent for simple drawing programs or for creating various types of figures and/or illustrations and they require only a minimum of programming information. In the Turtle demonstration (TURTLE.C), two complex figures are generated as examples, using very simple instructions, then a series of turtle characters and a logo illustration are created using the **turtle_write** function.

The maze used in the demo in Chapter 10, could also have been drawn using turtle graphics. A random maze could also be created using turtle graphics and a generation algorithm. In chief, turtle graphics are simply a programming tool, an alternative to the line functions in Turbo C graphics and an entry point for creating complex forms from simple algorithms.

turtle_write

Syntax: turtle_write(xaxis, yaxis, scale, color, workstr)

The **turtle_write** function draws characters defined using a simple instruction set that may be employed to create your own fonts, special characters, logos or other graphic elements.

The character set used in the turtle demo comprises only eight characters and is designed primarily to demonstrate how a font can be created. In general, turtle characters are similar to the stroked character fonts provided with Turbo Pascal and Turbo C (see Chapter 17 — **The Turbo Font Editor**) though the character images and methods used here are neither as sophisticated, nor as extensive.

The **turtle_write** and **drawchar** functions could be implemented by a variety of methods: the character definitions could be condensed, stored in binary files or redesigned to include curve calculations (though curves are not provided by the turtle functions) for smooth, rounded characters. The method used was chosen primarily for simplicity and for ease of demonstration.

Because curves are not supported, the strokes comprising a character are limited to unit steps in the eight directions shown in Figure 11-1.

Figure 11-2 shows two turtle characters — *e* and *i* — diagrammed as vector strokes with the **turtle_write** instructions by each stroke.

The beginning and end points for each character are shown as a register mark (a circle enclosing a cross mark). For the character **e**, the complete instruction string reads:

pba*ma6b2c4d2e2f2g4edc3bcef2g4h2*pb2a3*mbc2dfg2h* pd7

Note: the italicized instructions are executed pen down, the others pen up.

Each stroke begins as a direction and may be followed by a number 2..0 indicating how many steps are to be executed in this direction. If no number follows the direction key, only one step is executed; thus a 1 would be redundant and is not used. A zero is used for 10 steps and distances greater than 10 steps are coded as multiple instructions. Thus, a move right of 16 steps would be coded as *c8c8* rather than *c16*.

Figure 11-2: Plot for Characters "e" and "i"

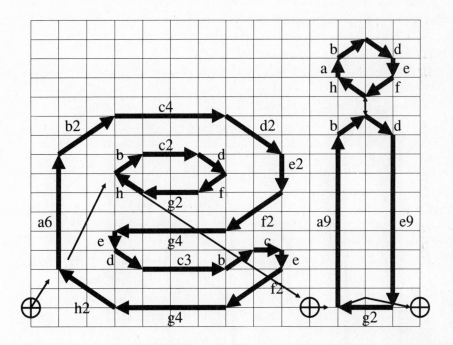

In addition to the directions, two other instructions, *p* and *m,* are used. In the instruction string for **e**, the instruction *p* calls **pen_up** so that the next two move instructions, *ba*, are executed without drawing a line. The instruction *m* calls **pen_down** and the following instruction groups draw the outside of the character. Next, another **pen_up** is followed by *b2a3* to position the turtle to draw the eye of the character and the final three instructions, *pd7*, move the turtle, without drawing, to the terminating position. The turtle ends on the same horizontal as it began, but is one pixel beyond the character, leaving a thin margin on both sides.

The character **i** is coded as: pc*ma9b*pam*habdefp*em*de9g2*pc3. You should be able to follow the coding for these two characters in Figure 11-2.

Following are the rest of the characters used in the Turtle demonstration, together with their code strings:

Figure 11-3: Plot for Characters "l" and "r"

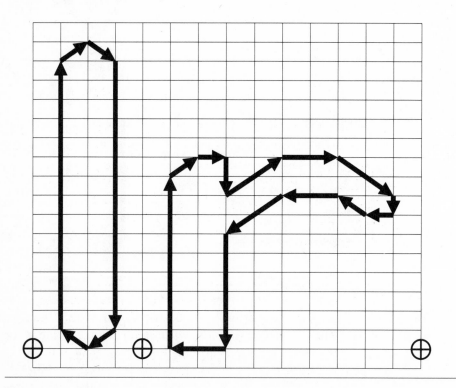

The **l** is coded as: pb*ma7a7bde7e7fh*pdc2
The **r** is coded as: pc*ma9bce2b2c2d2eghg2f2e6g2*pc9
The **t** is coded as: pb2c*ma8g3hbc3a3bde3c3dfg3e7dcdfg2h2*pd2c5

Notice that the character **t** begins at a point inside the left-most extent of the cross bar (as shown by the register mark). This offset provides kerning to allow the character to fit better with other letters, creating a smoother appearance.

Figure 11-4: Plot for Character "t"

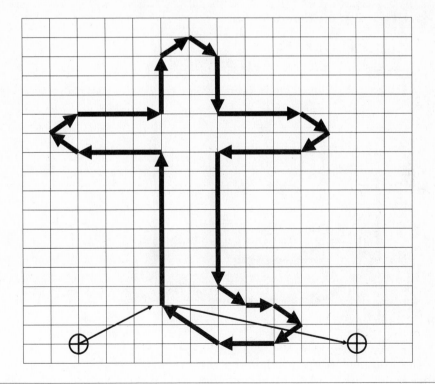

Characters may be kerned either left or right and, in many cases, special kerning is assigned to pairs of letters to make them visually fit together. For example, the characters AV are usually kerned to allow the left top of the V to overlap the bottom right of the A. No provision has been made here for pair kerning, but it is frequently used in typesetting.

The **u** is coded as: pba*ma7bde6dc2ba6bde7deghfg4h2*pd2c7

In this case, the character **u** ends immediately at the tail on the right, instead of allowing a pixel margin. Like the kerning on the **t**, this provides a better visual appearance when the character is written as part of a word.

Figure 11-5: Plot for Character "u"

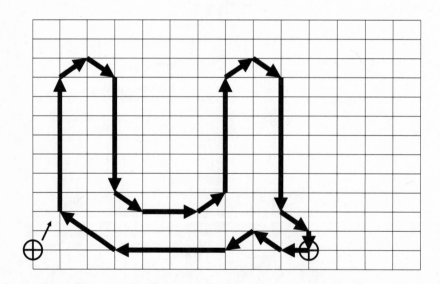

The character **w** is considerably wider than any of the others shown but still receives only a one pixel right and left margin. When written together, as the demo program will show, the characters present a smooth, proportional appearance.

Figure 11-6: Plot for Character "w"

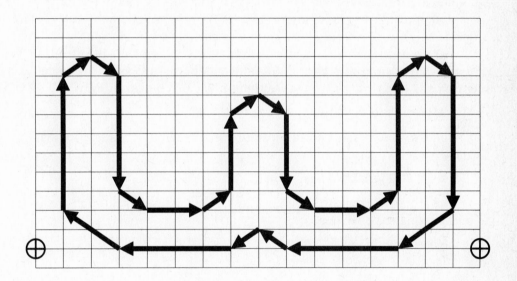

As executed in the demo program, the **turtle_write** function is called with five arguments: the x and y screen position (in turtle coordinates), a scaling factor, a color argument and the string to be written.

```
void turtle_write( int x, int y, int scale, int color, char workstr[100] )
{
        int   i;
        char logostr[125]=    "pcma8a8b2c8c8c8e8e8f2g8g8g8a8a8c8c8c8"
                        "f2g0g0e5b2c0c0a5f2e3g9g9a3g2e5c7c8c7"
                        "f2g0g0e5b2c0c0a5f2e3g9g9a3g2e5c8c8c8pcd";
```

237

Note that, unlike most string functions, *workstr* is not a pointer to a string, but is an array of characters as is the local variable *logostr*. This handling is used because the **turtle_write** function will treat the various strings as arrays of elements and use individual elements as instructions. This could still be managed using pointers, but is simpler as shown.

The *logostr* array is defined in its declaration, but could also have been passed directly to the **drawstr** function from some other source. This handling was chosen only because it was convenient to the demonstration.

The *color* argument allows passing color settings with the string to be displayed. Also, a negative color value can be passed as an argument and will result in a random color selection for each character drawn.

```
if( color <= MaxColors ) set_pen_color( color );
```

The *scale* factor is a multiplier setting the size of the characters. Negative and zero *scale* factors are not allowed.

```
if( scale <= 0 ) scale = 1;
```

The initial screen position is set (x, y), then a loop runs through the length of the string to be written:

```
set_position( x, y );
for( i=0; i<=strlen(workstr); i++ )
{
        if( color < 0 ) set_pen_color( random( MaxColors ) + 1 );
```

As the loop proceeds, each element of the string to be written is sent, as a string of stroke instructions, directly to the **drawstr** function:

```
switch( workstr[i] )
{
        case ' ':    drawstr( scale, "pc6");                    break;
        case 'e':    drawstr( scale, "pbama6b2c4d2e2f2g4edc3bc"
                                    "ef2g4h2pb2a3mbc2dfg2hpd7" );
                break;
        case 'i':    drawstr( scale, "pcma9bpamhabdefpemde9g2pc3" );
```

```
                    break;
     case 'l':      drawstr( scale, "pbma7a7bde7e7fhpdc2" );
                    break;
     case 'r':      drawstr( scale, "pcma9bce2b2c2d2eghg2f2e6g2pc9" );
                    break;
     case 't':      drawstr( scale, "pb2cma8g3hbc3a3bde3c3dfg3"
                                    "e7dcdfg2h2pd2c5" );
                    break;
     case 'u':      drawstr( scale, "pbama7bde6dc2ba6bde7deghf"
                                    "g4h2pd2c7" );
                    break;
     case 'w':      drawstr( scale, "pbama7bde6dc2ba3bde3dc2b"
                                    "a6bde7f2g4hfg4h2pd2c6c7" );
                    break;
          }
     }
```

And, after each line is written, the logo illustration is added.

```
          drawstr( scale, logostr );
     }
```

The logo character is a figure known as a double bolix (a bolix is a type of visual paradox).

```
logostr =     pcma8a8b2c8c8c8e8e8f2g8g8g8a8a8c8c8c8
              f2g0g0e5b2c0c0a5f2e3g9g9a3g2e5c7c8c7
              f2g0g0e5b2c0c0a5f2e3g9g9a3g2e5c8c8c8pcd
```

Unlike most of the letter characters, the logo design could not be drawn in a single, continuous line. Two options were possible: one, to use the **pen_up** function to move to a new location in order to fill in necessary elements; or two, to simply trace over existing lines as required. Since, visually, the two options appear quite similar, the second was chosen and line elements are retraced as required until the figure is completed.

Figure 11-7: Plot for Author's Logo

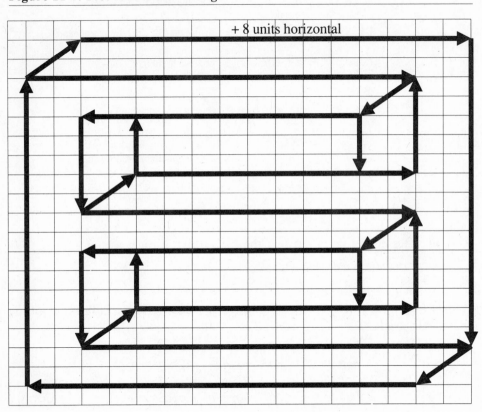

Display logos can also be created using a variety of drawing programs such as PC Paint, Microsoft Paint, GEM Draw or others, stored as disk files and subsequently accessed by your program (precise methods vary depending on the utility chosen). A turtle-created logo, however, offers greater flexibility because, as shown in the demo program, a turtle logo can be scaled to size.

Since individual turtle graphic elements can be defined by instruction strings, as shown with the sample alphabet, picture elements can also be created as turtle graphic instructions using either the **turtle_write** function or via an instruction handler designed to use the **forward**, **back**, **turn_right**, **turn_left** and **set_heading** functions if you need more flexible line elements.

Other Turtle Options

The turtle functions are not designed so much as to be used directly as to be called indirectly by other program applications. Turtle functions could, however, be easily interfaced to a mouse, joystick or to cursor keys for a drawing utility or combined with various algorithms to trace business data graphs in a moving presentation. They can also be used to create interactive graphic slide shows and to show different relations or connections between display elements in interactive stories or programmed instructions.

You might also experiment with revisions to permit separate x- and y-axis scaling. Currently, the **turtle_write** function is best suited to create 'balloon' or 'outline' typefaces. With minor additions to the **drawstr** function, however, the **floodfill** function could create solid letters or fill letters using various fillpatterns. Another enhancement might be an option to include color changes in the instruction strings.

The turtle functions are simply a tool set — feel free to enhance, change and revise these according to your needs and imagination.

Turtle Graphics With Plotters

In Chapter 15, a method of writing a color graphics screen to a graphics plotter are demonstrated ... but the results are neither fast nor satisfactory in all senses.

Because both turtle graphics and graphics plotters are stroke (line) oriented, essentially the same functions that are used here to drive the turtle, can also be adapted to duplicate the motions (with scaling adjustments, if necessary) on a graphics plotter.

If you need business graph displays in full color for slide and overhead projector applications, keep the turtle graphics and plotter in mind — they suit each other nicely.

```
/*      **********************************************        */
/*          TURTLE.I for Turbo C graphics — 28 turtle functions   */
/*      **********************************************        */

#include <math.h>

#define NORTH  0
#define EAST  90
#define SOUTH  180
#define WEST  270
#define PI    3.14159
#define FALSE  0
#define TRUE  1


double TAsp;
       int    direction, draw, pencolor, timeout, wrapoff,
              xhome, xpos, yhome, ypos, visible = 0,
              left, right, top, bottom;           /* turtle limits in abs screen coords */
void   *turtle;


void    back( int distance );
void    clear_turtle_screen();
void    correct_direction();
void    create_turtle();
void    drawstr( int scale,  char charstr[150] );
void    forward( int distance );
int     heading();
void    hide_turtle();
void    home();
void    init_turtle();
void    no_wrap();
void    pen_down();
void    pen_up();
```

```
double   rsin( int degrees );
double   rcos( int degrees );
void     set_heading( int degrees );
void     set_pen_color( int color );
void     set_position( int xaxis, int yaxis );
void     show_turtle();
void     step_turtle( int xmove, int ymove );
void     turn_left( int degrees );
void     turn_right( int degrees );
void     turtle_delay( int time );
int      turtle_where();
void     turtle_window( int xaxis, int yaxis, int width, int height );
void     wrap();
int      xcor();
int      ycor();

void create_turtle()
{
     int  i, j, k = getmaxcolor(), size;
     void *temp;
     size = imagesize( 1, 1, 5, 5 );
     temp = malloc( size );
     getimage( 1, 1, 5, 5, temp );
     putimage( 1, 1, temp, XOR_PUT );
     for( i=1; i<=5; i++ ) putpixel( i, 3, k );
     for( j=1; j<=5; j++ ) putpixel( 3, j, k );
     putpixel( 3, 3, 0 );
     turtle = malloc( imagesize( 1, 1, 5, 5 ) );
     getimage( 1, 1, 5, 5, turtle );
     putimage( 1, 1, turtle, XOR_PUT );
     putimage( 1, 1, temp, COPY_PUT );
     free( temp );
}

double rsin( int degrees )
```

```
{
    return( (double) sin( PI * degrees / 180 ) );
}


double rcos( int degrees )
{
    return( (double) cos( PI * degrees / 180 ) );
}


void clear_turtle_screen()
{
    struct  viewporttype  graphport;
    getviewsettings( &graphport );
    setviewport( left, top, right, bottom, 1 );
    clearviewport();
    setviewport( graphport.left,  graphport.top,
                    graphport.right, graphport.bottom, graphport.clip );
    if( visible ) putimage( xpos–2, ypos–2, turtle, XOR_PUT );
    home();
}


void correct_direction()
{
    while( direction > 360 ) direction –= 360;
    while( direction < 0 )   direction += 360;
}


void step_turtle( int xstep, int ystep )
{
    if( visible ) putimage( xpos–2, ypos–2, turtle, XOR_PUT );
    xpos = xstep;
    ypos = ystep;
    if( !wrapoff )
    {
```

```
        if( xpos < left ) xpos += right;
        else if( xpos > right ) xpos -= right;
        if( ypos < top ) ypos += bottom;
        else if( ypos > bottom ) ypos -= bottom;
        }
            if( draw && turtle_where() ) putpixel( xpos, ypos, pencolor );
            if( visible ) putimage( xpos-2, ypos-2, turtle, XOR_PUT );
            if( timeout && turtle_where() ) delay( timeout );
        }


void drawstr( int scale,  char charstr[150] )
{
        int  distance, j, k, x, y;

        for( j=0; j<=strlen(charstr); j++ )
        {
            distance = scale;
            switch( charstr[j] )
            {
                case 'a' :   x = 0;   y = -1;   break;
                case 'b' :   x = 1;   y = -1;   break;
                case 'c' :   x = 1;   y = 0;    break;
                case 'd' :   x = 1;   y = 1;    break;
                case 'e' :   x = 0;   y = 1;    break;
                case 'f' :   x = -1;   y = 1;   break;
                case 'g' :   x = -1;  y = 0;    break;
                case 'h' :   x = -1;  y = -1;   break;
                case 'm':    x = 0;   y = 0;    pen_down(); break;
                case 'p' :   x = 0;   y = 0;    pen_up();   break;
                case '2' :                     break;
                case '3': distance = scale * 2;  break;
                case '4': distance = scale * 3;  break;
                case '5': distance = scale * 4;  break;
                case '6': distance = scale * 5;  break;
                case '7': distance = scale * 6;  break;
```

```
            case '8':  distance = scale * 7;  break;
            case '9':  distance = scale * 8;  break;
            case '0':  distance = scale * 9;  break;
            default :  x = 0;  y = 0;
        }
        for( k=1; k<=distance; k++ ) step_turtle( xpos + x, ypos + y );
    }
}


void forward( int distance )
{
    int   i, xdistance, ydistance,
          xorg = xpos, yorg = ypos;
    double slope;


    xdistance = rsin( direction ) * distance;
    ydistance = rcos( direction ) * distance * TAsp;
    if( abs( xdistance ) > abs( ydistance ) )
    {
        slope = (double) ydistance / xdistance;
        if( xdistance > 0 )
            for( i=1; i<=xdistance; i++ )
                step_turtle( xorg + i, yorg + (int) ( i * slope ) );
        else
            for( i=-1; i>=xdistance; i-- )
                step_turtle( xorg + i, yorg + (int) ( i * slope ) );
    }
    else
    {
        slope = (double) xdistance / ydistance;
        if( ydistance > 0 )
            for( i=1; i<=ydistance; i++ )
                step_turtle( xorg + (int) ( i * slope ), yorg + i );
        else
            for( i=-1; i>=ydistance; i-- )
```

```
                    step_turtle( xorg + (int) ( i * slope ), yorg + i );
        }
}

void back( int distance )
{
        forward( distance * –1 );
}

int  heading()
{
        return( direction );
}

void hide_turtle()
{
        if( visible ) putimage( xpos–2, ypos–2, turtle, XOR_PUT );
        visible = FALSE;
        if( timeout ) delay( timeout );
}

void home()
{
        if( visible ) putimage( xpos–2, ypos–2, turtle, XOR_PUT );
        xpos = xhome;
        ypos = yhome;
        if( timeout ) delay(timeout);
        if( visible ) putimage( xpos–2, ypos–2, turtle, XOR_PUT );
}

void no_wrap()
{
        wrapoff = TRUE;
```

```
}

void pen_down()
{
    draw = TRUE;
}

void pen_up()
{
    draw = FALSE;
}

void set_heading( int degrees )
{
    direction = degrees;
    correct_direction();
}

void set_pen_color( int color )
{
    if( color < 0 ) color = 0;
    if( color > getmaxcolor() ) color = getmaxcolor();
    pencolor = color;
    setcolor( pencolor );
}

void set_position( int xaxis, int yaxis )
{
    if( visible ) putimage( xpos-2, ypos-2, turtle, XOR_PUT );
    xpos = xhome + xaxis;
    ypos = yhome - yaxis;
    if( timeout ) delay(timeout);
    if( visible ) putimage( xpos-2, ypos-2, turtle, XOR_PUT );
```

```
}

void show_turtle()
{
      if( !visible ) putimage( xpos–2, ypos–2, turtle, XOR_PUT );
      visible = TRUE;
      if( timeout ) delay( timeout );
}


void turn_left( int degrees )
{
      direction += degrees;
      correct_direction();
}


void turn_right( int degrees )
{
      direction –= degrees;
      correct_direction();
}


void turtle_window( int xaxis, int yaxis, int width, int height )
{
      int  xlimit = getmaxx() – 3,
           ylimit = getmaxy() – 3;

      left = xaxis – ( width  / 2 );
      while( left < 3 ) left++;
      right = left + width;
      while( right > xlimit ) right– –;

      top = yaxis – ( height / 2 );
```

```
    while( top < 3 ) top++;
    bottom = top + height;
    while( bottom > ylimit ) bottom--;

    setviewport( left, right, top, bottom, 0 );
    clearviewport();

    xpos = xhome = xaxis;
    ypos = yhome = yaxis;
}

int turtle_where()
{
    if( xpos >= left && xpos <= right &&
        ypos >= top  && ypos <= bottom   ) return( TRUE );
        else                               return( FALSE );
}

void turtle_delay( int time )
{
    timeout = time;
}

void wrap()
{
    wrapoff = FALSE;
}

int xcor()
{
    return(xpos-xhome);
}
```

```
int ycor()
{
      return( −1 * (ypos−yhome) );
}


void init_turtle()
{
      int   xasp, yasp, MaxX, MaxY;

      create_turtle();
      getaspectratio( &xasp, &yasp );
      TAsp = (double) xasp / (double) yasp * −1;
      MaxX = getmaxx();
      MaxY = getmaxy();
      turtle_window( MaxX/2, MaxY/2, MaxX, MaxY );
      set_pen_color( getmaxcolor() );
      show_turtle();
      turtle_delay( 0 );
      no_wrap();
      pen_down();
      set_heading( 0 );
}
          /* **************************************** */
          /*    TURTLE.C — Turtle Graphics Demo Program   */
          /* **************************************** */


#ifdef __TINY__
#error Graphics demos will not run in the tiny model.
#endif

#include <conio.h>
```

```
#include <stdio.h>
#include <stdlib.h>
#include <stdarg.h>
#include <graphics.h>
#include <gprint.i>
#include <fcntl.h>
#include "turtle.i"


int    GraphDriver;
int    GraphMode;
int    MaxColors;
int    ErrorCode = 0;


void Initialize()
{
    GraphDriver = DETECT;
    initgraph( &GraphDriver, &GraphMode, "" );
    ErrorCode = graphresult();
    if ( ErrorCode != grOk )
    {
        printf(" Graphics System Error: %s\n",
                    grapherrormsg( ErrorCode ) );
        delay( 10000 );
        exit( 1 );
    }
    MaxColors = getmaxcolor() + 1;
}


void Pause()
{
    while( kbhit() ) getch();
    getch();
}
```

```
void TurtleDemo()
{
    int  i, j;

    turtle_delay(10);
    set_heading( SOUTH );
    pen_up();
    forward( 100 );
    delay( 500 );

    turtle_delay(0);
    pen_down();
    set_heading( 45 );
    for( i=1; i<=15; i++ )
    {
        set_pen_color( i );
        for( j=1; j<=6; j++ )
        {
            forward(100 + i*3);
            turn_right(59);
        }
    }
    home();
    Pause();
    clear_turtle_screen();
    wrap();
    set_position( -100, -100 );
    set_heading( 45 );
    for( i=1; i<=15; i++ )
    {
        set_pen_color( i );
        for( j=1; j<=3; j++ )
        {
            forward( 200 );
            turn_left( 90 );
```

```
        }
        forward( 200 );
    }
    home();
    Pause();
}


void turtle_write( int x, int y, int scale, int color, char workstr[100] )
{
    int   i;
    char  logostr[125] = "pcma8a8b2c8c8c8e8e8f2g8g8g8a8a8c8c8c8"
                         "f2g0g0e5b2c0c0a5f2e3g9g9a3g2e5c7c8c7"
                         "f2g0g0e5b2c0c0a5f2e3g9g9a3g2e5c8c8c8pcd";


    if( color <= MaxColors ) set_pen_color( color );
    if( scale <= 0 ) scale = 1;
    set_position( x, y );
    for( i=0; i<=strlen(workstr); i++ )
    {
        if( color < 0 ) set_pen_color( random( MaxColors ) + 1 );
        switch( workstr[i] )
        {
            case ' ': drawstr( scale, "pc6");                    break;
            case 'e': drawstr( scale, "pbama6b2c4d2e2f2g4edc3bc"
                                      "ef2g4h2pb2a3mbc2dfg2hpd7" );        break;
            case 'i': drawstr( scale, "pcma9bpamhabdefpemde9g2pc3" );      break;
            case 'l': drawstr( scale, "pbma7a7bde7e7fhpdc2" );            break;
            case 'r': drawstr( scale, "pcma9bce2b2c2d2eghg2f2e6g2pc9" );   break;
            case 't': drawstr( scale, "pb2cma8g3hbc3a3bde3c3dfg3"
                                      "e7dcdfg2h2pd2c5" );                break;
            case 'u': drawstr( scale, "pbama7bde6dc2ba6bde7deghf"
                                      "g4h2pd2c7" );                      break;
            case 'w': drawstr( scale, "pbama7bde6dc2ba3bde3dc2b"
                                      "a6bde7f2g4hfg4h2pd2c6c7" );        break;
        }
    }
```

255

```
        }
        drawstr( scale, logostr );
}


void TurtleWriteDemo()
{
        randomize();
        turtle_delay( 10 );
        turtle_write( −300, −110, 5, MaxColors, "turtle write ");
        turtle_delay( 7 );
        turtle_write( −300, −20, 4, random(MaxColors)+1, "write turtle ");
        turtle_delay( 5 );
        turtle_write( −300,  55, 3, −1, "turtle write ");
        turtle_delay( 3 );
        turtle_write( −300, 110, 2, −1, "write turtle ");
        turtle_delay( 1 );
        turtle_write( −300, 150, 1, MaxColors, "turtle write turtle write "
                                              "turtle write turtle write turtle " );
        home();
        Pause();
}


void main()
{
        Initialize();
        init_turtle();
        show_turtle();
        TurtleDemo();
        TurtleWriteDemo();
        closegraph();
}
```

CHAPTER 12

IMAGE MANIPULATION AND IMAGE FILES

The basic principles required to store and retrieve an image as a disk file and other methods for manipulating an existing image will be covered in this chapter.

Structure of an Image

When Turbo C saves an image of a portion of the screen, the screen image is "coded" or compressed to minimize memory usage.

For example, assume an image that is 41 by 41 pixels in size. If each pixel value was stored as a char value, the image would require 1681 bytes of memory. In a monographic mode, each pixel location contains only two bits of real information: the video bit and the intensity bit. At the other extreme, in EGA/VGA color modes, each pixel contains six bits of information, the **RrGgBb** color bits (see Chapters 13 and 14 for more detail on color video data). Thus, instead of 1681 bytes, for an EGA/VGA system, only 1261 bytes of actual information are required to be saved and, for a monochrome image, only 421 bytes.

Turbo C, however, goes one step further and uses a data compression algorithm to minimize the memory requirements, reducing 1681 EGA/VGA pixels to a mere 990 bytes of image data (about a 42 percent savings over storing the image as chàr data). In monographic modes, similar compression results in even greater savings.

The data compression and deciphering is automatic and is handled whenever **getimage** and **putimage** are called — and there is no need to worry about the mechanisms involved. There is one item of information in the data image that is useful to know about: the first four bytes of data contain the x and y-axis size of the image coded as *X_lsb*, *X_msb*, *Y_lsb*, *Y_msb*.

For the example proposed, the first four bytes of the image would read *28h*, *00h*, *28h*, *00h* (28h = 40 decimal) with the least_significant_byte first and the most_significant_byte second. Notice also that the size value is not stored as 41, but as 40 — a minimum axis size of one being reasonably assumed.

Image Files: Storage and Retrieval

When you are using graphics images, instead of placing the code description for a series of images in your program, it is often more convenient to create an image, or several images, once. They can then be stored as external image files, and recalled when necessary for use in your application program.

For example, in a line-graph demo, four images could be used to represent four different types of stock or four different types of company. In a real application, this line graph might require dozens or even hundreds of image symbols, though only a few would be needed at any particular time. Instead of including the coding to create each of these in the application program and instead of wasting both the time to draw each image and the memory required to store all of the images, a more efficient approach would be to use a separate image creation utility program, store the images as external files and then read the image files for each *when_and if* it was required by the application.

This is all very simple to accomplish.

As mentioned previously, because the image size is included in the image (and therefore, in the image file), all you actually need to know in order to retrieve an image, is the filename.

The FILE_IMG.C Demo

The demo program FILE_IMG.C will show how this is accomplished; first, by creating a image (Flash); then by storing it as a diskfile (FLASH.IMG) and, finally, by retrieving FLASH.IMG as Flash2.

FILE_IMG declares two pointers:

```
void   *Flash, *Flash2;
```

It then initializes the graphics system and calls **CreateImage** for the actual demonstration. When done, **FILE_IMG** waits for a key entry, releases the memory allocated for the images and exits.

```
main()
{
        Initilize();
        CreateImage();
        Pause();
        free(Flash);
        free(Flash2);
        closegraph();
}
```

The **CreateImage** procedure is adapted from an earlier animation program, using one of the 'flash' images previously demonstrated.

```
void CreateImage()
{
        int  Size = 0, MaxColor = getmaxcolor();
        int  pflash[] = { 100, 40, 110, 60, 100, 70, 120, 65,
                        140, 80, 130, 60, 140, 50, 120, 55, 100, 40 };
        randomize();
        setcolor( random( MaxColor ) + 1 );
        setfillstyle( random(11) + 1, random ( MaxColor ) + 1 );
        fillpoly( sizeof( pflash )/( 2 * sizeof( int ) ), pflash );
```

The *Flash* image is, again, created by calling **SaveImage** but, in this application, **SaveImage** has been modified slightly to accept a fifth parameter, *Size*. *Size* is passed by address so that the value calculated will be returned for further use. This is not, of course, an absolute requirement since the **imagesize** function can be called at any time, but it is convenient and the size information will be needed by **FileImage**.

```
Flash = SaveImage( 100, 40, 140, 80, &Size );
```

The **FileImage** function is passed the image pointer (*Flash*), the size of the image (*Size* returned by **SaveImage**) and the filename where the image will be stored.

```
FileImage( Flash, Size, "FLASH.IMG" );
```

The **ReadImage** function requires only the filename, returning a pointer to the new image retrieved from the disk and last, for confirmation, the image retrieved is written to the screen.

```
Flash2 = ReadImage( "FLASH.IMG" );
putimage( 200, 200, Flash2, COPY_PUT );
}
```

The **SaveImage** procedure operates exactly as before, except for the added parameter, *size*.

```
void *SaveImage( int left, int top, int right, int bottom, unsigned *size )
{
        void  *image;
        *size = imagesize( left, top, right, bottom );
        image = malloc( *size );
        getimage( left, top, right, bottom, image );
        putimage( left, top, image, XOR_PUT );
        return( image );
}
```

The **FileImage** procedure is the key to storing an image on disk and it accepts three parameters: **image*, a pointer to the image to be written; *size*, the size of the image as calculated by the **imagesize** function, and the filename.

```
void FileImage( void *image, unsigned size, char *filename )
{
```

A file handle (stream) is declared and **fileopen** assigns the filename and indicates that this is a new file created for write.

```
        FILE  *f1 = fopen( filename, "w" );
```

The **fwrite** function references the pointer *image* to write *one* data item of *size* bytes to the stream pointed to by *f1*.

```
        fwrite( image, size, 1, f1 );
```

The **fflush** function is called to flush the stream (*f1*) and **fclose** closes the file.

```
        fflush( f1 );
        fclose( f1 );
}
```

That's it. The disk file was created, the image written and the file closed.

Using the **ReadImage** procedure, retrieving the image from the created file is almost as simple as creating and saving it; but, in this application, only one parameter is required: the filename. Using the filename and opening *f1* for read; and *tempimage*, a local pointer to reference the image, **ReadImage** declares three unsigned integers: *xaxis*, *yaxis* and *size*; and also a file handle, *f1*.

```
void *ReadImage( char *filename )
{
        unsigned xsize, ysize, size;
        FILE   *f1 = fopen( filename, "r" );
        void   *tempimage;
```

As mentioned previously, the screen size of the image is contained in the image data and; therefore, **imagesize** can be called locally to determine *size*. This is convenient because your program will not know how much memory is needed for an image retrieved from disk and memory *must be* allocated for this purpose.

The first trick is to read the image screen size (*xsize* and *ysize*) from the image data. Since this information is stored in reverse order with the least significant byte of each integer value appearing first and the most significant byte second, the data is read as byte values (type char) and **OR**'d to create an unsigned integer.

```
xsize = fgetc( f1 ) | (fgetc( f1 ) << 8);
ysize = fgetc( f1 ) | (fgetc( f1 ) << 8);
```

With these two values, the **imagesize** function can return *size*.

```
size = imagesize( 0, 0, xsize, ysize );
```

The image width and height and the memory size are written to the screen simply for demonstration purposes.

```
gprintxy( 10, 10, " xsize = %d, ysize = %d, imagesize = %d ",
                    xsize,      ysize,           size );
```

Once *size* is known, **malloc** allocates the necessary memory with *tempimage* pointed to the memory address.

```
tempimage = malloc( size );
```

Now, since the file pointer is already four bytes into the data, before the actual image can be retrieved, the file pointer must be reset to the start of the file using the **rewind** function.

```
rewind( f1 );
```

This done, the **fread** function is called in exactly the same manner as the **fwrite** function was called: the pointer *tempimage* is accessed to read *one* data item of *size* bytes from the stream pointed to by *f1*.

```
fread( tempimage, size, 1, f1 );
```

The **fclose** function closes down the file (no flush required) and the pointer value *tempimage* is returned to the calling function.

```
        close( f1 );
        return( tempimage );
}
```

It's done. Only a bit more work was required than when the image file was written. The image file was opened for read, the image screen size data was read, the memory size calculated and the memory allocated. Then the file was reset to the beginning and *size* bytes of image data were read into *tempimage*. Finally, after the file was closed, the image pointer was returned to the calling function.

Files With Multiple Images

While it is possible to write several images to a single file, it is not recommended — though it may be necessary for some applications.

Rather than offering any hard and fast rules for creating multiple image files, here are considerations and suggestions that should help when programming this type of application. They are not, however, guaranteed solutions.

First, will all the images be the same size? Or, will there be several different size images in a single file?

In either case, the handling can be similar, but if the images are all the same size (exactly the same size!), then positioning the file pointer to seek a specific image becomes simpler. If the images differ only slightly in size, then it may be worthwhile to make them all the size of the largest, for convenience.

If the images are all different sizes, then retrieval is a matter of reading successive images until the desired item is reached.

Or is it?

How are you going to retrieve the four bytes of information that tell you the screen image size and; therefore, the size of the data to read?

The **fseek** function offers assistance here but you will need to keep track of your file pointer (file position) with some accuracy. Remember, the data has no way to tell you that it is the beginning of an image and there are no reserved 'flag' bytes possible with graphics images — any value could occur in an image.

Second, how are you going to write multiple images to a file? The file append option, used when the file is opened, is the obvious choice but, when writing the file, should you add a few nulls between items? Or should you create a specific pattern of bits to insert between entries as a hopefully recognizable safety?

Actually, if your handling is accurate, such safeties shouldn't be necessary. And, if your handling isn't accurate, these probably won't help much anyway, so your best bet is not to depend on fancy insertions.

Last: if you do need multiple images in a single file, it can be done. And, it can be done easier in C (specifically Turbo C) than in Pascal or Basic. But it must be done carefully. And consistently.

Think of it as a challenge and have fun.

More Image Manipulation

The second principal topic in this chapter is image manipulation. Previously, in Chapter 10 on animation, images were rotated 180 degrees or flipped left for right — simple, transpositional manipulations in four basic directions.

But a mere four directions is a rather limited choice of orientations. What about a true image rotation? The computer is great at crunching numbers and can calculate coordinate transformations without raising a sweat, so why not use this capability?

The demo program, ROTATE.C, will show two types of rotation: direct image rotation and calculated image rotation.

Direct Image Rotation

In direct image rotation, an existing image is rotated pixel by pixel to create a second image, duplicating the first, but with a different orientation.

First, each pixel in the specified image area is tested, to see if it is non-zero — because there is no point in rotating background pixels.

If the pixel value is not zero — if it does contain visual information — then the pixel's position is read as an x-axis/y-axis offset from a center point. Nominally, an image is rotated geocentrically (self-centered), but provisions can also be made to rotate an image eccentrically by specifying the necessary zero point coordinates.

In either case, the pixel's position, as an x-axis/y-axis offset, is converted to an angle and a vector distance (the hypotenuse of a right triangle formed by the x and y distances — see **Vector Calculations**). The pixel angle is then incremented by the rotation angle and the vector distance reconverted to an x-axis/y-axis offset that becomes the new pixel position.

Since overwriting the original image would be self-defeating, each rotated pixel offset is plotted from a new center position to create a new, rotated image.

As ROTATE.C will demonstrate, the rotated image is not as smooth as the original. This is due to variations in the calculation that results in small changes in angles, both in the original pixel coordinates and the rotated vector angle, return fractional values that must finally be reduced to integer coordinates for the actual plot. Basically, the higher the screen resolution, the smoother the rotated image will appear, however, these calculated image rotations can not be smoothed entirely when carried out on a pixel by pixel basis.

Calculated Image Rotation

The second method of image rotation does not apply to all types of image but, for any image that is generated primarily using the Turbo C **arc** and **line** functions, the line and arc coordinates can be rotated, then a new image generated. These coordinate rotations are carried out in precisely the same manner as for direct image rotation.

One obvious exception does exist: the **ellipse** function cannot be rotated by rotating coordinates since there is no provision for circular elongation except directly along the x-axis or the y-axis. Also, the **circle** function, which is a special case of the **ellipse**, is not affected by coordinate rotation.

When coordinate rotation is practical, there are advantages: the resulting images are smoother than those produced by direct image rotation and creating the image is generally faster since fewer calculations are required.

Video Aspect Adjustments

As ROTATE.C will demonstrate (unless you are using a VGA system), the video aspect ratio also needs to be taken into account when rotating either pixels or image element coordinates. In some cases, however, as with the text legend in the center of the image, the rotated text is clearest when no aspect correction is applied (but the rest of the image is definitely distorted without correction).

The ROTATE.C Demo

The image rotation facilities demonstrated in this program are designed less as ''plug-in'' utilities than as a demonstration of how image rotation procedures can be created. Four basic methods are shown: direct (pixel) image rotation and calculated image rotation; both with and without video aspect correction.

Note: this demonstration is written primarily for EGA/VGA systems. The demo will run on CGA but the bottom portion of the display will be off of the screen.

To begin, the **main** procedure initializes the graphics system (and sets the video aspect ratio), then calls the **Show_Rotation** procedure with an angle (in degrees) for rotation. Acceptable values are *0..360*, though values outside of this range will be adjusted to fit.

```
main()
{
        Initialize();
        Show_Rotation( 135 );
        Pause();
        closegraph();
}
```

The **Show_Rotation** procedure creates a simple screen image, then demonstrates rotation using the four methods previously discussed.

```
void Show_Rotation(int degrees)
{
        int  i, j, x, y, Point, radius = 50;
        settextjustify( CENTER_TEXT, TOP_TEXT );
        outtextxy( 320, 10, "Original");
        x = 320;
        y = 100;
        circle( x, y, radius );
        line( x–radius, y+radius*AspR,
            x+radius, y–radius*AspR );
        line( x+radius, y–radius*AspR,
            x+radius, y–(radius–20)*AspR );
        line( x+radius, y–radius*AspR,
            x+radius–20, y–radius*AspR );
        outtextxy( 320, 100, "Horizontal?" );
```

In the original image, a circle is drawn with an arrow crossing it at an angle of 45 degrees and the question 'Horizontal?' is written across the center. This original image has been created in WHITE; but now, two colored circles will be written to the right and left to act as reference marks for the subsequent image rotations.

```
        setcolor(RED);
        x = 160;
        circle( x, y, radius );
        setcolor(GREEN);
```

```
x = 480;
circle( x, y, radius );
setcolor(WHITE);
```

Two captions are added to show the rotation angle selected:

```
x = 160; y = 30;
gprintf( &x, &y, "Figure rotated %d degrees", degrees);
gprintf( &x, &y, "without aspect correction");
x = 480; y = 30;
gprintf( &x, &y, "Figure rotated %d degrees", degrees);
gprintf( &x, &y, "using aspect correction");
```

Now, the original image is rotated using **Rotate_Point** to the left and **Adj_Rotate_Point** to the right.

```
for( i=-50; i<=50; i++ )
for( j=-50; j<=50; j++ )
{
        Point = getpixel( 320+i, 100+j );
        if( Point > 0 )
        {
            x = i;
            y = j;
            Rotate_Point( &x, &y, degrees );
            putpixel( 160+x, 100+y, Point );
            x = i;
            y = j;
            Adj_Rotate_Point( &x, &y, degrees );
            putpixel( 480+x, 100+y, Point );
        }
}
```

On the bottom half of the screen (not visible on CGA systems), two more captions are written for the coordinate rotation demonstrations.

```
x = 160; y = 180;
printf( &x, &y, "Coordinates rotated %d degrees", degrees);
```

```
gprintf( &x, &y, "without aspect correction");
x = 480; y = 180;
gprintf( &x, &y, "Coordinates rotated %d degrees", degrees);
gprintf( &x, &y, "using aspect correction");
```

The first coordinate rotation — in red, to the left — is done without using video aspect ratio corrections in the calculations. The *AspR* factor appearing here is the same as was used to correct the original figure, but does not further affect the values created by the **Rotate_Line** function.

Also, as you will notice, the text insertion that was rotated in the first half of this demonstration will not appear in this portion. Turbo C does not offer provisions for fractional rotation of the graphics text fonts. Also, except for 90° increments, the graphic text fonts tend to appear rather distorted even when direct image rotation is used.

```
setcolor(RED);
x = 160;  y = 250;
```

The x and y coordinates set the center point for the new image, and the original line formulas are repeated using the new reference point.

```
circle( x, y, radius );
Rotate_Line( x, y, degrees,
             x-radius, y+radius*AspR,
             x+radius, y–radius*AspR );
Rotate_Line( x, y, degrees,
             x+radius, y–radius*AspR,
             x+radius, y–(radius–20)*AspR );
Rotate_Line( x, y, degrees,
             x+radius,   y–radius*AspR,
             x+radius–20, y–radius*AspR );
```

The second coordinate rotation — in green, to the right — does use video aspect ratios in the coordinate calculation.

```
setcolor(GREEN);
x = 480;  y = 250;
circle( x, y, radius );
```

```
        Adj_Rotate_Line( x, y, degrees,
                        x–radius, y+radius*AspR,
                        x+radius, y–radius*AspR );
        Adj_Rotate_Line( x, y, degrees,
                        x+radius, y–radius*AspR,
                        x+radius, y–(radius–20)*AspR );
        Adj_Rotate_Line( x, y, degrees,
                         x+radius, y–radius*AspR,
                        x+radius–20, y–radius*AspR );
    }
```

In the **Rotate_Line** procedure, the *x* and *y* parameters are the center point, *degrees* is the angle for rotation and *x1*, *y1*, *x2* and *y2* are the begin and end points for the line to be rotated.

```
    void Rotate_Line( int x,  int y,  int degrees,
                    int x1, int y1, int x2, int y2 )
    {
```

The begin and end coordinate pairs are converted to offsets relative to the center point coordinates.

```
        x1 –= x;   y1 –= y;
        x2 –= x;   y2 –= y;
```

The offset pairs are rotated using **Rotate_Point**.

```
        Rotate_Point( &x1, &y1, degrees );
        Rotate_Point( &x2, &y2, degrees );
```

And a new line is drawn using the **line** function and passing parameters as the centerpoint coordinates, plus the x-axis and y-axis offsets returned by the **Rotate_Point** function.

```
        line( x+x1, y+y1, x+x2, y+y2 );
    }
```

The **Adj_Rotate_Line** procedure works the same way as **Rotate_Line** except for calling **Adj_Rotate_Point** instead of **Rotate_Point**.

```
void Adj_Rotate_Line( int x,  int y,  int degrees,
                      int x1, int y1, int x2, int y2 )
{
        x1 -= x;  y1 -= y;
        x2 -= x;  y2 -= y;
        Adj_Rotate_Point( &x1, &y1, degrees );
        Adj_Rotate_Point( &x2, &y2, degrees );
        line( x+x1, y+y1, x+x2, y+y2 );
}
```

The **Adj_Rotate_Point** function is an intermediate procedure calling the **Rotate_Point** function after adjusting the *Y_Off* (y-axis offset) value using the aspect ratio. In this case, the offset is being normalized to the same effective value it would have if plotted against the x-axis instead of being plotted on the y-axis (or, as if the x and y pixel sizes were the same).

```
void Adj_Rotate_Point( int *X_Off, int *Y_Off, int degrees )
{
        int    X0 = *X_Off;
        int    Y0 = *Y_Off / AspR;
        Rotate_Point( &X0, &Y0, degrees );
```

After **Rotate_Point** returns the rotated value, the y-axis value (*Y0*) is corrected for the screen aspect ratio.

```
        *X_Off =  X0;
        *Y_Off =  Y0 * AspR;
}
```

Both values (the coordinate pair) are returned to the calling function after rotation.

The **Rotate_Point** function carries out the actual calculations, accepting x-axis and y-axis offset values (which may be positive or negative distances) and the rotation angle in degrees.

```
void Rotate_Point( int *X_Off, int *Y_Off, int degrees )
{
        double  HypLen, R_Angle, O_Angle = 0;
```

```
int    Sign_X = 1,  Sign_Y = 1;
double X0 = (double) *X_Off + 0.5,
       Y0 = (double) *Y_Off + 0.5;
```

The offset parameters are accepted as local variables of type **double** and a decimal fraction of 0.5 is added to each. This fractional adjustment improves the results, following calculations, by helping smooth the final round-down corrections when the double values are returned as integers.

The angle *degrees* is only accepted as a positive rotation value.

```
degrees = abs( degrees );
```

Turbo C's **hypot** function conveniently returns a vector distance from the two offset values.

```
HypLen = hypot( X0, Y0 );
```

The vector angle is calculated, using the offset coordinates, as a value in radians.

```
if( abs(X0) > 0 ) O_Angle = atan2( (–1 * Y0), X0 );
else if( Y0 < 0 ) O_Angle = PI/2;
else              O_Angle = 3*PI/2;
```

If the absolute value of *X0* is greater than 0, then **atan2** returns the angle in radians. Alternatively — if *X0* is zero — then the y-axis offset is the determining factor and the angle can be either *PI/2* or *3*PI/2*, depending on whether the y-axis offset is positive or negative.

In the previous step, the **atan2** function returns values from *–PI* to *PI* and the angle (in radians) may have been returned as a negative value. If so, then the value in *O_Angle* is converted to a positive angle.

```
if( O_Angle < 0) O_Angle += 2*PI;
```

This conversion makes subsequent calculations easier but does not change the actual vector angle.

The value in *degrees* is also converted to a local parameter value in radians:

```
R_Angle = (double) degrees / 180 * PI;
```

And then the original angle (*O_Angle*) is added to the rotation angle (*R_Angle*).

```
R_Angle += O_Angle;
```

If the result is greater than *2*PI*, then *R_Angle* is returned to the normal range (*0..2*PI*).

```
if( R_Angle > 2*PI ) R_Angle -= 2*PI;
```

The next step is to check which quadrant *R_Angle* falls in and assign the necessary vector polarity because the vector coordinates will be calculated as absolute values and the *Sign_X* and *Sign_Y* flags will be used to determine the actual sign of the results. This is done as a correction for the fact that the calculated coordinate values will not match the coordinate values needed for screen positions (see **Vector Calculations** following).

```
if( ( R_Angle > PI/2 )  & ( R_Angle <= 3*PI/2 ) )    Sign_X = -1;
if( ( R_Angle > 0 )     & ( R_Angle <= PI ) )        Sign_Y = -1;
```

Now the vector distance (*HypLen*) and rotated vector angle (*R_Angle*) are returned to the new coordinate values (*X0* and *Y0*). Depending on which half of each quadrant's (see Figure 12-1) *R_Angle* falls in, either *X0* is calculated using the cosine or *Y0* is calculated using the sine of the angle with the other coordinate calculated as the remaining side of a right triangle.

```
if( ( ( R_Angle >=  PI/4 ) & ( R_Angle <= 3*PI/4 ) ) |
    ( ( R_Angle >= 5*PI/4 ) &  ( R_Angle <= 7*PI/4 ) ) )
{
        X0 = HypLen * cos( R_Angle );
        Y0 = sqrt( pow( HypLen, 2 ) - pow( X0, 2 ) );
}
else
{
```

```
        Y0 = HypLen * sin( R_Angle );
        X0 = sqrt( pow( HypLen, 2 ) – pow( Y0, 2 ) );
   }
```

Last, the absolute values of *X0* and *Y0* are multiplied by their sign and returned as *X_Off* and *Y_Off* coordinates.

```
      *X_Off = abs( X0 ) * Sign_X;
      *Y_Off = abs( Y0 ) * Sign_Y;
  }
```

Vector Calculations

You've seen how to rotate a point but haven't received any explanation about it. If your high school or college trig is a bit rusty, you may be wondering about the previous calculations.

First, a reminder about a few facts that you already know — but which you need to keep firmly in the forefront of your mind to understand what's happening here.

With computer graphics, all screen positions are described as x,y coordinates beginning with a 0,0 coordinate in the upper left corner of the screen. Yes, the upper left screen position is normally referenced as 1,1 in Turbo C or in Turbo Pascal but, to the computer, this is still the 0,0 reference point (and before DOS receives the C or Pascal coordinates they are changed to match this zero-origin system).

In screen coordinates, x-axis values increase from left to right and y-axis values increase from top to bottom. All of this should be very familiar to computer programmers.

In the Cartesian coordinate system (rectangular parallel coordinates), however, the x-axis values also increase from left to right (with negative values left of the 0,0 coordinate) but the y-axis values increase from bottom to top with the negative values on the y-axis lying below the 0,0 coordinate. Since the Cartesian coordinate system is well established (long predating computers) it has priority and; therefore, all trigometric conversions from x,y coordinate values assume Cartesian values initially. Likewise, all conversions from polar coordinates (vector angle and magnitude), yield results compatible with the Cartesian system — not the screen coordinate system.

Therefore, some minor — but important — adaptations will be necessary.

First, in order to rotate an image, a center point for rotation is required and this point becomes a new 0,0 reference point — but has no relationship to the screen origin 0,0 point. This center point reference is quite arbitrary, it is for local (program) reference only and can be anywhere on the screen (or even off the screen, if you desire).

Each point rotated, however, is now referenced in terms of an X and Y offset from this 0,0 coordinate. If the center point is located at screen coordinates 100,145 and the point to be rotated is at screen coordinates 50,175, then the rotation coordinates will be 50,30 (note: by convention, the x-axis coordinate is always given first and, the first coordinate is always the x-axis).

In Chapter 10, left-right and mirror image transformations were made quite simply by changing the sign of the offset (relative to a new center coordinate). True rotation, however, can not be accomplished this easily and requires something other than the x,y coordinate system.

To rotate a point, the point's x,y coordinates must first be converted to a polar vector. A vector consists of two values: an angle and a length and, for these purposes, the angle will always be in the range $0..2*PI$ ($0..360°$) and the length (magnitude) will always be a positive value. Negative vector angles and angles greater than $2*PI$ are possible and valid, as are negative vector magnitudes but, since these can always be normalized without loss of information, only normalized vectors are used in these calculations (besides, it's easier).

Note: since engineers were among the principal earlier users of computers — bless their little tinker-toy hearts — to prefer radian angles to degree/minute/second angles, computer trig functions commonly use angles expressed in radians instead of degrees.

Figure 12-1: Sine/Cosine Angle Values

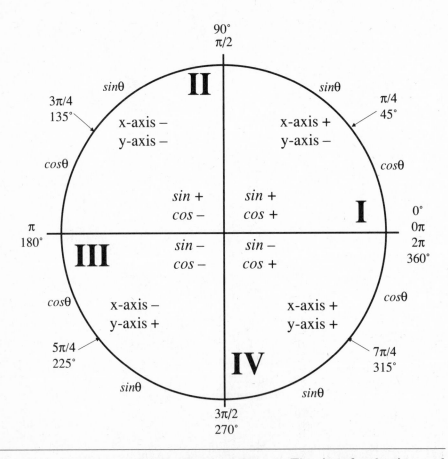

Angle values are shown both in radians and degrees. The signs for the sines and cosines of angles in each quadrant are shown for normal polar coordinates, while the x- and y-axis signs are shown for the screen coordinate system.

Both systems begin with a zero angle, 180° equals PI radians and 360° equals 2*PI radians and other angles are commonly expressed either as decimal radians or as radian fractions — see Figure 12-1.

Now back to calculating a polar (vector) coordinate from the screen position coordinates.

To get the vector magnitude (*HypLen*), C's **hypot** function is ready made:

```
HypLen = hypot ( X0, Y0);
```

And the **atan2** function very conveniently transforms the x,y coordinates into a vector angle — with one exception, an x-offset value of 0.

```
if( abs(X0) > ) O_Angle = atan2( (–1 * Y00, X0 );
```

Before covering the exception, however, there is another point to discuss.

Notice the –1 in the formula above? The value for *Y0* is precisely opposite in sign to what the **atan2** (or **atan**) functions expect. This is because (see Figure 12-1) the normal math functions treat positive values as 1st Quadrant points (i.e.– a positive value for *Y0* is expected to be above the 0,0 coordinate — as if the screen 0,0 point was at the bottom left corner of the screen).

Since this is a screen coordinate system, however, a positive vertical **value** is down and negative is up — therefore, *Y0* is multiplied by –1 to change its sign before the angle is calculated (this discrepancy between normal and screen coordinates will appear again in these calculations).

The **atan2** function is used rather than the **atan** function because the **atan** function is limited to angles in the range *–PI/2..PI/2* and requires large values for the x parameter involved. The **atan2** function returns values in the range *–PI..PI* and is accurate when the x parameter approaches 0 ... but not helpful when the x parameter equals zero (and the angles could be *PI/2* or *–PI/2*).

If the value of *X0* is zero, then the *Y0* parameter is used to determine the angle:

```
else if( Y0 < 0 )    O_Angle = PI/2;
else                 O_Angle = 3*PI/2;  { equals –PI/2 }
```

Now, because **atan2** returns the angle in radians in the range *–PI..PI*, the resulting *O_Angle* is normalized for convenience (remember, PI radians = 180°).

```
if( O_Angle < 0) O_Angle += 2*PI;
```

The x,y coordinates have been converted to a vector angle and magnitude (size, length, distance) that can be rotated. Rotation becomes a simple matter of adding the rotation angle to the vector angle (or subtracting the rotation angle, but here rotation has been limited to the counterclockwise direction). That's it, the vector has been rotated.

This has been the easy part — the vector must be restored to x,y coordinates before it can be used — which is the whole point of doing this. What remains, seems hard, but only requires a bit of care and explanation.

Again, please refer to Figure 12-1. Original angle and the rotation angle have already been summed together as *R_Angle*. If the value of *R_Angle* lies in the range *PI/2..3*PI/2*, then the vector is in the 2nd or 3rd quadrants and sign of X will be negative. (*Sign_X* and *Sign_Y* were initialized as +1.)

```
if( ( R_Angle > PI/2 ) & ( R_Angle <= 3*PI/2 ) ) Sign_X = –1;
```

Likewise, if the value of *R_Angle* lies in the range *0..PI*, the vector angle is in the 1st or 2nd quadrants and the sign of Y will be negative (in the screen coordinate system — which is the only one that counts here).

```
if( ( R_Angle > 0 ) & ( R_Angle <= PI ) ) Sign_Y = –1;
```

Normally, the sign of the sine (no, this is not a pun, simply an inescapable example of English homophones) of the angle would determine the sign of X. The sign of the cosine of the angle would determine the sign of Y — except that, first, in the screen coordinate system, this would be correct for X and invalid for Y and; second, the x,y results are going to be calculated in a slightly different manner.

If the angle lies in the range *PI/4..3*PI/4* or in the range *5*PI/4..7*PI/4*, then the x-axis value (*X0*) will be calculated using the cosine of the angle and the y-axis value will be calculated as the square root of the difference of the squares of the remaining sides (Pythagorean Theorem).

```
if( ( ( R_Angle >=  PI/4 ) & ( R_Angle <= 3*PI/4 ) ) |
   ( ( R_Angle >= 5*PI/4 ) & ( R_Angle <= 7*PI/4 ) ) )
{
        X0 = HypLen * cos( R_Angle );
        Y0 = sqrt( pow( HypLen, 2 ) – pow( X0, 2 ) );
}
```

Otherwise, the same calculations are carried out, but using the sine of the angle to find the y-axis value and Pythagoras' rule for the x-axis.

```
else
{
        Y0 = HypLen * sin( R_Angle );
        X0 = sqrt( pow( HypLen, 2 ) – pow( Y0, 2 ) );
}
```

The reason for this is accuracy. By using the **sin** and **cos** only within the angle ranges where they yield the greatest accuracy (using **sin** where the y-axis value is greater than the x-axis value and cos where the x-axis value is greater) and calculating the remaining value using the Pythagorean Theorem, the resulting position coordinates are as accurate as possible and the image rotation smoother. This is also why the local variables, $X0$ and $Y0$, are **double** rather than **integer** values.

Notice also the italicized $sin\theta$ and $cos\theta$ in Figure 12-1 show the ranges where each function yields the greater accuracy.

Now, because either the x or y value was calculated using the square root function, one of these is a positive value. (Since the square root of a number could be either positive or negative, **sqrt** always returns a positive value.) If only the **sin** and **cos** functions had been used, then the y-axis value could simply be inverted (multiplied by -1) to correct it for the screen coordinate system. This was not the case.

Instead, the absolute values of both *X0* and *Y0* are multiplied by the sign values determined earlier, then returned as screen coordinate integers.

```
*X_Off = abs( X0 ) * Sign_X;
*Y_Off = abs( Y0 ) * Sign_Y;
```

If this is confusing, please refer to the text and to Figure 12-1, remembering that the coordinate values used are screen coordinates, that the y-axis values are negative toward the top of the screen and that the angle increases in the counterclockwise direction. It really isn't a matter of difficulty, but of careful calculations and making allowance for the differences between the Cartesian coordinate system and the screen coordinate system.

And Other Image Rotation Options

When the direct image rotation was demonstrated, each pixel was tested and the background pixels ignored. Further selective rotation could be applied, however, and different color values rotated separately by different angles or in different directions.

Further, since in EGA/VGA modes the same color hues can be assigned to different palette entries and rotation made on the basis of the palette entry rather than the actual hue, it becomes practical to rotate one part of an image while leaving another portion — apparently the same color — unaffected.

Including Text Rotations

Earlier, in discussion of graphics text options, I pointed out the fact that only two text orientations were supported. Using the direct image rotation possibilities, even upside-down text becomes possible and, with care, some other text angles are practical (though not as convenient) as the directly supported text presentations.

Finally, these are tools for your usage — develop and employ them as you see fit. The possibilities, if not endless, are certainly vast and a bit of imagination could suggest a variety of options.

```
/*                    FILE_IMG.C — Saving an image as a data file                    */

#ifdef __TINY__
#error Graphics demos will not run in the tiny model.
#endif

#include <conio.h>
#include <stdio.h>
#include <stdlib.h>
#include <stdarg.h>
#include <graphics.h>
#include "gprint.i"

int       GraphDriver;
int       GraphMode;
double    AspectRatio;
int       xasp, yasp;
int       MaxColors;
int       ErrorCode = 0;
void      *Flash, *Flash2;

void Pause()
{
      while( kbhit() ) getch();
      getch();
}

void Initialize()
{
      GraphDriver = DETECT;
      initgraph( &GraphDriver, &GraphMode, "" );
      ErrorCode = graphresult();
      if ( ErrorCode != grOk )
      {
          printf(" Graphics System Error: %s\n",
                  grapherrormsg( ErrorCode ) );
          exit  ( 1 );
```

```
    }
    MaxColors = getmaxcolor() + 1;
    getaspectratio( &xasp, &yasp );
    AspectRatio = (double)xasp / (double)yasp;
}

void *SaveImage( int left, int top, int right, int bottom, unsigned *size )
{
    void  *image;

    *size = imagesize( left, top, right, bottom );
    image = malloc( *size );
    getimage( left, top, right, bottom, image );
    putimage( left, top, image, XOR_PUT );
    return( image );
}

void FileImage( void *image, unsigned size, char *filename )
{
    FILE  *f1 = fopen( filename, "w" );

    fwrite( image, size, 1, f1 );
    fflush( f1 );
    fclose( f1 );
}

void *ReadImage( char *filename )
{
    unsigned xsize, ysize, size;
    FILE   *f1 = fopen( filename, "r" );
    void   *tempimage;

    xsize = fgetc( f1 ) | (fgetc( f1 ) << 8);
    ysize = fgetc( f1 ) | (fgetc( f1 ) << 8);
    size = imagesize( 0, 0, xsize, ysize );
    gprintxy( 10, 10, " xsize = %d, ysize = %d, imagesize = %d ",
                            xsize,        ysize,          size );
```

```
        tempimage = malloc( size );
        rewind( f1 );
        fread( tempimage, size, 1, f1 );
        fclose( f1 );
        return( tempimage );
    }

void CreateImage()
    {
        int  Size = 0, MaxColor = getmaxcolor();
        int  pflash[] = { 100, 40, 110, 60, 100, 70, 120, 65,
                        140, 80, 130, 60, 140, 50, 120, 55, 100, 40 };

        randomize();
        setcolor( random( MaxColor ) + 1 );
        setfillstyle( random(11) + 1, random ( MaxColor ) + 1 );
        fillpoly( sizeof( pflash )/( 2 * sizeof( int ) ), pflash );
        Flash = SaveImage( 100, 40, 140, 80, &Size );
        FileImage( Flash, Size, "FLASH.IMG" );
        Flash2 = ReadImage( "FLASH.IMG" );
        putimage( 200, 200, Flash2, COPY_PUT );
    }

main()
    {
        Initialize();                    /*    set graphics mode    */
        CreateImage();                   /*    create and save image    */
        Pause();
        free(Flash);
        free(Flash2);
        closegraph();                            /*    restore text mode */
    }
```

```
/*          ROTATE.C — Rotating an image using Turbo-C Graphics          */

#ifdef __TINY__
#error Graphics demos will not run in the tiny model.
#endif

#include <conio.h>
#include <math.h>
#include <stdio.h>
#include <stdlib.h>
#include <stdarg.h>
#include <graphics.h>
#include <gprint.i>

const  double  PI = 3.14159254;

int    GraphDriver;                              /*      graphics device driver   */
int    GraphMode;                                /*      graphics mode value      */
double  AspR;                             /*   aspect ratio for screen pixels     */
int    xasp, yasp;                               /*      factors for aspect ratio */
int    MaxColors;                                /*      maximum colors available */
int    ErrorCode = 0;                     /*      reports any graphics errors      */

void Initialize()                  /*      initialize graphics system and report errors  */
{
    GraphDriver = DETECT;                        /*      request auto-detection    */
    initgraph( &GraphDriver, &GraphMode, "" );
    ErrorCode = graphresult();                   /*      test initialization results */
    if ( ErrorCode != grOk )         /*      if error occurred during init        */
    {
        printf(" Graphics System Error: %s\n",
                    grapherrormsg( ErrorCode ) );
        exit( 1 );
    }
    MaxColors = getmaxcolor() + 1;               /*      read max color range      */
    getaspectratio( &xasp, &yasp );              /*      read video aspect */
    AspR = (double)xasp / (double)yasp;          /*      calculate aspect ratio    */
```

285

```
}

void Pause()
{
    setcolor(WHITE);
    settextjustify( CENTER_TEXT, BOTTOM_TEXT );
    outtextxy( getmaxx()/2, getmaxy(), "press any key ..." );
    while ( kbhit() ) getch();
    getch();
    cleardevice();
}

void Rotate_Point( int *X_Off, int *Y_Off, int degrees )
{
    double  HypLen, R_Angle, O_Angle = 0;
    int     Sign_X = 1,  Sign_Y = 1;
    double  X0 = (double) *X_Off + 0.5,
            Y0 = (double) *Y_Off + 0.5;

    degrees = abs( degrees );           /*      allow positive rotation only     */
    HypLen = hypot( X0, Y0 );           /*          find offset vector distance   */
    if( abs(X0) > 0 ) O_Angle = atan2( (–1 * Y0), X0 );
        else if( Y0 < 0 )  O_Angle = PI/2;
        else     O_Angle = 3*PI/2;      /*        get angle in radians      */
    if( O_Angle < 0) O_Angle += 2*PI;   /*      positive angles only       */
    R_Angle = (double) degrees / 180 * PI;  /*          convert to radians*/
    R_Angle += O_Angle;                 /*       add original angle         */
    if( R_Angle > 2*PI ) R_Angle –= 2*PI;   /*         test range < 2*PI */

    if( ( R_Angle > PI/2 ) &            /*2nd or 3rd quadrant = –X        */
        ( R_Angle <= 3*PI/2 ) ) Sign_X = –1;
    if( ( R_Angle > 0 ) &               /*1st or 2nd quadrant = –Y*/
        ( R_Angle <= PI ) ) Sign_Y = –1;
    if( ( ( R_Angle >=  PI/4 ) & ( R_Angle <= 3*PI/4 ) ) |
        ( ( R_Angle >= 5*PI/4 ) & ( R_Angle <= 7*PI/4 ) ) )
    {
        X0 = HypLen * cos( R_Angle );
```

```
        Y0 = sqrt( pow( HypLen, 2 ) – pow( X0, 2 ) );
    }    else
    {
        Y0 = HypLen * sin( R_Angle );
        X0 = sqrt( pow( HypLen, 2 ) – pow( Y0, 2 ) );
    }
    *X_Off = abs( X0 ) * Sign_X;               /*    return rotated position   */
    *Y_Off = abs( Y0 ) * Sign_Y;               /*    with the appropriate sign */
}

void Adj_Rotate_Point( int *X_Off, int *Y_Off, int degrees )
{
    int    X0 = *X_Off;
    int    Y0 = *Y_Off / AspR;           /*    normalize aspect and rotate   */

    Rotate_Point( &X0, &Y0, degrees );
    *X_Off = X0;                         /*    return rotated position   */
    *Y_Off = Y0 * AspR;                  /*    with aspect ratio restored */
}

void Rotate_Line(   int x,  int y,  int degrees,
                    int x1, int y1, int x2, int y2 )
{
    x1 –= x;  y1 –= y;                    /*    convert coordinates relative  */
    x2 –= x;  y2 –= y;                    /*    to center of rotation         */
    Rotate_Point( &x1, &y1, degrees );
    Rotate_Point( &x2, &y2, degrees );
    line( x+x1, y+y1, x+x2, y+y2 );
}

void Adj_Rotate_Line(   int x,  int y,  int degrees,
                        int x1, int y1, int x2, int y2 )
{
    x1 –= x;  y1 –= y;                    /*    convert coordinates relative  */
    x2 –= x;  y2 –= y;                    /*    to center of rotation         */
    Adj_Rotate_Point( &x1, &y1, degrees );
    Adj_Rotate_Point( &x2, &y2, degrees );
```

287

```
        line( x+x1, y+y1, x+x2, y+y2 );
}

void Show_Rotation(int degrees)
{
        int  i, j, x, y, Point, radius = 50;

        settextjustify( CENTER_TEXT, TOP_TEXT );
        outtextxy( 320, 10, "Original");
        x = 320;
        y = 100;
        circle( x, y, radius );                        /*      in the original, the    */
        line( x–radius, y+radius*AspR,                 /*      arrow is drawn at 45     */
              x+radius, y–radius*AspR );               /*      degrees using cor–       */
        line( x+radius, y–radius*AspR,                 /*      rections for screen      */
              x+radius, y–(radius–20)*AspR );          /*          aspect ratio         */
        line( x+radius, y–radius*AspR,
              x+radius–20, y–radius*AspR );
        setcolor(RED);
        x = 160;
        circle( x, y, radius );                        /*      circle for reference     */
        setcolor(GREEN);
        x = 480;
        circle( x, y, radius );                        /*      circle for reference     */
        setcolor(WHITE);
        x = 160; y = 30;
        gprintf( &x, &y, "Figure rotated %d degrees", degrees);
        gprintf( &x, &y, "without aspect correction");
        x = 480; y = 30;
        gprintf( &x, &y, "Figure rotated %d degrees", degrees);
        gprintf( &x, &y, "using aspect correction");
        for( i=–50; i<=50; i++ )
            for( j=–50; j<=50; j++ )
            {
                Point = getpixel( 320+i, 100+j );
                if( Point > 0 )
```

```
        {
            x = i;
            y = j;
            Rotate_Point( &x, &y, degrees );
            putpixel( 160+x, 100+y, Point );
            x = i;
            y = j;
            Adj_Rotate_Point( &x, &y, degrees );
            putpixel( 480+x, 100+y, Point );
    }   }
x = 160; y = 180;
gprintf( &x, &y, "Coordinates rotated %d degrees", degrees);
gprintf( &x, &y, "without aspect correction");
x = 480; y = 180;
gprintf( &x, &y, "Coordinates rotated %d degrees", degrees);
gprintf( &x, &y, "using aspect correction");
setcolor(RED);
x = 160;  y = 250;
circle( x, y, radius );
Rotate_Line( x, y, degrees,
            x–radius, y+radius*AspR,
            x+radius, y–radius*AspR );
Rotate_Line( x, y, degrees,
            x+radius, y–radius*AspR,
            x+radius, y–(radius–20)*AspR );
Rotate_Line( x, y, degrees,
            x+radius, y–radius*AspR,
            x+radius–20, y–radius*AspR );
setcolor(GREEN);
x = 480;  y = 250;
circle( x, y, radius );
Adj_Rotate_Line( x, y, degrees,
            x–radius, y+radius*AspR,
            x+radius, y–radius*AspR );
Adj_Rotate_Line( x, y, degrees,
            x+radius, y–radius*AspR,
```

```
                            x+radius, y–(radius–20)*AspR );
        Adj_Rotate_Line(    x, y, degrees,
                            8 x+radius,   y–radius*AspR,
                            x+radius–20, y–radius*AspR );
}

main()
{
    Initialize();
    Show_Rotation( 90 );
    Pause();
    closegraph();
}
```

CHAPTER 13

COLORS AND COLOR SELECTION

This chapter is concerned primarily with colors and color selections in EGA/VGA modes and, secondarily with CGA and Monochrome systems.

This restriction is not intended as a put down of CGA or Monochrome video modes, but is simply a recognition of the fact that CGA systems have limited color capabilities and Monochrome systems have effectively none. Relatively little remains to be said concerning either of these (but see also **Grey-Scale Plotting** in Chapter 14).

Video Signal Cues

On Monochrome systems, graphic video output is limited to two bits of information per pixel: a video on/off and an intensity bit (see Table 13-1).

Table 13-1: System Video Attributes

BIT #	MONOCHROME	COLOR RGBI	COLOR EGA
0		Blue	Primary **B**lue
1		Green	Primary **G**reen
2		Red	Primary **R**ed
3	Video		secondary **b**lue
4	Intensity	Intensity	secondary **g**reen
5			secondary **r**ed

On CGA systems, the **RGBI** (**R**ed, **G**reen, **B**lue and **I**ntensity) color system is used with four bits of information per graphics pixel, but combinations are limited to four, predefined palettes of three colors plus background color (as shown in Table 13-3). The background color in each palette is BLACK by default, but can be selected from the entire range of 16 colors shown in Table 13-2.

Table 13-2: CGA Color Values

COLOR VALUES		4-BIT	COLOR	CONSTANT/
DEC	HEX	BINARY	COMPONENTS	COLOR NAME
0	0	0000	. . . .	BLACK
1	1	0001	. . . B	BLUE
2	2	0010	. . G .	GREEN
3	3	0011	. . G B	CYAN
4	4	0100	. R . .	RED
5	5	0101	. R . B	MAGENTA
6	6	0110	. R G .	BROWN
7	7	0111	. R G B	LIGHTGREY
8	8	1000	I . . .	DARKGREY
9	9	1001	I . . B	LIGHTBLUE
10	A	1010	I . G .	LIGHTGREEN
11	B	1011	I . G B	LIGHTCYAN
12	C	1100	I R . .	LIGHTRED
13	D	1101	I R . B	LIGHTMAGENTA
14	E	1110	I R G .	YELLOW
15	F	1111	I R G B	WHITE

On EGA/VGA systems, the **RrGgBb** color system uses six bits of information per pixel for a total of 64 colors/hues. The default colors for this palette are shown in Table 13-4.

CGA Colors

For CGA systems, 16 possible colors are supported, as shown in Table 13-2. In text modes, any of these colors can be selected as foreground color, though

COLORS AND COLOR SELECTION

only the first eight colors are valid as background. Using Turbo C graphics, the AT&T driver, modes ATT400C0..ATT400C3 and the MCGA driver, modes MCGAC0..MCGAC3, operate in the same fashion as CGA modes, CGAC0..CGAC3. Similarly, color operation in the CGAHI mode is duplicated by the MCGAMED, MCGAHI, ATT400MED and ATT400HI modes.

As shown in Table 13-2, each color is defined by four register bits controlling the red, green and blue hues and an intensity control. Each hue (color gun) has two settings: low and high intensity. When the Intensity bit is TRUE (ON), all color guns are set high. If Intensity is FALSE, all color guns respond as low.

Table 13-3: CGA Color Palette

PALETTE NUMBER 0 (CGAC0)

PALETTE COLOR	HEX	4-BIT BINARY	COLOR COMPONENTS	CONSTANT/ COLOR NAME
0	0	0000	. . . .	BLACK
1	A	1010	I . G .	LIGHTGREEN
2	C	1100	I R . .	LIGHTRED
3	E	1110	I R G .	YELLOW

PALETTE NUMBER 1 (CGAC1)

PALETTE COLOR	HEX	4-BIT BINARY	COLOR COMPONENTS	CONSTANT/ COLOR NAME
0	0	0000	. . . .	BLACK
1	B	1011	I . G B	LIGHTCYAN
2	D	1101	I R . B	LIGHTMAGENTA
3	F	1111	I R G B	WHITE

Table 13-3: continued

PALETTE NUMBER 2 (CGAC2)

PALETTE COLOR	HEX	4-BIT BINARY	COLOR COMPONENTS	CONSTANT/ COLOR NAME
0	0	0000	. . . .	BLACK
1	2	0010	. . G .	GREEN
2	4	0100	. R . .	RED
3	6	0110	. R G .	BROWN

PALETTE NUMBER 3 (CGAC3)

PALETTE COLOR	HEX	4-BIT BINARY	COLOR COMPONENTS	CONSTANT/ COLOR NAME
0	0	0000	. . . .	BLACK
1	3	0011	. . G B	CYAN
2	5	0101	. R . B	MAGENTA
3	7	0111	. R G B	LIGHTGREY

Thus BLUE is generated by turning on the Blue gun at low intensity; LIGHTBLUE also turns on the Blue gun but, because of the Intensity flag, is turned on high and produces a brighter color. In the same fashion, turning on both the Green and Blue guns produces CYAN; adding the Intensity signal produces LIGHTCYAN.

For a minor oddity, notice that enabling the Intensity signal alone (with the Red, Green and Blue guns off), still produces a response from all three of the color guns, though their output is very low, and the result is DARKGREY. You might consider this a 'bug' that has been turned into a 'feature' — and, in all probability, may have originated in exactly this fashion.

In graphics modes, the CGA system supports multiple colors only in the four low resolution, 320x200 pixel modes (C0, C1, C2 and C3). Each of these modes selects one of the predefined 4-color palettes shown in Table 13-3.

By default, the background color in each palette is BLACK but may be changed to any of the 16 CGA colors (see Table 13-2) using the **setbkcolor** function. The **setpalette** and **setallpalette** functions — used in EGA/VGA modes to change palette colors — are not applicable in CGA modes. There is, however, one exception: the function **setpalette(palette_index, color)** can be used with a *palette_index* of zero (background) as an alternative to the **setbkcolor** function.

Note: the CGA colors BLUE (value 1), DARKGREY (value 8) and LIGHTBLUE (value 9) do not appear in any of the defined palettes. These can, of course, be used as background colors.

CGA High Resolution

In any of the high resolution modes (CGAHI, MCGAMED or ATT400MED at 640x200 pixels, MCGAHI at 640x480 pixels or ATT400HI at 640x400 pixels), two colors are supported: a black background and a color foreground. The foreground color is selected from the 16 CGA colors using the **setbkcolor** function.

NO, this is not an error — due to a quirk in the CGA hardware, the **setbkcolor** function is used to select the CGAHI foreground color. The background color remains black.

All pixels with a value of 1 are displayed in the foreground color, pixels with a value of 0 remain black.

The IBM8514 and VGA Video Adapters

At the other extreme, the highest color resolution is provided by the IBM-8514 video card and the IBM8514 mode or by the VGA video card using the VGA256.BGI driver (see Appendix E), both of which are supported by the **setrgbpalette** function.

The **setrgbpalette** function allows custom color definition for a palette of 256 colors. To maintain compatibility, however, with other video adapters, the first 16 palette entries are predefined by the .BGI drivers to correspond to the default EGA/VGA color palette entries.

All 256 palette entries (numbered 0..255) can be individually defined by three integer color arguments: red, green and blue. While the arguments passed to the **setrgbpalette** function are integer values, only the six most-significant bits of the lower (LSB) byte are actually used to set the palette color value (values from 0 to 252 in steps of four, i.e.– arguments of 252, 253, 254 and 255 are treated identically since the six most-significant bits are the same and only the two most-significant bits differ).

Table 13-4: EGA/VGA Default Palette

PALETTE REGISTER	HEX	6-BIT	BINARY	COLOR COMPONENTS	CONSTANT/COLOR NAME
0	0	000	000	. . . . . .	EGA_BLACK
1	1	000	001	. . . . . B	EGA_BLUE
2	2	000	010	. . . . G .	EGA_GREEN
3	3	000	011	. . . . G B	EGA_CYAN
4	4	000	100	. . . R . .	EGA_RED
5	5	000	101	. . . R . B	EGA_MAGENTA
6	14	010	100	. g . R . .	EGA_BROWN
7	7	000	111	. . . R G B	EGA_LIGHTGREY
8	38	111	000	r g b . . .	EGA_DARKGREY
9	39	111	001	r g b . . B	EGA_LIGHTBLUE
A	3A	111	010	r g b . G .	EGA_LIGHTGREEN
B	3B	111	011	r g b . G B	EGA_LIGHTCYAN
C	3C	111	100	r g b R . .	EGA_LIGHTRED
D	3D	111	101	r g b R . B	EGA_LIGHTMAGENTA
E	3E	111	110	r g b R G .	EGA_YELLOW
F	3F	111	111	r g b R G B	EGA_WHITE

EGA/VGA Color

EGA/VGA video modes offer a palette of 16 colors selected from a spectrum of 64 possible hues. In actual fact, VGA systems are capable of wider color ranges, having 256 color registers and 256K possible hues. When using Turbo C procedures, they are effectively limited to the EGA color range, though they still support the higher resolutions. For information on developing special handling for VGA color systems, see Appendix E — The VGA256.BGI Driver.

For the present, the topic is restricted to color handling within the capabilities of Turbo C and restricted to the EGA color range of 64 hues.

The EGA/VGA modes also begin with a default palette of 16 hues. Unlike the CGA color system using 4-bit colors, each EGA/VGA color is defined by a 6-bit value. This is commonly called an **RrGgBb** color system.

The **RrGgBb** color system provides two flags (and two signals) for each of the three color guns: a primary **R**ed and secondary **r**ed, a primary **B**lue and secondary **b**lue and a primary **G**reen and secondary **g**reen. (By custom, the primary color is capitalized and the secondary is in lowercase.)

If you prefer, you can think of the **RrGgBb** system as analogous to the **RBGI** system except that the secondary colors act as individual intensity flags for each of the primary color guns.

Just as DARKGREY was created in CGA by turning on the Intensity flag but leaving off all of the color flags, EGA_DARKGREY turns on the **rgb** (intensity) flags while leaving the **RGB** (primary) color guns turned off. On the other hand, where the CGA system created BROWN by mixing the Red and Green guns, EGA_BROWN is created by mixing the Red color gun with the green intensity flag — effectively by mixing Red with a very low Green to produce a deeper Brown.

And, aside from the EGA_BROWN, the default palette colors for EGA/VGA are the same as the CGA colors except that three intensity signals (**rgb**) are used in place of a single intensity flag — gang-controlling all three color guns.

A Wider Range Of Hues

One of the advantages of EGA/VGA, in addition to being able to use 16 colors in high resolution modes, is being able to select your palette from 64 separate hues.

Table 13-5: EGA Yellows

DEC	COLOR VALUES HEX	6-BIT BINARY	SECONDARY AND PRIMARY COMPONENTS	
06	06h	000 110	. . .	R G .
14	0Eh	001 110	. . b	R G .
18	12h	010 010	. g .	. G .
22	16h	010 110	. g .	R G .
26	1Ah	011 010	. g b	. G .
30	1Eh	011 110	. g b	R G .
38	26h	100 110	r . .	R G .
46	2Eh	101 110	r . b	R G .
54	36h	110 110	r g .	R G .
55	37h	110 111	r g .	R G B
62	3Eh	111 110	r g b	R G .

To be perfectly frank, some of these 64 colors are not particularly appealing and the precise tone of a particular hue is subject to the color balance adjustments on the monitor used — but beauty is, as always, in the eye and monitor of the beholder.

For an example of the range of color, Table 13-5 shows 11 varieties of 'yellow', ranging from a color value of 06 which matches the CGA BROWN to a color value of 62 which corresponds to EGA_YELLOW.

Looking at the color components shown in Table 13-5, you will notice all of the yellows include Green and, with two exceptions, blend Red. In one case, color value 18, the color is actually high intensity Green — but, depending on the surrounding colors and background, this may be recognized as either Yellow, Green or Chartreuse. The precise recognition and label applied to any color is largely a matter of subjective perception.

Manipulating Color/Hue

In the EGA/VGA color system, specific color values can be created by manipulating the combinations of primary and secondary flags for each color gun. Effectively, each of the three color guns has four settings — completely off, low intensity (color off, intensity on), normal (color on, intensity off) and high (color on, intensity on) — for a total of 4^3 or 64 colors.

And, if you need to manipulate colors directly, these bit-values can be set directly to build a specific color value, then assign the created value to the EGA/VGA palette.

For example, suppose that you need three 'pure' greens. Bit 1 controls the Green color gun (bit 0, at the right, is blue) and bit 4 is the Green intensity flag, so the three pure greens — in order of intensity — would be 16 (010 000 or .g. . . .), 2 (000 010 or . . . .G.) and 18 (010 010 or .g. .G.).

The first green (color value 16) is a dark green, appearing almost khaki against some backgrounds. The second (color value 2) is a fairly pure green and corresponds to EGA_GREEN, while the third green (color value 18) is a bright or chartreuse green and, depending on surroundings, appears almost yellow (and, if you noticed, is also included in the yellows in Table 13-5).

But there is another green that does not appear among these possibilities. This fourth green is EGA_LIGHTGREEN, color value 58 (111 010 or **rgb** .G.). In this case, the **rgb** produces DARKGREY (which — since we're working with light emission and not color absorption/reflection — is also soft white). The dark grey is added to the Green color gun for a lighter green without overbalancing into chartreuse.

To show some of these relationships and to provide a convenient method of examining the variety of possible colors, two demo programs, **COLCUBE.C** and **COLORS.C,** are provided.

Please note: both of these demo programs will operate only on EGA/VGA capable systems. No provision has been made to adapt these two programs for CGA system, they are for high resolution color systems only.

The Color Relations Cube

The **COLCUBE.C** program uses the default color palette to create a doubled cube showing the relationships between the primary and secondary colors.

The physical spectrum, as seen in the rainbow or displayed by a prism, begins with Red, proceeding to Orange, Yellow, Green, Blue and ending with Violet. But, to create our computer color spectrum, we have only the Red, Green and Blue colors to work with. These three primary colors are, however, the three that the eye best perceives and, by combining these as light, the eye perceives colors that are not actually present.

In the case of a TV signal, these same three colors are used to generate everything from subtle ranges of flesh tones to the intense flashing headlines favored by automobile dealers on late-night movie ads. The TV, using analog signals, is able to offer finer gradations and combinations of primary colors than the computer which, in EGA/VGA mode, is limited to four values.

Notice the figure created by **COLCUBE.C** (see Figure 13-1) has four main axes: red, green, blue and white (or intensity). The human retina has three types of color receptors believed to correspond to these three primary colors. However, color perception is not limited simply to recognition of these three values but also to the relative intensity of each and the balance between these.

A balanced combination of all three colors is perceived as grey or white, depending on overall intensity (see Chapter 14 — **Colors and Grey-Scales**).

As mentioned previously, how colors are perceived is affected by other colors surrounding them and **COLCUBE** shows this effect by swapping the

Figure 13-1: Color Cube

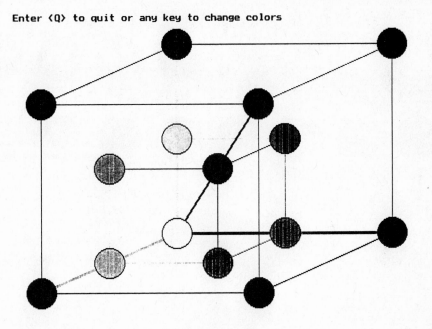

The graphics image was created by COLORCUB.C on an EGA screen, then downloaded to a laserjet printer in GREYSCALE mode using the LJ-GRAPH utility demonstrated in Chapter 14.

Figure 13-2: Colors Demo

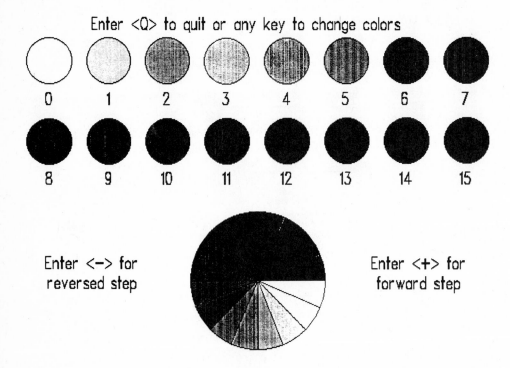

The graph was created in color on an EGA screen, then downloaded to a laserjet printer in GREYSCALE mode using the LJ-GRAPH utility demonstrated in Chapter 14.

EGA_BLACK and EGA_WHITE colors between palette color 0 (background) and palette color 15.

The COLORS.C Demo

The **COLORS.C** demo (see Figure 13-2) is pretty simple overall, beginning with three global variables: *radius* which sets the size for the display circles, *StepForward* which is used as a Boolean flag to determine whether the colors are incremented or decremented and *palette* which is the color palette structure. The structure type *palettetype* is defined in GRAPHICS.H.

```
int        radius = 30;
int        StepForward = 1;
           struct palettetype palette;
```

The **main** procedure starts the graphics system using the same **Initialize** procedure as virtually all of the other programs in this book. If you haven't figured out how **Initialize** works by this point, there's little point in offering another description of the setup procedures at this time.

The **settextjustify** and **settextstyle** procedures pick a font and text justification for the screen display, then write the appropriate messages to the screen.

```
main()
{
        Initialize();
        settextjustify( CENTER_TEXT, CENTER_TEXT );
        settextstyle( SANS_SERIF_FONT, HORIZ_DIR, 1 );
        outtextxy( 320, 10, "Enter <Q> to quit or any key to change colors " );
        outtextxy( 100, 250, "Enter <–> for" );
        outtextxy( 100, 270, "reversed step" );
        outtextxy( 540, 250, "Enter <+> for" );
        outtextxy( 540, 270, "forward step" );
```

Next, a special palette is created by the **Initialize_Colors** procedure. **Show_Colors** writes 16 colored circles in two rows, **Color_Wheel** creates a pie chart with the same 16 colors and, with the screen set up and drawn, **Step_Colors** is ready to show you through the 64 EGA/VGA color values.

```
Initialize_Colors();
Show_Colors();
Color_Wheel();
Step_Colors();
closegraph();
}
```

In the **Initialize_Colors** procedure, instead of using the default EGA/VGA palette colors, the palette entries are reset to color values 0..15 — the first 16 colors. The **setpalette** function assigns the unsigned integer values to the index elements in the *palette* structure.

```
void Initialize_Colors()
{
        int  i;
        for( i=0; i<=15; i++ ) setpalette( i, i );
}
```

The **Show_Colors** procedure uses a single loop from 0 through 7 to draw 16 circles in two rows across the top portion of the screen.

```
void Show_Colors()
{
        int  i;
        for( i=0; i<=7; i++ )
{
```

The first row of circles use the first eight palette colors: (*palette.color[0]..palette.color[7]*). At the moment, these are also the first eight possible color values, but it is the palette entry value that is assigned to the screen pixels, not the color value contained by each palette entry.

```
setfillstyle( SOLID_FILL, i );
circle( 80*i+40, 50, radius );
floodfill( 80*i+40, 50, getcolor() );
```

The **Label_Colors** function labels each colored circle with the color value — not the palette item number.

```
          Label_Colors( i );
```

The second row of circles takes the second set of palette item assignments (*palette.color[8]..palette.color[15]*).

```
          setfillstyle( SOLID_FILL, i+8 );
          circle( 80*i+40, 130, radius );
          floodfill( 80*i+40, 130, getcolor() );
          Label_Colors( i+8 );
       }
    }
```

The **Label_Colors** procedure is called with one argument specifying the palette entry number, then reads the value in *palette.colors[i]* and writes this value on the screen next to the colored circle. While the rest of the screen will not be rewritten as colors change, the labels for the specific color values are rewritten each time a palette entry is changed.

```
void Label_Colors( int i )
{
       if( i > 7 )gprintxy( 80*i–600, 135+radius, " %d ", palette.colors[i] );
       else gprintxy( 80*i+40,  55+radius, " %d ", palette.colors[i] );
}
```

The **Color_Wheel** function draws a second display in the form a of pie graph that has 16 slices filled with the 16 palette colors.

```
void Color_Wheel()
{
       int  i;
       for( i=0; i<=15; i++ )
       {
              setfillstyle( SOLID_FILL, 15–i );
```

```
            pieslice( 320, 270, i*22.5, (i+1)*22.5, radius*3 );
        }
    }
```

And the last element in this demo is the **Step_Colors** procedure.

```
void Step_Colors()
{
        int  i, this_color, Done = 0;
        char Ch;
```

The *Done* variable was initialized as 0 (False), setting up a loop condition that will continue until *Done* becomes non-zero. Until then, **Step_Colors** waits for a keyboard entry.

An entry of 'Q' or 'q' increments *Done* to allow an exit; an entry of '−' or '+' selects a direction for the colors to change.

```
    while( !Done )
    {
        Ch = getch();
        if( (toupper(Ch) == 'Q') ) Done++;
        if( Ch == '−' ) StepForward = 0;
        if( Ch == '+' ) StepForward = 1;
        if( !Done )
        {
```

Any keyboard entry which has not set the exit condition allows a second loop to increment or decrement the current palette color values. The loop steps through the 16 palette entries with *this_color* taking the value of each palette entry (*palette.colors[i]*) in turn, then *this_color* is incremented or decremented as appropriate with a final test to insure that the resulting color value remains within the range 0..63.

```
            for( i=0; i<=15; i++ )
            {
                this_color = palette.colors[i];
                if( StepForward ) this_color++;
                else              this_color− −;
```

```
if( this_color < 0 )   this_color = 63;
if( this_color > 63 ) this_color = 0;
```

Finally, **setpalette** sets *palette.colors[i]* to the new color value, **getpalette** updates the *palette* record, **Label_Colors** updates the screen label and a delay of 30 milliseconds is executed before the loop continues.

```
setpalette( i, this_color );
getpalette( &palette );
Label_Colors( i );
delay(30);
        }
    }
}
}
```

When you run this demo, notice the screen colors change *immediately* when a new value is passed to **setpalette**. If you would like to see a more pronounced demonstration of this effect, increase the value in *delay(30);* and add another delay before updating the color label on screen.

Remember: the only action required to change a screen color is to assign a new value to the appropriate palette entry. This action will update the entire screen on the next sweep refresh cycle, regardless of window or viewport settings or which video page is currently active.

This speed of change also allows other effects. For example, you could define several palettes as an array of type palette — for example: *struct palettetype alt_palette[10]* declares an array of 10 alternate palettes numbered 0..9. These alternate color palettes can be used to save any array of colors desired.

```
for(i=0; i<=16; i++)
    palette.colors[i] = alt_palette[ new_palette ].colors[i];
```

The loop can assign any of these as *new_palette* to the active *palette* definition.

Note: Turbo C does not allow the direct assignment of arrays in the form: *palette = alt_palette[new_palette]*. While this assignment will *appear* to work — no error condition occurs and the structure *palette* will contain new values — the screen colors will not change and will continue to use the default palette. Fair warning.

In conclusion, here is a pair of (pun intended) colorful demo programs. Take them apart and play with them for a while. Try a few experiments and see what happens. If nothing else, the results should be interesting.

Also, have a shot at "building" color values as previously described, these results can also be interesting. Also, try using the shift operators (<< and >>) directly on the color values (not on the palette entry numbers). The effects are unusual.

Take a bit of time, relax, play with the color assignments and see what happens. You might find something fascinating or useful — or both.

```
/*            COLORCUB.C — Color Chart for EGA Mode/Palettes          */
#ifdef __TINY__
#error Graphics demos will not run in the tiny model.
#endif

#include <conio.h>
#include <stdio.h>
#include <stdlib.h>
#include <stdarg.h>
#include <graphics.h>
#include "gprint.i"

int   GraphDriver;                              /*      graphics device driver   */
int   GraphMode;                    /*      graphics mode value       */
int   MaxColors;                                /*      maximum colors available */
int   ErrorCode = 0;                /*      reports any graphics errors       */
int   radius = 20;
int   xoff[3] = { 235,  380,  525 };
int   yoff[3] = { 230,  135, 40 };
int   zxoff[3] = {  0,  −90, −180 };
int   zyoff[3] = {  0,   30, 60 };
int   Colors;

void Initialize()                   /*      initialize graphics system and report errors */
{
    GraphDriver = DETECT;                       /*      request auto-detection    */
    initgraph( &GraphDriver, &GraphMode, "" );
    ErrorCode = graphresult();                  /*      test initialization results */
    if ( ErrorCode != grOk )        /*      if error occurred during init       */
    {
        printf(" Graphics System Error: %s\n",
                    grapherrormsg( ErrorCode ) );
        exit( 1 );
    }
}
```

```
void set_circle( int x, int y, int z, int color )
{
    setfillstyle( SOLID_FILL, color );
    setlinestyle( SOLID_LINE, 0, 1 );
    setcolor( EGA_WHITE );
    circle( xoff[x] + zxoff[z], yoff[y] + zyoff[z], radius );
    setcolor( EGA_BLACK );
    circle( xoff[x] + zxoff[z], yoff[y] + zyoff[z], radius / 2 );
    floodfill( xoff[x] + zxoff[z] + 1, yoff[y] + zyoff[z] + 1, EGA_WHITE );
    setcolor( EGA_LIGHTGREY );
}

void cline( int x1, int y1, int z1, int x2, int y2, int z2, int wt )
{
    setlinestyle( SOLID_LINE, 0, wt );
    line( xoff[x1] + zxoff[z1],  yoff[y1] + zyoff[z1],
          xoff[x2] + zxoff[z2],  yoff[y2] + zyoff[z2]  );
}

void Color_Cube()
{
    setcolor(EGA_RED);
    cline( 0, 0, 0, 1, 0, 0, 3 );
    cline( 1, 0, 0, 2, 0, 0, 3 );
    cline( 1, 0, 0, 1, 1, 0, 1 );
    cline( 1, 0, 0, 1, 0, 1, 1 );
    set_circle( 1, 0, 0, EGA_RED );
    setcolor(EGA_BLUE);
    cline( 0, 0, 0, 0, 1, 0, 3 );
    cline( 0, 1, 0, 0, 2, 0, 3 );
    cline( 0, 1, 0, 1, 1, 0, 1 );
    cline( 0, 1, 0, 0, 1, 1, 1 );
    set_circle( 0, 1, 0, EGA_BLUE );
    setcolor(EGA_GREEN);
    cline( 0, 0, 0, 0, 0, 1, 3 );
    cline( 0, 0, 1, 0, 0, 2, 3 );
```

```
    cline( 0, 0, 1, 1, 0, 1, 1 );
    cline( 0, 0, 1, 0, 1, 1, 1 );
    set_circle( 0, 0, 1, EGA_GREEN );
    setcolor(EGA_LIGHTGREY);
    cline( 0, 0, 0, 1, 1, 1, 3 );
    cline( 1, 1, 1, 2, 2, 2, 3 );
    set_circle( 0, 0, 0, EGA_BLACK );
    cline( 0, 1, 1, 1, 1, 1, 1 );
    set_circle( 0, 1, 1, EGA_CYAN );
    cline( 1, 1, 0, 1, 1, 1, 1 );
    set_circle( 1, 1, 0, EGA_MAGENTA );
    cline( 1, 0, 1, 1, 1, 1, 1 );
    set_circle( 1, 0, 1, EGA_BROWN );
    set_circle( 1, 1, 1, EGA_LIGHTGREY );
    setcolor(EGA_LIGHTRED);
    cline( 2, 0, 0, 2, 2, 0, 1 );
    cline( 2, 0, 0, 2, 0, 2, 1 );
    set_circle( 2, 0, 0, EGA_LIGHTRED );
    setcolor(EGA_LIGHTBLUE);
    cline( 0, 2, 0, 0, 2, 2, 1 );
    cline( 0, 2, 0, 2, 2, 0, 1 );
    set_circle( 0, 2, 0, EGA_LIGHTBLUE );
    setcolor(EGA_LIGHTGREEN);
    cline( 0, 0, 2, 2, 0, 2, 1 );
    cline( 0, 0, 2, 0, 2, 2, 1 );
    set_circle( 0, 0, 2, EGA_LIGHTGREEN );
    cline( 2, 2, 0, 2, 2, 2, 1 );
    set_circle( 2, 2, 0, EGA_LIGHTMAGENTA );
    cline( 0, 2, 2, 2, 2, 2, 1 );
    set_circle( 0, 2, 2, EGA_LIGHTCYAN );
    cline( 2, 0, 2, 2, 2, 2, 1 );
    set_circle( 2, 0, 2, EGA_YELLOW );
    set_circle( 2, 2, 2, EGA_WHITE );
}

void Color_Switch()
```

```
    {
        int  Done = 0;
        char Ch;
        while( !Done )
        {
            Ch = getch();
            if( (toupper(Ch) == 'Q') ) Done++;
            if( Colors )
            {
                setpalette( 0, EGA_BLACK );
                setpalette( 15, EGA_WHITE );
                Colors = 0;
            }
            else
            {
                setpalette( 0, EGA_WHITE );
                setpalette( 15, EGA_BLACK );
                Colors = 1;
            }
        }
    }

    main()
    {
        Initialize();
        Colors = 1;
        outtextxy( 10, 10,
                    "Enter <Q> to quit or any key to change colors" );
        Color_Cube();
        Color_Switch();
        closegraph();                           /*      restore text mode */
    }                                           /*      end COLCUBE.C*/
```

```
/*          COLORS.C — Color Chart for EGA/VGA Mode/Palettes           */

#ifdef __TINY__
#error Graphics demos will not run in the tiny model.
#endif

#include <conio.h>
#include <stdio.h>
#include <stdlib.h>
#include <stdarg.h>
#include <graphics.h>
#include "gprint.i"

int  GraphDriver;                              /*      graphics device driver    */
int  GraphMode;                    /*     graphics mode value              */
int  MaxColors;                                /*      maximum colors available */
int  ErrorCode = 0;                  /*     reports any graphics errors      */
int  radius = 30;
int  StepForward = 1;
struct palettetype palette;

void Initialize()                  /*     initialize graphics system and report errors */
{
    GraphDriver = DETECT;                      /*      request auto-detection     */
    initgraph( &GraphDriver, &GraphMode, "" );
    ErrorCode = graphresult();                 /*      test initialization results  */
    if ( ErrorCode != grOk )         /*     if error occurred during init     */
    {
        printf(" Graphics System Error: %s\n",
                    grapherrormsg( ErrorCode ) );
        exit( 1 );
    }
}

void Label_Colors( int i )
{
    if( i > 7 ) gprintxy( 80*i-600, 135+radius, " %d ", palette.colors[i] );
```

```
        else gprintxy( 80*i+40,   55+radius, " %d ", palette.colors[i] );
}

void Show_Colors()
{
      int  i;

      getpalette( &palette );
      for( i=0; i<=7; i++ )
      {
          setfillstyle( SOLID_FILL, i );
          circle( 80*i+40, 50, radius );
          floodfill( 80*i+40, 50, getcolor() );
          Label_Colors( i );
          setfillstyle( SOLID_FILL, i+8 );
          circle( 80*i+40, 130, radius );
          floodfill( 80*i+40, 130, getcolor() );
          Label_Colors( i+8 );
      }
}

void Color_Wheel()
{
      int  i;
      for( i=0; i<=15; i++ )
      {
          setfillstyle( SOLID_FILL, 15–i );
          pieslice( 320, 270, i*22.5, (i+1)*22.5, radius*3 );
      }
}

void Step_Colors()
{
      int  i, Done = 0;
      char Ch;

      while( !Done )
```

```
{
    int      this_color;

    Ch = getch();
    if( (toupper(Ch) == 'Q') ) Done++;
    if( Ch == '−' ) StepForward = 0;
    if( Ch == '+' ) StepForward = 1;
    if( !Done )
    {
        for( i=0; i<=15; i++ )
        {
            this_color = palette.colors[i];
            if( StepForward ) this_color++;
            else              this_color−−;
            if( this_color < 0 ) this_color = 63;
            if( this_color > 63 ) this_color = 0;
            setpalette( i, this_color );
            getpalette( &palette );
            Label_Colors( i );
            delay(30);
        }
    }
}
}

void Initialize_Colors()
{
    int  i;

    for( i=0; i<=15; i++ ) setpalette( i, i );
}

main()
{
    Initialize();
    settextjustify( CENTER_TEXT, CENTER_TEXT );
```

```
        settextstyle( SANS_SERIF_FONT, HORIZ_DIR, 1 );
        outtextxy( 320, 10, "Enter <Q> to quit or any key to change colors " );
        outtextxy( 100, 250, "Enter <-> for" );
        outtextxy( 100, 270, "reversed step" );
        outtextxy( 540, 250, "Enter <+> for" );
        outtextxy( 540, 270, "forward step" );
        Initialize_Colors();
        Show_Colors();
        Color_Wheel();
        Step_Colors();
        closegraph();                           /*      restore text mode */
}
```

CHAPTER 14

GRAPHICS PRINTER OUTPUT

Printers

Computer graphics are wonderful on screen but, unless you can create these same graphics on paper, they can be quite frustrating. Pasting a computer terminal into a manuscript is close to impossible.

For text modes, the Shift-PrtSc (Shift-PrintScreen) key command is available to send an ASCII screen to the printer and several TSR utilities have been created to execute the same task for a graphics screen. These latter, however, if they can be found, have been notably less than satisfactory. Most work only with specific printers, operate only in specific modes and, when used, may occupy entirely too much resident memory and also prevent other applications from running.

In this chapter; therefore, two graphics screen print utilities are created providing monochrome outputs using the Epson (dot-matrix) and LaserJet printers (see Chapter 15 for color output using plotters). These graphic output utilities avoid the problems mentioned because they can be tailored for any output device, will adapt to different video modes and can be incorporated directly into your application program.

Because more people have color monitors on their systems than have color plotters, the LaserJet graphics driver offers, in addition to Portrait and Landscape modes, a Greyscale mode (with two options: normal and inverse grey scales) that translates colors to greys in 16 shades on output.

Please note: all of the graphics output devices shown here are generic drivers. They have been specifically designed to work with most dot-matrix, laserjet or plotter devices presently marketed or can be easily adapted to work with any devices that require variant handling codes. The 'standard' devices chosen — Epson dot-matrix printers, HP LaserJet Series II printers and HP Plotters — are also de facto industry standards and most devices, regardless of manufacturers' trademarks, use essentially the same control codes and operate in basically the same manner.

One output device type not covered here are the 'color' dot-matrix printers using multicolor ribbons or multicolor inkjets. These devices are not particularly different in theory or operation from the color-pen plotters appearing in Chapter 15 and, a specialty driver for this type of device is easily created.

Table 14-1: Graphics FX-85 Graphics Mode

MODE	DENSITY	DESCRIPTION	SPEED
0	Single	60 dpi	16 in/sec
1	Low Speed Double	120 dpi	8 in/sec
2	High Speed Double	120 dpi	16 in/sec[1]
3	Quadruple	240 dpi	8 in/sec[1]
4	CRT 1	80 dpi	8 in/sec[2]
5	One-to-one	72 dpi	12 in/sec[2]
6	CRT II	90 dpi	8 in/sec
7	Dual-Density	144 dpi	3 in/sec[3]

1. Does not print consecutive dots in any one row.

2. Matches screen density of Epson QX-10.

3. Plotter modes: provide one-to-one horizontal dot density.

Using the Epson Dot-Matrix Printers

The Epson FX-85 printer is used as the 'standard' device for dot-matrix printers. This insures compatibility with the MX and RX series and, for the most part, with the LX (ink jet) series, as well as the majority of other manufacturers of dot-matrix printers. Most, if not all, offer graphics modes compatible with the Epson, but you should consult your printer manual for the capabilities of any specific device and adapt the graphics driver as appropriate.

The FX-85 printer offers eight graphics operation modes as shown in Table 14-1. A word of caution: if you are using an Epson printer (or compatible) with the dip switch selection set to "IBM mode" or an IBM dot matrix printer, only graphics modes 0-3 will be available.

While Epson provides mode 4 (CRT I) to match the screen (pixel) density of the QX-10 computer monitor, none of these modes offers an exact match for either CGA or EGA/VGA screen modes. Some, however, provide a better match than others, but this is also dependent on your output orientation.

Portrait vs. Landscape Orientation

Both the laserjet and dot-matrix drivers offer a choice of Landscape or Portrait imaging. The Portrait orientation plots the screen's x-axis across the width of your paper and the y-axis along the length of the paper, producing a half-sheet image. The Landscape orientation matches the long axis of the paper to the screen's x-axis, plotting the screen's y-axis across the width of the paper and producing a single screen image per page. This, in general, is the preferred output orientation.

For each orientation and screen mode, there is a preferred dot-matrix mode to best match the screen image, as shown in Table 14-2.

Table 14-2: Preferred Dot-Matrix Modes for Graphics

DIRECTION	CGA	EGA	VGA
PORTRAIT	3 / 7	1 / 7	1 / 7
LANDSCAPE	0	0	5

Three criteria apply in printer mode selection for a graphics screen output.

First, the number of dots per inch (dpi) must be high enough to map the screen pixels within the physical page limits. Using a resolution of 60 dpi (mode 0) in Portrait orientation would require a paper width greater than eight inches. For a 13-inch wide printer, 60 dpi would be acceptable for plotting 640 pixels horizontal but, on an eight-inch printer, only 480 pixels would be plotted before the margins were exceeded.

Second, the dots per inch horizontal and the lines per inch vertical must be balanced to achieve an output image close to your screen image. The horizontal dpi can be varied, the vertical cannot (or not easily).

Third, since the image is plotted one to one (one pixel/one dot), the higher the printer density (dots per inch), the smaller the resulting image. For example, mode 3 will plot an entire screen image, in Portrait mode, in a width of only 2.7 inches (and in very distorted proportions).

The modes shown are not dictated by fiat. I suggest that you experiment with your own equipment, try the various modes and see first hand how each matches output and screen image. In this particular application, a picture is quite literally worth a thousand words.

Remember, though, the higher the number of dots per inch (dpi), the smaller the resulting image horizontally. If you need both the dense bit imaging and a larger image, for a dot matrix, rewrite the graphics driver to output two (or more) printer dots per screen pixel. See also **Grey Scaling** which uses 16 dots per pixel (at 300 dpi) for color conversion with a laserjet and compare this approach with Epson's mode 3 Quadruple density (240 dpi).

Note also, for CGA modes C0..C3 (low resolution), printer mode 0 works well in Portrait orientation.

Calculating The Dot-Matrix Graphics Character

When the dot-matrix printer is used for normal (alphanumeric) output, an 8-bit character code selects a 9x9 pin pattern from the printer's ROM character sets.

In graphics modes, however, only eight of these pins are used and an 8-bit character is sent for each horizontal printhead position with each bit of this character code controlling one of the active pins.

The graphics character is calculated with the top pin controlled by bit 7 of the character, the bottom pin controlled by bit 0. Three examples of graphic character calculations are shown in Figure 14-1.

Figure 14-1: Individual Pin Calculation

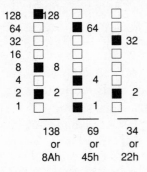

The graphics character code for the dot-matrix print head is calculated as an 8-bit character with bit 7 for the top pin (value 128) and bit 0 for the bottom pin (value 1). The character code sent is the sum of the values for the pins desired to print.

Graphics results are shown here in both decimal and hexadecimal codes.

On the dot-matrix, a series of graphics characters prints eight horizontal rows of dots, then the paper is advanced and the print head returned for the next row. Thus, in Portrait mode, each print line accounts for eight screen pixel rows and each character is generated from eight vertical pixels (see Figure 14-2).

In Landscape mode, the print direction and paper advance remain constant but the screen pixels are scanned as horizontal sets of eight pixels with a print line beginning at the top right of the screen and moving down. Subsequent print lines begin by scanning eight horizontal pixels at the top of the screen but with the horizontal scan position moved eight pixels left while final print line scans the left-most portion of the screen (see Figure 14-3).

Figure 14-2: Calculating Bit-Image Characters for the Dot-Matrix

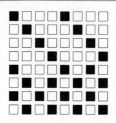

In PORTRAIT mode, the pixels would be read as eight vertical sets (left to right) as 8Ah, 45h, 22h,15h, 8Ah, 45h, 2Ah and 15h and transmitted in this order.

In LANDSCAPE mode, the pixels would be read as eight horizontal sets (top to bottom) as 11h, 22h, 44h, 88h, 51h, AAh, 55h and AAh and tranmitted in this order. Remember, the high order bit is to the right, the low order bit to the left.

EP_Graph — Dot-Matrix Graphics Driver

To describe the **EP_Graph** function (dot-matrix driver) as simplicity itself would be demeaning to a very smooth programming function. The **EP_Graph** function is precisely this: very simple and very smooth.

Before calling **EP_Graph**, however, I suggest defining two constants that will be used by the calling function to specify the output orientation desired:

```
#define  PORTRAIT    0
#define  LANDSCAPE  1
```

Two parameters are required to call **EP_Graph**, *Mode* and *Direction*.

```
void EP_Graph( int Mode, int Direction )
{
```

The *Mode* parameter is a provision allowing you test different printer modes. If and when you've settled on a preferred printer graphics mode, this calling parameter can be eliminated with mode constants supplied in *both* the *case PORTRAIT* and *case LANDSCAPE* options.

Figure 14-3: Mapping Screen to Paper in LANDSCAPE Mode

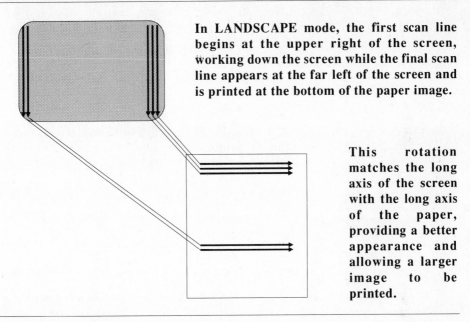

In **LANDSCAPE** mode, the first scan line begins at the upper right of the screen, working down the screen while the final scan line appears at the far left of the screen and is printed at the bottom of the paper image.

This rotation matches the long axis of the screen with the long axis of the paper, providing a better appearance and allowing a larger image to be printed.

Also, if you prefer to use only Landscape or Portrait orientation, the second parameter (*Direction*) can also be eliminated with the *switch* and *case* provisions rewritten for the preferred option.

In either case, a few local variables are required:

```
char  m;
int   i, j, k, Msb, Lsb,
      MaxX = getmaxx(),
      MaxY = getmaxy();
```

The last two variables, *MaxX* and *MaxY*, may duplicate similar declarations elsewhere in your program, but this will not interfere with their local declaration and these values will be needed.

323

```
setviewport( 0, 0, MaxX, MaxY, 0 );
```

If your calling program has other settings in effect — or if you want other settings in effect — this can be changed or eliminated. If you need to map a smaller area, it can be done by setting the limits to match the desired screen region — but be sure the data width specifications are set to match.

The printer should be set to graphics mode:

```
fprintf( stdprn, "\x1BA%c", 7 );
```

In Turbo C, *stdprn* is a predefined 'file' corresponding to LPT. If you need a different output port, change this designation accordingly.

The string $\x1BAn$ instructs the printer to set line spacing as $n/72$. In this case the *character* 07h specifies $7/72$ (about 82 dpi vertical spacing). Valid settings for **n** are 0..85.

Next, output orientation is selected as Portrait or Landscape:

```
switch( Direction )
{
    case PORTRAIT:
    {
```

The next step is to give the printer a graphics mode command and to specify how wide each line will be (how many dot positions will be plotted). The *Mode* value was specified when **EP_Graphic** was called and, in *PORTRAIT* orientation, this width would be the 640 pixels horizontally on the screen (assuming high resolution modes).

However, since the Epson printer can only accept 8-bit data, the 640 dot specification is reduced to two 8-bit arguments: *Lsb* and *Msb*. Since *MaxX* will have a value of 639 returned by **getmaxx**, the argument used to calculate *Lsb* and *Msb* is incremented by one.

```
Lsb = (MaxX+1) & 0x00FF;
Msb = (MaxX+1) >> 8;
```

And a loop begins at the top of the screen. Each loop, however, will plot eight vertical pixels.

```
for( j=0; j<=MaxY/8; j++ )
{
```

The arguments *Mode*, *Lsb* and *Msb* are passed as char values (unsigned 8-bit integers) with the \x1B* argument indicating that a graphics mode is being selected.

```
fprintf( stdprn, "\x1B*%c%c%c", Mode, Lsb, Msb );
```

This graphics mode setting is valid only for one line. After a graphics mode command and line length parameters are sent, the next *x* data bytes (set by the *Lsb* and *Msb* arguments) received are interpreted as graphics pin instructions — regardless of their contents! Thus, the graphics mode settings command initializes each and every graphics data line transmitted to the printer.

Now another loop begins, starting at the left screen margin and progressing across the screen to *MaxX*.

```
for( i=0; i<=MaxX; i++ )
{
```

The character *m* is set to null (0) at the start of each step, then an inner loop steps from *0* through *7* to read eight screen pixels (vertically).

```
m = 0;
for( k=0; k<8; k++ )
{
```

As the inner loop executes, the character *m* is shifted left one bit. If the current pixel is not *0* (black or background palette entry), then *m* is incremented (the rightmost or zero bit is set). As the loop continues and *m* is shifted left, each bit moves up and a new null bit becomes the low-order bit.

```
m <<= 1;
if( getpixel( i, j*8+k ) ) m++;
}
```

After the inner loop is finished, the resulting ''character'' is output to the printer.

```
        fprintf( stdprn, "%c", m );
    }
```

When the line is finished, the CR/LF codes are explicitly sent to the printer to advance the print head to the beginning of the next line.

```
        fprintf( stdprn, "\x0D\x0A" );
    }
}
```

And this process continues until the entire screen has been read — eight pixels at a time — and transferred to the printer in the form of a graphics character.

In the Landscape mode, the process is the same except that a different graphics string length is calculated using *MaxY* instead of *MaxX* and the screen image is read, starting at the top right and moving down and left, eight horizontal pixels at a byte (pun intended).

```
case LANDSCAPE:
{
        Lsb = MaxY & 0x00FF;
        Msb = MaxY >> 8;
        for( j=0; j<MaxX; j+=8 )
        {
                fprintf( stdprn, "\x1B*%c%c%c", Mode, Lsb, Msb );
```

Unlike the Portrait mode, here the screen image is read beginning at the bottom of the screen and working up.

```
        for( i=MaxY; i>=0; i-- )
        {
            m = 0;
            for( k=0; k<8; k++ )
            {
                m <<= 1;
```

```
            if( getpixel( j+k, i ) ) m++;
        }
        fprintf( stdprn, "%c", m );
        }
        fprintf( stdprn, "\x0D\x0A" );
    }
  }
}
```

Finally, after the entire screen image has been transmitted to the printer, a formfeed is sent to advance the paper.

```
    fprintf( stdprn,"\f" );
}
```

This completes the image transmission process. All very simple.

Using The LaserJet Printer

A graphics screen dump to a laserjet printer is no more difficult than printing to a dot-matrix — but there are differences both in the capabilities of the laserjet and in how the laserjet is treated.

First, the laserjet is capable of printing a finer dot-image than a dot-matrix printer — up to 300 dpi — but most laserjets also support four distinct dot resolutions: 75 dpi, 100 dpi, 150 dpi and 300 dpi. At 75 dpi, the image dots are 16 times as large (4x4) as the dots produced at 300 dpi and, naturally, only $1/16$ as much information can be mapped to a page. Similarly, the 100 dpi and 150 dpi resolutions create dot sizes which are submultiples of the 300 dpi.

Second, the resolution used does not affect the output speed. The time required to generate a graphics output is determined only by the amount of bit information sent to the printer (transmission time) and not by the resolution setting used by the printer to map the information to the page. The same image generated at 300 dpi and at 75 dpi will require the same output time.

Third, the dot resolution selected does not directly affect the relative x/y-axis spacing. While the x-axis spacing is determined by the dot resolution, the y-axis line spacing is directly under the control of the program. Thus screen aspect ratios can be matched on output with excellent results and, if desired, deliberate distortions can be introduced.

In sum, since the laserjet labors under fewer *mechanical* constraints than a dot-matrix, the resulting output is capable both of much higher resolution and of more faithful reproduction of the original video screen image.

Because of this lack of mechanical constraints, the laserjet is controlled in a different manner than a dot-matrix with two principal differences in operation.

First, each row (or column) of screen pixels is mapped one for one to the laserjet output scan. Thus, in Portrait mode, instead of reading successive groups of eight vertical pixels, as was done for the dot matrix, the screen image is read by rows, with each successive eight pixels transmitted as a graphics character and 80 characters creating one row of graphics dots on the page. The dpi resolution is selected and it determines the horizontal spacing between the dots.

Second, since there is no physical printhead involved, each graphics string output must be prefaced with position instructions explaining where on the page the dot image is to appear. However, as mentioned before, this is precisely the element which makes it possible for the aspect of the output image to match the screen image faithfully.

The LaserJet Screen Print Utility

The utility functions in LJ-GRAPH.I provide three modes for transferring your screen image to paper: Landscape, Portrait and Greyscale. The first two modes, Landscape and Portrait, provide a fast monochrome output in 75 and 100 dpi resolutions. The third mode, Greyscale, 'translates' screen colors into either four (CGA Low Resolution) or 16 (EGA/VGA) shades of grey (see Table 14-3).

Table 14-3: LaserJet Graphic Screen Dump Modes

MODE	APPROXIMATE DATA	RESOLUTION	TIME
LANDSCAPE	50,000 bytes	75 DPI	~1 minute
PORTRAIT	40,000 bytes	100 DPI	~1 minute
GREYSCALE	600,000 bytes	300 DPI	~6 minutes

As you will note, the Greyscale mode requires a fair amount of time — slightly more than six minutes — to output some 600,000 bytes of information describing a color screen. The image produced is effectively the same resolution and size as in Landscape mode except that each pixel has been mapped to a 16-bit (4x4) grey dot image The practice and options in grey scaling will be discussed further in this chapter (see **Sixteen- and Four-Tone Grey Scale Palettes**).

The same screen in either Landscape or Portrait mode requires slightly more than one minute. These times will vary, of course, depending on CPU speeds and other machine capabilities but the values given above provide a general rule for time requirements.

Three other considerations should be kept in mind.

First, if you do not have a laserjet immediately available, the screen dump output can be redirected to a disk file and then sent directly from disk to a laserjet at a later time using the DOS **PRINT** command.

Second, multiple copies of a screen image can be printed without requiring multiple transmission times. Adding a multicopy command to the output print image will be discussed later in this chapter.

Third, *do not* attempt to use the Greyscale mode with CGA monochrome graphics. There is simply no point, the results will be a very pale image and the Landscape mode will produce much more satisfactory results in about $1/6$ the time.

LaserJet Instruction Codes

Table 14-4 shows a sample series of laserjet graphic output instructions with each command sequence appearing on a separate line and with comments. In actual practice, the command sequences are not separated by any CR/LF sequences unless they happen to appear as graphics dot commands.

Each command sequence begins with the ESCape character ([1]B) followed by a series of ASCII characters that define the command and any parameters included in the command. For example, the sequence [1]B*t300R, sets 300 dpi resolution with the parameter *300* sent as a plain-text ASCII sequence and never as a code or value sequence as was used with the dot-matrix codes.

The DeciPoint Position Instructions

The laserjet supports three separate print cursor position modes: row, dot and decipoint. For this application, only the decipoint coordinate system will be used.

First, however, a bit of background explanation. Printers (meaning people rather than devices) have traditionally used a pica and point system to measure type sizes with six picas equalling one inch and 12 points to the pica. Thus, there are 72 points to the inch and the dot-matrix printer standard also provides for spacing in $1/2$ inch increments.

But laserjet uses a dot size of T $1/30$ of an inch, requiring a finer position increment than a mere point size and the laserjet's dot coordinate system provides this spacing in $1/300$ inch steps.

An even finer degree of positioning, however, is provided by the decipoint coordinates. A decipoint is $1/10$ of a point or $1/720$ of an inch and, to carry precision one degree further, the decipoint measurements also allow a decimal fraction (as 1234.5 decipoints) for a precision of $1/7200$ of an inch.

And the 'decipoint.decimal' is the position coordinate system which will be used to control the graphics print positions — which should be sufficient positioning to satisfy even the most finicky programmer.

Table 14-4: An Example of LaserJet Output Instructions

^1_BE	reset
^1_B&l1H	select paper feed from tray
^1_B&l0O	reset 0 origin for printer cursor position
^1_B*p0X	cursor position 0 dots horizontal
^1_B*p0Y	cursor position 0 dots vertical
^1_B*t300R	300 dpi resolution
^1_B&a1228.8h1180.8V	cursor position, horizontal & vertical decipoints
^1_B*r1A	start graphics at current cursor
^1_B*b23W 0F FF FF FF FF FF FF FF FF FF FF FF FF FF FF FF FF FF FF FF FF FF F8	
	transfer 23 bytes graphic data
^1_B*rB	end graphics
^1_B&a1228.8h1183.2V	position cursor, horizontal & vertical decipoints
^1_B*r1A	start graphics at current cursor
^1_B*b23W 01 F0 20 20 20 20 20 20 20 20 20 20 20 20 20 20 20 20 20 20 20 20 27 80	
	transfer 23 bytes graphic data
^1_B*rB	end graphics
⋮	(*graphics instructions continue*)
^1_B*rB 0C	end graphics + form feed (0Ch)
^1_B&l0O	reset 0 origin printer cursor position (*default*)
^1_B(8U	primary symbol set Roman-8 (*default*)
^1_B(s0p10h12vsb3T	reset primary font values (*defaults*)
^1_B&l1H	select paper feed from tray (*default*)
(*end of printer instructions*)	

One other bit of information: the 0,0 coordinate is a position roughly 1/2 inch down from the top of the page and 1/2 inch from the left. All decipoint measurements are made from this coordinate location.

Using 300 dpi resolution, each dot is nominally 0.0033... inches in diameter and, converting this measurement to decipoints, yields a basic vertical increment of 2.4 decipoints. For 150 dpi, this increment would be doubled to 4.8; at 100 dpi, becoming 7.2 decipoints and; at 75 dpi, the vertical increment becomes 9.6 decipoints.

These basic printer scan line increments are adjusted according to the screen pixel aspect ratios to insure that the proportions of the final print image match the screen appearance.

Note also that the printer cursor position command consists of a single instruction preface followed by two values: the x and y coordinates. Since the 'h' character identifying the preceding as a horizontal decipoint position coordinate is lowercase, the instruction preface does not have to be repeated. The second coordinate is ended with a capital 'V' indicating that the current command sequence is being terminated.

If you will look at the next to the last command sequence in Table 14-4, the sequence begins with a single instruction preface (^{1}B(s)) followed by a series of values and lowercase instruction indicators with the final instruction indicator in uppercase as a terminator. This format is used frequently when several commands sharing the same instruction preface sequence are being sent.

Additional information and explanation on the laserjet printer control sequences can be found in the **LaserJet series II Printer User's Manual**, Appendix A or in the **LaserJet series II Printer Technical Reference Manual** — both available from Hewlett-Packard.

Writing Graphics Characters to the LaserJet

Before the graphics data is transmitted, the printer cursor position is set using the horizontal and vertical decipoint coordinates, then the ^{1}B$*r1A$ sequence confirms that graphics output will begin at the cursor setting.

The next command sequence, ^{1}B$*b\#\#W$, tells the printer to treat the next ## characters as graphics characters. Just as the 300 dpi resolution figure was sent as plain text instead of using code characters (as was done with the dot-matrix), the number of data characters to be transmitted will also be sent as plain-text ASCII. That is, if 80 graphics characters will follow, then the ## markers will read an ASCII '80' instead of the 'P' character which would have been used with the dot-matrix. See Figure 14-5 for examples.

Figure 14-4: Calculating Bit-Image Characters for the LaserJet

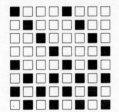

In **PORTRAIT** mode, the eight horizontal sets of pixels would be read as **88h, 44h, 22h, 11h, 8Ah, 55h, AAh and 55h.** As with the dot-matrix, each set of eight pixels is transmitted as a single graphics character and each set would be transmitted on a separate line.

In **LANDSCAPE** mode, the pixels would be read as eight vertical sets as **15h, 2Ah, 45h, 8Ah, 15h, 22h, 45h and 8Ah.** Again, each eight pixels are transmitted as a single graphics character and each vertical set shown here would be transmitted on a separate line.

As before, the information is transmitted in the form of 8-bit characters and for the laserjet, these bit-images are calculated precisely the same as for the dot-matrix images except for the direction and order of screen pixels read for each mode (see Figure 14-4).

Note: while the **transmit graphics data** command explicitly stated how many bytes (characters) of graphics data would be sent, an **end graphics** command string is still sent after the data transfer is complete. Granted, this appears redundant, but it is safe and adds little overhead to the data transmitted.

When all of the graphics data has been sent, the final **end graphics** command will be followed by the character 0Ch, the standard form feed character, instructing the laserjet to eject the page.

The four code sequences following the form feed character are simply housekeeping sequences to reset the laserjet to default values.

Sixteen and Four Tone Grey-Scale Palettes

In addition to the direct mapping modes (Landscape and Portrait), the provided Greyscale mode maps each screen pixel on output to a 'grey' 4x4 dot image, the 'grey' value being determined by the palette color number of the screen pixel. This is not a true grey-scale conversion (see **True-Color Grey-Scale Palettes**), but simply an arbitrary mapping providing 16 'greys' for EGA/VGA color screens and four 'greys' for CGA low-resolution color screens.

This grey-scale conversion is accomplished by setting an output resolution of 300 dpi, then scanning each screen pixel four times and outputting 16 dots (four per line on four lines) for each screen pixel. The resulting print image is the same size and aspect as created by the Landscape mode except that the screen colors are now approximated as shades of grey.

There are flaws in this particular method of grey-scaling.

First, since this is an arbitrary 'grey' mapping, the darker colors are assigned the lightest 'greys' and WHITE is printed as an almost solid black. The grey palette result for LIGHTGREY is out of order, being one dot lighter than the grey palette result assigned to DARKGREY (assuming the default EGA/VGA color palette). This light to dark scaling was arbitrarily chosen as 'normal' since it leaves the screen background printed as white.

An option is provided to invert the grey-scale results such that the background will be printed as black and the WHITE will be plotted as white on the page. This inversion, however, will not correct the minor discrepancy between the grey tones assigned to the LIGHTGREY and DARKGREY default palette entries.

Second, if new colors are assigned to the EGA/VGA palette, the gray-scale values will not change to accommodate these colors. If the palette color entry number two is assigned a bright green, it will still be grey-scaled according to the palette entry number and not the color value assigned.

Third, the 'shades of grey' provided may or may not be easily distinguished from each other and two adjacent shades of grey may be almost exactly the same in appearance, depending on the output device and the state of the ink (toner) cartridge used.

Figure 14-5: Bit Patterns for 16-level Grey-Scale Palette

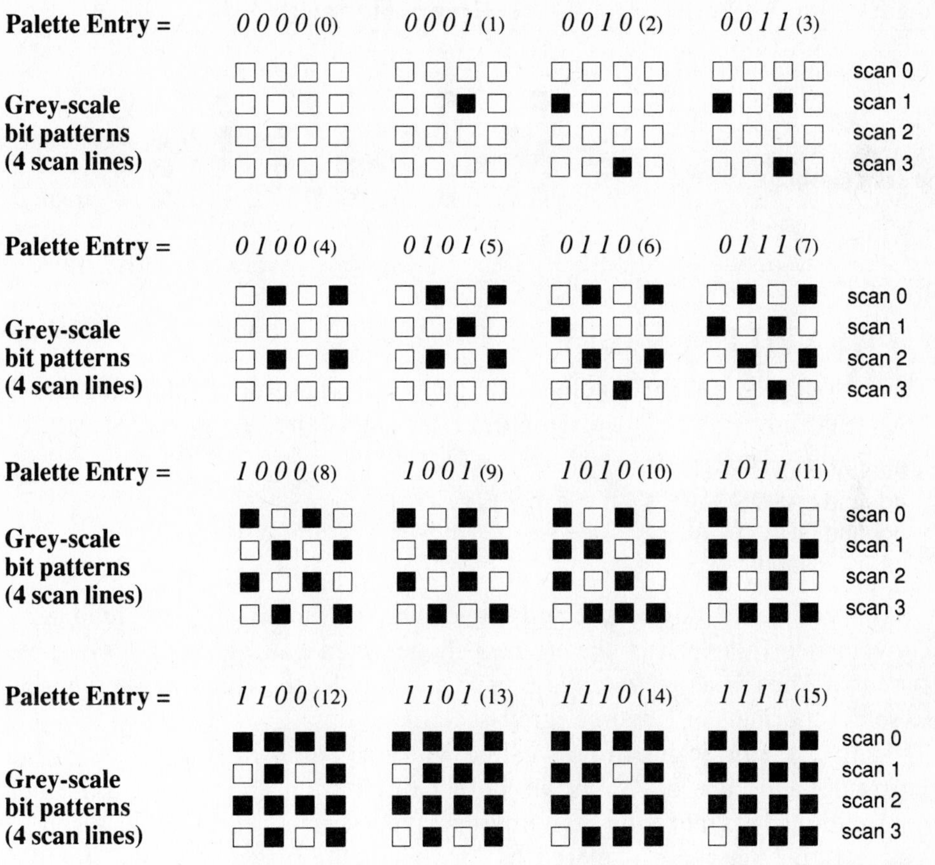

Palette Entry =	0 0 0 0 (0)	0 0 0 1 (1)	0 0 1 0 (2)	0 0 1 1 (3)	
					scan 0
Grey-scale					scan 1
bit patterns					scan 2
(4 scan lines)					scan 3

Palette Entry =	0 1 0 0 (4)	0 1 0 1 (5)	0 1 1 0 (6)	0 1 1 1 (7)	
					scan 0
Grey-scale					scan 1
bit patterns					scan 2
(4 scan lines)					scan 3

Palette Entry =	1 0 0 0 (8)	1 0 0 1 (9)	1 0 1 0 (10)	1 0 1 1 (11)	
					scan 0
Grey-scale					scan 1
bit patterns					scan 2
(4 scan lines)					scan 3

Palette Entry =	1 1 0 0 (12)	1 1 0 1 (13)	1 1 1 0 (14)	1 1 1 1 (15)	
					scan 0
Grey-scale					scan 1
bit patterns					scan 2
(4 scan lines)					scan 3

These are, however, the closest approximation to 16 shades of grey that it is possible to create within the limitations of the laserjet and the requirement of mapping an entire 640x350 (or larger) graphics screen.

Figure 14-6 shows the 'grey' bit-maps assigned to each palette entry.

Figure 14-6: Bit Patterns for 4-level Grey-Scale Palette

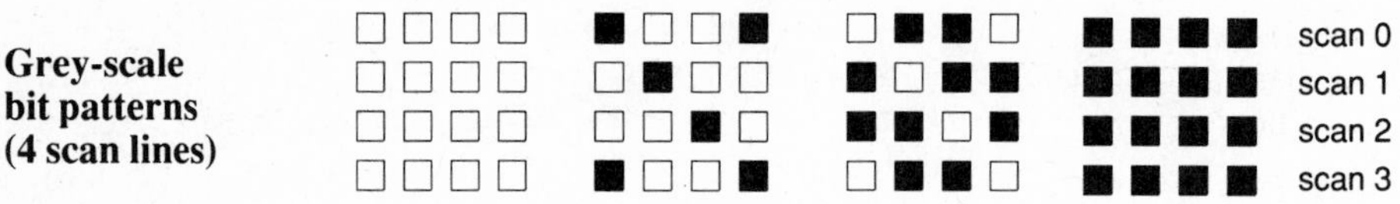

Grey-scale
bit patterns
(4 scan lines)

scan 0
scan 1
scan 2
scan 3

LJ-GRAPH.I

The LJ-GRAPH's utility include file contains the Laserjet Graphics driver functions and begins by declaring three constants and one global variable.

```
#define PORTRAIT 0
#define LANDSCAPE 1
#define GREYSCALE 2
int      Negative;
```

The constants Portrait, Landscape and Greyscale are provided as a convenience in selecting the desired mode when calling the **LJ_Graphic** function. The variable *Negative* is used as a flag by the **Grey-Scale** function to select 'normal' or 'inverse' grey-scale mapping.

The **LJ_Graphic** function is called with one parameter, *Mode*, selecting Portrait, Landscape or Greyscale output orientation and resolution. Since your calling program may not provide x and y screen limits and a screen aspect ratio, these are declared as local variable along with the doubles *xprint*, *yprint* and *prstep* and the character variables *m* and *resolution*.

```
void LJ_Graphic( int Mode )
{
        int    i, j, k, p, q, xasp, yasp,
               MaxX = getmaxx() + 1,
               MaxY = getmaxy() + 1;
        double xprint, yprint, prstep, AspR;
        char   m, resolution[3];
```

Also, two character strings, *graph_ends* and *graph_init* are defined.

The argument \x1B is the ESCape character (in hexadecimal format) but, if you have the disk version of these programs, ESCape will appear on screen as a low-lighted [character (*ctrl-[*). Also, the ESCape character (or any control character) can be entered directly by using the Turbo C editor's Control-Prefix entry (usually *Alt-P*), then entering the [key.

```
        static char graph_init[] =
               "\x1BE\x1B&l1H\x1B&lO\x1B*p0X\x1B*p0Y\x1B*t";
        static char graph_ends[] = "\x1B*rB";
```

The *graph_init* character string breaks down into several commands as shown in Figure 14-5. The final portion of the string, 1B*t, is the preface to the 'set resolution' command which will be completed before the sequence is transmitted.

Now, the **LJ_Graphic** function checks the screen aspect ratio, then restores the viewport settings to the full screen.

```
        getaspectratio( &xasp, &yasp );
        AspR = (double) xasp / (double) yasp;
        setviewport( 0, 0, MaxX, MaxY, 0 );
```

The **switch** command uses the *Mode* argument to select the desired output operation.

```
        switch( Mode )
        {
            case PORTRAIT:
            {
```

In Portrait mode, the output x/y coordinates are set using initial *decipoint* values.

```
xprint = 690.0;
yprint = 500.0;
```

The string sequence '100' is copied to the string variable *resolution* and the completed initialization string is sent to the printer.

```
strcpy( resolution, "100" );
fprintf( stdprn, "%s%sR", graph_init, resolution );
```

These two commands can be rewritten — if desired — as a single command:

```
fprintf( stdprn, "%s100R", graph_init );
```

This command could also be written as:

```
fprint( stdprn, "%s%3dR", graph_init, 100 );
```

Now the *prstep* variable is set to match the printer aspect ratio to the screen aspect ratio.

```
prstep = 7.2 / AspR;
```

So far, this has all been setup and initialization for the printer and for values used while the graphics loops execute. Now it's time to read the video screen and send the output information to the printer.

Because this is Portrait mode, the loop begins at the top of the screen sends a printer cursor position command, then increments the *yprint* coordinate by the value in *prstep*.

```
for( j=0; j<=MaxY; j++ )
{
    fprintf( stdprn, "\x1B&a%–*.1fh%–*.1fV",
                    format( xprint ), xprint,
                    format( yprint ), yprint );
    yprint += prstep;
```

Notice that two parameters are used for the x coordinate and two for the y coordinate. The parameter provided by *format(xprint)* is a width statement specifying how many places will be created in the %−*.1f number string. C is notorious for formatting floating point numbers in all number to string conversions. Since any leading or trailing spaces would confuse the laserjet, the **format** function has been created to return an integer value, setting the string format to exclude leading or trailing blanks.

Next, commands are send to start graphics at the printer cursor and to specify the number of graphics characters that will follow. Happily, C is not fanatical about formatting integers with extra spaces, so no width parameter is required.

```
fprintf( stdprn, "\x1B*r1A\x1B*b%dW", MaxX/8 );
```

Now the printer is expecting a string of *MaxX/8* graphics characters and two loops, the first from *0* to *MaxX/8* and the second from *0* to *7*, read a series of screen pixels, creating a graphics character describing each eight pixels and sending the final character to the printer.

```
for( i=0; i<MaxX/8; i++ )
{
    m = 0;
    for( k=0; k<8; k++ )
    {
        m <<= 1;
        if( getpixel( i*8+k, j ) ) m++;
    }
    fprintf( stdprn, "%c", m );
}
```

When these two loops are completed and the current row of pixels has been mapped to the printer, the *graph_ends* string is sent, then the loop continues with the next row of pixels.

```
        fprintf( stdprn, "%s", graph_ends );
    }
} break;
```

In the Landscape mode, the initial setup is much the same except that a resolution of 75 dpi is selected and the printer line spacing is adjusted accordingly.

```
case LANDSCAPE:
{
    xprint = 1000.0;
    yprint = 1000.0;
    strcpy( resolution, "75" );
    prstep = 9.6 * AspR;
    fprintf( stdprn, "%s%sR", graph_init, resolution );
```

The main loop, however, runs from screen left to screen right and the graphics strings will be created by reading a column of screen pixels instead of a row. Since *MaxY* may not be an even multiple of eight (EGA supports a vertical resolution of 350 pixels), *MaxY+4* is used to set the number of graphics characters that will be sent; otherwise, a few rows at the bottom of the screen may not be mapped to the printer.

```
for( j=0; j<MaxX; j++ )
{
    fprintf( stdprn, "\x1B&a%–*.1fh%–*.1fV",
                        format( xprint ), xprint,
                        format( yprint ), yprint );
    yprint += prstep;
    fprintf( stdprn, "\x1B*r1A\x1B*b%dW", (int) ( MaxY+4 ) / 8 );
```

The loop reading the screen pixels, however does not require the addition to the *MaxY* variable, the <= specification is sufficient to insure that all of the screen is read. Now, the loop proceeds as previously explained except that the horizontal pixel positions read are at *MaxX–j* where *j* is looping from *0* to *MaxX*. This inversion is necessary; otherwise, the printed result would be a mirror image of the screen.

```
for( i=0; i<=MaxY/8; i++ )
{
```

```
                m = 0;
                for( k=0; k<8; k++ )
                {
                    m <<= 1;
                    if( getpixel( MaxX–j, i*8+k ) ) m++;
                }
                fprintf( stdprn, "%c", m );
            }
            fprintf( stdprn, "%s", graph_ends );
        }
    }   break;
```

The third mode is the Greyscale mode. This operates almost exactly the same as the Landscape mode except that a resolution of 300 dpi is used and each screen pixel is mapped to a 4x4 grey-scale image.

```
case GREYSCALE:
{
        xprint = 1000.0;
        yprint = 1000.0;
        strcpy( resolution, "300" );
        prstep = 2.4 * AspR;
        fprintf( stdprn, "%s%sR", graph_init, resolution );
```

The grey-scale mapping is accomplished by adding a loop to read each screen pixel four times for four separate print lines.

```
        for( j=0; j<=MaxX; j++ )
        for( p=0; p<4; p++ )
        {
            fprintf( stdprn, "\x1B&a%–*.1fh%–*.1fV",
                            format( xprint ), xprint,
                            format( yprint ), yprint );
            yprint += prstep;
```

Because only two screen pixels are read for each graphics character output to the printer, the length of the graphics string is specified as *MaxY/2* instead of *(MaxY+4)/8*.

```
fprintf( stdprn, "\x1B*r1A\x1B*b%dW", MaxY/2 );
for( i=0; i<=MaxY/2; i++ )
{
    m = 0;
```

And *k* is looped from *0* to *1* while *m* is shifted left four places, then OR'd with the integer value returned by the **Grey_Scale** function for the current screen pixel.

```
for( k=0; k<=1; k++ )
{
    m <<= 4;
    m |= Grey_Scale( p, getpixel( MaxX–j, i*2+k ) );
}
    fprintf( stdprn, "%c", m );
}
    fprintf( stdprn, "%s", graph_ends );
}
    }   break;
} /* end of Switch */
```

The final housekeeping — sending a formfeed command and resetting the printer to its default state — is reserved until the **switch** statement is ended, instead of duplicating this instruction set for each of the three modes.

```
fprintf( stdprn, "\x0C\x1B&lO\x1B(8U\x1B(sp10h12vsb3T\x1B&l1H" );
}
```

Selecting Multiple Copies on Output

One convenient option has not been provided in the **LJ_Graph** utility: the provision to print multiple copies of a screen image.

This provision can be very simple. Before sending the final command set, the sequence beginning with \x0C, simply include the following command line:

```
fprintf( stdprn, "\x1B&l%dX", Number_Of_Copies );
```

The parameter *Number_Of_Copies* can be any value from *1* to *99* and the laserjet will print the specified quantity from a single download.

The format Function

The **format** function accepts a double value, returning an integer value to specify the number of integer places for a numerical string. The integer variable *width* begins with a value of *6* providing for four integer places, one decimal character and one place following the decimal.

If the value of *position* is less than 1000, *width* is decremented, then *position* is tested again against values of 100 and 10. The final value for *width* is returned to the calling function.

```
int format( double position )
{
        int width = 6;

        if( position < 1000.0 ) width– –;
        if( position < 100.0 )  width– –;
        if( position < 10.0 )   width– –;
        return( width );
}
```

The Grey_Scale Function

The **Grey_Scale** function is called with two parameters: *scanline,* that specifies which of the four scan lines is being created for the current pixel; and *palette_entry*, the color palette number read from the current screen pixel.

```
int Grey_Scale( int scanline, int palette_entry )
{
```

The local variable *grey* is initially set to zero. When **Grey_Scale** is finished, the value in *grey* will be returned to the calling function.

```
int grey = 0;
```

Provision is made here for a four-step grey scale for use with CGA low-resolution color modes. Since *palette_entry* for CGA modes can only have values from *0* to *3*, only two tests are required for each *scanline* and, if *palette_entry* AND'd with the test value provides a True boolean result, the variable *grey* is OR'd with the appropriate bit map value.

Notice that the values OR'd with *grey* for each case total 15. If both tests for each case are True, then the *grey* value returned will have all bits set and the plotted value will be a black square. If only one of the tests returns True, one of the two grey-shade values will be returned; if neither returns True, the plotted value will be a blank square for the tested pixel.

```
if( GraphDriver == CGA )
{
    switch( scanline )
    {
        case 0: {  if( palette_entry & 1 ) grey |=  9;
                   if( palette_entry & 2 ) grey |=  6;
                } break;
        case 1: {  if( palette_entry & 1 ) grey |=  4;
                   if( palette_entry & 2 ) grey |= 11;
                } break;
        case 2: {  if( palette_entry & 1 ) grey |=  2;
                   if( palette_entry & 2 ) grey |= 13;
                } break;
        case 3: {  if( palette_entry & 1 ) grey |=  9;
                   if( palette_entry & 2 ) grey |=  6;
                } break;
    }  }
```

If the GraphDriver is not CGA, then the 16-shade grey-scale is created. Again, notice that the sum of the values for each test — except *case 3* — is 15. Since one dot in the grey-scale pattern is not used by any of the sixteen grey shades, *case 3* omits the value 8, for a total of 7 (bits 4, 2 and 1).

In each test, only one bit in *palette_entry* is used. Look back at Figure 14-5 and notice that the grey-scale palettes for 1, 2, 4 and 8 are the critical dot patterns used here and all of the other dot patterns are a combination of these four, allowing a very simple decision tree to create 16 progressive dot patterns.

```
else
{ switch( scanline )
        {
                case 0: { if( palette_entry & 4 ) grey |= 5;
                          if( palette_entry & 8 ) grey |= 10;
                        } break;
                case 1: { if( palette_entry & 1 ) grey |= 2;
                          if( palette_entry & 2 ) grey |= 8;
                          if( palette_entry & 8 ) grey |= 5;
                        } break;
                case 2: { if( palette_entry & 4 ) grey |= 5;
                          if( palette_entry & 8 ) grey |= 10;
                        } break;
                case 3: { if( palette_entry & 2 ) grey |= 2;
                          if( palette_entry & 8 ) grey |= 5;
                        } break;
        } }
```

Next, if the flag variable *Negative* has been set, the bit pattern in *grey* is XOR'd with 0Fh to invert the results. This changes the default grey-scale that begins with the lightest pattern for a palette-entry of 0 and proceeds to return the darkest pattern for a palette-entry of 15, to a grey-scale that returns a dark grey-scale pattern for low palette colors and a blank grey-scale pattern for WHITE (palette entry 15).

```
if( Negative ) grey ^= 0x0F;
```

345

Last, the value in *grey* is returned to the calling function.

```
    return( grey );
}
```

The Print_Pause Function

The **Print_Pause** function is a simple utility to write a screen prompt and wait for a key response to select one of the three output modes supported by **LJ_Graphic**.

```
void Print_Pause( int Invert )
{
        char Ch;
        int  Done = 0;
        if( Invert ) Negative = 1; else Negative = 0;
        PromptLine( "Enter <P>ortrait, <L>andscape, <G>reyscale"
                            " — any other key to exit ..." );
        while( !Done )
        {
            while( kbhit() ) getch();
            Ch = getch();
            switch( toupper(Ch) )
            {
                case 'P' : LJ_Graphic( PORTRAIT );  break;
                case 'L' : LJ_Graphic( LANDSCAPE ); break;
                case 'G' : LJ_Graphic( GREYSCALE ); break;
                default  : Done++;
            }
        }
}
```

If you would like to use this prompt utility in another application, several approaches can be used without overwriting the existing screen.

One method would be to use the **getimage** function to save the area of the screen which the prompt will overwrite, then use **putimage** to restore the original screen before calling **LJ_Graphic** or exiting.

Another approach is to switch active video pages, write the prompt information on the alternate page and then return to the original screen.

The PromptLine Function

The **PromptLine** function should already be familiar. **PromptLine** is called with a message string, draws a box at the bottom of the screen, centers the message in the box, and returns to the calling function for further action.

```
void PromptLine( char *msg )
{
        int   height, MaxX = getmaxx(), MaxY = getmaxy();

        setcolor( getmaxcolor() );
        settextstyle( DEFAULT_FONT, HORIZ_DIR, 1 );
        settextjustify( CENTER_TEXT, TOP_TEXT );
        height = textheight( "H" );
        bar( 0, MaxY–( height+4 ), MaxX, MaxY );
        rectangle( 0, MaxY–( height+4 ), MaxX, MaxY );
        outtextxy( MaxX/2, MaxY–(height+2), msg );
}
```

More on Colors and Color Mapping

CAVEAT: Color — like beauty — is largely in the eye of the beholder. We may well differ in our perceptions of color and color values. You are perfectly free to rewrite or adapt the following color translation suggestions to better fit your own chromatic perceptions.

True-Color Grey Scale Palettes

In the GREYSCALE option used in **LJ_Graph**, the grey-scale palette was mapped according to the palette item numbers assigned to the screen pixels, and not by the actual screen colors. But, since the default palette colors are already arranged more or less in order of intensity, this is a minor discrepancy in most cases.

If you do need a more accurate color to grey-scale mapping, there are several possible approaches.

One approach would be to read the palette color values (not the palette item numbers), order the color values assigned to the palette entries and create a color-to-grey-scale translation map. The drawback to this approach, unfortunately, is that these color values do not reflect actual color (visual) intensities and a secondary translation table would have to be manually prepared to provide some basis for ordering.

An easier approach is to 'decipher' the palette color values and create an 'intensity' value for each color, then order the color-to-grey mapping according to these intensities.

To attempt this, however, some basis is necessary to say which color is more intense than another. Of the three primary colors (red, blue and green), the human eye perceives green most strongly, red next and blue the least. A grey-scale formula reflecting the perception of the human eye yields: *grey = 0.30 * R + 0.59 * G + 0.11 * B.*

But the EGA/VGA color palette values have two flags for each color, primary **R**ed and secondary **r**ed, primary **G**reen and secondary **g**reen and primary **B**lue and secondary **b**lue, so a formula is needed that can calculate a grey value from six flags (colors) instead of only three.

If the secondary colors are arbitrarily assigned $1/3$ of the base value and the primary colors are assigned $2/3$, then a new formula yields: *grey = 0.30 * (r + 2 * R) / 3 + 0.59 * (g + 2 * G)/3 + 0.11 * (b + 2 * B)/3.*

Figure 14-7 shows grey-scale percentages generated using this formula. The default palette EGA/VGA colors are labeled with the actual color values appearing in the left column.

Examining the grey-scale order, notice that the sequence of grey values does not match the sequence generated by the color values, nor the sequence of greys generated by the default conversion in the **Grey_Scale** function. Here the grey sequence is strictly according to perception intensity and DARKGREY falls midway in the low intensity colors between MAGENTA and CYAN — just as might be expected of an average grey tone. Similarly, the LIGHTGREY color falls between the LIGHTMAGENTA and LIGHTGREEN shades and, you might also note, the LIGHTBLUE appears just slightly lighter than BROWN.

As mentioned earlier, there is no hard and fast rule saying that this is the only grey-scale conversion formula possible and, if this does not suit your application or perceptions, please feel free to experiment with the conversion formula. One hint: the simplest method of experimentation would be to use a good spreadsheet, create your formula, apply it to the rRgGbB color bits and have the spreadsheet sort the results for your examination.

If all else fails, see Chapter 15 — **Graphics Plotter Output**.

Figure 14-7: True Color Grey-Scale Conversion

VALUE	r	R	g	G	b	B	%	EGA COLOR	VALUE	r	R	g	G	b	B	%	EGA COLOR
0							0	BLACK	11			□		□	□	503	
8			□				37		29		□	□	□		□	507	
1						□	73	BLUE	42	□		□		□		530	
32	□						100		60	□	□	□	□			533	LIGHTRED
9			□			□	110		35	□				□	□	567	
40	□		□				137		53	□	□		□		□	570	
33	□					□	173		18		□			□		590	
16		□					197		6				□	□		593	
4				□			200	RED	43	□		□		□	□	603	
41	□		□			□	210		61	□	□	□	□		□	607	LIGHTMAGENTA
24		□	□				233		26		□	□		□		627	
12			□	□			237		14			□	□	□		630	
17		□				□	270		19		□			□	□	663	
5				□		□	273	MAGENTA	7				□	□	□	667	LIGHTGREY
48	□	□					297		50	□	□			□		690	
36	□			□			300		38	□			□	□		693	
25		□	□			□	307		27		□	□		□	□	700	
13			□	□		□	310		15			□	□	□	□	703	
56	□	□	□				333	DARKGREY	58	□	□	□		□		727	LIGHTGREEN
44	□		□	□			337		46	□		□	□	□		730	
49	□	□				□	370		51	□	□			□	□	763	
37	□			□		□	373		39	□			□	□	□	767	
2					□		393	GREEN	22		□		□	□		790	
20		□		□			397	BROWN	59	□	□	□		□	□	800	LIGHTCYAN
57	□	□	□			□	407	LIGHTBLUE	47	□		□	□	□	□	803	
45	□		□	□		□	410		30		□	□	□	□		827	
10			□		□		430		23		□		□	□	□	863	
28		□	□	□			433		54	□	□		□	□		890	
3					□	□	467	CYAN	31		□	□	□	□	□	900	
21		□		□		□	470		62	□	□	□	□	□		927	YELLOW
34	□				□		493		55	□	□		□	□	□	963	
52	□	□		□			497		63	□	□	□	□	□	□	1000	WHITE

```
/*          EP-GRAPH.I — graphics output driver for dot-matrix printers          */

#define  PORTRAIT  0
#define  LANDSCAPE  1

void Print_Graph( int Mode, int Direction )
{
    char  m;
    int   i, j, k, Msb, Lsb,
            MaxX = getmaxx(),
            MaxY = getmaxy();

    setviewport( 0, 0, MaxX, MaxY, 0 );
    fprintf( stdprn, "\x1BA%c", 7 );                    /* sets line spacing to 7/72 inch */
    switch( Direction )
    {
        case PORTRAIT:
        {
            Lsb = MaxX & 0x00FF;                        /*  MaxX modulo 256    */
            Msb = MaxX >> 8;                            /*  (int) MaxX / 256   */
            for( j=0; j<=MaxY/8; j++ )
            {
                fprintf( stdprn, "\x1B*%c%c%c", Mode, Lsb, Msb );
                for( i=0; i<=MaxX; i++ )
                {
                    m = 0;
                    for( k=0; k<8; k++ )
                    {
                        m <<= 1;                        /* shift m left one bit */
                        if( getpixel( i, j*8+k ) ) m++; /* if pixel on, bit on   */
                    }
                    fprintf( stdprn, "%c", m );
                }
                fprintf( stdprn, "\x0D\x0A" );          /* use CR/LF codes vs \n flag */
            }
        }
```

```
        case LANDSCAPE:
        {
            Lsb = MaxY & 0x00FF;                              /*  MaxY modulo 256    */
            Msb = MaxY >> 8;                                  /*  (int) MaxY / 256    */
            for( j=0; j<MaxX; j+=8 )
            {
                fprintf( stdprn, "\x1B*%c%c%c", Mode, Lsb, Msb );
                for( i=MaxY; i>=0; i-- )
                {
                    m = 0;
                    for( k=0; k<8; k++ )
                    {
                        m <<= 1;                              /* shift m left one bit */
                        if( getpixel( j+k, i ) ) m++;         /* if pixel on, set bit */
                    }
                    fprintf( stdprn, "%c", m );
                }
                fprintf( stdprn, "\x0D\x0A" );                /* use CR/LF codes vs \n flag */
            }
        }
    }
    fprintf( stdprn,"\f" );                                   /* form feed to advance paper */
}                                                             /* end EP-GRAPH.I */
```

```
/*        LJ-GRAPH.I — graphics output driver for laserjet printers        */
void PromptLine( char *msg )
{
    int  height, MaxX = getmaxx(), MaxY = getmaxy();

    setcolor( getmaxcolor() );                      /* Set current color to white     */
    settextstyle( DEFAULT_FONT, HORIZ_DIR, 1 );
    settextjustify( CENTER_TEXT, TOP_TEXT );
    height = textheight( "H" );                     /* Determine current height       */
    bar( 0, MaxY−( height+4 ), MaxX, MaxY );
    rectangle( 0, MaxY−( height+4 ), MaxX, MaxY );
    outtextxy( MaxX/2, MaxY−(height+2), msg );
}

#define  PORTRAIT  0                  /* definitions for Print_Graph */
#define  LANDSCAPE 1                  /* image orientation           */
#define  GREYSCALE 2                  /* and color to grey scale     */
int     Negative;                     /* flag for grey scale order   */

int format( double position )
{
    int width = 6;

    if( position < 1000.0 ) width− −;
    if( position < 100.0 )  width− −;
    if( position < 10.0 )   width− −;
    return( width );
}

int Grey_Scale( int scanline, int palette_entry )
{
    int grey = 0;
    if( GraphDriver == CGA && GraphMode != CGAHI )
    {
        switch( scanline )
        {
```

```
            case 0: { if( palette_entry & 1 ) grey |=  9;        /* sets bits 1.1. */
                      if( palette_entry & 2 ) grey |=  6;        /* sets bits .1.1 */
                    } break;
            case 1: { if( palette_entry & 1 ) grey |=  4;        /* sets bits ...1 */
                      if( palette_entry & 2 ) grey |= 11;        /* sets bits 111. */
                    } break;
            case 2: { if( palette_entry & 1 ) grey |=  2;        /* sets bits 1... */
                      if( palette_entry & 2 ) grey |= 13;        /* sets bits .111 */
                    } break;
            case 3: { if( palette_entry & 1 ) grey |=  9;        /* sets bits .1.1 */
                      if( palette_entry & 2 ) grey |=  6;        /* sets bits 1.1. */
                    } break;
    }   }
    else
    { switch( scanline )
        {
            case 0: { if( palette_entry & 4 ) grey |=  5;        /* sets bits .1.1 */
                      if( palette_entry & 8 ) grey |= 10;        /* sets bits 1.1. */
                    } break;
            case 1: { if( palette_entry & 1 ) grey |=  2;        /* sets bits ..1. */
                      if( palette_entry & 2 ) grey |=  8;        /* sets bits 1... */
                      if( palette_entry & 8 ) grey |=  5;        /* sets bits .1.1 */
                    } break;
            case 2: { if( palette_entry & 4 ) grey |=  5;        /* sets bits .1.1 */
                      if( palette_entry & 8 ) grey |= 10;        /* sets bits 1.1. */
                    } break;
            case 3: { if( palette_entry & 2 ) grey |=  2;        /* sets bits ..1. */
                      if( palette_entry & 8 ) grey |=  5;        /* sets bits .1.1 */
                    } break;
    }   }
    if( Negative ) grey ^= 0x0F;              /* inverts grey scale bit patterns */
    return( grey );
}

void LJ_Graphic( int Mode )
{
```

```
int   i, j, k, p, q, xasp, yasp,
      MaxX = getmaxx() + 1,
      MaxY = getmaxy() + 1;
static  char  graph_ends[] = "\x1B*rB";
static  char  graph_init[] =
              "\x1BE\x1B&l1H\x1B&lO\x1B*p0X\x1B*p0Y\x1B*t";
double  xprint, yprint, prstep, AspR;
char    m, resolution[3];

getaspectratio( &xasp, &yasp );
AspR = (double) xasp / (double) yasp;
setviewport( 0, 0, MaxX, MaxY, 0 );
switch( Mode )
{
    case PORTRAIT:
    {
        xprint = 690.0,                               /* initial page print positions */
        yprint = 500.0,
        strcpy( resolution, "100" );                  /* select 100 DPI resolution    */
        prstep = 7.2 / AspR;                          /* adjust to match screen image */
        fprintf( stdprn, "%s%sR", graph_init, resolution );
        for( j=0; j<=MaxY; j++ )
        {
            fprintf( stdprn, "\x1B&a%-*.1fh%-*.1fV",
                            format( xprint ), xprint,
                            format( yprint ), yprint );
            yprint += prstep;
            fprintf( stdprn, "\x1B*r1A\x1B*b%dW", MaxX/8 );
            for( i=0; i<MaxX/8; i++ )
            {
                m = 0;
                for( k=0; k<8; k++ )
                {
                    m <<= 1;                           /* shift m left one bit */
                    if( getpixel( i*8+k, j ) ) m++;    /* if pixel on, bit on  */
                }
```

```
                        fprintf( stdprn, "%c", m );
                }
                fprintf( stdprn, "%s", graph_ends );
        }
} break;

case LANDSCAPE:
{
        xprint = 1000.0;                          /* initial page print positions */
        yprint = 1000.0;
        strcpy( resolution, "75" );                   /* select 75 DPI resolution    */
        prstep = 9.6 * AspR;                      /* adjust to match screen image */
        fprintf( stdprn, "%s%sR", graph_init, resolution );
        for( j=0; j<MaxX; j++ )
        {
                fprintf( stdprn, "\x1B&a%-*.1fh%-*.1fV",
                                format( xprint ), xprint,
                                format( yprint ), yprint );
                yprint += prstep;
                fprintf( stdprn, "\x1B*r1A\x1B*b%dW", (int) ( MaxY+4 ) / 8 );
                for( i=0; i<=MaxY/8; i++ )
                {
                        m = 0;
                        for( k=0; k<8; k++ )
                        {
                                m <<= 1;                             /* shift m left one bit */
                                if( getpixel( MaxX-j, i*8+k ) ) m++;       /* if pixel, bit on */
                        }
                        fprintf( stdprn, "%c", m );
                }
                fprintf( stdprn, "%s", graph_ends );
        }
}    break;

case GREYSCALE:
{
```

```
        xprint = 1000.0;                              /* initial page print positions */
        yprint = 1000.0;
        strcpy( resolution, "300" );                     /* select 300 DPI resolution   */
        prstep = 2.4 * AspR;                           /* adjust to match screen image */
        fprintf( stdprn, "%s%sR", graph_init, resolution );
        for( j=0; j<=MaxX; j++ )
        for( p=0; p<4; p++ )
        {
            fprintf( stdprn, "\x1B&a%-*.1fh%-*.1fV",
                            format( xprint ), xprint,
                            format( yprint ), yprint );
            yprint += prstep;
            fprintf( stdprn, "\x1B*r1A\x1B*b%dW", MaxY/2 );
            for( i=0; i<=MaxY/2; i++ )
            {
                m = 0;
                for( k=0; k<=1; k++ )
                {
                    m <<= 4;                            /* shift m left four bits */
                    m |= Grey_Scale( p, getpixel( MaxX-j, i*2+k ) );
                }
                fprintf( stdprn, "%c", m );
            }
            fprintf( stdprn, "%s", graph_ends );
        }
    }   break;
    }
    /* end of Switch */
    fprintf( stdprn, "\x0C\x1B&lO\x1B(8U\x1B(sp10h12vsb3T\x1B&l1H" );
                                                        /* close operations */
}

void Print_Pause( int Invert )
{
    char Ch;
    int  Done = 0;
```

```
if( Invert ) Negative = 1; else Negative = 0;
PromptLine( "Enter <P>ortrait, <L>andscape, <G>reyscale"
            " -- any other key to exit ..." );
while( !Done )
{
    while( kbhit() ) getch();
    Ch = getch();
    switch( toupper(Ch) )
    {
        case 'P'  : LJ_Graphic( PORTRAIT );  break;
        case 'L'  : LJ_Graphic( LANDSCAPE ); break;
        case 'G' : LJ_Graphic( GREYSCALE ); break;
        default   : Done++;
    }
}
}
```

CHAPTER 15

GRAPHICS PLOTTER OUTPUT

Recording Color Images

Previously, I've shown how a graphics screen could be output to a printer
(either dot-matrix or laserjet). A great deal of the demo programs in this
book, however, have been using colors, while the printer outputs have only
been black-on-white or at best, grey-scaled. So, what about color output
devices?

Aside from cameras — which do not depend on programming — only two
types of devices are currently available for recording color images from
computer screens: color printers and color plotters.

Color Printers

Color printers — which use multicolor ribbons to create color images — are
relatively limited in resolution and in the range of colors that can be created.
Since several different models are available (though none are common) and
since no standard presently exists for these devices, I am not going to cover
them in much detail. I should say though that the dot-matrix driver can be
easily modified for color recognition (see the grey-scale options in Chapter
14 and the **Match_Color** procedure in PLOTTER.I in this chapter) and
plotting ... within its limited reproduction capabilities.

Color Plotters

The second — and preferred — choice for reproducing a color image is a
color plotter such as the Hewlett-Packard ColorPro. A monocolor plotter can

also be used if provision is made to swap pen colors as appropriate (or the color plotter's color range can be extended with provision for swapping pen carousels), but the initial assumption here will be a plotter with an eight-pen carousel using — by virtue of being an industry standard — the HP Graphics Language instruction set.

Caveat

The color plotter was not designed nor intended to be used as a bit-mapped output device ... but it comes closer to fitting this application than does anything else presently available. With a certain amount of care and accommodation, it is capable of providing hard copy color reproduction, but it does so with two principal drawbacks; slow operation and limited color correspondence.

If you are already familiar with plotter operation, you may skip this explanation, but for those who are not, here's how a plotter works.

Plotter Operation

Plotters use special pens (hard-nib, fiber-tip or roller-ball) to draw images directly on a sheet of paper or transparent film. Some plotters move the pen along two axes while the paper remains fixed on a flat platen (flatbed). Others move the pen along one axis and the paper along the second axis (gritwheel). The simplest plotters can use only one pen at a time, requiring manual assistance to change drawing colors and others hold 3, 4, 6 or 8 pens (usually in a carousel) and select pens according to software instructions.

Because the plotter is a mechanical device — physically moving a drawing pen across a sheet of paper and raising and lowering the pen to draw a single line at a time, the plotter is slower than other graphics output devices.

Likewise, plotter resolutions vary, ranging from resolutions of 0.00008 inch to a more common resolution of 0.004 inch with repeatability (accuracy of registration on subsequent plots) usually falling in the +\–0.004 inch range.

In operation, the plotter is designed to draw a line between two points specified by coordinate pairs (from xstart/ystart to xend/yend). This line is drawn by simultaneously by moving the pen along both axes (or by moving both pen and paper simultaneously) and the resulting line is a direct (analog) output as opposed to the stepped-pixel (digital) line created on a CRT (or a laserjet).

The Hewlett-Packard Graphics Language (HPGL) provides an instruction set for communicating with the plotter to create images directly (not by recreating screen images) and, *for most applications*, is both faster and smoother than using a plotter screen dump. For more information on HP plotter capabilities and the HPGL instruction set, refer to the **HP ColorPro Graphics Plotter Programming Manual**, available from Hewlett-Packard.

Plotting The CRT

It isn't always practical to program an image directly. To map a CRT image to a plotter, individual screen pixels are recreated as a series of short lines, using one pen (drawing color) at a time and repeating the operation for each color used in the reproduction. Thus, for an EGA/VGA screen filled with an essentially random color dot pattern, a complete screen output in full color can require four to six hours (and this using a relatively *fast* plotter).

This is, however, the worst case example. For more common displays, by drawing adjacent pixels of a single color as a single continuous line, a full screen display can be recreated, in color, in only 30 to 45 minutes.

Note: the PLOTTER.I utility was tested during development using the screen image generated by the COLORCUB.C demo program (see Chapter 13). The first working version of the PLOTTER.I utility required two hours, nine minutes and 33 seconds to complete. With refinements, the same image can now be completed in a mere 32 minutes.

Plotter Colors

The second drawback mentioned in using a color plotter to copy a screen image, was a limited color palette on the plotter. Using the ColorPro plotter, 10 pen colors are available (yellow, orange, red, red-violet, violet, blue, aqua, green, brown and black) and pen colors can be combined to yield some additional hues.

Because the pen carousel can only hold eight pens, the yellow, red-violet, red, green, blue, violet, brown and black pens were chosen for demonstration and should be inserted in the carousel in this order to match the instructions in the PLOTTER.I utility.

The principal colors and color combinations are shown in Table 15-1.

Table 15-1: Pen Color Combinations Using Plotter

Pen Colors[1]	Yellow	Red/Violet	Red	Green	Blue	Violet	Brown	Black
Yellow	YELLOW							
Red/Violet	*	LTMAGENTA				**Resulting Colors**		
Red	LTRED	*	RED					
Green	LTGREEN	*	*	GREEN				
Blue	*GREEN*	*BLUE*	*	*CYAN*	LTBLUE			
Violet	*	*	*	*BLUE*	BLUE	MAGENTA		
Brown	*BROWN*	*VIOLET*	*RUST*	*	GREY	*	BROWN	
Black	BLACK	BLACK	BLACK	BLACK	BLACK	BLACK	BLACK	BLACK

1. All color equivalents are only approximations. COLOR NAMES in caps correspond to named EGA/VGA colors. *Italic color names* are other resulting hues. Asterisks indicate unnamed (or unnameable) color combinations.

Several of the possible color combinations are not particularly useful in emulating EGA/VGA palette colors. Quite a few of these combinations result in muddy hues and others do not match hues in the EGA/VGA default color palette.

Also, I have not been able to create good plotter equivalents for all colors. In the PLOTTER.I utility, the EGA/VGA default palette is mapped as shown in the Table 15-2.

Table 15-2: Mapping EGA/VGA Colors to Plotter Colors

EGA/VGA COLORS	PEN COLOR(S)
YELLOW	yellow
LIGHTRED	yellow, red
LIGHTGREEN	yellow, green
LIGHTMAGENTA	red-violet
RED	red
GREEN	green
CYAN	green, blue
LIGHTCYAN	green, blue
LIGHTBLUE	blue
BLUE	blue, violet
DARKGREY	blue, brown
LIGHTGREY	blue, brown
MAGENTA	violet
BROWN	brown
WHITE	black

As you can see, the CYAN and LIGHTCYAN, and the DARKGREY and LIGHTGREY hues are identical. If you like, yellow can be added to the two lighter colors, but this will not greatly differentiate them. Also, the LIGHTMAGENTA (red-violet) and RED (red) do not appear clearly separated.

Also notice that WHITE (on the screen) is mapped to black on paper while the screen background (BLACK) is not mapped at all. You can change this and experiment with your own color combinations — you may well find a better set of colors to fit a specific application.

Ideally, better color combinations could be created if a better initial set of pen colors — beginning with lighter primary colors — was available. With the currently available pen colors, however, the hues shown are the best possible.

Also, the present order of pen colors is chosen so the lightest colors are drawn first and the light pens do not become contaminated by darker inks picked up from the paper.

Selecting The Plotter Serial Interface

The HP ColorPro plotter (and many others) uses a serial interface for communication. On the ColorPro, a dip switch on the back of the unit (between the power and RS-232C connectors) is used to select the serial baud rate, stop bits and parity information. The dip switch settings are shown in Table 15-3.

Table 15-3: HP Color Pro Switch Settings

BAUD RATE	1 STOP BIT				2 STOP BITS			
	B1	B2	B3	B4	B1	B2	B3	B4
75	-	-	-	-	1	0	0	0
110	-	-	-	-	0	1	0	0
150	1	1	0	0	-	-	-	-
200	0	0	1	0	-	-	-	-
300	1	0	1	0	1	1	0	1
600	0	1	1	0	0	0	1	1
1200	1	1	1	0	1	0	1	1
2400	0	0	0	1	0	1	1	1
4800	1	0	0	1	1	1	1	1
9600	0	1	0	1	0	0	0	0

PARITY	S1	S2	
none	0	0	(space parity)
none	0	1	(mark parity)
even	1	0	
odd	1	1	

And a Serial Curiosity

For reasons that I cannot explain (and no-one at Hewlett-Packard seems to know) all HP serial devices use a non-standard RS-232C serial port connection.

Unfortunately, this small factor *is not* explained in any of the HP manuals, but is left to your powers of deductive reasoning. If you have purchased your serial cables from HP, then they should work fine ... with HP devices ... but not with any other serial equipment such as modems, standard dot-matrix devices, etc.

One clue is provided, however — an unexplained diagram for a dummy modem appearing in an appendix in the user's manual.

Figure 15-1: RS-232C Dummy (Null) Modem

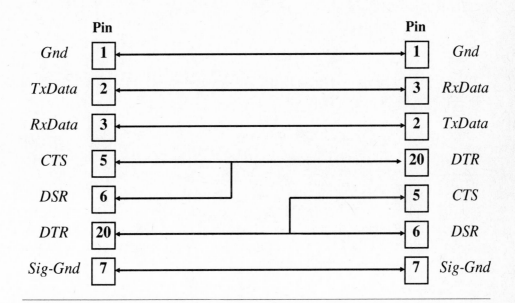

365

The special serial interface cabling required does correspond to the familiar ''dummy'' or null-modem cable (see Figure 15-1). If you do not look forward to manufacturing a null-modem cable, a simple null-modem connector can be purchased at your local computer or electronic supply store.

Using The PLOTTER.I Utility

The **Call_Plotter** procedure accepts a port argument and four screen coordinates for the area that will be output to the plotter.

```
void Call_Plotter( unsigned select_port,  int xstart, int ystart,
                                           int xend,  int yend )
{
    if( init_port( select_port ) & InitComm )
    {
        init_plotter();
        plot_screen( xstart, ystart, xend, yend );
        close_plotter();
    }
}
```

Note: no provisions are included to test errors in the port or screen coordinates passed as arguments.

Communicating With The Serial Port

Turbo C provides several predefined streams such as *stdprn* for the printer port (parallel or PRN:), *stdin* and *stdout* (the CON: device) and *stdaux* for the serial port (AUX:, typically COM1). These do not, however, allow you to direct communications to COM2, COM3 or COM4.

If you are like me, you probably already have the COM1 port (and maybe COM2) in use. While DOS will allow for the redirecting of your output to any of the ports, it is an awkward method of handling output.

Instead of worrying about these predefined output streams, the PLOTTER utility uses ROM Bios calls to communicate directly with the serial port selected and definitions are provided for COM1, COM2, COM3 and COM4.

Before communications can be opened, the desired serial port must be initialized with the desired baud rate, parity, stop bits and word len (see Table 15-4).

Table 15-4: Serial Port Initialization Parameter Values

BITS	7,6,5,	BAUD RATE	4, 3,	PARITY	2,	STOP BITS	1, 0	WORD LEN
	000 =	110	**00** =	SPACE	**0** =	1 BIT	**00** =	N/A
	001 =	150	**01** =	ODD	**1** =	2 BITS	**01** =	N/A
	010 =	300	**10** =	MARK			**10** =	7 BITS
	011 =	600	**11** =	EVEN			**11** =	BITS
	100 =	1200						
	101 =	2400						
	110 =	4800						
	111 =	9600						

Note: normal settings for ColorPro plotter are: 9600, none, 8 bits = 11100011 (E3h).

The **init_port** function is called with an argument that selects the port desired and returns an unsigned integer showing the port status. The *Init_Comm* parameter is defined in PLOTTER.I as *E3*h (see Table 15-4).

```
unsigned init_port( unsigned active_port )
{
    port = active_port;
    inreg.x.ax = InitComm;
    inreg.x.dx = port;
    call_port;
    return( inreg.x.ax );
}
```

Initializing The Plotter

The **init_plotter** procedure is used to set up values in order to map the screen to the plotter and to initialize the plotter for operation. Prior to initialization, the assumption is that the plotter has been turned on and loaded — operations that can only be executed manually from the plotter control panel.

When using the plotter, unlike the EP_GRAPH and LJ_GRAPH utilities, no provisions are required to match the screen aspect to the device. The four parameters *xplot1*, *yplot1*, *xplot2* and *yplot2*, defined in PLOTTER.I, match the active plot area to the physical screen proportions, while the *HStep* and *VStep* variables calculated in **init_plotter** (using the *MaxX* and *MaxY* variables read from the system) adjust the plotter increments to match the screen aspect ratio within the plotting area.

```
void  init_plotter()
{
     MaxX = getmaxx();
     MaxY = getmaxy();
     HStep = (double) xplot2 / MaxX;
     VStep = (double) yplot2 / MaxY;
```

The **writeport** procedure is first called to set the plotter to hardwire handshaking using the ESCape-'P3' sequence. Several other handshaking methods and protocols are supported if needed, including XOn/XOff, ENQuiry/ACKnowledge and software checking handshakes (see the **HP ColorPro Programming Manual** for details).

```
writeport( "[P3;" );
```

Next, the 'IN;' instruction is sent to set the plotter to its default conditions, cancelling any coordinate rotations, scaling or other settings.

```
writeport( "IN;" );
```

Finally, the 'SC' (scale) instruction is passed with the four predefined parameters setting up the P1 and P2 coordinate locations that define the corners of the active plotting area.

```
            writeport( "SC%d,%d,%d,%d;\n",
                   xplot1, yplot1, xplot2, yplot2 );
    }
```

Figure 15-2: Plotter Page Layout

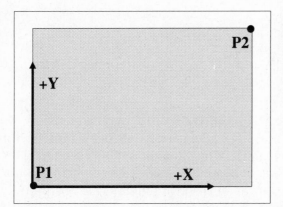

The plotter uses the landscape mode by default with the 0,0 origin point in the lower-left corner of the page.

The shaded region defined by P1 and P2 is the active plot area.

By default, the plotter expects all measurements to be in ''plotter units''. A plotter unit (pu) is defined (for the ColorPro) as 0.025 mm or 0.00098 inches (40 pu = 1 mm or 1016 pu = 1 inch). Remember, however, that the plotter is only accurate to 0.004 inches or about four plotter units.

Plotting The Screen

The **plot_screen** procedure is called with four parameters that select the screen area to be mapped to the plotter. The **plot_screen** procedure begins by selecting a pen from the carousel, then reading the graphics screen by rows and columns, looking for pixels matching the pen selection. (The screen

369

is read by column from left to right, each column being read from bottom to top.)

```
void  plot_screen( int xstart, int ystart, int xend, int yend )
{
        int  x, y, pen, pen_stat, retrace;
        for( pen=1; pen8; pen++ )
        {
            select_pen( pen );
            for( x=xstart; x<=xend; x++ )
            {
                pen_stat = 0;
                retrace = TRUE;
                for( y=yend; y<=ystart; y-- )
                {
```

As long as the pen is up (*pen_stat* = FALSE or 0), **plot_screen** begins by looking for a screen pixel that matches the current pen color (or which the current pen color is used to plot). When found, a plot absolute ('PA') command is sent with the plotter coordinates corresponding to the pixel coordinates followed by a pen down ('PD') instruction. If the *retrace* flag is true, a brief delay is executed to allow time for the pen to move from its previous position.

The *retrace* flag is reset at the beginning of each column scanned. The *y_ref* variable is updated with the y-axis plot coordinates, with each pen up instruction and the delay is calculated according to the distance the pen is required to move on retrace.

Finally, the pen status flag (*pen_stat*) is set to TRUE;

```
                if( !pen_stat && match_color( pen, getpixel( x, y ) ) )
                {
                    writeport( "PA%9.3f,%9.3f;PD;\n",
                            x*HStep, (MaxY-y)*VStep );
                    if( retrace )
                    {
                        delay((int)abs(y_ref-(y*VStep))/10);
```

```
                    retrace = FALSE;
                }
                pen_stat = TRUE;
            }
```

Now the scan continues, but this time, seeking a pixel that does not require the current pen color is being sought.

```
            if( pen_stat && !match_color( pen, getpixel( x, y ) ) )
            {
                y_ref = y * VStep;
                writeport( "PA%9.3f,%9.3f;PU;\n",
                                x*HStep, (MaxY–(y+1))*VStep );
                pen_stat = FALSE;
            }
        }
```

When found, the immediately preceding pixel location (which, presumably, did use the current pen color) is used to send a second set of plotter coordinates, again using the plot absolute ('PA') instruction, but ending with a pen up ('PU') instruction and setting *pen_stat* to FALSE. With this last instruction set completed, a line is drawn from the previous coordinate position to the present position.

Note also that the *y_ref* variable has also received the plotter y-axis position that may or may not be used subsequently to provide a retrace delay.

If, on the current scan, no pixel is found that does not use the present pen color (the line extends to the top of the screen), instructions are provided to complete the line at this point.

```
            if( pen_stat )
            {
                y_ref = y * VStep;
                writeport( "PA%9.3f,%9.3f;PU;\n",
                                x*HStep, (MaxY–(y+1))*VStep );
                pen_stat = FALSE;
            }
        }
```

Finally, when the graphics screen has been completely scanned, the *select_pen(0)* instruction returns the current pen to the carousel. The initial loop then proceeds to select the next pen in order and another scan begins.

```
        select_pen( 0 );
        }
}
```

The select_pen procedure

The **select_pen** procedure is called with one argument that indicates the pen number desired or, with a zero argument that instructs the plotter to return the present pen (if any) to the carousel.

```
void   select_pen( int pen )
{
        writeport( "SP%d;\n", pen );
        if( pen ) delay(5000);
}
```

If a fresh pen is being selected from the carousel, a five-second delay is provided to allow time for the pickup. No delay is provided when a pen is being returned to the holder.

The match_color function

The **match_pen** function is called, with the current pen number and the screen pixel value, and decides which screen pixel colors are plotted using the current pen color. If the pixel color (palette entry) matches the test conditions for the current pen number, **match_color** returns TRUE. Otherwise, the function returns FALSE.

```
int   match_color( int pen, int scolor )
{
        switch( pen )
        {
            case 1: if(   scolor == YELLOW ||
```

```
                    scolor == LIGHTRED ||
                    scolor == LIGHTGREEN )
                        return( TRUE );                break;
        case 2: if(  scolor == LIGHTMAGENTA )
                        return( TRUE );                break;
        case 3: if(  scolor == LIGHTRED ||
                    scolor == RED )
                        return( TRUE );                break;
        case 4: if(  scolor == LIGHTCYAN ||
                    scolor == LIGHTGREEN ||
                    scolor == CYAN ||
                    scolor == GREEN )
                        return( TRUE );                break;
        case 5: if(  scolor == LIGHTCYAN ||
                    scolor == LIGHTBLUE ||
                    scolor == CYAN ||
                    scolor == BLUE ||
                    scolor == LIGHTGREY ||
                    scolor == DARKGREY )
                        return( TRUE );                break;
        case 6: if(  scolor == MAGENTA ||
                    scolor == BLUE )
                        return( TRUE );                break;
        case 7: if(  scolor == BROWN ||
                    scolor == LIGHTGREY ||
                    scolor == DARKGREY )
                        return( TRUE );                break;
        case 8: if(  scolor == WHITE )
                        return( TRUE );                break;
        }
        return( FALSE );
}
```

For a CGA system, a new **match_color** function would be required using both the palette entry and the palette (Mode) selection. Remember: the color values here refer to only the EGA/VGA default palette entries — not to the actual color values that are assigned to the palette.

The writeport procedure

The **writeport** procedure accepts a character or format string with optional arguments for output to the active serial port.

```
void writeport( char *fmt, ... )
{
        va_list      argptr;
        char         str[140];
        int          i;
        unsigned     test;

        va_start( argptr, format );
        vsprintf( str, fmt, argptr );
```

In using formatted string handling and variable arguments, **writeport** is similar to the procedures **gprintf**, **gprintxy** and **gprintc,** which have been discussed previously.

In outputting the final string to a serial port, however, a slightly different handling is required. In this instance, the string (*str*) is sent to the plotter one character at a time, with the **plotter_ready** function called before each character is sent, to be sure that the plotter is ready to accept additional input.

```
        for(i=0; i<=strlen(str); i++)
        {
                while( !plotter_ready() ) ;
```

Once **plotter_ready** returns TRUE, the AH register is given the argument 01h (function 1 — write to serial port) and the AL register takes the character value.

```
                inreg.h.ah = 0x0100
                inreg.h.al = str[i]
```

The DX register receives the *port* argument.

```
inreg.x.dx = port;
```

The *call_port* function (defined as *int86(0x14, &inreg, &outreg)*) calls the ROM Bios interrupt 14h — Bios serial port services.

```
        call_port;
}
    va_end( argptr );
}
```

The plotter_ready procedure

The plotter has only a small buffer for input. The **plotter_ready** function; therefore, is used to test the selected serial port before information is sent.

```
int     plotter_ready()
{
        unsigned  result;
        inreg.x.ax = 0x0300;
        inreg.x.dx = port;
        call_port;
        delay(5);
        result = outreg.x.ax;
            if( result & 0x0010 ) return( TRUE );
            else                  return( FALSE );
}
```

Interrupt 14h, Function 03h asks the serial port and the device connected to the port for status information. The AH register returns the serial port status, the AL register returns information from the device connected to the port (such as a modem or, in this case, a serial plotter). The meaning of the bit flags returned are shown in Table 15-5.

Table 15-5: Serial Port Status Bytes

BIT	AH REGISTER	BIT	AL REGISTER
7	timed-out	7	receive line signal detected
6	tx shift register empty	6	ring indicator
5	tx hold register empty	5	data-set ready (DSR)
4	break detected	4	clear to send (CTS)
3	framing error	3	detect change in receive line signal
2	parity error	2	trailing edge ring indicator
1	overrun error	1	change in DSR status
0	data ready	0	change in CTS status

In this instance, only one bit is tested: the CTS (Clear To Send) status flag. If you have any trouble with a plotter not responding correctly, you might change the test conditions to check *60B0h,* which tests the serial port tx shift and hold registers and the DSR, CTS and receive line signals.

The close_plotter procedure

When the screen plot is completed, the **close_plotter** function is called to set the pen position to the P1 location. It returns the current pen to the carousel.

```
void  close_plotter()
{
    writeport( "PA0,0;SP0;\n" );
}
```

```
/*          PLOTTER.I — Include file for direct control of serial plotter          */

#include <dos.h>

#define call_port int86(0x14, &inreg, &outreg)            /*      serial port intr   */
#define COM1        0x0000                      /*    def port for COM1 device  */
#define COM2        0x0001                      /*    def port for COM2 device  */
#define COM3        0x0002                      /*    def port for COM3 device  */
#define COM4        0x0003                      /*    def port for COM4 device  */
#define InitComm    0x00E3                      /*    initialization parameters */
#define FALSE  0
#define TRUE   1

union REGS      inreg,   outreg;                          /*static registers used   */

double HStep, VStep;                                     /*x and y plot increments  */
int  xplot1 = 0,  yplot1 = 0;                            /*plotter origin points    */
int  xplot2 = 10250;                                     /*max x-axis plotter units */
int  yplot2 = 7479;                                      /*max y-axis plotter units */
int  MaxX, MaxY;                                         /*graphics screen size     */
int  port;                                               /*active port for plotter  */
int  y_ref;                                              /*plot position reference  */

/*                         Pen Positions Expected In Carousel              */
/*            pen colors    order        video palette                     */
/*            Yellow        1            14, 12, 10                         */
/*            Red-Violet    2            13                                 */
/*            Red           3            12, 4                              */
/*            Green         4            11, 10, 3, 2                       */
/*            Blue          5            11, 9, 8, 7, 3, 1                  */
/*            Violet        6            5, 1                               */
/*            Brown         7            6, 8, 7                            */
/*            Black         8            15                                 */

unsigned init_port( unsigned active_port )
{
    port = active_port;
```

```c
    inreg.x.ax = InitComm;              /*      initialization parameter  */
    inreg.x.dx = port;                  /*      which port to open        */
    call_port;
    return( inreg.x.ax );
}


int  plotter_ready()
{
    unsigned  result;
    inreg.x.ax = 0x0300;
    inreg.x.dx = port;
    call_port;
    delay(5);
    result = outreg.x.ax;
    if( result & 0x0010 ) return( TRUE );
    else                  return( FALSE );
}

void writeport( char *fmt, ... )
{
    va_list  argptr;                    /*      argument list pointer      */
    char    str[140];                   /*      buffer to build sting into */
    int    i;
    unsigned test;
    va_start( argptr, format );         /*      initialize va_functions    */
    vsprintf( str, fmt, argptr );       /*      add elements to str buffer */
    for(i=0; i<=strlen(str); i++)       /*      output string to plotter   */
    {
        while( !plotter_ready() ) ;     /*      wait for buffer space      */
        inreg.x.ah = 0x01
        inreg.x.al = str[i]
        inreg.x.dx = port;
        call_port;
    }
    va_end( argptr );                   /*      close va_functions         */
```

```
}

void  init_plotter()
{
    MaxX = getmaxx();
    MaxY = getmaxy();
    HStep = (double) xplot2/MaxX;
    VStep = (double) yplot2/MaxY;
    writeport( "[P3;" );                          /*EscP3 - initiate handshake*/
    writeport( "IN;" );                           /*      initialize plotter   */
    writeport( "SC %d, %d, %d, %d; \n",           /*      set scaling          */
                    xplot1, yplot1, xplot2, yplot2 );
}

void  close_plotter()
{
    writeport( "PA0,0;SP0;\n" );
}

void  select_pen( int pen )
{
    writeport( "SP%d;", pen );                    /*      select pen from carousel   */
    if( pen ) delay(5000);                        /*      allow time for pickup      */
}

int  match_color( int pen, int scolor )
{
    switch( pen )
    {
        case 1:  if(  scolor == YELLOW ||
                      scolor == LIGHTRED ||
                      scolor == LIGHTGREEN )
                                            return( TRUE ); break;
        case 2:  if( scolor == LIGHTMAGENTA )
                                            return( TRUE ); break;
        case 3:  if( scolor == LIGHTRED ||
```

```
                            scolor == RED )
                                                     return( TRUE );break;
            case 4:  if(  scolor == LIGHTCYAN ||
                          scolor == LIGHTGREEN ||
                          scolor == CYAN ||
                          scolor == GREEN )
                                                     return( TRUE );break;
            case 5:  if(  scolor == LIGHTCYAN ||
                          scolor == LIGHTBLUE ||
                          scolor == CYAN ||
                          scolor == BLUE ||
                          scolor == LIGHTGREY ||
                          scolor == DARKGREY )
                                                     return( TRUE );break;
            case 6:  if(  scolor == MAGENTA ||
                          scolor == BLUE )
                                                     return( TRUE ); break;
            case 7:  if(  scolor == BROWN ||
                          scolor == LIGHTGREY ||
                          scolor == DARKGREY )
                                                     return( TRUE ); break;
            case 8:  if(  scolor == WHITE )          return( TRUE ); break;
        }
        return( FALSE );
    }

    void  plot_screen( int xstart, int ystart, int xend, int yend )
    {
        int  x, y, pen, pen_stat, retrace;

        for( pen=1; pen<=8; pen++ )
        {
            select_pen( pen );
            for( x= xstart; x<=xend; x++ )
            {
            pen_stat = 0;
```

```
        retrace = TRUE;
        for( y=yend; y<=ystart; y− − )
        {
            if( !pen_stat && match_color( pen, getpixel( x, y ) ) )
            {
                writeport( "PA%9.3f,%9.3f;PD;\n",
                            x*HStep, (MaxY−y)*VStep );
                if( retrace )
                {                              /*        allow time for pen to retrace        */
                    delay((int)abs(y_ref−(y*VStep))/10);
                    retrace = FALSE;
                }
                pen_stat = TRUE;
            }
            if( pen_stat && !match_color( pen, getpixel( x, y ) ) )
            {
                y_ref = y * VStep;
                writeport( "PA%9.3f,%9.3f;PU;\n",
                            x*HStep, (MaxY−(y+1))*VStep );
                pen_stat = FALSE;
            }
        }   }
        if( pen_stat )                         /*        if the pen's still down at screen end */
        {
            y_ref = y * VStep;
            writeport( "PA%9.3f,%9.3f;PU;\n",
                        x*HStep, (MaxY−(y+1))*VStep );
            pen_stat = FALSE;
        }
    }
    select_pen( 0 );
    }
}

void Call_Plotter( unsigned select_port, int xstart, int ystart,
            int xend,   int yend )
{
```

```
        if( init_port( select_port ) & InitComm )
        {
            init_plotter();
            plot_screen( xstart, ystart, xend, yend );
            close_plotter();
        }
    }                                                    /*      end PLOTTER.I   */
```

CHAPTER 16

USING A MOUSE WITH GRAPHICS DISPLAYS

When an input device is required with a graphics display (text graphics excepted), the obvious choice is to use the mouse as the primary selection mechanism and the cursor keys (in the absence of a mouse) as a secondary device.

The mouse can be used in two different fashions. First, by reading the mouse output codes as an analog of the cursor keys and second, by directly incorporating a mouse driver in your program and directly interpreting mouse events.

Reading Mouse Events As Cursor Keys

This method uses the default mouse interface (the MOUSE.COM or MOUSE.SYS driver) supplied with the physical mouse hardware and requires little or no special provision by the programmer. When the mouse is moved left, the system receives the two codes (scan and char codes) *00h*, *48h* — just as if the left arrow key had been pressed. This assumes that the scan and char key codes are being read directly from the input device or port. Similarly, the left mouse button normally returns the same code (*0Dh*) as pressing the *Enter* key on the keyboard.

However, with a Logitech mouse (and many others), these key response codes can be reassigned or even interpreted as macro instructions (see your mouse manual for details) and it can be difficult to insure that the appropriate and desired responses will always be returned by the mouse software.

A Direct Mouse Interface

For most graphics applications, indirectly interpreting the mouse input (treating the mouse as a keyboard analog) is unreliable or unsatisfactory for several reasons: the mouse movement and key responses may not be assigned correctly, the information returned is less complete than can be read directly from the mouse, little or no control can be exercised over the mouse parameters, and the program loop time may produce too much delay in responding to the mouse movement.

For these reasons, most graphics applications seek to exercise a direct interface with the mouse device, allowing the program to set mouse parameters and to read mouse events and position directly.

The following mouse interface procedures allow you (via your program) to:
- restrict mouse movement to a specific screen area
- read the mouse screen position directly
- change the mouse response rates and adjust vertical and horizontal mouse to screen movement ratios
- read mouse keys as both make and break events and test individual key-down status
- select graphics mouse cursors or create new graphics mouse cursor patterns
- selectively hide or display the mouse cursor

Most of these capabilities will be demonstrated in the G-MOUSE.C program in this chapter.

Mouse Types

The mouse interface procedures are provided as an include file MOUSE.I in this chapter and are also available on disk, as source codes, together with the other utilities and demo programs appearing in this book. These mouse interface procedures can be used with both graphics and text applications, though only the graphics interface applications will be demonstrated here (the corresponding text interface applications are relatively simple, differ only in minor elements and require little explanation).

To begin, there are currently two basic types of mouse in use: the Microsoft (two button) mouse and the Logitech (three button) mouse. While mice with a variety of trademarks are available, most will conform to one of these two standards.

First, the basic Microsoft mouse supports 16 mouse functions (functions 0..15) and has two buttons, each producing a make and a break response capable of being read as pressed or released.

The Logitech mouse supports all features of the Microsoft mouse, but adds two additional mouse functions (functions 16 and 19) and a third (middle) button.

The procedures in MOUSE.I include both the Microsoft and Logitech mouse functions and the G-MOUSE.C program will operate with either type of mouse though the third button and functions 16 and 19 will not be supported by the Microsoft mouse.

Note: these mouse procedures presume the presence of two items: a hardware mouse and a mouse device driver — both of which are supplied by the mouse manufacturer or vendor. The hardware mouse may be either a serial or buss mouse and the mouse device driver may be either MOUSE.COM or MOUSE.SYS (normally both device drivers are supplied with each mouse).

Definitions and Constants

The **dos** header file is required to define the DOS registers used by the interface procedures and *call_mouse* is defined as a macro to access DOS interrupt function 33h (the Mouse interrupt function).

```
#include <dos.h>
#define  call_mouse int86(0x33, &inreg, &outreg)
```

385

The EVENTMASK, defined here as 7Fh, is a mask for accessing the mouse event register and will be explained further. The SOFTWARE and HARDWARE constants are provided to select text cursor types and the constants ON and OFF are provided as general purpose Boolean values.

```
#define EVENTMASK  0x7F
#define SOFTWARE   0
#define HARDWARE   1
#define OFF        0
#define ON         1
```

Variables and Structures

Two global variables are created in MOUSE.I and are used to track the graphics mouse cursor status.

```
int  m_cursor = ON, m_view = OFF;          /* mouse cursor status flags */
union REGS  inreg, outreg;                 /* static registers used */
```

And several data structures are defined for use by the mouse interface procedures (and are also used by the G-MOUSE.C demo).

The first structure, **m_result**, is provided to test the presence of mouse in the system and also returns the number of buttons on the mouse (2 or 3).

```
typedef struct   {   int present,
                         buttons;
                 }   m_result;
```

The **m_status** structure returns several values.

The *button_status* value is returned with bits 0-2 set if the corresponding button is down. On a Microsoft mouse, only bits 0-1 will be set, bit 0 corresponding to the left button, bit 1 to the right button. With a Logitech mouse, bit 2 corresponds to the center button.

The *button_count* value returns the number of times a specified button has been pressed (since the button status was last reset).

And the *xaxis* and *yaxis* values return the mouse cursor screen position at the time the specified button was pressed. Note: since the mouse cursor is not a single pixel point, the coordinates returned are the coordinates of the cursor ''hot spot''. See **Graphics Mouse Cursors** for further information.

```
typedef struct  {    int  button_status,
                     button_count,
                     xaxis, yaxis;
                }    m_status;
```

The **m_movement** structure returns two values: *x_count* is the net horizontal movement (in *mickeys* — mouse movement units, not screen pixels) since *x_count* was last reset. The *y_count* value is the corresponding vertical movement.

```
typedef struct  {    int x_count;
                     y_count;
                }    m_movement;
```

The **mouse_event** structure returns four unsigned integer values: the *flag* or mouse event register value selected by EVENTMASK, the *button* value showing which button was last pressed and the *xaxis* and *yaxis* values which show the coordinate location of the mouse cursor when the last mouse event occurred.

```
typedef struct  {    unsigned flag,
                     button,
                     xaxis, yaxis;
                }    mouse_event;
```

The *flag* register is read as a bit register and will normally contain only one bit set — the bit indicating the last mouse event that occurred.

And the global pointer **m_events** points to the **mouse_event** structure. Note: this is a global *far* pointer and will be referenced heavily in the G-MOUSE demo.

```
static mouse_event far *m_events;
```

Figure 16-1: The Flag Register Bits

The mask value 007Fh (EVENTMASK) excludes everything except bits 0..6 (unshaded) of the 16-bit register. These seven flag bits are defined as shown.

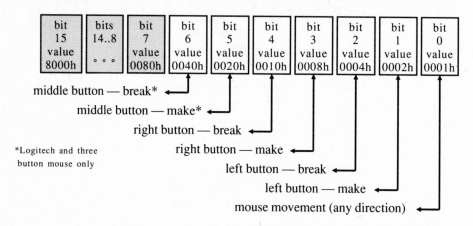

middle button — break*

middle button — make*

*Logitech and three button mouse only

right button — break

right button — make

left button — break

left button — make

mouse movement (any direction)

The **g_cursor** structure defines a pointer to the graphics mouse cursor pattern and the ''hot spot'' (*xkey* and *ykey*) coordinates relative to the upper-left corner of the cursor image. See **Graphics Mouse Cursors** for further details.

```
typedef struct  {    unsigned    *image,
                     xkey, ykey;
                )    g_cursor;
```

The Mouse Interface Functions

Eighteen basic mouse functions are discussed in this section. The two lightpen functions, however, are combined in a single procedure in this implementation.

The m_reset Function

Interrupt 33h, function 00h checks for the presence of the mouse, resets it to the default status, initializes the mouse driver and returns a pointer to the **m_result** data structure.

```
m_result *m_reset()
{
    static m_result  m;

    inreg.x.ax = 0;
    call_mouse;
    m.present = outreg.x.ax;
    m.buttons = outreg.x.bx;
    return ( &m );
}
```

The **m_result** structure contains a Boolean value, *present*, indicating the existence of the mouse driver and mouse hardware and the variable *buttons* showing how many buttons are present (2 or 3) if the mouse is present. The variable *present* will be 0 if no mouse is found, −1 if the mouse is found.

This function is always called to initialize the mouse or to reset the graphics mouse cursor to the default cursor image (the left slanted arrow image).

The m_show and m_hide Functions

The **m_show** procedure makes the mouse graphics cursor visible using interrupt 33h, function 01h. The **m_hide** procedure turns off the mouse graphics cursor using function 02h. Two Boolean tests have been included in each procedure.

The first flag, *m_cursor*, is used in implementing an analog of the **m_conceal** function and will be explained later.

The *m_view* flag is more immediately important and is used to determine if the mouse graphics cursor is already visible or not. Each time the mouse interrupt function is called to turn on the mouse cursor, an internal counter increments and, when the mouse cursor is turned off, this counter is decremented. If the counter result is one or greater, the mouse cursor is visible. If zero or less, the mouse cursor is hidden.

The problem that arises is, if the mouse cursor is turned on more than once, then more than one call to **m_hide** will be required to turn off the cursor and the reverse is true if the cursor were turned off more than once without being turned on again.

To simplify matters, the *m_view* variable is used as a Boolean flag. If *m_view* is set, the cursor is already visible and the call to **m_show** is simply ignored. Also, if **m_hide** is called and *m_view* is zero, the mouse cursor is already hidden and the function is not repeated. A call to **m_show** will always reveal a hidden cursor and a call to **m_hide** will always hide a visible cursor.

```
void m_show()
{
        if( m_cursor && !m_view )
        {
            inreg.x.ax = 1;
            call_mouse;
            m_view = ON;
        }
}

void m_hide()
{
        if( m_cursor && m_view )
        {
            inreg.x.ax = 2;
            call_mouse;
            m_view = OFF;
        }
}
```

All other mouse functions are independent of the visibility of the mouse cursor. The cursor continues to track the physical mouse motions even when invisible and drawing functions are not affected.

The m_pos Function

The **m_pos** function returns a pointer to the **m_status** data structure which shows the status of the buttons and the present x and y mouse cursor position. Bit 0 corresponds to the left button, bit 1 to the right button and bit 2 the middle button (Logitech only). If any button is down, the corresponding bit value is set (1). If the button is up, the bit value is zero.

```
m_status *m_pos()
{
        static m_status  m;
        inreg.x.ax = 3;
        call_mouse;
        m.button_status = outreg.x.bx;
        m.xaxis = outreg.x.cx;
        m.yaxis = outreg.x.dx;
        return (&m);
}
```

The m_moveto Function

The **m_moveto** function uses interrupt 33h, function 04h to set the mouse cursor to a specified screen position. The x-axis and y-axis values must be within the valid ranges for the current video mode.

Note: in text modes, the x-axis and y-axis values are still specified as pixel values, but they will be automatically rounded to the nearest character boundaries.

```
void  m_moveto( int xaxis, int yaxis )
{
        inreg.x.ax = 4;
```

```
        inreg.x.cx = xaxis;
        inreg.x.dx = yaxis;
        call_mouse;
    }
```

The m_pressed Function

The **m_pressed** function with an argument specifying one of the mouse buttons returns a pointer to the **m_status** structure containing information about the specific button and the present status of all buttons.

The **m_status** structure will contain the number of times a specified button has been pressed and the cursor coordinates when that button was last pressed. The button count and position information are reset by the call.

The **m_status** structure also reports the current status of all buttons with bit 0 set if the left button is down, bit 1 for the right button and bit 2 for the middle button (Logitech only).

```
m_status  *m_pressed( int button )
{
        static m_status  m;

        inreg.x.ax = 5;
        inreg.x.bx = button;
        call_mouse;
        m.button_status = outreg.x.ax;
        m.button_count = outreg.x.bx;
        m.xaxis = outreg.x.cx;
        m.yaxis = outreg.x.dx;
        return (&m);
}
```

The m_released Function

The **m_released** function is essentially the same as **m_pressed** except that the **m_status** data structure reports the cursor position when the specified button was released and how many times the button has been released. As with the **m_pressed** function, the current status of all buttons is also returned.

```
m_status  *m_released( int button )
{
        static m_status  m;

        inreg.x.ax = 6;
        inreg.x.bx = button;
        call_mouse;
        m.button_status = outreg.x.ax;
        m.button_count = outreg.x.bx;
        m.xaxis = outreg.x.cx;
        m.yaxis = outreg.x.dx;
        return (&m);
}
```

The m_xlimit and m_ylimit Functions

The **m_xlimit** and **m_ylimit** functions set minimum and maximum horizontal and vertical ranges for the mouse cursor, restricting cursor movement to the area defined. If the mouse cursor is outside of the specified range, the cursor position is corrected until it is within the valid screen area. If either minimum is larger than the corresponding maximum, the values are exchanged.

Note: if you are using EGA or VGA video, the default x and y mouse screen limits *may* or *may not* match the actual screen pixel size. Always use the **m_xlimit** and **m_ylimit** functions to set the actual required video margins.

```
void  m_xlimit( int min_x, int max_x )
{
        inreg.x.ax = 7;
        inreg.x.cx = min_x;
        inreg.x.dx = max_x;
        call_mouse;
}
```

```
void  m_ylimit( int min_y, int max_y )
{
        inreg.x.ax = 8;
        inreg.x.cx = min_y;
        inreg.x.dx = max_y;
        call_mouse;
}
```

The m_graphic_cursor Function

The **m_graphic_cursor** function allows a new graphics cursor image to be selected as the current (active) graphics cursor. The *xaxis* and *yaxis* values specify the target or "hot spot" location within the 16x16 pixel image. The *mask_Seg* and *mask_Ofs* values point to the cursor image.

Defining graphics cursor images is discussed in more detail later. See also the **Set_Graphic_Cursor** function.

```
void  m_graphic_cursor(  int xaxis,
                         int yaxis,
                         unsigned mask_Seg,
                         unsigned mask_Ofs )
{
        struct SREGS  seg;

        inreg.x.ax = 9;
        inreg.x.bx = xaxis;
        inreg.x.cx = yaxis;
        inreg.x.dx = mask_Ofs;
        seg.es     = mask_Seg;
        int86x( 0x33, &inreg, &outreg, &seg );
}
```

The Set_Graphic_Cursor Function

The **Set_Graphic_Cursor** function is supplied as a convenience and lets a simpler (single parameter) specification call any predefined graphics cursor.

```
void Set_Graphic_Cursor( g_cursor ThisCursor )
{
        m_graphic_cursor( ThisCursor.xkey,
                          ThisCursor.ykey,
                          _DS,
                          (unsigned) ThisCursor.image );
}
```

The m_text_cursor Function

The **m_text_cursor** function selects and defines the text cursor type (*text modes only*) and two text cursors are supported: a software cursor and a hardware cursor. A *type* argument of *0* selects the software cursor, *1* selects the hardware cursor. Since the topic of this book is graphics, the text mode function is included only in the interest of completeness and is not described in total detail.

The Software Cursor

The software text cursor is a character or a character attribute which replaces and/or changes the screen character cell where it is positioned. The software cursor is defined by two 16-bit values, the screen mask and the cursor mask.

First, the screen mask is AND'd with the screen character and attribute, then the cursor mask is XOR'd with the resulting image. For further details, experimentation is suggested.

The Hardware Cursor

The hardware cursor is the text cursor written to the screen by the video controller and is defined by the scan lines of the character cell as shown in Table 16-2.

```
void  m_text_cursor( int type, unsigned start, unsigned stop  )
{
        inreg.x.ax = 10;
        inreg.x.bx = type;
        inreg.x.cx = start;
        inreg.x.dx = stop;
        call_mouse;
}
```

Table 16-1: Software Text Cursor Marks

BIT	DESCRIPTION
15	BLINKING (1) OR NON-BLINKING (0) CHARACTER
14..12	BACKGROUND COLOR
11	FOREGROUND INTENSITY, HIGH (1) OR LOW (0)
10..8	FOREGROUND COLOR
7..0	CHARACTER CODE

The m_movement Function

The **m_movement** function returns a pointer to the **m_motion** structure which reports the horizontal and vertical step count (the distance the mouse has moved in *mickeys* or $1/200$ inch increments) since the last call to this function. Some mice report only 100 mickeys/inch, others 200 mickeys/inch and some as high as 320 mickeys/inch. The vertical and horizontal step count is reported as a signed integer value in the range $-32768..32767$ with positive values specifying motions from left to right or top to bottom (with the mouse cord pointing ''up'' or away from the user).

Table 16-2: Cursor Size Settings

VIDEO TYPE (MODE)	MONOCHROME (07h)	TEXT (00-03h)
DEFAULT START/STOP	9h / 0Ah	06h / 07h
BLOCK START/STOP	00h / 0Ah	00h / 0Bh

Because the total mouse distance which can be reported is a bit less than 14 feet (in any direction from a starting point of 0,0), this is quite adequate for virtually any application short of a computer odometer.

Note: the **m_speed** function causes a non-linear cursor motion response to the actual mouse motion. Since the **m_speed** function is enabled by default and, with fast mouse movement, can report as high as 400 steps per inch (mickeys), this acceleration can be disabled by passing an argument to **m_speed** setting a very large speed threshold such as *7FFFh*.

```
m_movement  *m_motion()          /* net cursor motion since last call */
{
        static m_movement  m;

        inreg.x.ax = 11;
        call_mouse;
        m.x_count = _CX;                    /* net x-axis movement */
        m.y_count = _DX;                    /* net y-axis movement */
        return (&m);
}
```

The m_inst_task Function

The **m_inst_task** function passes an event mask and the address of a user-defined subroutine which is called by the mouse driver when any of the events defined by the mask occur. The mask values passed to this event handler routine are shown in Figure 16-1 (preceding).

Note: **The Logitech Programmer's Reference Manual** includes a caution recommending that as little time as possible be spent in the event handler. In direct disregard of this advice, the **m_inst_task** function is demonstrated extensively in the MOUSE.C demo — in part to demonstrate where and how the event handler can be a bad idea as well as a good idea. Use it with caution.

```
void m_inst_task( unsigned mask,
                  unsigned task_seg,
```

```
                unsigned task_ofs )
        {
                struct SREGS  seg;

                inreg.x.ax = 12;
                inreg.x.cx = mask;
                inreg.x.dx = task_ofs;
                seg.es    = task_seg;
                int86x( 0x33, &inreg, &outreg, &seg );
        }
```

The m_lightpen Function

The mouse interrupt (*33h*) supplies two functions (*0Dh* and *0Eh*) to enable and disable lightpen emulation. The **m_lightpen** function combines these functions using a Boolean argument to turn the lightpen emulation on and off.

Lightpen emulation allows programs which expect a lightpen to be run using the mouse as the input device. When emulation is in effect, pressing the right and the left mouse button will simulate the pen-down state, while releasing both emulates the pen-up state.

If both a lightpen and mouse are present, emulation can be turned off.

```
void m_lightpen( int set )
{
        if( set ) inreg.x.ax = 13;
        else     inreg.x.ax = 14;
        call_mouse;
}
```

The m_move_ratio Function

The **m_move_ratio** sets the amount of mouse motion (*mickeys*) required to move the screen cursor eight pixels horizontally or vertically. The default values are eight mickeys per eight pixels horizontal and 16 mickeys per eight pixels vertical.

For a 200 mickey/inch mouse, these settings will require 3.2 inches horizontal movement and 2.0 inches vertical movement to cover a 640x200 pixel screen.

```
void m_move_ratio( int xsize, int ysize )
{
        inreg.x.ax = 15;
        inreg.x.cx = xsize;
        inreg.x.dx = ysize;
        call_mouse;
}
```

The m_conceal Function

The **m_conceal** function is implemented by the Logitech mouse (and compatibles) only and is not valid for the Microsoft mouse. The **m_conceal** function allows the user to define an area on the screen where the mouse cursor will automatically be turned off. This is reset by calling the **m_show** function.

```
void m_conceal( int left, int top, int right, int bottom )
{
        inreg.x.ax = 16;
        inreg.x.cx = left;
        inreg.x.dx = top;
        inreg.x.si = right;
        inreg.x.di = bottom;
        call_mouse;
}
```

Note: for EGA/VGA systems, depending on your version of mouse and mouse driver, this function may not operate correctly. For this reason, a different implementation of the **m_conceal** effect is shown in the

G_MOUSE.C demo. Remember, you may have an up-to-date mouse and driver — but your customer/user may not — accordingly, this function is not recommended.

The m_speed Function

The **m_speed** function is used to set a threshold speed (in mickeys/second), over which the mouse driver will add in an acceleration factor. Thus, if the mouse is moved quickly, the mouse cursor will move further for a given hand-movement distance than if moved slowly.

Some mouse drivers use a fixed acceleration of two; others (including Logitech) increase the acceleration factor as the speed of the mouse increases.

To cancel the acceleration effect, call **m_speed** with an argument of 7FFFh (unless, of course, your user is faster than a speeding bullet). In actual fact, a speed setting of 7FFFH is only about 9.3 MPH or 450 RPM on the ball (assuming a standard of 200 mickeys/inch).

To restore acceleration, call **m_speed** with a speed threshold of 0.

```
void m_speed( int speed )
{
        inreg.x.ax = 19;
        inreg.x.dx = speed;
        call_mouse;
}
```

The m_handler Function

The **m_handler** function is a convenient method of getting a handle on the mouse driver's data segment. But — warning — it can also be temperamental as will be shown further in the demo program G-MOUSE.C.

```
void far m_handler ()                    /*event handler called by device driver*/
{
        mouse_event far *save;           /*pointer to save area in diff segment*/
        unsigned a, b, c, d;                     /*temp storage of registers*/
        a =_AX;                                        /*save registers*/
        b =_BX;
        c =_CX;
        d =_DX;
        save = MK_FP(_CS-0x10, 0x00C0);       /*point to PSP user area*/
        save->flag =a;                        /*stuff registers into it*/
        save->button =b;
        save->xaxis =c;
        save->yaxis =d;
}
```

Mouse Graphics Cursors

In graphics modes, while a default mouse cursor is supplied (see Figure 16-5), a variety of alternate cursor patterns can also be defined (see Figures 16-6 through 16-10).

Writing the cursor image to the screen does not destroy existing screen information. The cursor image is written to overlie the screen image and, as the cursor moves, leaves the original image unaffected.

Table 16-3: Screen and Cursor Mask Effects

SCREEN MASK BIT	CURSOR MASK BIT	DISPLAY BIT
0	0	0
0	1	1
1	0	UNAFFECTED
1	1	INVERTED

The graphics cursor images consist of two masks, the *screen mask* and the *cursor mask*, each defined as a 16x16 pixel image pattern as shown following. These two masks determine the shape of the graphics cursor and its interaction with existing screen image. In use, the screen mask image is AND'd with the screen contents and the cursor mask is then XOR'd with the screen result as shown in Table 16-3.

Figure 16-2: Mouse Default Graphics Cursor Against Matching Background

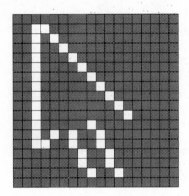

Left, the default graphics cursor is shown against a matching background. Against a contrasting background, only the cursor mask image would appear.

Below (left and right), the screen mask and cursor mask are shown separately.

Screen Mask

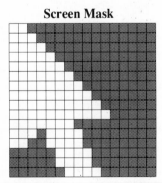

Cursor Mask

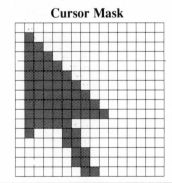

The default graphics cursor is the left-angled arrow pattern (see Figure 16-2). Here the screen mask is used to selectively block the background image around the cursor image, creating a border to make the cursor visible even when the background image color is the same.

The graphics cursor definition contains more than just the cursor image. It also contains two coordinates specifying the cursor's "hot spot" or target pixel. The cursor target values can be in the range −16..16, though normally coordinates in the range 0..15 would be chosen, as the negative coordinates lie outside (above and left) of the cursor image. In Figures 16-3 through 16-9, the graphics cursor target or "hot spot" is shown by small, crossed arrows. In all of the images defined here, the hot spot lies within the cursor image.

The ARROW Cursor

Figure 16-3 Arrow Graphics Cursor

Screen Mask Hex	Cursor Mask Hex
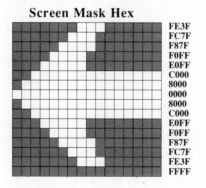	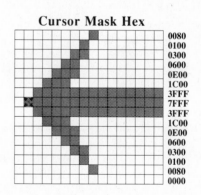

Screen Mask Hex

FE3F
FC7F
F87F
F0FF
E0FF
C000
8000
0000
8000
C000
E0FF
F0FF
F87F
FC7F
FE3F
FFFF

Cursor Mask Hex

0080
0100
0300
0600
0E00
1C00
3FFF
7FFF
3FFF
1C00
0E00
0600
0300
0100
0080
0000

```
static  unsigned  arrow_image[32] =
/* screen mask */ {    0xFE3F, 0xFC7F, 0xF87F, 0xF0FF,
                       0xE0FF, 0xC000, 0x8000, 0x0000,
                       0x8000, 0xC000, 0xE0FF, 0xF0FF,
```

```
                          0xF87F, 0xFC7F, 0xFF3F, 0xFFFF,
/* cursor mask */         0x0080, 0x0100, 0x0300, 0x0600,
                          0x0E00, 0x1C00, 0x3FFF, 0x7FFF,
                          0x3FFF, 0x1C00, 0x0E00, 0x0600,
                          0x0300, 0x0100, 0x0080, 0x0000  };
static g_cursor ARROW = { NULL, 1,  7 };
```

The CHECK Cursor

Figure 16-4: Check Graphics Cursor

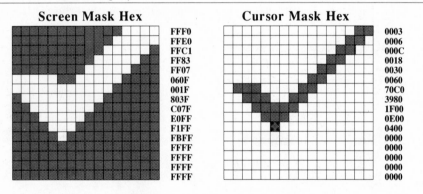

```
static  unsigned check_image[32] =
/* screen mask */    {    0xFFF0, 0xFFE0, 0xFFC1, 0xFF83,
                          0xFF07, 0x060F, 0x001F, 0x803F,
                          0xC07F, 0xE0FF, 0xF1FF, 0xFBFF,
                          0xFFFF, 0xFFFF, 0xFFFF, 0xFFFF,
/* cursor mask */         0x0003, 0x0006, 0x000C, 0x0018,
                          0x0030, 0x0060, 0x70C0, 0x3980,
                          0x1F00, 0x0E00, 0x0400, 0x0000,
                          0x0000, 0x0000, 0x0000, 0x0000  };
static g_cursor CHECK = { NULL, 5, 10 };
```

The CROSS Cursor

For the CROSS (cross-hairs) graphics cursor, notice that both an interior and exterior border are created, allowing the cursor image to be clearly visible against any background. Notice also that one pixel in the center of the screen mask — corresponding to the target pixel shown in the cursor mask — is also off-set. This insures that the existing screen pixel at the target position will always be visible and is not overwritten by either the screen or cursor masks.

Figure 16-5: Cross Graphics Cursor

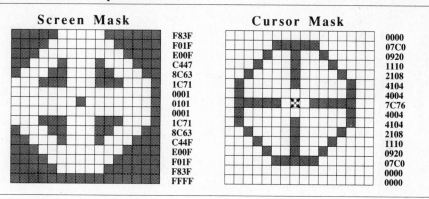

```
static  unsigned  cross_image[32] =
/* screen mask */  {     0xF83F, 0xE01F, 0xE00F, 0xC557,
                         0x8C63, 0x1C71, 0x0001, 0x0101,
                         0x0001, 0x1C71, 0x8C63, 0xC447,
                         0xE00F, 0xF01F, 0xF83F, 0xFFFF,
/* cursor mask */        0x0000, 0x07C0, 0x0920, 0x1110,
                         0x2108, 0x4104, 0x4004, 0x7C76,
                         0x4004, 0x4104, 0x2108, 0x1110,
                         0x0920, 0x07C0, 0x0000, 0x0000  };
static g_cursor CROSS = { NULL, 7,  7 };
```

The GLOVE Cursor

As with the CROSS cursor, the GLOVE cursor has an interior area where the background (the existing screen image) is allowed to show through. When you run the demo program (G-MOUSE.C), move the GLOVE cursor across a solid area and watch the effects. You might also redefine the GLOVE screen mask to blank this interior mask (set to zeros) and repeat the experiment.

Figure 16-6: Glove Graphics Cursor

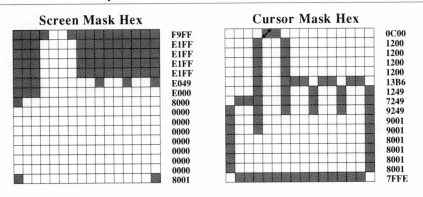

Screen Mask Hex	Cursor Mask Hex
F9FF	0C00
E1FF	1200
E1FF	1200
E1FF	1200
E1FF	1200
E049	13B6
E000	1249
8000	7249
0000	9249
0000	9001
0000	9001
0000	8001
0000	8001
0000	8001
0000	8001
8001	7FFE

```
static  unsigned  glove_image[32] =
/* screen mask */  {    0xF9FF, 0xE1FF, 0xE9FF, 0xE9FF,
                        0xE9FF, 0xE849, 0xE800, 0x8924,
                        0x0924, 0x0986, 0x0DFC, 0x2FFC,
                        0x3FFC, 0x3FFC, 0x0000, 0x8001,
/* cursor mask */       0x0C00, 0x1200, 0x1200, 0x1200,
                        0x1200, 0x13B6, 0x1249, 0x7249,
                        0x9249, 0x9001, 0x9001, 0x8001,
                        0x8001, 0x8001, 0x8001, 0x7FFE };
static  g_cursor  GLOVE = { NULL, 4,  0 };
```

The IBEAM Cursor

The IBEAM cursor is popular in graphics text applications such as Ventura Publisher's text (edit) modes where text information is presented using graphics-generated characters and the cursor is aligned with the text images.

Figure 16-7: Ibeam Graphics Cursor

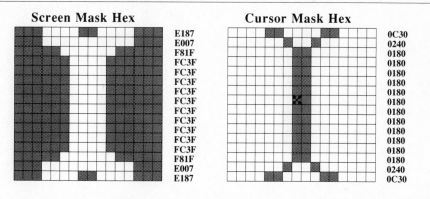

```
static  unsigned  ibeam_image[32] =
/* screen mask */  {     0xE187, 0xE007, 0xF81F, 0xFC3F,
                         0xFC3F, 0xFC3F, 0xFC3F, 0xFC3F,
                         0xFC3F, 0xFC3F, 0xFC3F, 0xFC3F,
                         0xFC3F, 0xF81F, 0xE007, 0xE187,
/* cursor mask */        0x0C30, 0x0240, 0x0180, 0x0180,
                         0x0180, 0x0180, 0x0180, 0x0180,
                         0x0180, 0x0180, 0x0180, 0x0180,
                         0x0180, 0x0180, 0x0240, 0x0C30  };
static g_cursor IBEAM = { NULL, 7,  7 };
```

The initialize_cursors Function

The last function provided in the MOUSE.I unit is the **initialize_cursors** function which simply assigns pointers to the defined cursor images, making these available for use. Notice the **static g_cursor** assignment (above) for each of these cursors has assigned the pointer element (defined in **g_cursor**) to a NULL pointer, while defining the target coordinates for each cursor image. Now these NULL pointers are simply being reassigned to the actual image locations.

```
void initialize_cursors()
{
        ARROW.image = arrow_image;
        CHECK.image = check_image;
        CROSS.image = cross_image;
        GLOVE.image = glove_image;
        IBEAM.image = ibeam_image;
}
```

The G-MOUSE Demo Program

The G-MOUSE program is written using the mouse event handler for purposes of demonstration. It is, however, somewhat temperamental and all of the processes demonstrated here can also be accomplished using the other mouse functions previously defined. For actual programming practices, the alternative choices are recommended.

This approach was chosen for demonstration to show what can be done and where the pitfalls lie even though it is not the optimum selection for all applications. The alternative functions, however, are all effectively self-explanatory and need little additional comment.

First, a look at how the demo program operates, then I'll mention a few elements of temperament for you to observe when running the program

The **Mouse_Demo** function is the key to the entire program and begins with a few local variables:

```
void Mouse_Demo()
{
        int         i, color, VStep, target[10], exit_time = 0, box_width = 100;
        void  *button_image;
        m_result *rodent;
```

The **Initialize** function has been amply discussed and appears in previous demos in essentially the same form.

```
        Initialize();
```

After the graphics have been initialized, values are assigned to *VStep* and *color*, and a button image is created. This image will later be employed to show which mouse key is in use.

```
        VStep = MaxY / 7;
        color = MaxColors;
        setfillstyle( CLOSE_DOT_FILL, color );
        target[0] = target[6] = target[8] = 2;
        target[1] = target[3] = target[9] = 2;
        target[2] = target[4] = box_width / 4;
        target[5] = target[7] = VStep / 2;
        fillpoly( 5, target );
        getimage( 1, 1, box_width/4, VStep/2, button_image );
        putimage( 1, 1, button_image, XOR_PUT );
```

The **Make_Screen** procedure sets up an initial screen image with a row of action boxes along the left of the screen and a row of color boxes along the top of the screen. If you are using CGA video and have a color monitor, I suggest rewriting the **Initialize** procedure to select one of the CGAC0..CGAC3 modes for this demo.

```
        Make_Screen( VStep, box_width );
```

Now the pointer **m_events**, which is defined by the **mouse_event** data structure, is pointed to the mouse interface event buffer location referenced by offset from the global **_psp** reference. The location referenced is furnished by DOS and is constant for all mouse types.

```
m_events = MK_FP( _psp, 0x00C0 );
```

The **initialize_cursors** function assigns memory location pointers to the cursor images and *rodent* calls the **m_reset** function to make sure that a mouse is present in the system and to reset the mouse handler.

```
initialize_cursors();
rodent = m_reset();
if( rodent–>present )
    {
```

If everything is fine (*present* did not return as zero), then we're ready to go, the event flag value is set to zero for a starting condition and **m_inst_task** is called with the EVENTMASK and the address of **m_handler**.

The constant EVENTMASK was set to 7Fh to include all mouse events as shown previously because we want to know about everything that happens with the mouse: was the mouse moved? were any buttons pressed? were any buttons released?

```
m_events–>flag = 0;
m_inst_task( EVENTMASK, FP_SEG( m_handler ), FP_OFF( m_handler ) );
```

A bit of housekeeping is required, turning on the mouse cursor, setting the screen limits for the mouse and initializing our exit flag.

```
m_show();
m_xlimit( 1, MaxX );
m_ylimit( 1, MaxY );
exit_time = 0;
```

The exit flag (*exit_time*) is used to loop until the exit option is selected by moving the mouse cursor to the upper left box on the screen and clicking the left mouse button within the box. Until then, the program will loop.

```
while( !exit_time )
    {
```

The loop always begins by resetting the event flag (*m_events–>flag*), then waiting for any mouse event to be reported. When a mouse event is reported, the *m_events–>flag* is tested to decide what response is required.

```
m_events–>flag = 0;
while(!m_events–>flag ) ;                    /*do nothing*/
switch( m_events–>flag )
{
```

The mouse cursor is moved automatically — the program does not need to handle this element because the mouse driver is already taking care of this event. We are, however, still interested in the mouse movement for other applications.

```
case 0x01: if( ( m_events–>xaxis > box_width ) &&
               ( m_events–>yaxis > bar_height ) )
```

If the mouse is within the drawing area (right of *box_width* and below *bar_height*), then a new decision is required: was either the left or right mouse button down?

```
switch( m_events–>button )        /* mouse moved */
{
```

Drawing A Pixel

If the left button is down (*m_events–>button* reports a 1), then it's time to draw a pixel at this position using the current *color* value. Before putting a pixel on the screen, the **m_hide** function is called to remove the mouse cursor. With the cursor image gone (the screen restored to its original condition) the **putpixel** function interrogates the *m_events* record for the cursor coordinates and writes to the pixel corresponding to the cursor's hot spot. Last, the cursor image is rewritten over the new screen image.

```
case 1:    m_hide();                   /* if left button */
           putpixel( m_events–>xaxis,
           m_events–>yaxis, color );
           m_show();                   break;
```

If the cursor image is not cancelled before writing the new pixel to the screen, the change would be lost as soon as the cursor was moved because the previous screen image — before the pixel was written — would be restored with the cursor movement.

If the right button is down, the same process is followed except that the current pixel is written in the background color — thus, the right button has been assigned for erasure.

```
        case 2:     m_hide();                        /* if right button */
                    putpixel( m_events–>xaxis,
                    m_events–>yaxis, 0 );
                    m_show();               break;
        }
```

Also note: instead of looking for a button being pressed in the form of a character value being set by the mouse, the test simply asked if the button were being held down — not if it were being pressed repeatedly after each incremental mouse movement. The latter — requiring a make and break of the button for each pixel movement — would be both very awkward and very slow and would defeat the entire purpose of using a mouse.

In other cases, however, action will only be taken on a specific *make* condition produced by a button being pressed but not by one which is held down.

Conditional Cursor Hide

Now, before a pixel was written (if the appropriate buttons was down), the screen position of the mouse cursor was tested to see if it was in the allowed drawing area. If it was not, then no action was taken to draw a pixel image but the mouse cursor image was not interrupted or altered (except for being moved by the mouse driver).

The **m_conceal** function was previously described as permitting an area to be selected in which the mouse cursor would not be shown. A note was added, however, indicating that this function was not reliable in all cases and was not supported at all by the Microsoft mouse. For this reason, an analog of the **m_conceal** function is used here to guard the lower left box on the screen.

This is an area of the screen where the **putimage** function will be writing the *button_image* to show which button(s) are currently pressed. If the mouse cursor image is allowed to appear in this area while a screen update is being executed, the results are difficult to describe but are definitely not desirable.

If you would like to see precisely what does happen, comment out this section of code in the G-MOUSE demo and experimenting. Also remember, before even a single pixel of the screen was updated in the previous drawing functions, the mouse cursor was turned off, then restored afterwards.

To guard the desired area, a simple test is repeated with each mouse movement and, if the mouse cursor enters the guarded area, then **m_hide** is called to turn off the cursor and the Boolean variable *m_cursor* is set to OFF, preventing both the **m_hide** and **m_view** functions from changing the cursor display further until the cursor is reenabled.

```
if( ( m_events–>xaxis <= box_width ) &&
  ( m_events–>yaxis >= 6*VStep ) )
{
    m_hide();
    m_cursor = OFF;
}
```

If the area condition test is not met (the cursor is not within the guarded area) a second test asks if the cursor has been deactivated (by testing *m_cursor*) and, if the cursor is not enabled, reenables it for display and then calls **m_show** to turn the cursor back on.

```
else
if( !m_cursor )
{
    m_cursor = ON;
    m_show();
};                              break;
```

413

This is all quite simple and several areas of the screen can be guarded, if necessary, by using multiple test conditions.

Also, you might notice that the button images will still show buttons being pressed or released even when the mouse cursor is in the protected area. The mouse is not disabled, only hidden to prevent a video foul-up.

Using Button Event Selection

In many cases, it may be desirable to act only when a button is specifically pressed — not merely when a button is being held down. When you run the G-MOUSE demo, you will see a series of labeled boxes along the left of the screen (and a series of color boxes across the top). The graphics cursor is allowed to move freely across these boxes but, even if a button is being held down while doing so, nothing is drawn in these areas.

The mouse cursor can, however, be moved to any of these and then specifically ''clicked on'' (using the left button) to select the option or color.

At the same time, when any button is ''clicked'' anywhere on the screen, the corresponding button image (lower left corner box) is updated to reflect the make or break condition.

And both of these tasks are accomplished using the mouse event report (*m_events–>flag*).

If the *m_events–>flag* reports the left button being pressed (a *make* condition — not merely being held down), then *button_image* is XOR'd over the box for the left button.

```
case 0x02: putimage( 5, VStep*6.25, button_image, XOR_PUT );
```

The left button *make* condition is used for several other selections. If the mouse cursor is left of *box_width* when the button is pressed (i.e. – within the labeled boxes), then a series of *if..else* tests check to see what response is appropriate.

```
if( m_events–>xaxis <= box_width )
{
    if( m_events–>yaxis < VStep ) exit_time++;
```

```
        else
        if( m_events–>yaxis < 2*VStep )
            Set_Graphic_Cursor( ARROW );
        else
        if( m_events–>yaxis < 3*VStep )
            Set_Graphic_Cursor( CHECK );
        else
        if( m_events–>yaxis < 4*VStep )
            Set_Graphic_Cursor( CROSS );
        else
        if( m_events–>yaxis < 5*VStep )
            Set_Graphic_Cursor( GLOVE );
        else
        if( m_events–>yaxis < 6*VStep )
            Set_Graphic_Cursor( IBEAM );
    } else
```

Otherwise, if the mouse cursor is in the color bar area, then a new *color* value is calculated from the cursor position.

```
    if( m_events–>yaxis <= bar_height )
        color = ( MaxColors *
                ( m_events–>xaxis – box_width – 3 ) /
                ( MaxX – box_width – 3 ) ) + 1;
break;
```

In this case, instead of using a complex *if..else* decision tree to pick colors, the cursor position is calculated — using the formula that was used to create the color boxes — to see what color the cursor would be on and to set the drawing color appropriately.

Showing the Buttons

The remaining cases — mouse event flags 04h..40h — are used here only to update the button images.

```
    case 0x04: putimage(   5, VStep*6.25,
```

```
                                button_image, XOR_PUT );
                   break;
        case 0x08:
        case 0x10:  putimage(  box_width/2+15, VStep*6.25,
                               button_image, XOR_PUT );
                   break;
        case 0x20:
        case 0x40:  putimage(  box_width/4+10, VStep*6.25,
                               button_image, XOR_PUT );
                   break;
        }
    }
```

Now, I've mentioned that there are some flaws which you should look for in using this event-handler system instead of the defined mouse functions and the preceding **switch** decision structure is the best spot to observe them.

Each **switch/case** is triggered by a single bit in the *m_events->flag* register and, if more than one bit were set, neither of the appropriate cases would be triggered because the integer value of *m_events->flag* would not correspond specifically to any of the **case** conditions stated. For example, if *m_events->flag* returns with both bits, 0 and 2, set and reporting that the left button was released *and* the mouse had moved, then neither the *case 0x01* nor the *case 0x04* conditions would be met — even though the event flag bits for both were set.

In the demo program, the most obvious result will be a button image which is out-of-step with the actual button condition, but you may also notice errors in color selection (that a color was not selected even though you did press the left button) or cursor pattern selection.

Again — please note — all of the preceding can be accomplished using mouse functions instead of using the event handler and this particular demo was designed to show problems to be avoided rather than the optimum handling.

The event handler is useful but must be written and employed carefully with a full knowledge and understanding of what is being trapped and why.

Now, after experimenting, try rewriting the **Mouse_Demo** procedure so that duplicate events are not singularly ignored.

```
/*       MOUSE.I: Turbo C source code for mouse interface functions      */


#include <dos.h>
#define  call_mouse int86(0x33, &inreg, &outreg)
                                         /* interrupt call for mouse device driver */
#define  EVENTMASK  0x7F         /* includes mouse movement, all buttons  */
#define  SOFTWARE   0                            /* text cursor types */
#define  HARDWARE   1
#define  OFF        0                       /* general boolean values */
#define  ON         1

int    m_cursor = ON, m_view = OFF;          /* mouse cursor status flags */

union REGS  inreg, outreg;                     /* static registers used */

typedef struct {  int present,                /* TRUE if mouse present  */
                      buttons;                /* # of buttons on mouse  */
              } m_result;

typedef struct {  int button_status,          /* bits 0-2 on if button down */
                      button_count,           /* # times button was clicked */
                      xaxis, yaxis;           /* mouse cursor position    */
              } m_status;

typedef struct {  int x_count,                /* net horizontal movement */
                      y_count;                /* net vertical movement   */
              } m_movement;                   /* returned by mMotion     */

typedef struct {  unsigned  flag,             /* mouse event record */
                           button,
                           xaxis, yaxis;
              } mouse_event;

typedef struct {  unsigned  *image,           /* graphics cursor descriptor */
                           xkey, ykey;
          } g_cursor;
```

```
m_result *m_reset()                           /* resets mouse default status, returns pointer to m_result */
                                              /* structure indicating if mouse installed and, if present, */
{                                             /* number of buttons — always call during initialization   */
    static m_result  m;

    inreg.x.ax = 0;                                       /* mouse function 0 */
    call_mouse;
    m.present = outreg.x.ax;
    m.buttons = outreg.x.bx;
    return ( &m );
}

void m_show()                                          /* renders mouse cursor visible */
{
    if( m_cursor && !m_view )
    {
        inreg.x.ax = 1;                                  /* mouse function 1 */
        call_mouse;
        m_view = ON;
    }
}

void m_hide()                                          /* conceals mouse cursor from view */
{
    if( m_cursor && m_view )
    {
        inreg.x.ax = 2;                                  /* mouse function 2 */
        call_mouse;
        m_view = OFF;
    }
}

m_status *m_pos()                             /* returns pointer to m_status structure with */
{                                             /* mouse cursor position and button status    */
    static m_status  m;
```

419

```
        inreg.x.ax = 3;                                /* mouse function 3 */
        call_mouse;
        m.button_status = outreg.x.bx;                   /* button status */
        m.xaxis = outreg.x.cx;                       /* x-axis coordinate */
        m.yaxis = outreg.x.dx;                       /* y-axis coordinate */
        return (&m);
    }

    void  m_moveto( int xaxis, int yaxis )
    {                                       /* mouse cursor to new position */
        inreg.x.ax = 4;                                /* mouse function 4 */
        inreg.x.cx = xaxis;
        inreg.x.dx = yaxis;
        call_mouse;
    }

    m_status  *m_pressed( int button )
                        /* returns button pressed info; current status (up/down), */
                        /* times pressed since last call, cursor position at last */
                        /* press — resets count and position info — button 0 is */
    {                   /* left, 1 right on Microsoft mouse, 2 center on Logitech */
      static m_status  m;

      inreg.x.ax = 5;                                  /* mouse function 5 */
      inreg.x.bx = button;                        /* request for specific button */
      call_mouse;
      m.button_status = outreg.x.ax;
      m.button_count = outreg.x.bx;
      m.xaxis = outreg.x.cx;
      m.yaxis = outreg.x.dx;
      return (&m);
    }

    m_status  *m_released( int button )          /* returns release info about button */
    {
      static m_status  m;
```

```
        inreg.x.ax = 6;                                          /* mouse function 6 */
        inreg.x.bx = button;                                /* request for specific button */
        call_mouse;
        m.button_status = outreg.x.ax;
        m.button_count = outreg.x.bx;
        m.xaxis = outreg.x.cx;
        m.yaxis = outreg.x.dx;
        return (&m);
}
void  m_xlimit( int min_x, int max_x )
                        /* Sets min and max horizontal range for mouse cursor. Moves */
                        /* cursor inside range if outside when called. Swaps values if */
                        /* min_x and max_x are reversed. */
{                                                                /* mouse function 7 */
        inreg.x.ax = 7;
        inreg.x.cx = min_x;
        inreg.x.dx = max_x;
        call_mouse;
}

void  m_ylimit( int min_y, int max_y )                      /* sets vertical boundaries */
{
        inreg.x.ax = 8;                                          /* mouse function 8 */
        inreg.x.cx = min_y;
        inreg.x.dx = max_y;
        call_mouse;
}

void  m_graphic_cursor( int  xaxis,                        /* Sets graphic cursor shape */
                        int yaxis,
                        unsigned mask_Seg,
                        unsigned mask_Ofs )
{
        struct SREGS  seg;

        inreg.x.ax = 9;                                          /* mouse function 9 */
            inreg.x.bx = xaxis;                             /* x-axis cursor hot spot */
```

```
        inreg.x.cx = yaxis;                              /* y-axis cursor hot spot */
        inreg.x.dx = mask_Ofs;
        seg.es   = mask_Seg;
        int86x( 0x33, &inreg, &outreg, &seg );
}

void  m_text_cursor( int type, unsigned start, unsigned stop )
                    /* Sets text cursor type, where 0 = software and 1 = hardware) */
                /* For software cursor, start and stop are screen and cursor masks */
{                   /* For hardware cursor, start and stop specify scanline start/stop */
        inreg.x.ax = 10;
        inreg.x.bx = type;
        inreg.x.cx = start;
        inreg.x.dx = stop;
        call_mouse;
}

m_movement *m_motion()                   /* reports net cursor motion since last call */
{
        static m_movement  m;

        inreg.x.ax = 11;
        call_mouse;
        m.x_count = _CX;                                  /* net x-axis movement */
        m.y_count = _DX;                                  /* net y-axis movement */
        return (&m);
}

void m_inst_task( unsigned mask,                  /* installs user-defined task to */
                  unsigned task_seg,                     /* execute on mouse  */
                  unsigned task_ofs )              /* events specified by mask */
{
  struct SREGS  seg;

  inreg.x.ax = 12;
  inreg.x.cx = mask;
  inreg.x.dx = task_ofs;
```

```
    seg.es    = task_seg;
    int86x( 0x33, &inreg, &outreg, &seg );
}

void m_lightpen( int set )                          /* initiates lightpen emulation    */
{
    if( set ) inreg.x.ax = 13;                      /* mouse function 13 (default) = ON */
        else  inreg.x.ax = 14;                      /* mouse function 14         = OFF */
    call_mouse;
}

void m_move_ratio( int xsize, int ysize )
{                                                   /* sets motion-to-pixel ratio with */
    inreg.x.ax = 15;                                /* defaults 8/8 horizontal, 16/8 vertical */
    inreg.x.cx = xsize;
    inreg.x.dx = ysize;
    call_mouse;
}

void m_conceal( int left, int top, int right, int bottom )
{                                                   /* LOGITECH ONLY — sets conditional area */
    inreg.x.ax = 16;                                /* where mouse will not appear during */
    inreg.x.cx = left;                              /* screen update operation */
    inreg.x.dx = top;
    inreg.x.si = right;
    inreg.x.di = bottom;
    call_mouse;
}

void m_speed( int speed )                           /* LOGITECH ONLY — speed threshold */
{                                                   /* (mickeys/second) for accelerated */
    inreg.x.ax = 19;                                /* mouse cursor movement response */
    inreg.x.dx = speed;
    call_mouse;
}

static  unsigned  arrow_image[32] =
```

```
/* screen mask */ {    0xFE3F, 0xFC7F, 0xF87F, 0xF0FF,
                       0xE0FF, 0xC000, 0x8000, 0x0000,
                       0x8000, 0xC000, 0xE0FF, 0xF0FF,
                       0xF87F, 0xFC7F, 0xFF3F, 0xFFFF,
/* cursor mask */      0x0080, 0x0100, 0x0300, 0x0600,
                       0x0E00, 0x1C00, 0x3FFF, 0x7FFF,
                       0x3FFF, 0x1C00, 0x0E00, 0x0600,
                       0x0300, 0x0100, 0x0080, 0x0000 };
static g_cursor ARROW = { NULL, 1,  7 };

static unsigned check_image[32] =
/* screen mask */ {    0xFFF0, 0xFFE0, 0xFFC1, 0xFF83,
                       0xFF07, 0x060F, 0x001F, 0x803F,
                       0xC07F, 0xE0FF, 0xF1FF, 0xFBFF,
                       0xFFFF, 0xFFFF, 0xFFFF, 0xFFFF,
/* cursor mask */      0x0003, 0x0006, 0x000C, 0x0018,
                       0x0030, 0x0060, 0x70C0, 0x3980,
                       0x1F00, 0x0E00, 0x0400, 0x0000,
                       0x0000, 0x0000, 0x0000, 0x0000 };
static g_cursor CHECK = { NULL, 5, 10 };

static unsigned cross_image[32] =
/* screen mask */ {    0xF83F, 0xE01F, 0xE00F, 0xC557,
                       0x8C63, 0x1C71, 0x0001, 0x0101,
                       0x0001, 0x1C71, 0x8C63, 0xC447,
                       0xE00F, 0xF01F, 0xF83F, 0xFFFF,
/* cursor mask */      0x0000, 0x07C0, 0x0920, 0x1110,
                       0x2108, 0x4104, 0x4004, 0x7C76,
                       0x4004, 0x4104, 0x2108, 0x1110,
                       0x0920, 0x07C0, 0x0000, 0x0000 };
static g_cursor CROSS = { NULL, 7,  7 };

static unsigned glove_image[32] =
/* screen mask */ {    0xF9FF, 0xE1FF, 0xE9FF, 0xE9FF,
                       0xE9FF, 0xE849, 0xE800, 0x8924,
                       0x0924, 0x0986, 0x0DFC, 0x2FFC,
                       0x3FFC, 0x3FFC, 0x0000, 0x8001,
```

```
/* cursor mask */        0x0C00, 0x1200, 0x1200, 0x1200,
                         0x1200, 0x13B6, 0x1249, 0x7249,
                         0x9249, 0x9001, 0x9001, 0x8001,
                         0x8001, 0x8001, 0x8001, 0x7FFE };
static g_cursor GLOVE = { NULL, 4,  0 };

static  unsigned  ibeam_image[32] =
/* screen mask */    {   0xE187, 0xE007, 0xF81F, 0xFC3F,
                         0xFC3F, 0xFC3F, 0xFC3F, 0xFC3F,
                         0xFC3F, 0xFC3F, 0xFC3F, 0xFC3F,
                         0xFC3F, 0xF81F, 0xE007, 0xE187,
/* cursor mask */        0x0C30, 0x0240, 0x0180, 0x0180,
                         0x0180, 0x0180, 0x0180, 0x0180,
                         0x0180, 0x0180, 0x0180, 0x0180,
                         0x0180, 0x0180, 0x0240, 0x0C30  };
static g_cursor IBEAM = { NULL, 7,  7 };

static mouse_event far *m_events;              /* Global far ptr to mouse event record */

void far m_handler()                           /* event m_handler called by device driver */
{
    mouse_event far *save;                     /* pointer to save area in diff segment */
    unsigned    a, b, c, d;                    /* temp storage of registers */

    a = _AX,                                              /* save registers */
    b = _BX,
    c = _CX,
    d = _DX;
    save = MK_FP( _CS–0x10, 0x00C0 );          /* point to PSP user area */
    save–>flag  = a;                           /* stuff registers into it */
    save–>button = b;
    save–>xaxis  = c;
    save–>yaxis  = d;
}

void initialize_cursors()                      /* initialize ptrs in cursor descriptors */
{
```

```
        ARROW.image = arrow_image;
        CHECK.image = check_image;
        CROSS.image = cross_image;
        GLOVE.image = glove_image;
        IBEAM.image = ibeam_image;
    }

    void Set_Graphic_Cursor( g_cursor ThisCursor )
    {
        m_graphic_cursor( ThisCursor.xkey,
                          ThisCursor.ykey,
                          _DS,
                          (unsigned) ThisCursor.image );
    }
```

/ end MOUSE.I */*

```
/*              G_MOUSE.C — Basic Graphics Mouse Demo               */

#ifdef __TINY__
#error Graphics demos will not run in the tiny model.
#endif

#include <conio.h>
#include <stdio.h>
#include <stdlib.h>
#include <stdarg.h>
#include <graphics.h>
#include <gprint.i>
#include <mouse.i>

int    GraphDriver;                             /* graphics device driver    */
int    GraphMode;                               /* graphics mode value       */
int    MaxColors;                               /* maximum colors available  */
int    ErrorCode = 0;                           /* reports any graphics errors */
int    MaxX, MaxY, bar_height = 50;

void Initialize()                    /* initialize graphics system and report errors */
{
    GraphDriver = DETECT;                          /* request auto-detection    */
    initgraph( &GraphDriver, &GraphMode, "" );
    ErrorCode = graphresult();                     /* test initialization results */
    if ( ErrorCode != grOk )                       /* if error occurred during init */
    {
        printf(" Graphics System Error: %s\n", grapherrormsg( ErrorCode ) );
        exit( 1 );
    }
    MaxX = getmaxx();
    MaxY = getmaxy();
    MaxColors = getmaxcolor();
}

void label_box( int left, int top, int right, int bottom, char *label )
{
```

427

```
        rectangle( left, top, right, bottom );
        outtextxy( left+(right−left)/2, top+(bottom−top)/2, label );
}

void Make_Screen( int step, int width )
{
        int  i, color_bar, color_step;

        settextstyle( TRIPLEX_FONT, 0, 1 );
        settextjustify( CENTER_TEXT, CENTER_TEXT );
        label_box( 1,   1,    width, step,  "Quit" );
        label_box( 1, step+1,   width, step*2, "Arrow" );
        label_box( 1, step*2+1, width, step*3, "Check" );
        label_box( 1, step*3+1, width, step*4, "Cross" );
        label_box( 1, step*4+1, width, step*5, "Glove" );
        label_box( 1, step*5+1, width, step*6, "IBeam" );
        label_box( 1, step*6+1, width, step*7, " L  M  R " );
        for( i=0; i<=2; i++ )
        rectangle( (width/4+5)*i+5,   step*6.25, (width/4+5)*(i+1), step*6.75 );
        settextstyle( DEFAULT_FONT, 0, 1 );
        settextjustify( LEFT_TEXT, CENTER_TEXT );
        switch( GraphDriver )
{
        case CGA  : if( GraphMode != CGAHI ) color_bar = 3;  break;
        case EGA  :
        case VGA  : color_bar = 15; break;
        default      : color_bar = 0;
}
if( color_bar )
{
        color_step = (MaxX − width+3) / color_bar;
        for( i=1; i<=color_bar; i++ )
        {
            setfillstyle( SOLID_FILL, i );
            rectangle( width+3 + color_step * (i−1), 1,
                        width+3 + color_step * i, bar_height );
```

```
                floodfill( width+7 + color_step * (i–1), 10, MaxColors );
        }
    }
}

void Mouse_Demo()
{
    int       i, color, VStep, target[10], exit_time = 0, box_width = 100;
    void      *button_image;
    m_result *rodent;

    Initialize();
    VStep = MaxY / 7;
    color = MaxColors;
    setfillstyle( CLOSE_DOT_FILL, color );
    target[0] = target[6] = target[8] = 2;
    target[1] = target[3] = target[9] = 2;
    target[2] = target[4] = box_width / 4;
    target[5] = target[7] = VStep / 2;
    fillpoly( 5, target );
    getimage( 1, 1, box_width/4, VStep/2, button_image );
    putimage( 1, 1, button_image, XOR_PUT );
    Make_Screen( VStep, box_width );
    m_events = MK_FP( _psp, 0x00C0 );
    initialize_cursors();
    rodent = m_reset();
    if( rodent–>present )
    {
        m_events–>flag = 0;
        m_inst_task( EVENTMASK,
                    FP_SEG( m_handler ), FP_OFF( m_handler ) );
        m_show();
        m_xlimit( 1, MaxX );
        m_ylimit( 1, MaxY );
        exit_time = 0;
        while( !exit_time )
```

```
    {
        m_events–>flag = 0;                              /* zero out the event flag */
        delay(10);
        while( !m_events–>flag );                        /* wait for a mouse event */
        switch( m_events–>flag )                         /* act on any mouse event */
        {
            case 0x01: if( ( m_events–>xaxis > box_width ) &&
                           ( m_events–>yaxis > bar_height ) )
                       switch( m_events–>button )        /* mouse moved */
                       {
                           case 1: m_hide();             /* if left button */
                                   putpixel( m_events–>xaxis,
                                           m_events–>yaxis, color );
                                   m_show();
                                   break;
                           case 2: m_hide();             /* if right button */
                                   putpixel( m_events–>xaxis,
                                           m_events–>yaxis, 0 );
                                   m_show();
                                   break;
                       }
                       /* alternative procedure replacing m_conceal ( conditional */
                          /* hide ) function — see text for additional explanation */
                       if( ( m_events–>xaxis <= box_width ) &&
                         ( m_events–>yaxis >= 6*VStep ) )
                       {
                           m_hide();
                           m_cursor = OFF;
                       }
                       else
                       if( !m_cursor )
                       {
                           m_cursor = ON;
                           m_show();
                       };
                       break;
```

```
case 0x02: putimage( 5, VStep*6.25, button_image, XOR_PUT );
          if( m_events->xaxis <= box_width )
          {
              if( m_events->yaxis < VStep )
                  exit_time++;
              else
              if( m_events->yaxis < 2*VStep )
                  Set_Graphic_Cursor( ARROW );
              else
              if( m_events->yaxis < 3*VStep )
                  Set_Graphic_Cursor( CHECK );
              else
              if( m_events->yaxis < 4*VStep )
                  Set_Graphic_Cursor( CROSS );
              else
              if( m_events->yaxis < 5*VStep )
                  Set_Graphic_Cursor( GLOVE );
              else
              if( m_events->yaxis < 6*VStep )
                  Set_Graphic_Cursor( IBEAM );
          } else
          if( m_events->yaxis <= bar_height )
          color = ( MaxColors *
                  ( m_events->xaxis – box_width – 3 ) /
                  ( MaxX – box_width – 3 ) ) + 1;
          break;
case 0x04: putimage( 5, VStep*6.25,
                  button_image, XOR_PUT );
          break;
case 0x08: putimage( box_width/2+15, VStep*6.25,
                  button_image, XOR_PUT );
          break;
case 0x10: putimage( box_width/2+15, VStep*6.25,
                  button_image, XOR_PUT );
          break;
case 0x20: putimage( box_width/4+10, VStep*6.25,
```

```
                                        button_image, XOR_PUT );
                            break;
                case 0x40: putimage( box_width/4+10, VStep*6.25,
                                        button_image, XOR_PUT );
                            break;
            }
        }
        closegraph();
        m_text_cursor( HARDWARE, 0x0000, 0x0007 );
        m_show();
    } else outtextxy( 10,10, "no mouse present" );
}

main()
{
    Mouse_Demo();
}
```

CHAPTER 17

THE TURBO FONT EDITOR

For Turbo C, Pascal and Prolog Stroked Graphics Fonts

The **Font Editor** is a utility designed to create or to edit stroked fonts for use with Turbo Pascal, Turbo C or Turbo Prolog using BGI graphics displays. The **Font Editor** utility consists of the editor program FE.EXE, and nine character fonts: EURO.CHR, GOTH.CHR, LCOM.CHR, LITT.CHR, SANS.CHR, SCRI.CHR, SIMP.CHR, TRIP.CHR and TSCR.CHR.

Also available from Borland, are a .BIN to .BGI conversion utility (DFONT.EXE, DFONT.C and FONT.H) and a .BGI Driver Toolkit (see Appendix D) and a new video driver VGA256.BGI (see Appendix E).

The following instructions apply to **Font Editor** revision 1.0.

Introduction to Stroked Fonts

Stroked fonts define characters as line sequence instructions (strokes) showing the outline composing the specific characters (see also Chapter 11 — **Turtle Graphics** — for another illustration of a stroked font creation). Alternatively, the standard text font displayed by your computer is a bitmap font with each character defined as a matrix of dots.

The advantage found in stroked fonts is that the characters can be arbitrarily scaled in size and in proportions without loss of resolution. Bitmap fonts can be enlarged, but only in simple multiples of the grid size for they suffer degradation of appearance as they're enlarged.

For example: if a bitmap font is enlarged four times, each dot in the original grid becomes a 4x4 pixel square in the enlargement, resulting in a jagged, stepped appearance (see Figure 17-1 — Stroked vs. Bitmap Characters).

Stroked fonts are not converted to dot patterns (pixels) until the desired font size and output device resolution are known. A stroked font can be sized without suffering in appearance. Also, stroked fonts can be output to devices with quite different resolution (such as 120 dpi dot-matrix printers or 300 dpi laserjet printers), without loss of stroke resolution.

Figure 17-1: Stroked vs. Bitmap

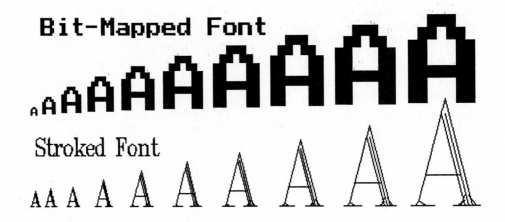

Further, the Font Editor can be used to create non-alphabetic or symbol fonts for specialized displays and applications. For example, in Chapter 9, bit images were created for use with the line graph display. Using FE, these same images could be created as a stroked symbol font, much more conveniently that writing bit-by-bit instructions. The resulting symbols are used, not only in the line graph display, but in a variety of applications and in any size desired (see Figure 17-2 — Special Symbol Font Characters).

Also, several new stroked fonts are available (see Table 17-1).

Figure 17-2: Special Symbol Font Characters (Runic Alphabet)

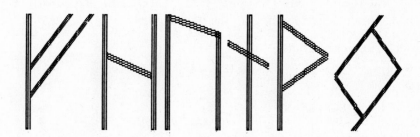

System Requirements

The Font Editor is compatible with most systems, but does impose a few minimum requirements.

Computer Requirements

Font Editor (FE.EXE) runs on IBM PCs, PC/XTs, PC/ATs and most compatibles. You must also copy the appropriate .BGI driver (this will be EGAVGA.BGI in most cases) to the same directory as FE.EXE or provide a path in your AUTOEXEC.BAT file to the directory containing the .BGI files.

Mouse Requirements

Font Editor requires a mouse supporting the Microsoft External Mouse Driver Interface (MM protocol). This includes the Microsoft, Mouse Systems and Logitech bus or serial mice.

435

If you are using another hardware mouse type, consult your mouse manual for installation instructions. The mouse driver (MOUSE.COM or MOUSE.SYS) must be installed in memory before calling **FE**. Normally, the mouse is loaded as a DOS device driver by definition in your CONFIG.SYS file (DEVICE = MOUSE.SYS) or in your AUTOEXEC.BAT (MOUSE<cr> or MOUSE 2<cr>), depending on the port used.

Table 17-1: Stroked Fonts

FILE NAME	FONT	NAME	VALUE
EURO.CHR*	EUROPEAN	–	–
GOTH.CHR	GOTHIC	GOTHIC_FONT[1]	4
LCOM.CHR*	TEXT (ROMAN)	–	–
LITT.CHR	SMALL	SMALL_FONT[1]	2
SANS.CHR	SANS-SERIF	SANS_SERIF_FONT[1]	3
SCRI.CHR*	SCRIPT	–	–
SIMP.CHR*	SIMPLEX	–	–
TRIP.CHR	TRIPLEX	TRIPLEX_FONT[1]	1
TSCR.CHR*	TEXT ITALIC	–	–

* New fonts supplied with **Font Editor** utility.

1. Font names and values defined in GRAPHICS.H header file.

Graphics Requirements

Font Editor also requires an Enhanced Graphics Adapter (EGA) or compatible and a color display. The graphics adapter card must have a minimum of 128K RAM installed.

Plotter Requirements

(Optional) **Font Editor** supports hardcopy output to one of the following Hewlett-Packard or compatible plotters:

- HP 7470
- HP 7475 (8 $1/2$ x 11 paper only)
- HP 7440 (ColorPro)

There are two considerations to keep in mind. First, when using a plotter and a serial mouse, two serial ports are required, one for the plotter and one for the mouse. When plotter output is requested, **FE** will prompt you for the port (COM1 or COM2) for the plotter and will then initialize the indicated serial port (see Chapter 15 for details on serial port initialization). Be sure that you indicate the correct port for the plotter or you may find the mouse no longer responds. After the plotter port is selected, **FE** will ask for initialization parameters, assuming 9600 baud, Even parity, 7 bits and 1 stop bit.

If other settings are desired, the serial port should be initialized using the DOS Mode command before calling **Font Editor**.

Second, the most common problem interfacing between an HP plotter and a non-HP computer is in the connecting cable. If you experience any problems in this area, Hewlett-Packard supplies a standard cable for this application, part number HP 17255D, or you can use straight-through RS-232C cabling together with a dummy (null) modem (see Chapter 15).

General Capabilities

Font Editor edits Borland stroked fonts (files with the .CHR extension shipped with Turbo C and Turbo Pascal or fonts supplied with the **Font Editor**). You can read in fonts, edit individual characters, preview characters on screen or, optionally, on a plotter and save the resulting font back to disk.

Font Editor Display

The **Font Editor** screen is divided into four major areas that are explained momentarily. Because each screen area reacts slightly differently with the mouse, mouse usage will be covered first.

Mouse Conventions

The left and right mouse buttons are treated identically.

Two major operations are performed using the mouse with **Font Editor**. The first is a click — a quick press-and-release of the mouse button when the graphics cursor is positioned on an object to select that object. The second is a "drag" — a press-hold-and-move operation used to slide objects or to define an area. When the drag operation is being used, the object "sticks" to the mouse cursor, moving with the cursor until the button is released.

Area Definition Using The Mouse

The mouse can be used to define an area within the work screen. The location where a mouse button is depressed marks one corner and the diagonally opposite corner is defined when the button is released.

If you define the starting corner erroneously, the error cannot be changed except by starting over (defining a new rectangle). The second corner, however, can be changed by moving the mouse before releasing the mouse button.

Using The Mouse In The Character Window

When the mouse is used in the Character (Edit) window, you will notice that the mouse moves in discreet steps, moving only between indicated intersection points where strokes can start and stop. The spacing of the grid points depends on the Zoom option and also on the size of the font being edited. For example, if you select LITT.CHR (SMALL_FONT), the grid points will be widely spaced (a 12x10 point grid), while selecting SANS.CHR (SANS_SERIF_FONT) will show a tightly spaced grid (a 44x33 point grid).

Escape From Plotter Output

Pressing any mouse button during a plotter output terminates the graphics plotter dump. This may, however, require you to hold the mouse button down for several seconds until the button status is recognized. Also, plotting will not halt immediately, but will continue until the drawing commands in its internal buffer are completed.

The Font Editor Menu

When using **Font Editor**, a series of menus are displayed as a line of text across the top of the screen for selection by mouse click.

Some items in the menu, such as *Load* and *Save,* perform a single function and, when the function is completed, display the same menu. Other items, such as *Edit*, display a new menu. All menus except the initial menu contain the item *Exit* which will return you to the previous menu.

The *Quit* item in the main menu returns to DOS. If changes have been made to the current font, a *Save* prompt will appear before exiting.

Selecting A Character For Editing

When **FE** is first called, a menu shows all of the .CHR fonts in the current directory. The first step is to use the mouse to select a font for editing. After selection, the display will shift to the edit screen. The font directory can also be called by selecting *Load* from the menu options across the top of the screen.

In the edit screen, to the right, a large rectangular area shows a 256 character display (using the extended ASCII character set — not the font currently being edited). Clicking on any character within this box selects this character for edit, displaying the current font's equivalent character in the Edit Window as a series of strokes and below the selection box as it would appear on screen with a size definition of 1. Characters can also be selected for edit by keyboard entry.

Within the selection window, the characters displayed appear in green if the current font contains a stroked character definition or in red if no stroked image has been defined for this character. The characters 00h (null), 20h (space) and FFh appear as blanks, but can be selected and defined as font characters.

The currently selected character is highlighted in the window (as bright green or bright red).

The Character Window

The character window is the large rectangular area on the left half of the screen (see Figure 17-3) where character editing takes place. The **Font Editor** will display the strokes comprising a selected character. An existing character may be edited or a new character created using the mouse to delete elements or to add new lines in this window.

Character Width/Spacing

Notice the small triangle along the baseline to the right. This marker shows the beginning position for the next character (the intercharacter spacing). The character width can be changed by dragging the triangle to a new position.

Kerning — the practice used by typesetters where inter-character spacing is adjusted to allow specific character pairs to fit together — is not supported per se, though character widths can be adjusted to create tightly or loosely spaced fonts as required.

Editing A Character

Character strokes are added or deleted by moving the mouse cursor to the desired starting point, pressing the button and dragging to the desired end point. If no stroke connected these points previously, then a new stroke is added; if one did exist, then it is deleted.

Figure 17-3: Edit Window Display

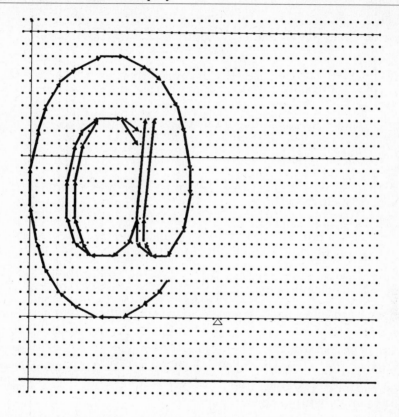

The vertical line along the left side of the grid shows the left edge of the
character. Four horizontal lines, beginning at the top, show the height of a
capital character (A, B etc.), the height of a lowercase character (a,c etc.), the
baseline and the descender depth (as for g, j or y).

Curves are not supported. Instead, curves and bends are created as a series of strokes as shown in Figure 17-3. Drawing a line where there was none before will add a stroke to the character definition. Drawing a line on top of an existing line erases that line from the character definition (leaving no line).

Combinations of adding and deleting strokes can be performed with a single line. For example, drawing a new stroke in the middle of an existing line erases that portion of the line, leaving two other lines corresponding to the end portions that were not drawn over.

The Small Character

The area in the lower right hand corner of the screen displays a small version of the current character (as would be displayed on the screen with a character size of 1). Note: the Small Character display is not affected by additions or deletions in the Edit window until the Update option is exercised.

This area is for information only; nothing is mouse selectable here.

The Update Selector Box

Changes — additions or deletions — to the currently edited character are not added to the stroke definition until specifically instructed by clicking on the *Update* option shown above the selection box.

While editing a character, the changes made to a character are saved in an edit buffer. To make the edits permanent, the mouse is used to select the *Update* option, writing the edit buffer to the actual character.

Clicking on the current character in the selection box will bring up a prompt asking if the strokes are to be added (or subtracted) from the current character. Clicking on a new character will display the same prompt before the new selection is displayed in the edit window.

NOTE: The edit actions on characters only affect the edit image, *not* the character stroke data. For example, suppose several lines are added to a character, but the character is not updated. Now, if the Edit option is selected from the menu and used to move the character, only the information in the character buffer will be affected, but the new lines added to the character image will not be moved. This applies to all of the edit functions, including move, flip, flop, reverse, shift, cut, and copy.

Editing Tools

This section gives a brief description of the **Font Editor** tools — see the **Command Reference** section for detailed descriptions of these commands.

Single Strokes

Single strokes can be added or deleted from a character image by moving the mouse cursor into the character window and performing a drag operation between the grid points where the stroke should be added or deleted. As the mouse is dragged, a line appears between the start point and the mouse cursor — a process known as "rubber banding" because the line appears to stretch or to shrink when following the cursor.

Drawing over an existing stroke, deletes the line and drawing over a portion of an existing line, deletes only a portion of the line.

Also, if the mouse cursor is moved outside the character window while rubber banding a line, the stroke will be cancelled.

Groups of Strokes

Because many characters share the same stroke groups, groups of strokes can be manipulated as a single object using the **Edit/Clipboard** commands. For example, the strokes defining the left hand part of a 'c' will probably be the same as those in the left-hand part of a 'd.'

The tools available in the **Clipboard** menu allow selection of a group of strokes from a character to be used again in that character or in another character. **Cut** and **Copy** move a group of characters into a holding buffer (the **Clipboard**). **Cut** removes the strokes from the current character, while **Copy** leaves the originals undisturbed.

Strokes are selected for **Clipboard** by rubber banding a rectangle around the strokes. Note: both end points of a given stroke must be completely inside the rectangle in order to be selected for a **Cut** or **Copy**.

The strokes in **Clipboard** are pasted into a character by selecting the **Paste** option which adds the contents to the character window. The strokes can be moved using a drag operation.

Paste does not empty **Clipboard**; the next paste operation will find the same strokes. **Cut** and **Copy** always change the contents of the **Clipboard**. **Delete** operates like **Cut**, except that the deleted strokes are not placed in **Clipboard**, just discarded. **Move** is similar to a combined **Cut** and **Paste** operation, except that the contents of **Clipboard** are not altered.

The contents of the Clipboard buffer can also be rotated using the commands under **Edit/Flip** to flip the contents upside down (horizontal axis) or right and left (vertical axis).

Whole Characters

Special techniques are provided for manipulating whole characters.

CopyChar (Edit menu) allows you to copy from one character within a single font to another, duplicating the selected character strokes as a new character.

For example, after creating a 'c', the 'c' could be copied to 'd' and edited to create the new character without repeating the strokes used for the 'c'.

Flip (Edit menu) allows you to flip a character upside down or right/left or both.

Shift (Edit menu) allows you to move a whole character right, left, up, or down.

For example, the characters, b, d, p, and q are usually just flipped versions of one another. You can draw one and use CopyChar and Flip to make the other three.

Whole Fonts

The commands under **Global** allow you to perform operations on the entire font. These are primarily concerned with inter-character spacing and usually, will be used as a part of the final editing process of a font.

LeftSpace will move every character in the font so that its left-most part is the specified distance from the left margin (the dark solid vertical line in the character window).

RghtSpace will set the character spacing marker of every character in the font to the distance specified to the right of the right-most stroke of each character.

BaseLine will shift every character up or down by the same amount so that the base line corresponds to zero.

Copy will allows selection of another font, copying characters from it into the current work font. Many characters — such as the graphic characters — will not change from one font to another and the **Copy** option saves the trouble of recreating these.

Font Editor Command Reference

In this section, the **Font Editor** menu commands and functions are described in detail.

Load — Loads an existing font file into **Font Editor**. A large rectangle will be drawn on the screen. There are two mouse sensitive areas within this rectangle: the file selector area and the file prompt line.

Clicking on the file prompt line will allow you to enter a new filename for loading and may include a new path. If the path/filename does not exist, you will be warned. If you confirm that the file does not exist, the file will be created and will become the default output file when the font is saved.

The file selector area contains a list of all of the files with the extension .CHR on the current drive/directory. As the mouse cursor is moved over these, the filenames will appear on the file prompt line. Clicking on one of these names will select the current file for load.

Show — The tools under **Show** simply show the appearance of the selected font but do not operate on or change the font.

Font shows all of the currently defined characters on the monitor and is also useful for a quick check of the inter-character spacing. Overlapping characters or gaps between characters will indicate errors in inter-character spacing.

String allows you to type a string of characters for display. Sometimes it is important to see two special characters together to determine the proper appearance and spacing.

When a line becomes full, display will continue on the next line or the Enter key can be used to force a new line. When the bottom of the screen is reached, the display does not scroll.

The **ESC**ape key is used to exit the String mode.

Plotter draws the current font on an HP plotter. See the section on Optional Hardware or Chapter 15 for a discussion of connecting the plotter.

When you select this tool, you will be asked if the plotter is COM1 or COM2. **Font Editor** must have the serial port on the PC configured to be able to communicate with the plotter. You may either let **FE** set the serial port to 9600 baud, Even parity, 7 data bits, and 1 stop bit (in which case the DIP switches on your plotter must be set for this configuration) or you may select NO to make **FE** skip this step.

If **FE** does not initialize the plotter's serial port, you must issue the DOS Mode command prior to starting **FE** to match your plotter's switch settings.

If you're using a serial mouse, be careful not to choose the serial port to which your mouse is connected.

Finally, you'll be asked to confirm plot. Have the paper loaded and the plotter ready before selecting YES.

If you start plotting and want to stop before the plot is complete, press and hold a mouse button until the screen clears.

Your plotter output will be labeled with the name of the file from which it came, and the page number. In the case of multiple page plots, **FE** will stop at the end of each page to allow you to load a new piece of paper.

Exit returns you to the main menu.

Global commands operate on an entire font, unlike most other commands which operate on a single character or stroke.

LeftSpace adjusts the space between the left-most stroke of a character and the vertical guide line shown in the character window. Typically, this should be set to zero for all fonts, so that an application that mixes fonts will maintain character spacing between font changes.

RghtSpace adjusts the character width mark of all the characters to the set value. The character width value set for each character is the number selected from sub-menu, plus the right most stroke of the character. This choice will therefore, provide uniform inter-character spacing for a proportionally spaced font.

Typically, this choice is issued for the entire font for proportional spacing, then selected characters — such as the numeric characters and the graphics character symbols which require the same total widths for column lineup — are adjusted individually,

BaseLine adjusts each character in the font up or down by the same amount. This option is exercised for an entire font so that all fonts refer to the same base line value. An application switching fonts will not have the baseline of the new font shifted up or down from the previous font.

Copy selects characters from a different font file. The source font file is selected as under the **Load** option.

When **Copy** is selected, you will see two character selector boxes on the screen: the left box corresponding to the source font selected, the right box corresponding to the working font.

Characters are copied individually by clicking on the character desired from the source character box, then clicking on the destination character in the right-hand character box.

To quit, select **Done** in the menu area.

Exit returns to the main menu.

Edit provides tools for editing whole characters or groups of strokes. The **Clipboard** functions under this heading are of particular importance.

CopyChar allows intra-font copying of characters by selecting source and destination characters within the working font. If a character already exists where you selected the destination character, then you will be asked if that character should be replaced.

Flip allows flipping either the current character or the contents of **Clipboard**.

Characters are flipped within the space that they occupy. For example, if a character only occupies the lower portion of the character cell, then the results — after flipping it vertically — will only occupy the lower portion of the character cell. The **Shift** option can be used to change positions.

The results of flipping the **Clipboard** will not be visible until it is pasted into the **Edit** window.

Shift moves a character one dot in any direction. It does not modify the inter-character spacing.

ShowAlso superimposes another character over the character currently being edited. The superimposed character's strokes and width marker are shown in RED where strokes match the edit character or in GREEN where they do not coincide.

The superimposed character will remain in the edit window until **Update** is executed or a new edit character is selected.

Clipboard contains all the tools for working on groups of strokes. The **Cut**, **Copy** and **Paste** options work by reading and writing a buffer area called the Clipboard. **Move** and **Delete** do not use the **Clipboard**.

Strokes are selected from the current character by rubber banding a rectangle around them. One corner of the rectangle is defined by the location where you press a mouse button, the diagonally opposite corner is defined by the position where the mouse button is released.

Remember, both end points of a stroke must lie completely within the rectangle in order to be selected.

For the **Move** and **Paste** options, when a region has been defined, the strokes contained in the region are copied within the window, to the right of the character width marker. The upper left corner of the strokes will be attached to the mouse cursor while a mouse button is pressed and will stay attached until the button is released.

Cut removes the selected strokes from the current character, placing them in the **Clipboard**. The previous contents of **Clipboard** are lost.

Copy copies the selected strokes from the current character to the clip board without changing the current character. The previous contents of **Clipboard** are lost.

Paste copies the contents of the **Clipboard** to the current character. The contents of the **Clipboard** are not changed.

Move moves the selected strokes to a new location: the equivalent of a **Cut** and **Paste** operation except that the contents (if any) of the **Clipboard** are not changed.

Delete cuts the selected strokes from the current character. This is equivalent to a **Cut** except that the contents of the **Clipboard** are not changed.

Exit returns to the Edit menu.

Exit returns to the Main menu.

Save writes the current font data to an output file. **Save** works like the **Load** command, drawing a large rectangle on the screen containing two mouse sensitive areas: the file selector area and the file prompt line.

Clicking on the file prompt line allows entry of a new filename and may include a new path. You will be warned if the file name entered does not exit. If you confirm that the file does not exist, the file will be created.

The file selector area contains a list of all of the files on the current drive/directory with the extension .CHR. As the mouse cursor is moved over this list, each filename will on the file prompt line. Clicking on one of these names will select the current destination file.

The options under **Window** control how the character editing window displays. These options do not change the characters, only the way that they are displayed.

The default values shown are set automatically when a font file is loaded. If **Font Editor** is called without selecting an initial font file (i.e. — by bypassing **Load**) these values must be set.

Zoom Out reduces the magnification used to display the character in the Edit window. Magnification is automatically set to show all characters in the character window as large as possible when the font file is loaded.

Zoom In increases the magnification used to display the character in the Edit window. Magnification is automatically set to show all characters in the character window as large as possible when the font file is loaded.

Magnification may be increased so that characters are larger than the window — parts of characters that would be outside the window are clipped to the window limits. This is useful while working on lowercase letters or the strokes that make up the serifs of a serif font.

Origin allows positioning the origin guide line anywhere within the character editing window.

While, for most fonts, this is drawn underneath the base line guide line and won't be visible, it is still moveable. Move the origin guide line towards the top of the window and zoom in to work on descending strokes or move the origin guide line to the bottom of the window to work on uppercase letters.

d-ht sets the descender height guide line in the character editing window. This has no effect on the character, character edits, or display of the character in the window. It is simply for your convenience.

b-ht sets the base line height guide line in the character editing window. This has no effect on the character, character edits, or display of the character in the window. It is simply for your convenience.

x-ht positions the x-height guide line (lowercase height) in the character editing window. This has no effect on the character, character edits, or display of the character in the window. It is simply for your convenience.

c-ht positions the character height guide line (uppercase height) in the character editing window. This has no effect on the character, character edits, or display of the character in the window. It is simply for your convenience.

ShowMovs shows each *move, draw, draw, ...* sequence in a different color so that some notion of how the character is being stroked can be gained. The sequence of colors shows the order in which strokes are generated.

This option defaults to off. Turning this option on may produce disquieting results when drawing in the character editing window. Its use is not recommended (but is interesting — if somewhat garish).

Grid shows the grid of points in the character editing on which stokes can begin and end. This option defaults ON.

Exit returns to the Main menu.

Quit returns to DOS; you will be asked if you want to save any edits.

Beginning a New Font from Scratch

Here are a few considerations for the user who wishes to start a new font from scratch. To begin a new font, start **Font Editor** and select a new font filename. The screen will show a character window with no characters defined (all character choices will be displayed in red). The four global parameters for the font are determined automatically by the font editor when a file is loaded or saved. These parameters are the Base Height, the Capital Height, the Descender Height, and the Lowercase Height (or x Height). The values for these are determined by examining the characters that a typographer would use to determine the same information.

Capital Height: This value is determined by examining the E Ligature character (144 decimal). This is the tallest of the European characters. If this character is undefined, the capital M is used as the capital height. If neither of these characters is defined, the value will default to 40 (of a maximum +/–64).

Base Height: This value is determined by examining the E Ligature or the Capital M. This value is used as the origin for the other three dimensions. If neither of these characters are defined, the value will default to 0 (of a maximum of +/–64).

Descender Height: This value is determined by examining the lowercase 'q' letter. If the lower case 'q' is undefined, the value will default to -7 (of a maximum of +/−64).

Lowercase Height (or x Height): This value is determined be examining the lowercase 'x' letter. If the lowercase 'x' is undefined, the value will default to the Capital Height divided by two.

To define the size and placement of the characters in the font, it is best to define the 'M', 'q', 'x', and E Ligature (if desired) as the first characters. The next time the font is loaded, the character dimensions will be used to define the size and placement of the character window for the font.

If you are defining a special symbol font, these parameters may or may not be relevant, but in most cases, as a minimum, the Base Height should be defined.

Using Custom Fonts

The original fonts supplied with Turbo C (or Turbo Pascal) are ''built-in'' the BGI Graphics library. Unlike the original fonts, however, user-created fonts (and the five new fonts supplied with the **Turbo Font Editor**) cannot be referenced directly but must first be installed in the internal font table.

The **installuserfont** function (Turbo C version 2.0 or later) is supplied for this purpose and returns a font ID number that can be used subsequently with **settextstyle** to identify the font.

The NEWFONTS.C demo program (at the end of this chapter) installs the five new fonts supplied with the **Turbo Font Editor** and prints a brief message to the screen with each font (see Figure 17-3).

Identifying The Fonts

The original fonts are identified by constant names in the GRAPHICS.H header file. For convenience and to provide compatibility, the new fonts are also identified by font names but, since no library constants exist for these, the font names are declared as variables with initial values of 0.

```
int LARGE_FONT = 0,          /* EURO.CHR */
    ROMAN_FONT = 0,          /* LCOM.CHR */
    SIMPLEX_FONT = 0,        /* SIMP.CHR */
    ITALIC_FONT = 0,         /* TSCR.CHR */
    SCRIPT_FONT = 0;         /* SCRI.CHR */
```

Figure 17-4: New Graphics Character Fonts

ABCDEFGHIJKL Large

ABCDEFGHIJKL Roman

ABCDEFGHIJKL Italic

ABCDEFGHIJKL Script

ABCDEFGHIJKL Simplex

An Install_Font Utility

Now, because the possibility always exists that the .CHR file required for a particular font may not even exist, a simple **Install_Font** function can be used.

Install_Font is called with the path/filename for the font desired and returns an integer identifying the entry in the internal font table. If the .CHR file for a specified font is not found, **Install_Font** can display a message and, instead of returning a negative error code, returns a zero value which provides a simpler Boolean test than the graphics error code.

```
int Install_Font( char *font_name )
{
    int  font_number;

    font_number = installuserfont( font_name );
    if( font_number  0 )
    {
        /* you can put an error message on the screen */
        return( 0 );
    }
    else return( font_number );
}
```

Loading Several Fonts

If more than one font is required, the simplest route is to assign all the fonts needed at one time. The integer values returned are assigned to the font variable names (LARGE_FONT, ROMAN_FONT, etc).

This does not require any excessive memory expenditure — only the font names are installed and the font information itself is loaded into memory only when the font is actually assigned using the **settextstyle** function.

```
void Load_Fonts()
{
    LARGE_FONT   = Install_Font( "EURO.CHR" );
    ROMAN_FONT  = Install_Font( "LCOM.CHR" );
    ITALIC_FONT    = Install_Font( "TSCR.CHR" );
    SCRIPT_FONT  = Install_Font( "SCRI.CHR" );
    SIMPLEX_FONT= Install_Font( "SIMP.CHR" );
}
```

Short and simple, that's it. Between the **Turbo Font Editor** and the preceding utility procedures, there's a world of possibilities for special displays and graphics features.

BGI Stroke File Format

The structure of Borland .CHR (stroked font) file follows, beginning at offset 00h with a header:

```
HeaderSize      equ     080h
DataSize        equ     (size of font file)
descr           equ     "Triplex font"
fname           equ     "TRIP"
MajorVersion equ        1
MinorVersion equ        0
db      'PK',8,8
db      'BGI ',descr,' V'
db      MajorVersion + '0'
db      (MinorVersion / 10) + '0', (MinorVersion mod 10) + '0'
db      ' - 19 October 1987', ODh, OAh
db      0,1Ah                   ; null & ctrl-Z = end
dw      HeaderSize              ; size of header
db      fname                   ; font name
dw      DataSize                ; font file size
db      MajorVersion,MinorVersion ; version #'s
db      1,0                     ; minimal version #'s
db      (HeaderSize - $) DUP (0) ; pad out to header size
```

The data for the file begins at offset 80h:

```
80h     '+'     flags stroke file type
81h-82h         number chars in font file (n)
83h             undefined
84h             ASCII value of first char in file
85h..86h        offset to stroke definitions (8+3n)
87h             scan flag (normally 0)
```

88h	distance from origin to top of capital
89h	distance from origin to baseline
90h	distance from origin to bottom descender
91h..95h	undefined
96h	offsets to individual character definitions
96h + 2n	width table (one word per character)
96h + 3n	start of character definitions

The individual character definitions consist of a variable number of words describing the operations required to render each character. Each word consists of an (x,y) coordinate pair and a two bit-opcode, encoded as shown following:

Table 17-2: Encoded Opcodes

BYTE 1	7	6..5..4..3..2..1..0	*BIT #*
	OP1	<7-BIT SIGNED X COORD>	
BYTE 2	7	6..5..4..3..2..1..0	*BIT #*
	OP2	<7-BIT SIGNED Y COORD>	

Table 17-3: Opcodes

OP1	OP2	MEANING
0	0	end of character definition.
1	0	move the pointer to (x,y)
1	1	draw from current pointer to (x,y)

```
/*              NEWFONTS.C — Using New Turbo .CHR Alphabets           */
#ifdef __TINY__
#error Graphics demos will not run in the tiny model.
#endif
#include <conio.h>
#include <stdio.h>
#include <stdlib.h>
#include <stdarg.h>
#include <graphics.h>
#include <fcntl.h>
#include "gprint.i"


int     GraphDriver;
int     GraphMode;
int     ErrorCode = 0;
int     LARGE_FONT = 0,              /* EURO.CHR -- install required */
        ROMAN_FONT = 0,              /* LCOM.CHR -- install required */
        SIMPLEX_FONT = 0,            /* SIMP.CHR -- install required */
        ITALIC_FONT = 0,            /* TSCR.CHR -- install required */
        SCRIPT_FONT = 0;             /* SCRI.CHR -- install required */


void Initialize()
{
        GraphDriver = DETECT;
        initgraph( &GraphDriver, &GraphMode, "" );
        ErrorCode = graphresult();
        if ( ErrorCode != grOk )
        {
        printf(" Graphics System Error: %s\n", grapherrormsg( ErrorCode ) );
        exit( 1 );
        }
}
```

```
void Pause()
{
        if( kbhit() ) getch();
        getch();
}


int Install_Font( char *font_name )
{
        int  font_number;
        font_number = installuserfont( font_name );
        if( font_number  0 )
        {
            gprintxy( 10, 10, "%s not loaded", font_name );
            Pause();
            return( 0 );
        }
        else return( font_number );
}


void Display_Alphabet( int font, int vpos, char *name )
{
        settextstyle( font, HORIZ_DIR, 4 );
        gprintxy( 50, vpos, "ABCDEFGHIJKL %s", name );
}


void Load_Fonts()
{
        LARGE_FONT   = Install_Font( "EURO.CHR" );
        ROMAN_FONT   = Install_Font( "LCOM.CHR" );
        ITALIC_FONT  = Install_Font( "TSCR.CHR" );
        SCRIPT_FONT  = Install_Font( "SCRI.CHR" );
        SIMPLEX_FONT = Install_Font( "SIMP.CHR" );
}
```

```
void Show_New_Fonts()
{
        Load_Fonts();
        setcolor(WHITE);
        settextjustify( LEFT_TEXT, TOP_TEXT );
        Display_Alphabet( LARGE_FONT,   20, "Large"   );
        Display_Alphabet( ROMAN_FONT,   80, "Roman"   );
        Display_Alphabet( ITALIC_FONT,  120, "Italic" );
        Display_Alphabet( SCRIPT_FONT,  160, "Script" );
        Display_Alphabet( SIMPLEX_FONT, 200, "Simplex" );
}


main()
{
        Initialize();
        cleardevice();
        Show_New_Fonts();
        Pause();
        closegraph();
}
```

GRAPHICS FUNCTIONS — QUICK REFERENCE

Color/Palette Functions

getbkcolor	returns current background color setting
getcolor	returns current drawing color
getmaxcolor	returns maximum valid color value
getpalette	returns palette information
setallpalette	changes all palette colors as specified
setbkcolor	sets current background color using the palette
setcolor	sets current drawing color using the palette
setpalette	changes one palette color

Drawing Functions

arc	draws circular arc
bar	draws a bar
bar3d	draws a 3-D bar
circle	draws a circle
drawpoly	draws the outline of a polygon
ellipse	draws an elliptical arc
fillellipse	draws and fills a closed ellipse
fillpoly	draws and fills a polygon
floodfill	fills a bonded region
getarccoords	returns coordinates of last call to **arc** function

getaspectratio	returns current graphic aspect ratio
getfillpattern	copies user-defined fill pattern to memory
getfillsettings	returns information about fill pattern and color
getlinesettings	returns current line style, pattern and thickness
line	draws line between two specified points
linerel	draws line relative distance from CP
lineto	draws line from CP to specified offset (x,y)
pieslice	draws and fills in pie slice
rectangle	draws a rectangle
sector	draws and fills elliptical pie slice
setaspectratio	sets (adjusts) new graphic aspect ratio
setfillpattern	selects user-defined fill pattern
setfillstyle	sets fill pattern and color
setlinestyle	sets the current line width and style
setwritemode	sets graphics line write mode

Error Functions

grapherrormsg	returns error message string
graphresult	returns error code for failed graphic operation

Bit Image Functions

getimage	saves bit image from specified region into memory
imagesize	returns bytes required to store bit image
putimage	places bit image on screen
setgraphbufsize	changes the size of the internal graphics buffer

Mode Functions

closegraph	shuts down the graphics system
detectgraph	checks hardware to determine driver and mode
getdrivername	returns graphics driver name
getgraphmode	returns current graphics mode
getmodename	returns graphics mode name
getmoderange	returns range of modes for specified driver
graphdefaults	resets all graphic settings to default values
_graphfreemem	user-modifiable graphic memory deallocation
_graphgetmem	user-modifiable graphic memory allocation
initgraph	initializes graphics system
installuserdriver	installs user-defined graphics driver
registerbgidriver	registers linked-in graphics driver code
restorecrtmode	restores screen mode to original (text) settings
setgraphmode	sets system to graphics mode, clears screen

Pixel Functions

getpixel	returns color value of specified pixel
putpixel	plots pixel at specified point

Screen Position Functions

getmaxx	returns maximum x-axis screen coordinate (max CP)
getmaxy	returns maximum y-axis screen coordinate (max CP)
getx	returns current position's (CP) x coordinate
gety	returns current position's (CP) y coordinate

moverel	moves current position (CP) to a relative distance
moveto	moves current position (CP) to (x,y)

Screen/Page Functions

cleardevice	clears the graphics screen
setactivepage	sets active page for graphics output
setvisualpage	sets the visual graphics page number

Text Functions

gettextsettings	returns current graphics text settings
gprintf	displays formatted string in viewport at (x,y)
gprintxy	displays formatted string in viewport at (x,y)
installuserfont	installs user-defined graphics font
outtext	displays string in viewport (graphics window)
outtextxy	displays string in viewport at (x,y)
registerbgifont	registers linked-in stroked font code
settextjustify	sets text justification
settextstyle	sets current text characteristics
setusercharsize	user-defined character size for stroked fonts
textheight	returns the height of a string in pixels
textwidth	returns the width of a string in pixels

Viewport (Graphics Window) Functions

clearviewport	clears the current viewport (window)
getviewsettings	returns current viewport (window) settings
setviewport	sets current viewport for graphics output

arc

```
int     xcenter, ycenter, startangle, endangle, radius;
arc( xcenter, ycenter, startangle, endangle, radius );
```

Draws circular arc; startangle and endangle are in degrees (0..360); xcenter, ycenter and *radius* in pixels. See also **circle**, **ellipse**, **getaspectratio** and **pieslice**.

bar

```
int     left, top, right, bottom;
bar( left, top, right, bottom );
```

Draws a filled-in rectangular bar using current fill pattern and color. For an outlined bar, use **bar3d** with depth zero. See also **bar3d**, **getcolor**, **getfillsettings**, **getlinestyle** and **rectangle**.

bar3d

```
int     left, top, right, bottom, depth, topflag;
bar3d( left, top, right, bottom, depth, topflag );
```

Outlines a three-dimensional rectangular bar using current line style and color, then fills in results using current fill pattern and color. The bar's depth is given in pixels (normally about 25 percent of width). If the topflag parameter is zero, no top is added, allowing bars to be stacked. See also **bar**, **getcolor**, **getfillsettings**, **getlinestyle** and **rectangle**.

circle

```
int     xcenter, ycenter, radius;
circle( xcenter, ycenter, radius );
```

Draws a circle using current color, centered at coordinates given with specified radius (in pixels). See also **arc**, **ellipse**, **getaspectratio** and **pieslice**.

cleardevice

```
cleardevice();
```

Erases the entire graphics screen, moves the current position (CP) to home (0,0). See also **clearviewport**.

clearviewport

```
clearviewport();
```

Erases the current viewport, moving current position (CP) to home position (0,0) within the viewpoint setting. See also **getviewsettings** and **cleardevice**.

closegraph

```
closegraph();
```

Uses **_graphfreemem** to deallocate memory reserved for graphics system and restores screen to text mode detected when **initgraph** was called. See also **restorecrtmode** and **setgraphmode**.

detectgraph

```
int     graphdriver, graphmode;
detectgraph( &graphdriver, &graphmode );
```

Normally called by **initgraph**, **detectgraph** checks the hardware and returns values for the graphics driver and highest valid mode. See also **initgraph**.

drawpoly

```
int     points;
int     poly[] = { 100,100, 200,100, 200,200, 100,200, 100,100 };
drawpoly( points, poly );
```

Draws the outline of a polygon using current color setting; *points* gives the number of vertices for the polygon; *poly* points to a sequence of integer pairs, each pair defining the x/y coordinates of one vertex of the polygon. In order to draw a closed figure with *n* vertices, *points* = *n+1* and the *nth* (final) coordinate pair is equal to the *0th* (first) coordinate pair.

If an error occurs, **graphresult** returns –6. See also **getlinesettings**, **getcolor**and **fillpoly**.

ellipse

```
int      xcenter, ycenter, startangle, endangle, xradius, yradius;
ellipse( xcenter, ycenter, startangle, endangle, xradius, yradius );
```

Draws an elliptical arc centered at (x,y) with separate x-axis and y-axis radii. The start and end angles are given in degrees. For a complete (closed) ellipse, use a start angle of 0° and an end angle of 360°. Uses current color. See also **arc**, **circle** and **pieslice**.

farmalloc

```
void     far   *bitimage;
int      xleft, ytop, xright, ybottom;
bitimage = farmalloc( imagesize( xleft, ytop, xright, ybottom ) );
```

Allocates memory for a pixel image (or other application), returning a pointer to the memory location. Use **farmalloc** for small data models and include <alloc.h> header file to allocate a far pointer. See also **malloc**.

fillellipse

```
int       xcenter, ycenter, xradius, yradius;
fillellipse( xcenter, ycenter, xradius, yradius );
```

The **fillellipse** function (Turbo C version 2.0 or later) draws an ellipse using xcenter, ycenter as the center point and xradius and yradius as the horizontal and vertical axes, filling the ellipse with the current fill color and fill pattern. Unlike the **ellipse** function, start and end angle arguments are not supported and an elliptical arc cannot be drawn. See **sector**.

fillpoly

```
int     points;
int     poly[] = { 100,100, 200,100, 200,200, 100,200, 100,100 };
fillpoly(points, poly );
```

Draws and fills a polygon using current fill style and color settings; *points* gives the number of vertices for the polygon; *poly* points to a sequence of integer pairs, each pair defining the x/y coordinates of one vertex of the polygon. In order to draw a closed figure with *n* vertices, *points = n+1* and the *nth* (final) coordinate pair is equal to the *0th* (first) coordinate pair.

If an error occurs, **graphresult** returns −6. See also **drawpoly**, **getfillsettings** and **getcolor**.

floodfill

```
int     xpoint, ypoint, bordercolor;
floodfill( xpoint, ypoint, bordercolor );
```

Fills a bounded (enclosed) region defined by the specified bordercolor, beginning at (x,y), a point within the area to be filled and using the current fill pattern and color. If the start point is outside a bounded region, the exterior will be filled. If a break occurs in the line defining the region, then the fill will ''leak''.

For future compatibility, **fillpoly** is recommended where possible instead of **floodfill**.

If an error occurs, **graphresult** will return a value of −7. See also **drawpoly**, **getfillsettings** and **getlinesettings**.

getarccoords

```
struct arccoordstype   arcinfo;
getarccoords( &arcinfo );
```

Returns the coordinates of the last call to **arc**. The structure *arccoordstype* is defined in GRAPHICS.H as:

```
struct      arccoordstype { int x, y;
                            int xstart, ystart, xend, yend; };
```

This structure defines the center point (x,y), the starting point (xstart, ystart) and the end point (xend, yend) of the arc. These values can be used to draw chords or other lines meeting the ends of the arc and are used by the **pieslice** function.

getaspectratio

```
int      xasp, yasp;
getaspectratio( &xasp, &yasp );
```

Returns x- and y-axis aspects. The aspect ratio is calculated as *xasp/yasp* and is used as a scaling factor by the **arc**, **circle** and **pieslice** routines to make circles on the screen appear round.

Each graphics driver and graphics mode has an associated aspect ratio determined by the relative height and width of the pixels. For example, with the VGA graphics system, where each pixel is square, xasp = yasp and the aspect ratio is one. The y aspect factor is normalized to 10,000 and, in general, xasp <= 10,000 (most pixels are taller than they are wide).

getbkcolor

```
int      backcolor = getbkcolor();
```

Returns current background color setting. See also **getcolor** and **setbkcolor**.

getcolor

```
int      forecolor = getcolor();
```

Returns current foreground color setting. See also **getbkcolor** and **setcolor**.

getdrivername

The **getdrivername** function (version 2.0 or later) returns a pointer to a string identifying the current graphics driver.

```
char    *driver_name;
driver_name = getdrivername();
```

getfillpattern

```
char    fillpatterninfo[8];
getfillpattern( &fillpatterninfo );
```

Copies a user-defined fill pattern to memory. See **setfillpattern**.

getfillsettings

```
struct   fillsettingtype fillinfo;
getfillsettings( &fillinfo );
```

Returns information about current fill pattern. The structure *fillsettingtype* is defined in GRAPHICS.H as:

```
struct   fillsettingtype {   int pattern;
                             int color;    };
```

See also **getfillpattern**, **setfillpattern** and **setfillstyle**.

getgraphmode

```
int     modenow;
modenow = getgraphmode();
```

Returns the current graphics mode set by **initgraph** or **setgraphmode**. See also **getmoderange**.

getimage

```
include <alloc.h>
void    far *bitimage;
int     xleft, ytop, xright, ybottom;
bitimage = farmalloc( imagesize( xleft, ytop, xright, ybottom ) );
getimage( xleft, ytop, xright, ybottom, bitimage );
```

Save bit image from specified region into memory. The four integer parameters define the area to be saved. Use **imagesize** to get memory requirements, then allocate memory for image storage (memory allocation must be less than 64K). For compatibility with small data models, instead of **malloc**, the **farmalloc** function is used allocate memory but **alloc.h** must be included. See also **imagesize** and **putimage**.

getlinesettings

```
struct      linesettingstype lineinfo;
getlinesettings( &lineinfo );
```

Fills *lineinfo* with the current line style, pattern (*upattern*) and thickness. The structure *linesettingstype* is defined in GRAPHICS.H as:

```
struct      linesettingstype {    int linestyle;
                                  unsigned upattern;
                                  int thickness;         };
```

See also **setlinestyle**.

getmaxcolor

```
int      MaxColors = getmaxcolor() + 1;
```

Returns the maximum valid color (palette size −1) for the current graphics mode. See also **setcolor**.

getmaxx

```
int      MaxX = getmaxx();
```

Returns the maximum x-axis screen coordinate (max CP) for the current graphics driver and mode. See also **getmaxy** and **getx**.

getmaxy

```
int      MaxY = getmaxy();
```

Returns the maximum x-axis screen coordinate (max CP) for the current graphics driver and mode. See also **getmaxx** and **gety**.

getmodename

```
char    *mode_name;
mode_name = getmodename();
```

The **getmodename** function (version 2.0 or later) returns a pointer to a string identifying the current graphics mode.

getmoderange

```
int     graphdriver, lomode, himode;
getmoderange( graphdriver, &lomode, &himode );
```

Provides the lowest and highest valid mode values for the specified *graphdriver*. If the *graphdriver* specified is invalid, *lomode* and *himode* return set to −1.

getpalette

```
struct  palettetype palette;
getpalette( &palette );
```

Fills *palette* with current palette information (settings). The structure *palettetype* is defined in GRAPHICS.H as:

```
struct  palettetype {   unsigned char size;
                        signed char colors[MAXCOLORS + 1]; };
```

Palette.size gives the number of colors valid for the current graphics driver and mode, *palette.color* is an array of *size* of bytes containing the color numbers for each entry in the palette. See also **setallpalette** and **setpalette**.

getpixel

```
int     x, y;
color = getpixel( x, y );
```

Returns the color value of the indicated pixel at (x,y). See also **getimage** and **putpixel**.

gettextsettings

```
struct      textsettingstype textinfo;
gettextsettings( &textinfo );
```

Fills *textinfo* with the current text font, direction, size and horizontal and vertical justification. The structure *textsettingstype* is defined in GRAPHICS.H as:

```
struct      textsettingstype {    int font;      int direction;
                                  int charsize;
                                  int horiz;     int vert; };
```

See also **outtext**, **textheight** and **settextstyle**.

getviewsettings

```
struct      viewporttype    viewport;
getviewsettings( &viewport );
```

Fills *viewport* with graphics window coordinates and clipping flag. The structure *viewporttype* is defined in GRAPHICS.H as:

```
struct      viewporttype    {    int left, top, right, bottom;
                                 int clipflag;                    };
```

The viewport's corners appear as absolute screen coordinates. If clipflag is non-zero, all lines, etc., will be truncated at the margins of the current viewport; otherwise, line drawings, etc. will extend across the entire screen. See also **clearviewport**, **initgraph**, **setgraphmode** and **setviewport**.

getx

```
int               xpos = getx();
```

Returns the current position x (CPX) coordinate relative to the viewport. See also **gety**, **getviewsettings**, **moverel** and **moveto**.

gety

```
int     ypos = gety();
```

Returns the current position y (CPY) coordinate relative to the viewport. See also **getx**, **getviewsettings**, **moverel** and **moveto**.

gprintf (not included in GRAPHICS.LIB)

```
include <stdarg.h>
void gprintf( int *xloc, int *yloc, char *fmt, ... )
{
        va_list  argptr;
        char     workstr[140];
        struct   textsettingstype textinfo;
        gettextsettings( &textinfo );
        va_start( argptr, format );
        vsprintf( workstr, fmt, argptr );
        outtextxy( *xloc, *yloc, workstr );
        if ( textinfo.direction == HORIZ_DIR )
                *yloc += textheight( workstr ) + 2;
        else    *xloc += textheight( workstr ) + 2;
        va_end( argptr );
}
```

The **gprintf** routine is the graphics equivalent of **printf**. This routine is not included in the GRAPHICS.LIB, but must be entered by the programmer.

Text output is handled in both horizontal and vertical orientations. In horizontal orientation, the x-axis CP remains unchanged while the y-axis CP is moved down by the height of the workstring, plus two pixels. In vertical orientation, the x-axis CP is incremented by the width of the string plus two pixels, while the y-axis CP is not altered.

Otherwise, the actual text output is handled by **outtextxy**; see text for further notes. See also **gettextsettings**, **outtext**, **setcolor**, **settextsettings**, **textheight** and **textwidth**.

Remember, the length of the *fmt* argument should not exceed 140.

gprintxy (not included in GRAPHICS.LIB)

```
void gprintxy( xloc, yloc, fmtstr, ... )
```

The **gprintxy** routine works as per **gprintf** but accepts coordinate arguments directly and does not return an adjusted screen position for next string output. This routine is not included in the GRAPHICS.LIB but must be entered by the programmer. See text for further notes. See also **gettextsettings**, **outtext**, **setcolor**, **settextsettings**, **textheight** and **textwidth**.

graphdefaults

```
graphdefaults();
```

Resets all graphic settings to the default values; including restoring viewport to entire screen, setting CP to (0,0), resetting default palette, background and drawing colors, default fill style and pattern, default text font and justification.

grapherrormsg

```
char     *ErrMsg = grapherrormsg( ErrorCode );
```

Returns a pointer to the string indicated by the ErrorCode. See also **graphresult**.

_graphfreemem

```
unsigned    size;
int         *memptr;
_graphfreemem( &memptr, size );
```

Normally **_graphfreemem** is called by **closegraph** to deallocate the memory reserved for drivers, fonts and internal buffers. By default, **_graphfreemem** calls the **free** function but custom memory management can be created by defining a new **_graphfreemem**. See also **_graphgetmem**.

_graphgetmem

```
unsigned   size;
_graphgetmem( size );
```

Normally **_graphgetmem** is called by **initgraph** to allocate memory space for graphic drivers, graphic character fonts and internal buffers. By default, **_graphgetmem** uses the **malloc** function to set memory allocation but custom memory management can be created by defining a new **_graphgetmem** function. See also **_graphfreemem**.

graphresult

```
int      ErrorCode = graphresult();
```

Returns an error code for the last failed graphics operation. See also **grapherrormsg**.

imagesize

```
unsigned   size = imagesize(ulx, uly, lrx, lry);
```

Returns the size in bytes required to store the bit image according to the size specified. If the size required for the image is greater than 64K, a value of −1 (0xFFFF) is returned. See also **getimage** and **putimage**.

initgraph

```
int      graphdriver = DETECT,   graphmode;
char    *driverpath;
initgraph( &graphdriver, &graphmode, driverpath );
```

Initializes graphics system by loading graphics driver, and putting system in graphics mode. When *graphdriver* is set to DETECT (0), **detectgraph** is called to test the system's graphics adapter and select the highest resolution mode valid. If no graphics hardware is detected, *graphdriver* is set to –2 and **graphresult** will also return –2.

A common error occurs in setting pathstring as: char *driverpath = "C:\TURBOC\BGI"; instead of: char *driverpath = "C:\\TURBOC\\BGI";

A specific *graphdriver* can also be assigned. The *driverpath* must specify the directory where the .BGI drivers and .CHR fonts are located. See also **detectgraph** and **closegraph**.

installuserdriver

```
driver = installuserdriver( "DRIVER", detect_driver() );
```

The **installuserdriver** function (version 2.0 or later) allows installation of a custom or vendor-added device driver to the BGI internal table. See **Appendix D** for information on creating custom BGI drivers.

installuserfont

```
int     USER_FONT = 0;
USER_FONT = installuserfont( "\FontPath\FontName.CHR" );
```

The **installuserfont** function (version 2.0 or later) loads a .CHR (stroked) font which is not built into the BGI system, returning an font ID number which can be passed to **settextstyle** to select the font. Up to 20 external fonts can be installed at any time. If the internal font table is full, a value of -11 (*grError*) is returned.

See also Chapter 17 — **The Turbo Font Editor**.

line

```
int     xstart, ystart, xend, yend;
line( xstart, ystart, xend, yend );
```

Draws a line between the points specified using the current color, line style and thickness without changing the current position (CP). See also **linerel** and **lineto**.

linerel

```
int    xdev, ydev;
linerel( xdev, ydev );
```

Draws a line from the current position to another point separated from CP by the distance *xdev*, *ydev*; uses the current color, line style and thickness and updates CP to the new position. See also **line** and **lineto**.

lineto

```
int    x, y;
lineto(x,y);
```

Draws a line from the current position to the point specified by (x,y), using the current color, line style and thickness. Resets CP to (x,y). See also **line** and **linerel**.

malloc

```
void    *bitimage;
int     xleft, ytop, xright, ybottom;
bitimage = malloc( imagesize( xleft, ytop, xright, ybottom ) );
```

Allocates memory for a pixel image (or other application), returning a pointer to the memory location. For small data models, see **farmalloc**.

moverel

```
int    xdev, ydev;
moverel( xdev, ydev );
```

Moves CP the relative distance specified by (*xdev,ydev*). See also **moveto**.

moveto

```
int     x, y;
moveto( x, y );
```

Moves CP to the absolute point specified by (*x,y*). See also **moverel**.

outtext

```
outtext( "Display string for viewport" );
```

Displays string in viewport (graphics window) beginning at CP, using current font, color, charsize, direction and text justification. If horizontal justification is LEFT_TEXT and direction is HORIZ_DIR, CP's x-axis coordinate is advanced by *textwidth(textstring)* — otherwise CP is not altered. See also **gettextsettings**, **gprintf**, **outtextxy**, **setcolor**, **settextsettings**, **textheight** and **textwidth**.

outtextxy

```
int     x, y;
outtextxy( x, y, "Display string for viewport" );
```

Displays string in viewport (graphics window) beginning at position specified by (*x,y*), using current font, color, charsize, direction and text justification. CP's coordinates are not changed. See also **gettextsettings**, **gprintf**, **outtext**, **setcolor**, **settextsettings**, **textheight** and **textwidth**.

pieslice

```
int     xcenter, ycenter, startangle, endangle, radius;
pieslice( xcenter, ycenter, startangle, endangle, radius );
```

Draws and fills in a pie slice, centered at (*xcenter,ycenter*) through the arc specified by the start and end angles (in degrees). The pie slice is outlined in the current drawing color, then filled using the current fill pattern and color. See also **arc**, **circle**, **ellipse** and **getaspectratio**.

putimage

```
void    far *bitimage;
int         xleft, ytop, ops;
putimage( xleft, ytop, bitimage, ops );
```

Writes a previously saved bit image to the screen with the upper-left corner of the image appearing at (*xleft,ytop*). The *ops* parameter controls how each image pixel (color) is combined with the existing screen pixels.

See also **imagesize**, **getimage**, **farmalloc** and **malloc**.

putpixel

```
int     xpos, ypos, color;
putpixel( xpos, ypos, color );
```

Sets the pixel specified by (*xpos,ypos*) to the color indicated.

rectangle

```
int     xleft, ytop, xright, ybottom;
rectangle( xleft, ytop, xright, ybottom );
```

Draws a rectangle in the current line style, thickness and color. See also **bar**.

registerbgidriver/registerfarbgidriver

```
int     GraphicDriver;
if ( registerbgidriver( GraphicDriver ) < 0 ) exit(1);
```

The **registerbgidriver** function is used to register a linked-in graphics driver. If the specified graphics driver is not found, a negative error code is returned; otherwise, the internal driver number is returned. The **registerfarbgidriver** should not be called unless the /**F** option is used with the BGIOBJ.EXE utility (see Appendix D — **Turbo C Utilities** in the **Turbo C Reference Guide**). See **Appendix D** (this book) for information on creating linked-in graphics drivers.

registerbgifont/registerfarbgifont

```
int     GraphicFont;
if ( registerbgifont( GraphicFont ) < 0 ) exit(1);
```

The **registerbgifont** function is used to register a linked stroked font character set. If the specified font is not found, a negative error code is returned; otherwise, the registered font number is returned. The **registerfarbgidriver** should not be called unless the **/F** option is used with the BGIOBJ.EXE utility (see **Appendix D — Turbo C Utilities** in the **Turbo C Reference Guide**). See also **Appendix F** (this book) for information on creating linked-in fonts.

restorecrtmode

```
restorecrtmode();
```

Resets video to text mode detected by **initgraph**. May be used with **setgraphmode** to switch back and forth between graphics and text modes. See also **initgraph**.

sector

```
int     xcenter, ycenter, startangle, endangle, xradius, yradius;
sector( xcenter, ycenter, startangle, endangle, xradius, yradius );
```

The **sector** function creates an elliptical arc, draws lines from the end points to the center point and then fills in the completed figure. The sector outline is drawn using the current drawing color and current line style for the radius lines, then filled using the current fill pattern and fill color (see **floodfill**). Screen aspect ratio adjustment is automatic.

See also **arc**, **circle**, **ellipse**, **fillellipse**, **getaspectratio** and **pieslice**.

setactivepage

```
int     pagenum;
setactivepage( pagenum );
```

Selects graphics page *pagenum* for output. This may or may not be the active visual page (see **setvisualpage**), but all graphics output will be directed to this page. Only EGA, VGA and Hercules graphics cards currently support multiple graphics (or text) pages. It is useful for animation.

setallpalette

```
struct  palettetype newpalette;
setallpalette( &newpalette );
```

Makes *newpalette* the current palette. All color changes are affected immediately. The colors for *newpalette* must be assigned using **setpalette**. See also **getpalette**.

setbkcolor

```
int      backcolor;
setbkcolor( backcolor );
```

The argument *backcolor* can be a name or value.

setcolor

```
int      forecolor;
setcolor( forecolor );
```

Sets the current drawing color using *palette.color[forecolor]*. See **setpalette** for color names and predefined palettes; see also **getcolor** and **setbkcolor**.

setfillpattern

```
int      color;
char    diamond[8] = {  0x10, 0x38, 0x7C, 0xFE,
                        0x7C, 0x38, 0x10,  0x00};
setfillpattern( &diamond, color );
```

Selects an 8x8 user-defined fill pattern. *diamond* is a sequence of eight bytes, each byte corresponding to eight pixels in the pattern. One bits turn on pixel, zero bits turn off pixel. The example pattern *diamond* creates a small 7x7 diamond pattern with a one pixel border at right and bottom. See also **getfillpattern**, **getfillstyle** and **setfillstyle**.

setfillstyle

```
setfillstyle( SOLID_FILL, GREEN );
```

Sets current fill pattern and color.

setgraphbufsize

```
unsigned      bufsize, oldbufsize;
oldbufsize = setgraphbufsize( bufsize );
```

Several of graphics routines use a memory buffer created by **initgraph** via **_graphgetmem**. The default size is 4K (4096 bytes), but can be decreased to save space or increased if more buffer memory is required. The **setgraphbufsize** function must be called *before* calling **initgraph**.

setgraphmode

```
int      graphmode;
setgraphmode( graphmode );
```

Resets system to graphics mode, clearing the screen. Graphics mode must have been previously initialized by **initgraph**. See also **restorecrtmode**.

setlinestyle

```
unsigned      linepattern;
int              style, width;
setlinestyle( style, linepattern, width );
```

Sets current line width and style. See also **getlinesettings.**

setpalette

```
int       palette_index, color;
setpalette( palette_index, color );
```

With any of the 320x200 pixel video graphics modes (CGA, MCGA or AT&T), color selections are limited to predefined 4-color palettes: C0, C1, C2 and C3. In each palette, the background color (index 0) can be user-defined but colors 1..3 cannot be changed. In other graphics modes, all colors can be redefined.

The IBM-8514 graphics card and IBM8514 driver support a color palette of 256 colors from a total of 262,144 (256K) color values. No symbolic constants are defined for this driver but the IBM-8514 card can also emulate VGA modes (as IBM8514LO but the VGA driver is recommended for better compatibility — see **initgraph**). Each color is defined by three six-bit values for the Red, Green and Blue components. See **setrgbpalette**.

setrbgpalette

```
int       colornum, valuered, valueblue, valuegreen;
setrbgpalette( colornum, valuered, valueblue, valuegreen );
```

The **setrbgpalette** routine is provided for use with the IBM8514 driver. The *colornum* argument sets the palette color (0..255) to be defined by the *valuered*, *valueblue* and *valuegreen* arguments. Only the six most significant bits of the low byte of each color argument are used (values from 0 to 252 in steps of four, i.e.– arguments of 252, 253, 254 and 255 are treated identically since the six most significant bits are the same).

The other palette manipulation routines in the graphics library are not valid with the IBM8514 driver in IBM8514HI (1023x768 pixel) mode. This includes **setallpalette**, **setpalette** and **getpalette**. Also, the **floodfill** routine is not valid with this driver and mode.

settextjustify

```
int     hjustify, vjustify;
settextjustify( hjustify, vjustify );
```

Sets horizontal and vertical text justification. Default settings are LEFT_TEXT, TOP_TEXT (0,2).When justification is set as *LEFT_TEXT* and *direction = HORIZ_DIR*, the current position's *x* setting is advanced after a call to **outtext** or **gprintf** by **textwidth(string)**. See also **settextstyle**.

settextstyle

```
int     font, direction, charsize;
settextstyle( font, direction, charsize );
```

Sets current graphics text characteristics according to *font*, *direction* and *charsize* selected. Normally, only one font is kept in memory at any time but multiple fonts can be linked using the BGIOBJ utility. Except for DEFAULT_FONT which is built into the graphics system, the .CHR files for the selected font must be in the directory or subdirectory indicated by initgraph as driverpath or linked and registered using registerbgifont.

Graphics Text Direction is horizontal by default but can be set to vertical (rotated 90° counterclockwise).

For bit-mapped font(s): *charsize* may be 0..10. Zero and one display 8x8 pixel rectangles, 2 = 16x16 pixel rectangle, etc., up to 10 times normal size.

For stroked fonts: *charsize = 0* magnifies the stroked font by the default factor of four or by the user-defined size factors set by **setusercharsize**. A maximum magnification of 10 is valid.

If invalid values are passed to **settextjustify**, **graphresult** will return −11 (*general error*) and the current text settings will remain unchanged. See also **settextjustify**, **textheight** and **textwidth**.

setusercharsize

```
int     xmult, xdiv, ymult, ydiv;
setusercharsize( xmult, xdiv, ymult, ydiv );
```

Provides user-defined character magnification for stroked fonts. These values are active only if **settextstyle** is called to set *charsize = 0*. The scaled width is defined as *xmult/xdiv*; the scaled height is defined as *ymult/ydiv*. See also **gettextsettings**.

setviewport

```
int     xleft, ytop, xright, ybottom, clipflag;
setviewport( xleft, ytop, xright, ybottom, clipflag );
```

The viewport's coordinates are absolute screen coordinates. If clipflag is non-zero, all lines, etc., will be truncated at the viewport margins; otherwise, line drawings, etc., will extend across the entire screen. See also **clearviewport**, **initgraph**, **setgraphmode** and **getviewsettings**.

setvisualpage

```
int     pagenum;
setvisualpage( pagenum );
```

Selects graphics page *pagenum* for active visual page and may or may not the active graphics page (see **setactivepage**). Only EGA, VGA and Hercules graphics cards currently support multiple graphics (or text) pages. Useful for animation.

setwritemode

```
int     writemode;
setwritemode( writemode );
```

The **setwritemode** function sets the screen writing mode for line drawing in graphics modes. Two constants are defined for *writemode*:

```
COPY_PUT =  0   (default)
XOR_PUT  =  1
```

Note: **setwritemode** currently works only with **line**, **linerel**, **lineto**, **rectangle** and **drawpoly**.

textheight

```
int     charheight = textheight( "H" );
```

Returns the height of a string in pixels, using the current font size, scaling factors and text direction. This may be the height of a single character or the height of an entire string. See also **textwidth**.

textwidth

```
int     charwidth = textwidth( "H" );
```

Returns the width of a string in pixels, using the current font size, scaling factors and text direction. This may be the width of a single character or the width of an entire string. See also **textheight**.

GRAPHICS CONSTANTS AND VARIABLES

Appendix B contains additional constants used in this book.

Table B-1: Operators for putimage

OP NAME	VALUE	ACTION
COPY_PUT*	0	MOV
XOR_PUT*	1	XOR
OR_PUT	2	OR
AND_PUT	3	AND
NOT_PUT	4	NOT

* COPY_PUT and XOR_PUT operators are also used by the **setlinemode** function.

Miscellaneous Structure Definitions

```
struct pointtype {  int x, y; };
struct viewporttype {   int left, top, right, bottom;
                        int clip;                   };
struct arccoordstype { int x, y;
                       int xstart, ystart, xend, yend };
```

Additional Constants Used In Modules Defined In This Book

The following are constants declared for general use by one or more modules in this book.

Table B-2: Constants Declared for General Use

NAME	VALUE	COMMENTS
PI	3.14159	utility definition
FALSE	0	general utility
TRUE	1	general utility

Table B-3: Constants Used by LJ_GRAPH.I and EP_GRAPH.I

NAME	VALUE	COMMENTS
PORTRAIT	0	select print orientation
LANDSCAPE	1	select print orientation
GREYSCALE*	2	color to grey-scale conversion

*LJ-Graph only

Table B-4: Constants Used in PLOTTER.I

NAME	VALUE	COMMENTS
COM1	0	serial port selection
COM2	1	serial port selection
COM3	2	serial port selection
COM4	3	serial port selection
InitComm	E300h	init parameters for serial port

Table B-5: Constants Used in Animate1.C and Animate2.C

NAME	VALUE	COMMENTS
RIGHT	0	image movement
LEFT	1	image movement
UP	2	image movement
DOWN	3	image movement

Table B-6: Constants Declared in Turtle Graphics Module

NAME	VALUE	COMMENTS
NORTH	0°	turtle movement direction
EAST	90°	turtle movement direction
SOUTH	180°	turtle movement direction
WEST	270°	turtle movement direction

MOUSE AND TURTLE FUNCTIONS

Following are functions defined in the TURTLE.I and G_MOUSE.I include files in this book.

Mouse Functions — Quick Reference

m_conceal	conditional hide mouse (Logitech mouse only)
m_graphic_cursor	sets graphic cursor shape
m_hide	conceals mouse cursor from view
m_inst_task	installs user-defined task
m_lightpen	turns lightpen emulation on/off
***m_motion**	reports net cursor motion since last call
m_move_ratio	sets mouse motion to pixel ratio
m_moveto	moves mouse cursor to new position
***m_pos**	returns cursor position and button status
***m_pressed**	returns pressed info about button
***m_released**	returns release info about button
***m_reset**	resets mouse default status
m_show	renders mouse cursor visible
m_speed	sets speed threshold (Logitech mouse only)
m_text_cursor	sets text cursor type
m_xlimit	sets x-axis minimum/maximum for mouse cursor

m_ylimit	sets y-axis minimum/maximum for mouse cursor
Set_Graphic_Cursor	selects graphic cursor (uses **m_graphic_cursor**)

Turtle Functions — Quick Reference

back	moves mouse backwards distance specified
clear_turtle_screen	clears turtle view screen
correct_direction	returns angle in 0..360 degree range
create_turtle	creates turtle cursor image
drawstr	draws figure from instruction string
forward	moves mouse forward distance specified
heading	returns current heading
hide_turtle	conceals turtle cursor
home	moves turtle cursor to home position
init_turtle	initializes turtle settings
no_wrap	turns off turtle wrap
pen_down	sets turtle to draw
pen_up	stops turtle from drawing
rsin	returns sine of angle in degrees
rcos	returns cosine of angle in degrees
set_heading	sets turtle heading (degrees)
set_pen_color	sets turtle pen color
set_position	moves turtle position relative to home
show_turtle	makes turtle cursor visible
step_turtle	moves turtle by steps (pixels)
turn_left	turns turtle heading left (degrees)

turn_right	turns turtle heading right (degrees)
turtle_delay	controls turtle speed
turtle_where	reports turtle cursor within window
turtle_window	sets turtle window
wrap	turns turtle wrap on
xcor	reports turtle x-axis position
ycor	reports turtle y-axis position

Mouse Constants, Functions and Structure Definitions

Table C-1: Mouse Constants

TYPE	VALUE	USAGE
SOFTWARE	0	text cursor types
HARDWARE	1	text cursor types
OFF	0	general usage
ON	1	general usage

Structure Definitions

m_result

```
struct     { int present,          /*     TRUE if mouse present  */
                 buttons;           /*     # of buttons on mouse  */
           }    m_result;
```

m_status

```
struct     { int button_status,    /*     bits 0-2 on if button down  */
                 button_count,      /*     # times button was clicked  */
                 xaxis, yaxis;      /*     mouse cursor position        */
           }    m_status;
```

m_movement

```
struct  { int x_count,                      /*       net horizontal movement   */
              y_count;                       /*       net vertical movement     */
        }   m_movement;
```

mouse_event

```
struct  { unsigned  flag,                   /*       mouse event record        */
                    button,                 /*       button(s) pressed         */
                    xaxis, yaxis;           /*       cursor position           */
        }   mouse_event;
```

g_cursor

```
struct  { unsigned  *image,                 /*       cursor descriptor */
                    xkey, ykey;             /*       cursor hotspot    */
        }   g_cursor;
```

Mouse Graphics Cursors

```
g_cursor   ARROW = { NULL, 1, 7 };
g_cursor   CHECK  = { NULL, 5, 10};
g_cursor   CROSS  = { NULL, 7, 7 };
g_cursor   GLOVE  = { NULL, 0, 4 };
g_cursor   IBEAM  = { NULL, 7, 7 };
```

Mouse Functions

initialize_cursors

```
initialize_cursors();
```

Initializes pointers to graphics mouse cursor descriptions.

m_conceal   (Logitech mouse or compatible)

```
int            xleft, ytop, xright, ybottom;
m_conceal( xleft, ytop, xright, ybottom );
```

Calls mouse function 16, defining a screen area where the mouse cursor will be automatically concealed. Calling **m_show** clears the conditional settings.

m_graphic_cursor

```
m_graphic_cursor( GLOVE.xkey, GLOVE.ykey, _DS, GLOVE.image );
```

Uses mouse function 9 to set graphic mouse cursor (default cursor is angled arrow). The *xkey* and *ykey* values describe the cursor's 'hot-spot'. Five cursor images are predefined, others can be easily added.

m_hide

```
m_hide();
```

Calls mouse function 2, concealing mouse cursor from view — see **m_show**.

m_inst_task

```
m_inst_task( mask, seg_task, ofs_task );
```

Uses mouse function 12 to install a user-defined task that will be executed by one or more mouse events as specified by the mask value.

m_lightpen

```
m_lightpen( ON );
```

Uses mouse function 13 to turn on lightpen emulation (default setting) and mouse function 14 to turn off emulation.

*m_motion

```
m_movement      m;
m = m_motion();
```

Uses mouse function 11, returning pointer to *m_movement* reporting net cursor motion since last call to this function.

m_move_ratio

```
int     xstep, ystep;
m_move_ratio( xstep, ystep );
```

Uses mouse function 15 to set mouse movement to pixel (cursor) motion ratio. Default values are 16 vertical, 8 horizontal.

m_moveto

```
int     xaxis, yaxis;
m_moveto( xaxis, yaxis );
```

Calls mouse function 4, moving move mouse cursor to defined position.

*m_pos

```
m_status   m;
m = m_pos();
```

Calls mouse function 3, returning pointer to *m_status* structure containing mouse cursor position and button status.

*m_pressed

```
int     button;
m_status m;
m = m_pressed( button );
```

Calls mouse function 5 for information on specified button. Returns a pointer to the *m_status* structure containing the current status of the button specified (up or down), the number of times the button was pressed since last call, and the cursor position the last time the button was pressed. Resets the count and position information. Button 0 is left, button 1 is right (Microsoft mouse) and button 2 is the center (Logitech only).

*m_released

```
int             button;
m_status m;
m = m_released( button );
```

Calls mouse function 6 for information on specified button. Returns a pointer to the *m_status* structure containing the current status of the button specified (up or down), the number of times the button was pressed since last call, and the cursor position the last time the button was pressed. Resets the count and position information. Button 0 is left, button 1 is right (Microsoft mouse) and button 2 is the center (Logitech only).

*m_reset

```
m_result     m;
m = m_reset();
```

Calls mouse function 0, initializing or resetting mouse to default status. Returns pointer to *m_result* structure indicating if mouse is installed and, if mouse is present, the number of buttons on the mouse. This function is always called during mouse initialization.

m_show

```
m_show();
```

Calls mouse function 1, making mouse cursor visible — see **m_hide**.

m_speed   (Logitech mouse or compatible)

```
int     speed;
m_speed( );
```

Calls mouse function 19, setting a speed threshold (in mickeys/second) for accelerated cursor movement. A normal setting is 300 mickeys/second (012Ch); maximum is 32767 mickeys/second (7FFFh).

m_text_cursor

```
unsigned   s_start, s_stop;
m_text_cursor( HARDWARE, s_start, s_stop );
```

Uses mouse function 10 to set text cursor type (SOFTWARE = 0, HARDWARE = 1). For software cursor, s_start and s_stop are the screen and cursor masks. For hardware cursor, s_start and s_stop specify scan line start/stop (i.e.– cursor shape).

m_xlimit

```
int      x_min, x_max;
m_xlimit( x_min, x_max );
```

Uses mouse function 7 to set horizontal mouse boundaries, limiting screen mouse movement. If mouse cursor is outside of this range, the cursor is moved inside the boundary specified. If *x_min* is larger than *x_max*, values are swapped.

m_ylimit

```
int      y_min, y_max;
m_ylimit( y_min, y_max );
```

Uses mouse function 8 to set vertical mouse boundaries, limiting screen mouse movement. If mouse cursor is outside of this range, the cursor is moved inside the boundary specified. If *y_min* is larger than *y_max*, values are swapped.

Set_Graphic_Cursor

```
Set_Graphic_Cursor( GLOVE );
```

Alternative, shorthand method of selecting graphic mouse cursor. Calls **m_graphic_cursor** function.

Turtle Functions

back

```
int     distance;
forward( distance );
```

Moves turtle specified distance in one pixel steps. Movement is opposite current turtle direction; if pen is down, draws a line using current drawing color. See also **forward**.

create_turtle

```
create_turtle();
```

Creates turtle cursor image, normally called only by **init_turtle** function.

clear_turtle_screen

```
clear_turtle_screen();
```

Clears turtle screen and resets turtle cursor to home position.

correct_direction

```
int     angle;
correct_direction( &angle );
```

Restricts angle to 0..360 degree range. See also **set_heading**, **turn_left** and **turn_right**.

drawstr

```
char    logostr[] = instruction_string;
int     scale;
drawstr( scale, logostr );
```

Deciphers instruction string to draw character, figure or logo using turtle graphics. Scale acts as multiplier setting size of figure drawn.

If the instruction string is longer than 150 characters, the figure will be truncated.

forward

```
int     distance;
forward( distance );
```

Moves turtle specified distance in one pixel steps. Movement is in current turtle direction; if pen is down, draws a line using current drawing color. See also **back**.

heading

```
int     angle;
angle = heading();
```

Returns the current turtle heading. See also **set_heading**, **turn_left** and **turn_right**.

hide_turtle

```
hide_turtle();
```

If turtle cursor is visible, hides cursor. See also **show_turtle**.

home

```
home();
```

Resets turtle cursor to turtle home position (normally at the center of the turtle window). See also **set_position**.

init_turtle

```
init_turtle();
```

Calls **create_turtle** to generate turtle cursor, reads video aspect ratio and screen size, sets up initial turtle window and home position and sets default turtle values and flags. Defaults include: pen color equals maximum valid color for video mode; turtle cursor visible; turtle delay zero (fast turtle); screen wrap off; pen down; and turtle heading NORTH.

no_wrap

```
no_wrap();
```

Turns off turtle screen wrap. Allows turtle movement outside of turtle window but drawing is restricted to window area. See also **wrap**.

pen_down

```
pen_down();
```

Puts turtle pen down in drawing position. Turtle movement will draw a line using current pen color. See also **pen_up**.

pen_up

```
pen_up();
```

Raises turtle pen, allowing movement without drawing. See **pen_down**.

rsin

```
double      sin_angle;
int         angle;
sin_angle = rsin( angle );
```

Returns the sine of an angle in degrees.

rcos

```
double      cos_angle;
int         angle;
cos_angle = rcos( angle );
```

Returns the cosine of an angle in degrees.

set_heading

```
int     degrees;
set_heading( degrees );
```

Sets turtle heading in degrees. Angles are corrected to 0..360 degree range. See also **turn_left** and **turn_right**.

set_pen_color

```
int     color;
set_pen_color( color );
```

Sets current turtle-draw color. Argument is checked against valid color range. Color can be passed as 0 background to erase.

set_position

```
int     xaxis, yaxis;
set_position( xaxis, yaxis );
```

Sets turtle cursor to position specified. Coordinates are relative to turtle home position (normally center of turtle window). See **home**.

show_turtle

```
show_turtle();
```

If turtle cursor is not visible, restores cursor image at current position. See **hide_turtle**.

step_turtle

```
int     xstep, ystep;
step_turtle( xstep, ystep );
```

Moves turtle cursor, drawing if the pen is down and turtle is within turtle window. Adjusts position at window limits if screen wrap is in effect.

turn_left

```
int     degrees;
turn_left( degrees );
```

Turns turtle heading to left number of degrees specified. Resulting angle is in 0..360 degree range. A negative argument turns turtle heading to right.

turn_right

```
int     degrees;
turn_right( degrees );
```

Turns turtle heading to right number of degrees specified. Resulting angle is in 0..360 degree range. A negative argument turns turtle heading to left.

turtle_window

```
int     xcenter, ycenter;
int     xwidth, yheight;
turtle_window( xcenter, ycenter, xwidth, yheight );
```

Sets turtle window with center at absolute screen coordinates *xcenter,ycenter*. The window will be *xwidth* pixels wide, *yheight* pixels high unless margins exceed physical screen limits. A three pixel margin is reserved at top and left for the turtle cursor image requirements. The turtle cursor is set to the home position.

turtle_where

```
if( turtle_where() ) ...
```

Returns TRUE (1) if turtle cursor is within the turtle window.

turtle_delay

```
int     timeout;
turtle_delay( timeout );
```

Sets turtle speed using time delay executed between turtle steps.

wrap

```
wrap()
```

Turns off turtle wrap, allowing turtle cursor to move outside of turtle window.

xcor

```
int     xaxis;
xaxis = xcor();
```

Returns the turtle cursor x-axis position (relative to the home position).

ycor

```
int     yaxis;
yaxis = ycor();
```

Returns the turtle cursor y-axis position (relative to the home position).

APPENDIX D

THE BGI DRIVER TOOLKIT

Creating Device Drivers for the Borland Graphics Interface

The BGI Driver Toolkit is available at no charge on an ''as is'' basis to users of Turbo Pascal, Turbo C and Turbo Prolog. The BGI Driver Toolkit also includes a .BIN to .BGI conversion utility (DFONT.EXE, DFONT.C and FONT.H) and a 'debug' driver.

   Also available from Borland are the Turbo Font Editor (see Chapter 17) with nine graphics character fonts: EURO.CHR, GOTH.CHR, LCOM.CHR, LITT.CHR, SANS.CHR, SCRI.CHR, SIMP.CHR, TRIP.CHR and TSCR.CHR; and a new VGA 256-color .BGI driver (see Appendix E).

The BGI Driver Toolkit

Copyright (c) 1988 Borland International
Revision 1
September 15, 1988

Note: This information and the accompanying program files are supplied on an "as is" basis at no charge to registered users of Borland's Turbo Pascal, Turbo C, and Turbo Prolog products.

Introduction

The Borland Graphics Interface (BGI) is a fast, compact, and device-independent software package for graphics development built into the Turbo Pascal, Turbo C, and Turbo Prolog language products. Device independence is achieved via loadable device-specific drivers called from a common Kernel. This document describes basic BGI functionality, as well as the steps necessary to create new device drivers. Accompanying this document are files containing sample code and other pertinent information.

Table D-1: Sample Code Files

FILE NAME	FILE DESCRIPTION
BH.C	BGI loader header building program source
BH.EXE	BGI loader header building program
DEVICE.INC	structure and macro definition file
DEBVECT.ASM	vector table for sample (DEBUG) driver
DEBUG.C	main module for sample driver
MAKEFILE	build file
BUILD.BAT	a batch file for make-phobics
TEST.C	C program demonstrating how to register and load a new device driver.
DFONT.EXE	a .BIN to .BGI conversion utility
DFONT.C	C source code for the conversion utility
FONT.H	header file used by DFONT

BGI Run-time Architecture

Programs produced by Borland languages create graphics via two entities acting in concert: the generic BGI Kernel and a device-specific driver. Typically, an application built with a Borland compiler will include several device driver files on the distribution disk (extension .BGI) so that the program can run on various types of screens and printers. Graphics requests (e.g.– draw line, draw bar, etc.) are sent by the application to the BGI Kernel, which in turn makes requests of the device driver to actually manipulate the hardware.

A BGI device driver is a binary image; that is, a sequence of bytes without symbols or other linking information. The driver begins with a short header, followed by a vector table containing the entry points to the functions inside.

The balance of the driver comprises the code and data required to manipulate the target graphics hardware.

All code and data references in the driver must be near (i.e.– small model, offset only), and the entire driver, both code and data, must fit within 64K. In use, the device driver can count on its being loaded on a paragraph boundary. The BGI Kernel uses a register-based calling convention to communicate with the device driver (described in detail below).

BGI Graphics Model

When considering the functions list below, keep in mind that BGI performs most drawing operations using an implicit drawing or tracing color (COLOR), fill color (FILLCOLOR), and pattern (FILLPATTERN). For example, the PIESLICE call accepts no pattern or color information, but uses the previously set COLOR value to trace the edge of the slice, and the previously set FILLCOLOR and FILLPATTERN values for the interior.

For efficiency, many operations take place at the position of the current pointer, or CP. For example, the LINE routine accepts only a single (x,y) coordinate pair, using the CP as the starting point of the line and the passed coordinate pair as the ending point. Many functions (LINE, to name one) affect CP, and the MOVE function can be used to explicitly adjust CP. The BGI coordinate system places the origin (pixel 0,0) at the upper left-hand corner of the screen.

Header Section

The device header section, which must be at the beginning of the device driver, is built using macro BGI defined in file DEVICE.INC. The BGI macro takes the name of the device driver to be built as an argument. For example, a driver named DEBUG would begin as shown here:

```
CSEG   SEGMENT PARA PUBLIC 'CODE'      ; any segment naming may be used
       ASSUME   DS:CSEG, CS:CSEG       ;cs=ds
       CODESEG
```

```
INCLUDE   DEVICE.INC          ; include the device.inc file
BGI       DEBUG               ; declare the device header section
```

The device header section declares a special entry point known as EMULATE. If the action of a device driver vector is not supported by the hardware of a device, the vector entry should contain the entry EMULATE. This will be patched at load-time to contain a jump to the Kernel's emulation routine. The routines will emulate the action of the vector, breaking the request into simpler primitives. If the hardware has functionality to draw polygons, the polygon vector will contain the address of the routine to dispatch the polygon data to the hardware and appears as follows:

```
dw     offset   POLYGON       ; Vector to the Polygon Routine
```

If, as is often the case, the hardware doesn't have the functionality to display polygons, the vector would instead contain the EMULATE vector:

```
dw     EMULATE               ; Polygon functions must be emulated
```

The Kernel has emulation support for some vectors:

Table D-2: Vector Emulation Support

VECTOR	SUPPORT
POLYGON	rendering polygons
BARFILL	filling rectangles
PATBAR	pattern filling of rectangles
ARC	elliptical arc rendering
PIESLICE	elliptical pie slices
FILLED_ELLIPSE	filled ellipses
SYMBOLS	line marking symbols
FILLSTYLE	solid filling styles
TSTYLE	text drawing styles
TEXT	hardware text rendering
TEXTSIZ	scaling of hardware text

The Driver Status Table

BGI requires that each driver contain a Driver Status Table (DST) to determine the basic characteristics of the device which the driver addresses. As an example, the DST for a CGA display is shown here:

```
STATUS      STRUC
STAT   DB   0                 ; Current Device Status (0 = No Errors)
DEVTYP      DB    0           ; Device Type Identifier (must be 0)
XRES   DW   639               ; Device Full Resolution in X Direction
YRES   DW   199               ; Device Full Resolution in Y Direction
XEFRES      DW    639         ; Device Effective X Resolution
YEFRES      DW    199         ; Device Effective Y Resolution
XINCH  DW   9000              ; Device X Size in inches*1000
YINCH  DW   7000              ; Device Y Size in inches*1000
ASPEC  DW   4500              ; Aspect Ratio = (y_size/x_size) * 10000
            DB    8h
            DB    8h          ; for compatibility, use these values
            DB    90h
            DB    90h
STATUS      ENDS
```

The BGI interface has a system for reporting errors to the BGI Kernel and to the higher level code developed using Borland's language packages. It is done using the STAT field of the Driver Status Table. This field should be filled in by the driver code if an error is detected during the execution of the device installation (INSTALL). The error codes are predefined in the header file GRAPHICS.H for Turbo C and in the Graphics unit for Turbo Pascal.

Table D-3: BGI Error Codes

ERROR MESSAGE	VALUE	
grOk	= 0	NORMAL OPERATION, NO ERRORS
grNoInitGraph	= −1	
grNotDetected	= −2	
		(continued)

Table D-3: Continued

ERROR MESSAGE	VALUE	
grFileNotFound	= −3	
grInvalidDriver	= −4	
grNoLoadMem	= −5	
grNoScanMem	= −6	
grNoFloodMem	= −7	
grFontNotFound	= −8	
grNoFontMem	= −9	
grInvalidMode	= −10	
grError	= −11	GENERIC DRIVER ERROR
grIOerror	= −12	
grInvalidFont	= −13	
grInvalidFontNum	= −14	
grInvalidDeviceNum	= −15	

The next field in the Device Status Table, DEVTYP, describes the class of the device that the driver controls; for screen devices, this value is always 0.

The next four fields, XRES, YRES, XEFRES, and YEFRES contain the number of pixels available to BGI on this device in the horizontal and vertical dimensions, minus one. For screen devices, XRES=XEFRES and YRES=YEFRES. The XINCH and YINCH fields are the number of inches horizontally and vertically into which the device's pixels are mapped, times 1000. These fields in conjunction with XRES and YRES permit device resolution (DPI, or dots per inch) calculation.

$$\text{Horizontal resolution (DPI)} = (XRES+1) / (XINCH/1000)$$
$$\text{Vertical resolution (DPI)} = (YRES+1) / (YINCH/1000)$$

The ASPEC (aspect ratio) field is effectively a multiplier/divisor pair (the divisor is always 10000) that is applied to Y coordinate values to produce aspect-ratio adjusted images (e.g.– round circles). For example, an ASPEC field of 4500 implies that the application will have to transform Y coordinates by the ratio: 4500/10000 when drawing circles to that device if it expects them to be round. Individual monitor variations may require an additional adjustment by the application.

The Device Driver Vector Table

The routines in the device driver are accessed via a vector table. This table is at the beginning of the driver and contains 16-bit offsets to subroutines and configuration tables within the driver. The vector table is shown below.

VECTOR_TABLE

```
DW      INSTALL         ; Driver initialization and installation
DW      INIT            ; Initialize device for output
DW      CLEAR           ; Clear graphics device; get fresh screen
DW      POST            ; Exit from graphics mode, unload plotter, etc
DW      MOVE            ; Move Current Pointer (CP) to (X,Y)
DW      DRAW            ; Draw Line from (CP) to (X,Y)
DW      VECT            ; Draw line from (X0,Y0) to (X1,Y1)
DW      POLY            ; Define polygon
DW      BAR             ; Filled rectangle from (CP) to (X,Y)
DW      PATBAR          ; Patterned rectangle from (X,Y) to (X1,Y1)
DW      ARC             ; Define ARC
DW      PIESLICE        ; Define an elliptical pie slice
DW      FILLED_ELLIPSE  ; Draw a filled ellipse
DW      PALETTE         ; Load a palette entry
DW      ALLPALETTE      ; Load the full palette
DW      COLOR           ; Set current drawing color/background
DW      FILLSTYLE       ; Filling control and style
DW      LINESTYLE       ; Line drawing style control
DW      TEXTSTYLE       ; Hardware Font control
DW      TEXT            ; Hardware Draw text at (CP)
DW      TEXTSIZ         ; Hardware Font size query
DW      FLOODFILL       ; Fill a bounded region
DW      GETPIX          ; Read a pixel from (X,Y)
DW      PUTPIX          ; Write a pixel to (X,Y)
                                              (continued)
```

VECTOR_TABLE: (Continued)

DW	BITMAPUTIL	; Bitmap Size query function
DW	SAVEBITMAP	; BITBLT from screen to system memory
DW	RESTOREBITMAP	; BITBLT from system memory to screen
DW	SETCLIP	; Define a clipping rectangle
DW	COLOR_QUERY	; Color Table Information Query
DW	RESERVED	; Reserved for Borland's use (0)
DW	SYMBOL	; Draw a Graphics Symbol

```
;
; 32 additional vectors are reserved for Borland's future use.
;
```

DW	RESERVED	; Reserved for Borland's use (1)
DW	RESERVED	; Reserved for Borland's use (2)
DW	RESERVED	; Reserved for Borland's use (3)
.		
.		
.		
DW	RESERVED	; Reserved for Borland's use (30)
DW	RESERVED	; Reserved for Borland's use (31)
DW	RESERVED	; Reserved for Borland's use (32)

```
;
; Any vectors following this block may be used by
; independent device driver developers as they see fit.
;
```

Vector Descriptions

The following information describes the input, output, and function of each of the functions accessed through the device vector table.

```
DW      offset INSTALL   ; device driver installation
```

The Kernel calls the INSTALL vector to prepare the device driver for use. A function code is passed in AL. The following function codes are defined:

Install Device

—>Install Device:	AL = 00
Input:	CL = Mode Number for device
	CH = Auto-Detect maximum device number
Return:	ES:BX —> Device Status Table
	(see STATUS structure, preceding)

The **Install Device** function is intended to inform the driver of the operating parameters which will be used. The device should not be switched to graphics mode (see INIT). On input, CL contains the mode in which the device will operate, and CH contains the maximum device number which will be used. An example of the use of the maximum device number is a graphics board with four modes, the last two of which require extended hardware. The Auto-Detect routine would check for the additional hardware, and if it is not present, would set the Maximum Device Number to limit entering the modes requiring the additional hardware.

The return value from the Install Device function is a pointer to a Device Status Table (described earlier).

Mode Query

—>Mode Query:	AL = 001h
Input:	Nothing
Return:	CX The number of modes supported by this device.

The **Mode Query** function is used to inquire the maximum number of modes supported by this device driver. This value is effected by the setting of the Auto-Detect Maximum Device Number as set in the Install Device function.

Mode Names

—>Mode Names:	AL = 002h	
Input:	CX	The mode number for the query.
Return:	ES:BX	—> a Pascal string containing the name

The **Mode Names** function is used to inquire the ASCII form of the mode number present in CX. The return value in ES:BX points to a Pascal string describing the given mode.

Note: A Pascal, or _length_, string is a string in which the first byte of data is the number of characters in the string, followed by the string data itself. To ease access to these strings from C, the strings should be followed by a zero byte, although this zero byte should not be included in the string length. The following is an example of this format:

```
NAME: db      16, '1280 x 1024 Mode', 0
```

INIT

```
DW          offset   INIT          ; Initialize device for output
Input:      ES:BX                  —> Device Information Table
Return:     Nothing
```

This vector is used to change an already INSTALLed device from text mode to graphics mode. This vector should also initialize any default palettes and drawing mode information as required. The input to this vector is a device information table (DIT). The format of the DIT is shown below and contains the background color and an initialization flag. If the device requires additional information at INIT-time, these values can be appended to the DIT. There in no return value for this function. If an error occurs during device initialization, the STAT field of the Device Status Table should be loaded with the appropriate error value.

```
; ************** Device Information Table definition **************
struct      DIT
            DB      0           ; Background color for initializing screen
            DB      0           ; Init flag; 0A5h = don't init;
                                ; anything else = init
            DB      64 dup 0    ; Reserved for Borland's future use
                                ; additional user information here
DIT         ends
```

CLEAR

```
DW          offset  CLEAR       ; Clear the graphics device
Input:      Nothing
Return:     Nothing
```

This vector is used to clear the graphics device to a known state. In the case of a CRT device, the screen is cleared. In the case of a printer or plotter, the paper is advanced, and pens are returned to station.

POST

```
DW          offset  POST        ; Exit from graphics mode
Input:      Nothing
Return:     Nothing
```

This routine is used to close the graphics system. In the case of graphics screens or printers, the mode should be returned to text mode. For plotters, the paper should be unloaded and the pens should return to station.

MOVE

```
DW          offset  MOVE        ; Move the current drawing pointer
Input:              AX          the new CP x coordinate
                    BX          the new CP y coordinate
Return:     Nothing
```

Set the Driver's current pointer (CP) to (AX,BX). This function is used prior to any of the TEXT, ARC, SYMBOL, DRAW, FLOODFILL, BAR, or PIESLICE routines to set the position where drawing is to take place.

DRAW

```
DW          offset  DRAW        ; Draw a line from the (CP) to (X,Y)
Input:              AX          the ending x coordinate for the line
                    BX          the ending y coordinate for the line
Return:     Nothing
```

517

Draw a line from the CP to (X,Y). The current LINESTYLE setting is used. The current pointer (CP) is updated to the line's endpoint.

VECT

DW	VECT	; Draw line from (X1,Y1) to (X2,Y2)
Input:	AX	X1; The beginning X coordinate for the line
	BX	Y1; The beginning Y coordinate for the line
	CX	X2; The ending X coordinate for the line
	DX	Y2; The ending Y coordinate for the line
Return:	Nothing	

Draw a line from the (X1,Y1) to (X2,Y2). The current LINESTYLE setting is used to draw the line. Note: CP is *not* changed by this vector.

POLY

DW	POLY	; Define polygon.
Input:	ES:BX	—> polygon
	CX = number of points in polygon	
	AX = 6	outline polygon in current color
	AX = 7	outline and fill polygon in current color, fill color and fill pattern
	AX = 8	fill polygon in current fill color and fill pattern
Return:	Nothing	

The polygon entry point is usually EMULATEd. Users with hardware capable of accepting polygon data in a single operation should contact Borland's technical support department for more information.

BAR

DW	BAR	; fill and outline rectangle (CP),(X,Y)
Input:	AX	X — right edge of rectangle
	BX	Y — bottom edge of rectangle
	CX	3D = width of 3D bar (ht = .75 * wdt);

		0 = no 3D effect
	DX	3D bar top flag;
		if CX <> 0 and DX = 0, draw a top
Return:	Nothing	

Fill and outline a bar (rectangle), using the current COLOR, FILLCOLOR, and FILLPATERN. The current pointer defines the upper, left corner of the rectangle and (X,Y) is lower, right. An optional 3D shadow effect (intended for business graphics programs) is obtained by making CX nonzero. DX then serves as a flag indicating whether a top should be drawn on the bar.

PATBAR

DW	PATBAR	; fill rectangle (X1,Y1), (X2,Y2)
Input:	AX	X1 — the rectangle's left coordinate
	BX	Y1 — the rectangle's top coordinate
	CX	X2 — the rectangle's right coordinate
	DX	Y2 — the rectangle's bottom coordinate
Return:	Nothing	

Fill (but don't outline) the indicated rectangle with the current fill pattern and fill color.

ARC

DW	ARC	; Draw an elliptical arc
Input:	AX	Starting angle of the arc in degrees (0..360)
	BX	Ending angle of the arc in degrees (0..360)
	CX	X radius of the elliptical arc
	DX	Y radius of the elliptical arc
Return:	Nothing	

ARC draws an elliptical arc using the (CP) as the center point of the arc, from the given start angle to the given end angle. To get circular arcs, the

application (not the driver) must adjust the Y radius as follows: *YRAD :=*
XRAD * (ASPEC/10000) where ASPEC is the aspect value stored in the DST.

PIESLICE

DW	PIESLICE	; Draw an elliptical pie slice
Input:	AX	Starting angle of the slice in degrees (0..360)
	BX	Ending angle of the slice in degrees (0..360)
	CX	X radius of the elliptical slice
	DX	Y radius of the elliptical slice
Return:	Nothing	

PIESLICE draws a filled elliptical pie slice (or wedge) using CP as the center
of the slice, from the given start angle to the given end angle. The current
FILLPATTERN and FILLCOLOR is used to fill the slice and it is outlined
in the current COLOR. To get circular pie slices the application (not the
driver) must adjust the Y radius as follows: *YRAD := XRAD * ASPEC/10000*
where ASPEC is the aspect value stored in the driver's DST.

FILLED_ELLIPSE

DW	FILLED_ELLIPSE	; Draw a filled ellipse at (CP)
Input:	AX	X Radius of the ellipse
	BX	Y Radius of the ellipse
Return:	Nothing	

This vector is used to draw a filled ellipse. The center point of the ellipse is
assumed to be at the current pointer (CP). The AX Register contains the X
Radius of the ellipse, and the BX Register contains the Y Radius of the
ellipse.

PALETTE

DW	PALETTE	; Load a color entry into the Palette
Input:	AX	The index number and function code for load

BX   The color value to load into the palette
Return: Nothing

The PALETTE vector is used to load single entries into the palette. The register AX contains the function code for the load action and the index of the color table entry to be loaded. The upper two bits of AX determine the action to be taken. The table below tabulates the actions. If the control bits are 00, the color table index in (AX AND 03FFFh) is loaded with the value in BX. If the control bits are 10, the color table index in (AX AND 03FFFh) is loaded with the RGB value in (Red=BX, Green=CX, and Blue=DX). If the control bits are 11, the color table entry for the background is loaded with the value in BX.

Table D-4: Register AX Actions

CONTROL BITS	COLOR VALUE AND INDEX
00	register bx contains color, ax is index
01	not used
10	red=bx, green=cx, blue=dx, ax is index
11	register bx contains color for background

ALLPALETTE

DW   ALLPALETTE   ; Load the full palette
Input: ES:BX   —> array of palette entries
Return: Nothing

The ALLPALETTE routine loads the entire palette in one driver call. The register pair ES:BX points to the table of values to be loaded into the palette. The number of entries is determined by the color entries in the Driver Status Table. The background color is not explicitly loaded with this command.

COLOR

DW	COLOR	; Load the current drawing color.
Input:	AL	Index number of the current drawing color
	AH	Index number of the fill color
Return:	Nothing	

The COLOR vector is used to determine the current drawing color. The value in AL is the index into the palette of the new current drawing color. The value in the AH register is the color index of the new fill color. All primitives are drawn with the current drawing color until the color is changed.

The fill color is used for the interior color for the bar, polygon, pie slice, and floodfill primitives.

FILLSTYLE

DW	FILLSTYLE	; Set the filling pattern
Input:	AL	Primary fill pattern number
	ES:BX	If the pattern number is 0FFh, this points to user-defined pattern mask.
Return:	Nothing	

Sets the fill pattern for drawing. The fill pattern is used to fill all bounded regions (BAR, POLY, and PIESLICE). The numbers for the predefined fill patterns are as follows:

Table D-5: Predefined Fill Patterns

CODE	DESCRIPTION	8 BYTE FILL PATTERN
0	No Fill	000h, 000h, 000h, 000h, 000h, 000h, 000h, 000h
1	Solid Fill	0FFh, 0FFh, 0FFh, 0FFh, 0FFh, 0FFh, 0FFh, 0FFh
2	Line Fill	0FFh, 0FFh, 000h, 000h, 0FFh, 0FFh, 000h, 000h
3	Lt Slash Fill	001h, 002h, 004h, 008h, 010h, 020h, 040h, 080h
4	Slash Fill	0E0h, 0C1h, 083h, 007h, 00Eh, 01Ch, 038h, 070h
5	Backslash Fill	0F0h, 078h, 03Ch, 01Eh, 00Fh, 087h, 0C3h, 0E1h

(continued)

Table D-5: (Continued)

CODE	DESCRIPTION	8 BYTE FILL PATTERN
6	Lt Bkslash Fill	0A5h, 0D2h, 069h, 0B4h, 05Ah, 02Dh, 096h, 04Bh
7	Hatch Fill	0FFh, 088h, 088h, 088h, 0FFh, 088h, 088h, 088h
8	XHatch Fill	081h, 042h, 024h, 018h, 018h, 024h, 042h, 081h
9	Interleave Fill	0CCh, 033h, 0CCh, 033h, 0CCh, 033h, 0CCh, 033h
10	Wide Dot Fill	080h, 000h, 008h, 000h, 080h, 000h, 008h, 000h
11	Close Dot Fill	088h, 000h, 022h, 000h, 088h, 000h, 022h, 000h
0FFh	User is defining the pattern of the fill.	

In the case of a user-defined fill pattern, the register pair ES:BX point to eight bytes of data arranged as a 8x8 bit pattern to be used for the fill pattern.

LINESTYLE

DW	LINESTYLE	; Set the line drawing pattern
Input:	AL	Line pattern number
	BX	User-defined line drawing pattern
	CX	Line width for drawing
Return:	Nothing	

Set the current line drawing style and the width of the line. The line width is either one pixel or three pixels in width. The following table defines the default line styles:

Table D-6: Default Line Styles

CODE	DESCRIPTION	16-BIT PATTERN	HEXIDECIMAL
AL = 0	solid line style	1111111111111111b	FFFFh
AL = 1	dotted line	1100110011001100b	CCCCh
AL = 2	center line	1111110001111000b	FC78h
AL = 3	dashed line	1111100011111000b	F8F8h
AL = 4	user-defined line style		

523

If the value in AL is four, the user is defining a line style in the BX register. If the value in AL is not four, then the value in register BX is ignored.

TEXTSTYLE

DW	TEXTSTYLE	; Hardware text style control
Input:	AL	Hardware font number
	AH	Hardware font orientation
		0 = Normal, 1 = 90 Degree, 2 = Down
	BX	Desired X Character size *
	CX	Desired Y Character size *
Return:	BX	Closest X Character size available *
	CX	Closest Y Character size available *
		* in graphics units

The TEXTSTYLE vector is used to define the attributes of the hardware font for output. The parameters that are affected are the selection of which hardware font to be used, the orientation of the font for output, the desired height and width of the font output. All subsequent text will be drawn using these attributes.

If the desired size is not supported by the current device, the closest available match to the desired size should be used. The return value from this function gives the dimensions of the font (in pixels) that will actually used.

For example, if the desired font is 8x10 pixels, and the device supports 8x8 and 16x16 fonts, the closest match will be the 8x8. The output of the function will be BX = 8, and CX = 8.

TEXT

DW	TEXT	; Hardware text output at (CP)
Input:	ES:BX	—> ASCII text of the string
	CX	The length (in characters) of the string.
	AL	Horizontal Justification Point
		0 = Left, 1 = Center, 2 = Right
	AH	Vertical Justification Point

		0 = Bottom, 1 = Center, 2 = Top
Return:	BX	The width of the string in graphics units.
	CX	The height of the string in graphics units.

This function is used to send hardware text to the output device. The text is output to the device beginning at the (CP). The placement of the text with respect to the (CP) is determined by the two bytes in AX. The value in AL is the horizontal justification flag. If the value is 0, the (CP) defines the left-most edge of the text string, if the value is 1, the (CP) defines the center of the text string, and if the value is 2, the (CP) defines the right-most edge of the text string. The value in AH is the vertical justification flag. If the value is 0, the (CP) defines the bottom edge of the text string, if the value is 1, the (CP) defines the center of the text string, and if the value is 2, the (CP) defines the top edge of the text string. The following diagram demonstrates the justification point placement:

Table D-7: Justification Point Placement

	LEFT	CENTER	RIGHT
TOP	AL=0, AH=2	AL=1, AH=2	AL=2, AH=2
CENTER	AL=0, AH=1	AL=1, AH=1	AL=2, AH=1
BOTTOM	AL=0, AH=0	AL=1, AH=0	AL=2, AH=0

TEXTSIZ

DW	TEXTSIZ	; Determine the height and width of text
		; strings in graphics units.
Input:	ES:BX	—> ASCII text of the string
	CX	The length (in characters) of the string.
Return:	BX	The width of the string in graphics units.
	CX	The height of the string in graphics units.

This function is used to determine the actual physical length and width of a text string. The current text attributes (set by TEXTSTYLE) are used to determine the actual dimensions of a string without displaying it. The application can thereby determine how a specific string will fit and reduce or increase the font size as required. There is NO graphics output for this vector. If an error occurs during length calculation, the STAT field of the Device Status Record should be marked with the device error code.

FLOODFILL

```
DW        FLOODFILL    ; Fill a bounded region using a flood fill
Input:    AX           The x coordinate for the seed point
          BX           The y coordinate for the seed point
          CL           The boundary color for the Flood Fill
Return:   Nothing      (Errors are returned in Device Status STAT field).
```

This function is called to fill a bounded region on bitmap devices. The (X,Y) input coordinate is used as the seed point for the flood fill. (CP) becomes the seed point. The current FILLPATTERN is used to flood the region.

GETPIXEL

```
DW        GETPIXEL     ; Read a pixel from the graphics screen
Input:    AX           The x coordinate for the seed point
          BX           The y coordinate for the seed point
Return:   DL           The color index of the screen pixel read
```

GETPIXEL reads the color index value of a single pixel from the graphics screen. The color index value is returned in the DL register.

PUTPIXEL

```
DW        PUTPIXEL     ; Write a pixel to the graphics screen
Input:    AX           The x coordinate for the seed point
          BX           The y coordinate for the seed point
          DL           The color index of the pixel read from the
                       screen.
Return:   Nothing
```

PUTPIXEL writes a single pixel with the color index value contained in the DL register.

BITMAPUTIL

```
DW          BITMAPUTIL          ; Bitmap Utilities Function Table
Input:      Nothing
Return:     ES:BX               —> BitMap Utility Table.
```

The BITMAPUTIL vector loads a pointer into ES:BX, which is the base of a table defining special case entry points used for pixel manipulation. These functions are currently only called by the ellipse emulation routines that are in the BGI Kernel. If the device driver does not use emulation for ellipses, this entry does not have to be implemented. This entry was provided because some hardware requires additional commands to enter and exit pixel mode, thus adding overhead to the GETPIXEL and SETPIXEL vectors. This overhead affected the drawing speed of the ellipse emulation routines. These entry points are provided so that the ellipse emulation routines can enter pixel mode and remain in pixel mode, for the duration of the ellipse rendering process.

The format of the BITMAPUTIL table is as follows:

```
DW  offset  GOTOGRAPHIC
                  ; Enter pixel mode on the graphics hardware
DW  offset  EXITGRAPHIC
                  ; Leave pixel mode on the graphics hardware
DW  offset  PUTPIXEL
                  ; Write a pixel to the graphics hardware
DW  offset  GETPIXEL
                  ; Read a pixel from the graphics hardware
DW  offset  GETPIXBYTE
                  ; Return a word containing the pixel depth
DW  offset  SET_DRAW_PAGE
                  ; Select page in which to draw primitives
```

```
DW    offset   SET_VISUAL_PAGE
                        ; Set the page to be displayed
DW    offset   SET_WRITE_MODE
                        ; XOR Line Drawing Control
```

The parameters of these functions are as follows:

GOTOGRAPHIC   ; Enter pixel mode on the graphics hardware

This function is used to enter the special Pixel Graphics mode.

EXITGRAPHIC   ; Leave pixel mode on the graphics hardware

This function is used to leave the special Pixel Graphics mode.

PUTPIXEL   ; Write a pixel to the graphics hardware

This function has the same format as the PUTPIXEL entry.

GETPIXEL   ; Read a pixel from the graphics hardware

This function has the same format as the GETPIXEL entry.

GETPIXBYTE   ; Return a word containing the pixel depth

This function returns the number of bits per pixel (color depth) of the graphics hardware in the AX register.

SET_DRAW_PAGE   ; Select alternate output graphics pages (if any)

This function takes the desired page number in the AL register and selects alternate graphics pages for output of graphics primitives.

SET_VISUAL_PAGE   ; Select the visible alternate graphics pages (if any)

This function takes the desired page number in the AL register and selects alternate graphics for displaying on the screen.

```
SET_WRITE_MODE       ; XOR Line drawing mode control.
```

XOR Mode is selected if the value in AX is one, and disabled if the value in AX is zero.

SAVEBITMAP

```
DW        SAVEBITMAP         ; Write from screen to system memory
Input:    ES:BX              —> write buffer in system memory
          SI                 Starting X coordinate of screen block
          DI                 Starting Y coordinate of screen block
          CX                 Ending X coordinate of screen block
          DX                 Ending Y coordinate of screen block
Return:   Nothing
```

The SAVEBITMAP routine is a block copy routine that copies screen pixels from a defined rectangle as specified by (SI,DI)–(CX,DX) to the system memory.

RESTOREBITMAP

```
DW        RESTOREBITMAP      ; Write system memory to the screen.
Input:    ES:BX              —> buffer in system memory
          SI                 Starting X coordinate of screen block
          DI                 Starting Y coordinate of screen block
          CX                 Ending X coordinate of screen block
          DX                 Ending Y coordinate of screen block
          AL                 Write mode for block writing
Return:   Nothing
```

The RESTOREBITMAP vector is used to load screen pixels from the system memory. The routine reads a stream of bytes from the system memory into the rectangle defined by (SI,DI)–(CX,DX). The value in the AL register defines the mode that is used for the write. The following table defines the values of the available write modes:

Table D-8: Write Mode Values

PIXEL OPERATION	CODE
OVERWRITE MODE	0
LOGICAL XOR	1
LOGICAL OR	2
LOGICAL AND	3
COMPLEMENT	4

SETCLIP

DW	SETCLIP	; Define a clipping rectangle
Input:	AX	Upper Left X coordinate of clipping rectangle
	BX	Upper Left Y coordinate of clipping rectangle
	CX	Lower Right X coordinate clipping rectangle
	DX	Lower Right Y coordinate clipping rectangle
Return:	Nothing	

The SETCLIP vector defines a rectangular clipping region on the screen. The registers (AX,BX)–(CX,DX) define the clipping region.

COLOR_QUERY

DW   offset COLOR_QUERY ; Device Color Information Query

This vector is used to inquire the color capabilities of a given piece of hardware. A function code is passed into the driver in AL. The following function codes are defined:

—>	Color Table Size	
	AL = 000h	
Input :	None:	
Return:	BX	The size of the color lookup table
	CX	The maximum color number allowed

The COLOR TABLE SIZE query is used to determine the maximum number of colors supported by the hardware. The value returned in the BX register is the number of color entries in the color lookup table. The value returned in the CX register is the highest number for a color value. This value is usually the value in BX, minus one however, there can be exceptions.

```
—>  Default Color Table
            AL = 001h
Input:      Nothing
Return:     ES:BX          —> default color table for the device
```

The DEFAULT COLOR TABLE function is used to determine the color table values for the default (power-up) color table. The format of this table is a byte containing the number of valid entries, followed by the given number of bytes of color information.

SYMBOL

```
DW          SYMBOL         ; Draw a graphics symbol at (CP)
Input:      AL             Code number of symbol (see below)
Return:     Nothing
```

This vector is used to write a "symbol" (or marker — an indicator for representing points on a line graph) to the output device. The symbol is written at the current pointer (CP).

Table D-9: Vector Symbols

SYMBOL NUMBER	DESCRIPTION
0	filled square
1	plus sign
2	eight pointed star
3	an unfilled square
4	an 'x' character
5	a filled triangle
	(continued)

Table D-9: (Continued)

SYMBOL NUMBER	DESCRIPTION
6	an hourglass
7	six pointed star
8	square with an 'x' inside
9	shadowed cross
10	vertical line
11	horizontal line

Device Driver Construction Particulars

The source code for a sample, albeit unusual, BGI device driver is included with this Toolkit to assist developers in creating their own. The demonstration driver is provided in two files, DEBVECT.ASM and DEBUG.C. This "Debug" driver doesn't actually draw graphics, but instead simply sends descriptive messages to the console screen (via DOS function call 9) upon receiving commands. Instead of simply playing back commands, your own driver would be structured similarly, but would access control ports and screen memory to perform each function.

Cookbook

1. Compile or assemble the files required.

2. Link the files together, making sure that the device vector table is the first module within the link.

3. Run EXE2BIN on the resulting .EXE or .COM file to produce a .BIN file. There should be no relocation fixups required.

4. Run program BH (provided with the toolkit) on the .BIN file to produce the .BGI file.

5. The resulting driver is now ready for testing. Examine the file TEST.C for an example of installing, loading, and calling a newly-created device driver.

Examples

```
; To call any BGI function from assembly language include the structure below and
; use the CALLBGI macro.

CALLBGI  MACRO  P
         MOV          SI,$&P                    ; Put opcode in (SI)
         CALL         CS:DWORD PTR BGI_ADD      ; BGI_ADD points to driver
         ENDM

; e.g., to draw a line from (10,15) to (200,300):

         MOV          AX, 10
         MOV          BX, 15
         MOV          CX, 200
         MOV          DX, 300
         CALLBGI      VECT

; To index any item in the status table include the status table structures below and
; use the BGISTAT macro.

BGISTAT  MACRO  P                               ; get ES:<SI> —> BGI STATUS
         LES          SI, CS:DWORD PTR STABLE   ; get location of status to SI
         ADD          SI, $&P                   ; offset to correct location
         ENDM

; e.g., to obtain the aspect ratio of a device:

         BGISTAT ASPEC
         MOV    AX, ES:[SI]                      ; (AX) = Y/X *10000
```

APPENDIX E

A VGA 256-COLOR .BGI DRIVER

In addition to the Font Editor utility and the custom .BGI package, Borland has provided a new VGA driver (VGA256.BGI) which supports the full VGA color resolution with a 256 hue palette employing the Hue-Saturation-Intensity (HSI) color model.

Available from Borland, the VGA utility package consists of five programs: the VGA256.BGI driver, the HSI.EXE and HSI.PAS color hue demonstration and VGADEMO.EXE and VGADEMO.PAS.

The VGADEMO is the principal demonstration (and does work on non-VGA systems though without the full range of 256 colors). The VGADEMO program includes demonstrations of several graphics functions which are new to Turbo C version 2.0 (or Turbo Pascal version 5.0), including the **setaspectratio**, **fillellipse**, **sector** and **setwritemode** functions. The **256 Color** and **SetRGBPalette** demos, of course, will only execute correctly on systems with VGA or compatible video cards. On an EGA system, for example, these two demo segments execute but are restricted to the EGAVGA default palette of 16 colors.

Of particular interest to the programmer, in the HSI or VGADEMO programs. are the **VGASetAllPalette** procedure and the **DetectVGA256** function. While the source codes for both demo programs are written in Pascal, C programmers should have little difficulty converting these for C applications.

THE GRAPHIC CHARACTER FONTS

Ten graphics character fonts are shown following. Fonts 0..4 are graphics character fonts distributed with Turbo C, Turbo Pascal and Turbo Prolog. Fonts 5..9 are provided with the Turbo Font Editor (see Chapter 17).

The font illustrations following were created by writing each font to the screen (EGA — 640x350) as shown, then hard-copied to a laserjet printer at a 75 DPI resolution (LANDSCAPE mode) using the screen-dump procedures demonstrated in Chapter 14.

The exact appearance of each font will vary depending on screen resolution and character magnification. For example, note characters B0h..B2h which show some distortion toward the bottom of the character where the stroke instructions "slip" slightly as they are mapped to the pixel image. This is normal and expected and is usually not visually apparent on the screen.

Also, the overall appearance of the characters on screen is generally smoother — due to tendency of illuminated pixels to visually "melt" together — than they appear on paper.

Note: The versions of fonts 1..4 shown here are the expanded versions of the original distribution fonts as distributed with the Turbo Font Editor utility.

Table F-1: Graphics Character Fonts

FONT	FONT NAME	TYPE
0	DEFAULT_FONT	BIT-MAPPED
1	TRIPLEX_FONT	STROKED
2	SMALL_FONT	STROKED
3	SANS_SERIF_FONT	STROKED
4	GOTHIC_FONT	STROKED
5	SCRIPT_FONT	STROKED
6	SIMPLEX_FONT	STROKED
7	ITALIC_FONT	STROKED
8	ROMAN_FONT	STROKED
9	LARGE_FONT	STROKED

Note: Font numbers and font titles for fonts 5..9 are not predefined. The font numbers shown were arbitrarily assigned by installuserfont in the order each font was assigned to the internal font table while preparing these figures. The font names are equally arbitrary, but are intended as descriptive mnemonics.

Font Number: 0 (DEFAULT_FONT), Bit-mapped
Source File: (built-in to GRAPHICS.LIB), Size = 3

Font 0	0	1	2	3	4	5	6	7	8	9	A	B	C	D	E	F
0		☺	☻	♥	♦	♣	♠	•	◘	○	◙	♂	♀	♪	♫	☼
1	►	◄	↕	‼	¶	§	▬	↨	↑	↓	→	←	∟	↔	▲	▼
2		!	"	#	$	%	&	'	(	)	*	+	,	-	.	/
3	0	1	2	3	4	5	6	7	8	9	:	;	<	=	>	?
4	@	A	B	C	D	E	F	G	H	I	J	K	L	M	N	O
5	P	Q	R	S	T	U	V	W	X	Y	Z	[	\	]	^	_
6	`	a	b	c	d	e	f	g	h	i	j	k	l	m	n	o
7	p	q	r	s	t	u	v	w	x	y	z	{	¦	}	~	⌂

Font Number: 0 (DEFAULT_FONT), Bit-mapped
Source File: (built into GRAPHICS.LIB), Size = 3

Font Number: 1 (TRIPLEX_FONT), Stroked
Source File: TRIP.CHR, Size = 3

Font 1	0	1	2	3	4	5	6	7	8	9	A	B	C	D	E	F
0																
1																
2		!	"	#	$	%	&	'	(	)	*	+	,	−	.	/
3	0	1	2	3	4	5	6	7	8	9	:	;	<	=	>	?
4	@	A	B	C	D	E	F	G	H	I	J	K	L	M	N	O
5	P	Q	R	S	T	U	V	W	X	Y	Z	[	\	]	^	_
6	`	a	b	c	d	e	f	g	h	i	j	k	l	m	n	o
7	p	q	r	s	t	u	v	w	x	y	z	{	|	}	~	△

Font Number: 1 (TRIPLEX_FONT), Stroked
Source File: TRIP.CHR, Size = 3

Font 1	0	1	2	3	4	5	6	7	8	9	A	B	C	D	E	F
8	Ç	ü	é	â	ä	à	å	ç	ê	ë	è	ï	î	ì	Ä	Å
9	É	æ	Æ	ô	ö	ò	û	ù	ÿ	Ö	Ü	ø	£	Ø	₧	ƒ
A	á	í	ó	ú	ñ	Ñ	ª	º	¿	⌐	¬	⅓	¼	¡	«	»
B			│	┤	╡	╢	╖	╕	╣	║	╗	╝	╜	╛	┐
C	└	┴	┬	├	─	┼	╞	╟	╚	╔	╩	╦	╠	═	╬	╧
D	╨	╤	╥	╙	╘	╒	╓	╫	╪	┘	┌					
E	α	β	Γ	π	Σ	σ	µ	γ	Φ	θ	Ω	δ	∞	ø	ε	∩
F	≡	±	≥	≤	⌠	⌡	÷	≈	°	·	·	√	ⁿ	ε	∎	

Font Number: 2 (SMALL_FONT), Stroked
Source File: LITT.CHR, Size = 7

Font 2	0	1	2	3	4	5	6	7	8	9	A	B	C	D	E	F
0																
1																
2		!	"	#	$	%	&	'	(	)	*	+	,	-	.	/
3	0	1	2	3	4	5	6	7	8	9	:	;	<	=	>	?
4	@	A	B	C	D	E	F	G	H	I	J	K	L	M	N	O
5	P	Q	R	S	T	U	V	W	X	Y	Z	[	\	]	^	_
6	`	a	b	c	d	e	f	g	h	i	j	k	l	m	n	o
7	p	q	r	s	t	u	v	w	x	y	z	{	|	}	˜	Δ

Font Number: 2 (SMALL_FONT), Stroked
Source File: LITT.CHR, Size = 7

Font 2	0	1	2	3	4	5	6	7	8	9	A	B	C	D	E	F
8	Ç	ü	é	â	ä	à	å	ç	ê	ë	è	ï	î	ì	Ä	Å
9	É	æ	Æ	ô	ö	ò	û	ù	ÿ	Ö	Ü	ø	£	Ø	₧	ƒ
A	á	í	ó	ú	ñ	Ñ	ª	º	¿	⌐	¬	½	¼	¡	«	»
B	▦	▦	▨	│	┤	╡	╢	╖	╕	╣	║	╗	╝	╜	╛	┐
C	└	┴	┬	├	─	┼	╞	╟	╚	╔	╩	╦	╠	═	╬	╧
D	╨	╤	╥	╙	╘	╒	╓	╫	╪	┘	┌	█	▄	▌	▐	▀
E	α	β	Γ	π	Σ	σ	µ	γ	Φ	θ	Ω	δ	∞	ø	∈	∩
F	≡	±	≥	≤	⌠	⌡	÷	≈	°	∙	·	√	ⁿ	²	■	

Font Number: 3 (SANS_SERIF_FONT), Stroked
Source File: SANS.CHR, Size = 3

Font 3	0	1	2	3	4	5	6	7	8	9	A	B	C	D	E	F
0																
1																
2		!	"	#	$	%	&	'	(	)	*	+	,	-	.	/
3	0	1	2	3	4	5	6	7	8	9	:	;	<	=	>	?
4	@	A	B	C	D	E	F	G	H	I	J	K	L	M	N	O
5	P	Q	R	S	T	U	V	W	X	Y	Z	[	\	]	^	_
6	'	a	b	c	d	e	f	g	h	i	j	k	l	m	n	o
7	p	q	r	s	t	u	v	w	x	y	z	{			}	~	△

Font Number: 3 (SANS_SERIF_FONT), Stroked
Source File: SANS.CHR, Size = 3

Font 3	0	1	2	3	4	5	6	7	8	9	A	B	C	D	E	F
8	Ç	ü	é	â	ä	à	à	ç	ê	ë	è	ï	î	ì	Ä	Å
9	É	œ	Æ	ô	ö	ò	û	ù	ÿ	Ö	Ü	ø	£	Ø	₧	ƒ
A	á	í	ó	ú	ñ	Ñ	ª	º	¿	⌐	¬	½	¼	¡	«	»
B	▒	▓	▒	│	┤	╡	╢	╖	╕	╣	║	╗	╝	╜	╛	┐
C	└	┴	┬	├	─	┼	╞	╟	╚	╔	╩	╦	╠	═	╬	╧
D	╨	╤	╥	╙	╘	╒	╓	╫	╪	┘	┌	█	▄	▌	▐	▀
E	α	β	Γ	π	Σ	σ	µ	τ	Φ	θ	Ω	δ	∞	ø	∈	∩
F	≡	±	≥	≤	⌠	⌡	÷	≈	°	∙	·	√	ⁿ	²	■	

Font Number: 4 (GOTHIC_FONT), Stroked
Source File: GOTH.CHR, Size = 3

Font 4	0	1	2	3	4	5	6	7	8	9	A	B	C	D	E	F
0																
1																
2		!	"	#	$	%	&	'	(	)	*	+	,	−	.	/
3	0	1	2	3	4	5	6	7	8	9	:	;	<	=	>	?
4	@	A	B	C	D	E	F	G	H	I	J	K	L	M	N	O
5	P	Q	R	S	T	U	V	W	X	Y	Z	[	\	]	^	_
6	`	a	b	c	d	e	f	g	h	i	j	k	l	m	n	o
7	p	q	r	s	t	u	v	w	x	y	z	{	|	}	~	△

Font Number: 4 (GOTHIC_FONT), Stroked
Source File: GOTH.CHR, Size = 3

Font 4	0	1	2	3	4	5	6	7	8	9	A	B	C	D	E	F
8	Ç	ü	é	â	ä	à	å	ç	ê	ë	è	ï	î	ì	Ä	Å
9	É	æ	Æ	ô	ö	ò	û	ù	ÿ	Ö	Ü	ø	£	Ø	₧	ƒ
A	á	í	ó	ú	ñ	Ñ	ª	º	¿	⌐	¬	½	¼	¡	«	»
B																
C	└	┴	┬	├	─	┼	╞	╟	╚	╔	╩	╦	╠	═	╬	╧
D																
E	α	β	Γ	π	Σ	σ	µ	τ	Φ	Θ	Ω	δ	∞	φ	ε	∩
F	≡	±	≥	≤	⌠	⌡	÷	≈	°	•	·	√	ⁿ	²	■	

Note: Characters B0h..BFh and D0h..DFh were missing from the pre-release version of the GOTH.CHR font used to prepare these figures.

Font Number: 9 (LARGE_FONT), Stroked
Source File: EURO.CHR, Size = 1

Font 9	0	1	2	3	4	5	6	7	8	9	A	B	C	D	E	F
0																
1																
2		!	"	#	$	%	&	'	(	)	※	+	,	–	.	/
3	0	1	2	3	4	5	6	7	8	9	:	;	<	=	>	?
4	@	A	B	C	D	E	F	G	H	I	J	K	L	M	N	O
5	P	Q	R	S	T	U	V	W	X	Y	Z	[	\	]	^	_
6	`	a	b	c	d	e	f	g	h	i	j	k	l	m	n	o
7	p	q	r	s	t	u	v	w	x	y	z	{	|	}	~	⌂

Font Number: 9 (LARGE_FONT), Stroked
Source File: EURO.CHR, Size = 1

Font 9	0	1	2	3	4	5	6	7	8	9	A	B	C	D	E	F
8	Ç	ü	é	â	ä	à	å	ç	ê	ë	è	ï	î	ì	Ä	Å
9	É	æ	Æ	ô	ö	ò	û	ù	ÿ	Ö	Ü	ø	£	Ø	₧	ƒ
A	á	í	ó	ú	ñ	Ñ	ª	º	¿	⌐	¬	½	¼	¡	«	»
B	░	▒	▓	│	┤	╡	╢	╖	╕	╣	║	╗	╝	╜	╛	┐
C	└	┴	┬	├	─	┼	╞	╟	╚	╔	╩	╦	╠	═	╬	╧
D	╨	╤	╥	╙	╘	╒	╓	╫	╪	┘	┌	█	▄	▌	▐	▀
E	α	β	Γ	π	Σ	σ	µ	τ	Φ	Θ	Ω	δ	∞	ø	∈	∩
F	≡	±	≥	≤	⌠	⌡	÷	≈	°	∙	·	√	ⁿ	²	■	

INDEX